Global Security Governance

Global Security Governance demarcates the barriers and pathways to major power security cooperation and provides an empirical analysis of threat perception among the world's major powers.

Divided into three parts and using a common analytical framework for the changing security agenda in Canada, France, Germany, Italy, Japan, the Russian Federation, the United States, the United Kingdom and the EU, each chapter:

- Examines the national 'exceptionalism' that accounts for foreign and security policy idiosyncrasies
- Defines the range of threats preoccupying the government, foreign policy elites and public
- Assesses the institutional and instrumental preferences shaping national security policies
- Investigates the allocation of resources between the various categories of security expenditure
- Details the elements of the national security culture and its consequences for security cooperation.

By combining a coherent theoretical framework with strong comparative case studies *Global Security Governance* contributes to the ongoing reconceptualization of security and definition of threat and provides a basis for reaching tentative conclusions about the prospects for global and regional security governance in the early twenty-first century. These features make it ideal reading for all students of security studies.

Emil J. Kirchner is Jean Monnet Professor of European Integration at the University of Essex. He is Associate Editor of the *Journal of European Integration*.

James Sperling is Professor of Political Science at the University of Akron, Ohio, USA.

Global Security Governance

Competing perceptions of security
in the 21st century

**Edited by Emil J. Kirchner
and James Sperling**

LONDON AND NEW YORK

First published 2007 by Routledge
2 Park Square, Milton Park, Abingdon, Oxon OX14 4RN

Simultaneously published in the USA and Canada
by Routledge
270 Madison Ave, New York, NY 10016

Routledge is an imprint of the Taylor & Francis Group, an informa business

Typeset in Times by
GreenGate Publishing Servies, Tonbridge, Kent
Printed and bound in Great Britain by
Antony Rowe Ltd, Chippenham, Wiltshire

British Library Cataloguing in Publication Data
A catalogue record for this book is available from the British Library

Library of Congress Cataloging in Publication Data
Global security governance : competing perceptions of security in the 21st
century / [edited] by Emil J. Kirchner and James Sperling.
       p. cm.
    Includes bibliographical references.
    ISBN-13: 978-0-415-39161-0 (hardback)
    ISBN-10: 0-415-39161-X (hardback)
    ISBN-13: 978-0-415-39162-7 (pbk.)
    ISBN-10: 0-415-39162-8 (pbk.)
    [etc.]
        1. Security, International. 2. National security. I. Kirchner, Emil
Joseph. II. Sperling, James.
JZ5588.G583 2007
355'.033–dc22
                                                        2006025446

ISBN 978–0–415–39161–0 (hbk)
ISBN 978–0–415–39162–7 (pbk)
ISBN 978–0-203–96470–5 (ebk)

Contents

List of tables

Contributors

Emil J. Kirchner is Professor of European Studies and Jean Monnet Chair at the University of Essex. His current main interests include European security policy, regional and global governance, and cross-border cooperation. His recent publications include (co-authored) *Studies on Policies and Policy Processes of the European Union* (2003); (co-authored) 'The New Security Threats in Europe: Theory and Evidence', *European Foreign Affairs Review* 2002; and (co-edited) *Committee Governance in the European Union* (2000).

James Sperling is Professor of Political Science at the University of Akron. He is editor of *Germany at 55: Berlin ist nicht Bonn?* (2004) and *Two Tiers or Two Speeds? The European security order and the enlargement of the European Union and NATO* (1999); and co-editor of *EU Enlargement and New Security Challenges in the Eastern Mediterranean* (2004) and *Limiting Institutions? The Challenge of Security Governance in Eurasia* (2003).

Osvaldo Croci is Associate Professor of International Politics at Memorial University in St. John's Newfoundland. His research interests focus on foreign and security policies in the Atlantic area, particularly those of Canada and Italy. Together with Amy Verdun, he has recently edited *The Transatlantic Divide: Foreign and security policies in the Atlantic Alliance from Kosovo to Iraq* (2006); and *The European Union in the Wake of Eastern Enlargement: Institutional and policy-making challenges* (2006).

Paolo Foradori currently teaches International Relations and European Studies at the University of Trento. His main research interests are international relations theory and security studies. His most recent publications include (co-authored) 'Italy and the politics of European Defence: playing the logic of multilevel network', *Modern Italy* 2004; 'Sfide globali e risposte nazionali: le trasformazioni della sicurezza nell'era dell'interdipendenza', in Foradori and Scartezzini (eds) *Globalizzazione e processi di integrazione sovranazionale: l'Europa, il Mondo* (Rubbettino 2006); and (co-edited) *Managing a Multilevel Foreign Policy: The EU in international affairs* (Forthcoming).

Haruhiro Fukui is Professor Emeritus at the Department of Political Science, University of California. His research interests include Japanese politics and foreign policy, and international politics in East Asia. His latest publications include 'Hirohito' and 'Japan' in Krieger (ed.) *The Oxford Companion to Politics of the World,* 2nd edn (2001); (co-authored) 'Japan', in Kesselman *et al.* (eds) *Introduction to Comparative Politics,* 3rd edn (2003); and (co-authored) 'Foreign policy by coalition: deadlock, compromise, and anarchy', in *International Studies Review,* Special Issue 2001.

Vladimir I. Ivanov is Deputy Chief Regional Representative of Rosneft Oil company. He was formerly Director of Research and Senior Economist at the Economic Research Institute for Northeast Asia (ERINA). His research interests cover economic, social, political and security issues of Northeast Asia and the larger Asia-Pacific region, including Russia's relations with her neighbours and energy security. His latest publications include 'Russia and Japan beyond 2005', *ERINA Report* 2005; and 'Russia's energy politics: focusing on new markets in Asia', in a forthcoming monograph by the Korea Economic Institute.

Elke Krahmann is Senior Lecturer in International Relations in the Department of Politics at the University of Bristol. She has published widely on international foreign and security policy, including *New Threats and New Actors in International Security* (2005); and *Multilevel Networks in European Foreign Policy* (2003). A forthcoming research monograph will examine the privatization of military services in Europe and North America, while her current ESRC-funded project analyses the theoretical implications of the commodification of security.

Katja Mirwaldt is a PhD candidate in the Department of Government, University of Essex. Her research interests are cross-border cooperation in Europe and Germany's relations with Poland and the Czech Republic.

Liselotte Odgaard is Associate Professor at the Department of Political Science, University of Aarhus. Her research interests include international relations, foreign policy analysis, security/strategic studies, Sino–US security relations, and the balance of power in the Asia-Pacific. Her recent publications include *The Balance of Power in Asia-Pacific Security* (Routledge 2006); 'The South China Sea: ASEAN's security concerns about China', *Security Dialogue* 2003; and *Maritime Security between China and Southeast Asia: Conflict and cooperation in the making of regional order* (2002).

Paolo Rosa is Researcher of Political Sociology at the Department of Sociology and Social Research of the University of Trento. His main research interests include foreign policy analysis and Italian and EU foreign policy. His most recent publication is (edited) *Le relazioni internazionali contemporanee: il mondo dopo la guerra fredda* (2003).

Alexander Siedschlag is Professor of European Security Policy at the University of Innsbruck. His research interests include transatlantic security policy, German foreign and security policy, European Security and Defence Policy (ESDP), NATO, theories of international politics, and qualitative methods in security studies. His recent publications include 'International non-proliferation policy and the United Nations security system after 9/11 and Iraq' in Köchler (ed.) *The Use of Force in International Relations. Challenges to Collective Security* (International Progress Organization 2006); and (edited) *Methoden der sicherheits politischen Analyse* (2006).

Thierry Tardy is a faculty member and the Director of the European Training Course at the Geneva Center for Security Policy. His area of expertise covers crisis management, UN peace operations, French security policy, EU–UN relations, and European security issues. His recent publications include (edited) *Peace Operations after 11 September 2001* (Frank Cass 2004); and 'EU–UN cooperation in peacekeeping: a promising relationship in a constrained environment', in Ortega (ed.) *The EU and the UN: Partners in effective multilateralism* (2005).

Amy Verdun is Professor and Jean Monnet Chair at the University of Victoria. Her current research interests include European integration and governance, including matters surrounding integration theory, policy-making, political economy, and security matters. Her most recent books include (co-edited) *The Transatlantic Divide: Foreign and security policies in the Atlantic Alliance from Kosovo to Iraq* (2006); (co-edited) *The European Union in the Wake of Eastern Enlargement: Institutional and policy-making challenges* (2006); and *Britain and Canada and their Large Neighboring Monetary Unions* (2006).

Preface

Global Security Governance provides an empirical analysis of threat perception among the world's major powers. This collection of essays was designed to make a positive contribution to the ongoing reconceptualization of security and definition of threat, to identify the range of threat perceptions of the major powers as well as the patterns of interaction characterizing their policies, and to provide the basis for reaching some tentative conclusions about the prospects for global and regional security governance. It is our hope that this collection demarcates the barriers and pathways to major power security cooperation in the twenty-first century.

The end of the Cold War not only changed the geopolitical milieu, but the content and form of threats facing the great powers. Three other events have reinforced these developments. First, there has been an asynchronous evolution of the state in the international system. The emergence of the post-Westphalian state in the Atlantic basin and the attending perforation of the state's 'wall of defensibility' contrasts with the largely intact Westphalian states of Eurasia and the Pacific basin. Second, 11 September 2001 pushed transnational terrorism to the top of the security agenda and introduced another source of tension between the United States, its allies and adversaries. The Canadians, Europeans and Japanese, for example, generally view terrorism as an intelligence and policing problem, whereas the United States has treated it as an unconventional threat susceptible to a conventional military solution. Third, the American-led invasion of Iraq in 2003 revealed the deep chasm separating the European and North American powers with respect to the use of force. Not only did the war tear at the fabric of the Atlantic Alliance, but it divided Europe against itself. These differences should not obscure the general consensus that terrorism, regional conflicts and instability, state failure, the proliferation of weapons of mass destruction, and even the environment represent a common threat requiring joint action. Yet, deep differences exist with respect to the origins of those threats, the way in which those threats should be addressed, and the relative utility of the traditional and civilian instruments of statecraft. Those differences, in turn, limit the potential for regional and global security cooperation.

The chapters in this book provide an empirically grounded comparative analysis of the changing security agenda in nine countries and the European Union (EU).

The introduction employs security governance as the analytical framework for understanding the current security challenges that confront the G8 member states (Canada, France, Germany, Italy, Japan, the Russian Federation, the United States and the United Kingdom), China, and the EU. The introduction explores a series of questions, including: What are the conditions for, and functions and instruments of global or regional security governance? How do the requirements for meeting the tasks of global security governance change depending on the functional objectives and operational (geographical and institutional) milieu? How does the target of security (state or society) affect the instruments and institutional configurations of governance? The substantive chapters (2–11) rely upon a common analytical framework. Each author examines the national 'exceptionalism' that accounts for foreign and security policy idiosyncrasies, identifies the range of threats preoccupying the government, foreign policy elites and public, assesses the institutional and instrumental preferences shaping national security policies, investigates the allocation of resources between the various categories of security expenditure, and details the elements of the national security culture and its consequences for security cooperation.

The conclusion, which draws on the empirical data presented in the substantive chapters, answers three relatively straightforward questions: What factors facilitate or bar regional security cooperation? Should the major powers seek the ambitious goal of global security cooperation or must they settle instead for the less ambitious task of regional security cooperation? Are these powers only capable of ensuring that their respective geopolitical neighbourhoods are more or less secure? Towards answering these questions, four variables will be compared across Europe, the Transatlantic area, Eurasia and the Asia-Pacific: the national assessment of threats and their origins; the dominant pan-regional interaction pattern of the major powers; the balance struck between the civilian and traditional forms of statecraft; the patterns of convergence and divergence in national security cultures. The values taken on by those four variables, in turn, identify the vertices of conflict and interstices of regional and global security cooperation in the early twenty-first century.

Acknowledgements

The book has benefited from the presentation of research at a number of workshop and conference venues and from the comments of colleagues on the individual chapters. Workshops at the University of California, San Diego in 2002, and at the United Nations University in Bruges in 2003 contributed to our understanding of which questions should be asked in the new security environment. Special thanks are owed to William and Marsha Chandler at UCSD and to Luc van Langenhove at the United Nations University in Bruges, all of whom were instrumental in organizing and sponsoring those gatherings. Draft chapters were first presented at the Standing Conference on International Relations of the ECPR at The Hague in September 2004 and at the GARNET workshop in Trento in September 2005, which was graciously hosted by Paolo Foradori and Riccardo Scartezinni. Research and travel support was provided by the Network on Global and Regional Governance (GARNET), which is financed by the European Commission's Sixth Framework Programme. We are deeply indebted to all participants of the workshops and conferences, several of whom are also contributors to this book, for their helpful comments and suggestions. Similar thanks are owed to the two anonymous reviewers for Routledge.

Besides institutional and financial support, this book would not have been possible without the support of many individuals. We wish to thank especially Katja Mirwaldt and Susan Sydenham for their editorial assistance at different stages of the book. Jim Sperling would also like to thank Professor Tom Weingeist and Dr Chet Patel at the Eye Institute, University of Iowa Medical School, for making it possible for him to continue writing as well as Pam and Terry Trimpe for their friendship and hospitality during his trips to Iowa City.

Our deepest thanks must go to our families for their encouragement and support.

Emil J. Kirchner and Jim Sperling, July 2006

Abbreviations

ABM	Anti-Ballistic Missile
ACNS	Advisory Council on National Security – Canada
ACP	African, Caribbean and Pacific countries
ADB	Asian Development Bank
ARF	ASEAN Regional Forum
ASEAN	Association of Southeast Asian Nations
AU	African Union
BMDP	Ballistic Missile Defence Programme – Canada
BMVg	Bundesministerium der Verteidigung (Federal Ministry of Defence – Germany)
BSEC	Black Sea Economic Cooperation
CARICOM	Caribbean Community
CBRN	Chemical, Biological, Radiological and Nuclear weapons
CBSA	Canada Border Services Agency
CCFR	Chicago Council on Foreign Relations
CEE	Central and Eastern Europe
CFET	Conventional Forces in Europe Treaty
CFSP	Common Foreign and Security Policy
CIREFI	Centre for Information, Discussion and Exchange on the Crossing of Frontiers and Immigration
CIS	Commonwealth of Independent States
CIVCOM	Committee for Civilian Aspects of Crisis Management
CSIS	Canadian Security and Intelligence Service
DAC	Development Assistance Committee
DCI	Director of Central Intelligence – US
DICOD	French Ministry of Defence Information Services
DND	Department of National Defence – Canada
DoD	Department of Defense – United States
ECOMOG	Economic Community of West African States Monitoring Observer Group
ECOWAS	Economic Community of West African States
ENP	European Neighbourhood Policy
ESDI	European Security and Defence Identity

ESDP	European Security and Defence Policy
ESS	European Security Strategy
EU	European Union
EUFOR	European Force
FSU	Former Soviet Union
G7	Group of Seven (Canada, France, Germany, Italy, Japan, UK and US)
G8	Group of Eight (Canada, France, Germany, Italy, Japan, Russia, UK and US)
GU(U)AM	Georgia, Ukraine, (Uzbekistan,) Azerbaijan and Moldova
HR/SG	High Representative and Secretary General of the Council of Ministers
IAEA	International Atomic Energy Agency
IBET	Integrated Border Enforcement Team – Canada
IFOR	Implementation Force
IFRI	Institut français des relations internationales (French Institute of International Relations)
IISS	International Institute for Stategic Studies
IMF	International Monetary Fund
IMU	Islamic Movement of Uzbekistan
INF	Intermediate-range Nuclear Force
INSET	Integrated National Security Enforcement Team – Canada
IRA	Irish Republican Army
IRPA	Immigration and Refugee Protection Act – Canada
ISAF	International Security Assistance Force
ITAC	Integrated Threat Assessment Centre – Canada
JDA	Japanese Defence Agency
KAIPTC	Kofi Annan International Peacekeeping Training Centre
KFOR	Kosovo Force
MAE	Ministero degli Affari Esteri (Italian Ministry of Foreign Affairs)
MERCOSUR	Mercado Común del Cono Sur (Southern Cone Common Market)
MIC	Monitoring and Information Centre
MoD	Ministry of Defence – UK
MOFA	Ministry of Foreign Affairs – Japan
MP	Member of Parliament
MPL	Military Programme Law – France
NATO	North Atlantic Treaty Organization
NGO	Non-Governmental Organization
NIPC	National Infrastructure Protection Center – United States
NORAD	North American Aerospace Defence Command
NPC	National People's Congress – China
NPT	Non-Proliferation Treaty
NSA	National Security Agency
NSHS	National Strategy for Homeland Security – United States
NSS	National Security Strategy – United States

OAS	Organization of American States
ODA	Official Development Assistance
OECD	Organization for Economic Cooperation and Development
OSCE	Organization for Security and Co-operation in Europe
PCO	Privy Council Office – Canada
PfP	Partnership for Peace
PKO	Peace Keeping Operations
PLA	People's Liberation Army – China
PSEP	Department of Public Safety and Emergency Preparedness – Canada
PSTC	Peace Support Training Centre
RCMP	Royal Canadian Mounted Police
SCO	Shanghai Cooperation Organization
SDF	Self-Defence Force – Japan
SDR	Strategic Defence Review – UK
SFOR	Stabilization Force
SHDCS	Strategy for Homeland Defense and Civil Support – United States
SIGINT	Signals Intelligence – Canada
SISDE	Civil Intelligence – Italy
SISMI	Military Intelligence – Italy
START	Strategic Arms Reduction Treaty
TEU	Treaty on European Union
UK	United Kingdom
UN	United Nations
UNDP	United Nations Development Programme
UNEP	United Nations Environment Programme
USA	United States of America
WHO	World Health Organization
WMD	Weapons of Mass Destruction
WTO	World Trade Organization

Introduction

1 Regional and global security

Changing threats and institutional responses

Emil J. Kirchner

An increasing number of state and non-state actors have displayed an indifference to international norms and law as well as conventional forms of conflict resolution, and have demonstrated a preparedness to adopt offensive strategies that have the potential to challenge the traditional security architecture. The terrorist attacks on New York and Washington in 2001, Madrid in 2004 and London in 2005, have underscored the need for reconstructing global and regional systems of security governance. Barriers to that task include different threat assessments by the major powers, divergent perceptions of security threats to states, and divergent strategic choices (ranging from unilateralism to a robust multilateralism) for meeting today's security challenges. Similarly, the major states have variable inclinations towards relying upon 'hard power' and 'soft power' to resolve those security challenges (Nye 2003). The aim of this and subsequent chapters is a comparative analysis of the great and middle-ranked powers' changing security agendas and their responses to the challenges of global and regional security governance. A further objective is to examine the dominant characteristics of national security cultures. The investigation will be based on the perceptions of governments, parliaments, security experts and the public of the G8 countries (Canada, France, Germany, Italy, Japan, the Russian Federation, the United Kingdom and the United States) and China.[1] These countries play leading roles in regional and global security and their views on the subject of security threats and institutional response are important for assessing the prospects of international security governance. The growing importance of the EU as a security actor, its role within the G8, and its relationship with NATO, the UN and the US in the field of security are reason for devoting an extra chapter to it. The analysis will enable a greater understanding of the problem of security governance in three different regional contexts: Europe, Trans-Atlantic and Asia-Pacific. It will also lend itself to a reconceptualization of threat, the state, and the institutional framework for understanding those threats. Security governance can be defined as an intentional system of rule that involves the coordination, management and regulation of issues by multiple and separate authorities, interventions by both public and private actors, formal and informal arrangements, and purposefully directed towards particular policy outcomes.[2]

The study of security governance is complicated by three unresolved problems. First, there is presently neither a satisfactory typology of the security threats[3] confronting Europe, nor a conceptual consensus on what constitutes a security threat (content), the way in which threats are manifested (form), the source of threat (agency), and the role of institutions as mediators of conflict (structure). Second, the state is undergoing an asynchronous evolution in the Atlantic and Pacific basins. The emergence of the post-Westphalian state in the Atlantic basin and the perforation of the state's 'wall of defensibility' contrasts with the largely intact Westphalian states of the Pacific basin. Third, the changed nature of the state and new security threats suggest four readily identifiable contagion mechanisms: the interaction density among European polities; the widespread presence of underdeveloped civil societies or failed state structures along its periphery; the geographic propinquity between the stable and unstable states of Eurasia; and the pervasiveness of cyberspace, which has transcended national boundaries. In terms of European regional governance, the first two mechanisms are of particular importance.

Moreover, in the post-Cold War period new challenges have arisen to the management of global and regional security governance. While, in the past, most threats to states came from other states, non-state actors have increasingly posed major threats in the minds of policy-makers. In the contemporary climate, open economies and open societies have improved economic welfare but have also made the tasks of pursuing security more difficult. Control of territory is no longer the only or most important priority.

In this context, two major challenges need particular attention. First, policy-makers must determine if long-standing western security arrangements can be extended outwards. Second, policy-makers must determine whether the new security governance system will be cooperative or competitive and whether it will be based on alliances or ad hoc balancing. The first challenge requires efforts to overcome the heterogeneity of the international system and the lack of international norms. Such efforts beg the question of whether it is possible to come up with a system, either regionally or globally, consistent both with norms of local countries and Western norms. And, if so, the additional question would be: what are the boundaries of the new regional or global security system(s)? Norm sharing would appear more easily attainable in a regional than a global context, as higher levels of economic and social interactions prevail regionally than globally;[4] but for this assumption to hold the incidence of interstate threats within a region must be low. The second challenge raises issues about the suitability of global or regional security arrangements, and the role of international security institutions in dealing with the contemporary security environment. To the extent that most of the threats are not limited to local places and that crossborder spillovers are possible, regional responses seem logical. The EU enlargement process with regard to Greece, Spain and Portugal initially, with Central and Eastern European countries recently, and with the Western Balkan countries currently provides a good example of regional solutions. But how far EU enlargement can be extended and to what extent regional responses are feasible or possible in other parts of the globe remain as yet unanswered questions.[5] Similarly, international institutions, such as the UN, perform an increasing role in conflict prevention, peacekeeping and peace-building. But the record is mixed in different regions of the globe and states have different views on the relevance and effectiveness of international security institutions.[6]

It is the task of this and of subsequent chapters to identify areas of divergent and convergent interests among the nine countries plus the EU that may facilitate or inhibit international security cooperation. Before moving on to these tasks some consideration will be given to the current state of security studies; the relevance of the regional component in security arrangements and the role of international institutions in the management of security governance.

The contemporary security context[7]

The concept of security can be defined in different ways, ranging from relatively restrictive definitions building on military defence (security from war and conquest) to more inclusive definitions of security that consider a wider range of threats against human life. The latter category includes political security (security from extreme political oppression and persecution), economic security (security from hunger and deprivation), social and cultural security (cultural survival and minority rights), and environmental security (security from environmental degradation and disasters).

The emergence of new security threats in Europe suggests that we can no longer conceive of security in terms of a policy choice that can be fruitfully framed by a framework that is restricted to specific dyads of states. This point is confirmed in the findings of Kirchner and Sperling (2002), from which two observations can be drawn. First, states play a relatively minor role as protagonists in the present security system. Agency is attributed overwhelmingly to non-state actors that are beyond the reach of states or the traditional instruments of statecraft. Second, threats against the state are indirect rather than direct. The new security threats are generally aimed at society and threaten the social contract instead of the state's ability to govern. Threats can therefore no longer be disaggregated into the capabilities and intentions of states; primacy can no longer be attributed to the state as either agent or object (Snyder 1991). Rather, security threats have now acquired a system-wide significance that requires an alternative conceptualization. Restricting the definition of security to the traditional concern with territorial integrity or the protection of ill-defined 'national interests' would exclude threats to the social fabric of domestic or international societies.[8] Moreover, the evolution of the territorial state has left states vulnerable to new categories of threat.

The expansion of the security agenda is controversial and contested. Criteria are required to distinguish analytically a security threat from other potential sources of disorder in the international system and its component parts. Buzan *et al.* (1998) offer a definition of security that incorporates the various elements of the new security agenda, but nonetheless stays rooted in the traditional meaning generally ascribed to security by international relations scholars. They argue that 'security is about survival. It is when an issue is presented as posing an existential threat to a designated referent object.'[9] What makes something an existential threat (and thus demanding an extraordinary response) is therefore heavily dependent upon what the 'referent object' is (Buzan *et al.* 1998: 21). This means, logically, that states are not necessarily the only referents; neither are states the only possible sources of threat. Securitization theory thus opens up the possibility of thinking about security across different levels of analysis and in different issue areas. If 'security' is about surviving threats, then the act of surviving threats can be linked to almost all entities ranging from the level of the individual, as in human security, all the way upwards to the global level. Security threats are thus not necessarily consigned strictly to military, that is interstate, issues.

The military sector has traditionally been concerned with the security of the state and its armed forces as referents. The problem with traditional studies is in viewing essentially all military activity as matters of security. The truth is, however, that not all military affairs are matters of security, just as not all matters of security are related to military affairs. For instance, advanced powers have often deployed their militaries to support humanitarian aid or peacekeeping operations. Yet in these instances it is clear that their states of origin are not the referent objects under existential threat. Neither do these examples comprise 'extraordinary' measures, but are frequently considered routine activities in which the militaries of more advanced countries participate.

These discrepancies in traditional security studies are thus what motivate the multi-sector approach endorsed by the Copenhagen School that also incorporates political, economic, societal and environmental issues within the security domain (Buzan 1991). In the political sector, existential threats have traditionally been considered as threats to a state's sovereignty or prevailing ideology; but political threats can also arise in issues of influence, self-determination, or of political authority and legitimacy. In the circumstances of globalization, this becomes increasingly salient as a whole new range of potential referent objects (and threats) arise, from local political entities or societies, to international regimes, to supranational organizations, such as the European Union, as focused upon in recent governance work (Webber *et al.* 2004; Krahmann 2003). What is important in this context of different sectors (political, societal or economical etc.) and different levels (local, national or global) is to recognize the different types of interaction and, therefore, different types of referent objects (Buzan *et al.* 1998: 7). In the military sector, for instance, interaction is determined by relationships of armed force and coercion. The political sector is characterized by relationships of influence, authority and legitimacy. Relationships in the economic sector are concerned with finance, trade, the control of resources and means of production. The societal sector is concerned with collective identities, while the environmental sector is about the interaction of human civilization and the various levels of the global ecosystem. The logical extension of the multi-sector approach to security means that 'referent objects other than the state [are] allowed into the picture' (Buzan *et al.* 1998: 8).

Determinants of the new security agenda

These conceptual clarifications help to relate to the novel nature of the threats posed to the European system of governance and the prominence of non-state actors as the primary source of threat. But further precision is required. A security threat can be said to exist only if the threat posed to national, societal or systemic security is one of high intensity. The intensity of a threat is determined by five variables: the specificity of the threat, the closeness of the threat in time and space, the high probability of the threat being realized, and the seriousness of consequences the threat will have for the state, society or system (Buzan 1991: 134–40). These criteria do not address the more problematic task of establishing a hierarchy of threat. More specifically, even though the new security threats satisfy the threat criteria outlined, the problem of establishing a hierarchy of threat has become more pressing.

The analytical solution to the problem posed by the new security agenda could take any number of forms. A first approach would be a general dismissal of the 'new' security agenda as the response of those seeking to provide an alternative rationale for the continuation of NATO as a security organization as well as those who would favour an expansive remit for international institutions in the false hope of mitigating international anarchy. A second category of response would assume the position that these threats have persisted throughout the modern period and it is only the absence of great power conflict that has pushed these issues to the surface. Put somewhat differently, it is only now that the Cold War has ended that sufficient attention and intellectual resources can be paid to these long-standing threats to societal, state and systemic stability. A third category of response, and the one which appears most relevant, focuses on the changed structure of the European state system and the changing nature of the European state. The 'connectedness' of the European state system, facilitated by the success of the post-war institutions of European economic and political integration, has made these states easily penetrated by malevolent non-state and state actors: geography, technological innovations, particularly the revolution in information technologies and the linking of national economies and societies by the world wide web, convergence around the norms of political and economic openness, and the rising 'dynamic density' – defined by John Ruggie (1986: 148) as the 'quantity, velocity, and diversity of transactions' – of the Euro-Atlantic area.

It is the very elements of the contemporary state system, particularly the pressure towards norm convergence within Europe conjoined by the openness of both European states and societies, that provide the opportunities for the externalization of domestic disequilibria. This development has of necessity altered the conception of security threats away from the narrow concern with national defence to a broader understanding and concern with security. There has been a reorientation towards broad and collective milieu goals that has displaced particularistic and national goals of traditional statecraft. These structural changes in the nature of the European state and state system mitigates the conceit that there has been a qualitative change in the interrelationships between European states and societies that requires a re-examination of the nature and sources of security threats in the new century. One can even go a step further and suggest that as a consequence of globalization the same process is gradually happening at the global level, which thus requires more governance at that level as well.

A host of non-state actors exist in the management of security, particularly in the European context, involving private firms, national non-governmental organizations, international non-governmental organizations and international security organizations such as the United Nations, NATO, the Organization for Security and Co-operation in Europe (OSCE) and the EU. International organizations, NGOs and private companies are becoming increasingly drawn into security policy-making and implementation (Krahmann 2003: 11; Webber *et al.* 2004; Higgott 2005).

To determine the relative importance of state and non-state actors as agents of security requires empirical research, which needs to be directed to a number of questions. First, what type of threats do states perceive as important and with what intensity? What probability of occurrence do they assign to different type of threats? Second, are the anticipated targets state structures, societal structures, or non-combatants? Third, are the anticipated geographic sources subregional, regional or global in kind? Fourth, is the agency or actor of threat seen as a state or non-state?

A study by Kirchner and Sperling (2002) has identified twelve types of threats,[10] of which ethnic factionalism and migratory pressures emerged (in 1999) as the two threats with the highest probability of occurrence. With the onset of a spate of terrorist activities since September 2001, there is a likelihood that the ranking of security threats found by Kirchner and Sperling will have changed. An application of the typology of security threats provided by Kirchner and Sperling (2002) to the nine countries plus the EU will therefore enable both an update and an expansion of the countries under investigation.

It will further provide an opportunity to tease out the convergent and divergent points in threat perception among the different countries, as well as within the EU, and to explore possible reasons for these differences. This will not only help to establish comparisons for the transatlantic region, but to some extent also for the EU, as four of the leading EU actors are members of the G8. In part for this reason, and in part because of the growing prominence of the EU as a security actor, an examination of the security threat perception by the EU will also be made.

Regional security governance

Knowledge on these issues will allow greater understanding of the nature of security threats and the issues that are likely to dominate the security agenda whether nationally, regionally or globally. However, it is only one side of the coin and needs to be complemented with information on the range of policy responses that can relieve the symptoms as well as the underlying causes of those threats. It is the task of this volume to shed light on the perceptions of nine countries and the EU on policy responses along the following lines. First, is the preference for uni-, bi- or multilateral responses to the threats identified? Second, are there preferences for institutional response, and if so, are these of a (sub)regional, transatlantic, transpacific, or global kind?

The diversity and complexity of the new security threats outruns the capacities of states to respond unilaterally. Issues of efficiency and effectiveness compel states to cooperate with a variety of NGO and international actors, as well as to draw upon their resources and expertise, in responding to the 'emergence' of these threats. These observations appear to be borne out by the recent profusion of transnational cooperative networks and institutions (Graybow and O'Brien 2000; see also Hurrell and Woods 1999; Alagappa 1995).

A regional security governance focus expresses the inherent territoriality of contemporary international security, but also provides the contexts that give meaning to local security problems and issues, as well as widening the analytical focus to (potentially) incorporate actors other than states (Buzan and Wæver 2003). Regional security governance can be self-standing or connected with the UN. The UN encourages member states to make 'every effort' to achieve peaceful settlement of local disputes through regional arrangements to keep the Security Council informed of their activities and seek its authorization to conduct enforcement measures (UN Charter: Ch. VIII, Art. 52). But as Williams (2005: 171) shows, regional arrangements have engaged in enforcement activities often without Security Council authorization, as was the case with ECOWAS in Liberia in 1990 and again in 2003.

Because of its economic power and need to respond to conflicts in neighbouring states as well as to attacks of international terrorism (e.g. the events of 11 September 2001, Madrid 2004 and London 2005), the EU has emerged as an important regional (and potentially global) actor in the field of security (Bretherton and Vogler 1999). By being able to dispose over a spectrum of economic, political and military tools, the EU can effectively engage in different security functions such as conflict prevention, peace enforcement, peacekeeping and peace-building. The extent to which the EU's security role can be expanded is subject to both internal and external factors, which are interconnected. External factors can be a stimulant for an expansion, as was the case with the EU response to the Kosovo conflict. But as shown over the disunity on the US intervention in Iraq in 2003, external factors can also impede expansion. In spite of this setback there is a high density of interactions among security actors within the EU, both state and non-state, and a high degree of institutionalization and routinization in dealing with security matters, which is not found elsewhere in the world.

In other regions, only initial stages of regional security exist. In Africa two regional organizations should be mentioned: the African Union (AU) and the Economic Community of West African States (ECOWAS). However, both organizations suffer from severe institutional deficiencies and shortcuts in resources. On the AU, the most significant litmus test of its capability to proactively promote security on the African continent so far constitutes its mission in Darfur, which commenced in April 2004 with fewer than 500 peacekeepers. Since October 2005, the AU has employed more than 7,000 troops, mostly Rwandans and Nigerians. Financial and logistical support comes from the EU, the US and others. The AU mission's main task is to protect civilians, to assist humanitarian agencies and monitor the ceasefire with the Janjaweed rebels. However, due to the limited number of troops, inadequate equipment and logistics, and internally conflicting political interests, the AU has not been able to guarantee security in the Darfur region. In general, the capabilities of the AU would have to be strengthened significantly to do justice to the expectations of the international community for a reliable institutional response to crises in Africa.

As one of the most advanced subregional groups in the developing world dealing with security issues, particularly with conflict management and prevention, the picture is a bit brighter in the case of ECOWAS. Its Monitoring Observer Group (ECOMOG) was involved in a range of West African crisis situations, notably in Liberia, Sierra Leone and Guinea-Bissau. Since 1990 ECOWAS, through ECOMOG operations, has become able to contain and even end conflict and violence in Western Africa. Although ECOMOG's activities by no means went continuously smoothly, it might nevertheless serve as a 'prototype or future model' for security activities by African countries within African countries (cf. Ero 2000). But because Nigeria has been the driving force of ECOMOG's undertakings, using it as a tool for its own interests in the region, it is surely not a tool of an African community of equals, and not all actors within the region 'favour ECOMOG as a model for regional security' (Ero 2000). Therefore, even though the international community very much welcomes the concept of ECOMOG, it is clear that this form of regional governance does not necessarily solve more security concerns than it creates in the long run.

Another example of regional security governance is the Caribbean Community (CARICOM). Despite its mainly economic roots, the CARICOM has taken a range of steps towards political community in recent years. A notable demonstration of its role also in security questions has been given by its engagement towards its member state Haiti. In 2000, for instance, CARICOM conducted an observer mission for the elections in Haiti, with the aim to contribute towards the practice of good governance and the securing of democracy in the community. Concerned about the worsened security situation in the country, CARICOM sent a Special Mission to Haiti in February 2002 to assess the state of affairs and prepare possible steps to strengthen the government. When violence erupted in the country in spring 2004, CARICOM undertook considerable efforts to resolve the crisis in Haiti. It brought the case of Haiti to the world community, not least by bringing in the UN Security Council, and presented plans to deal with the rapidly deteriorating political and security situation. CARICOM was also involved in the post-conflict phase, particularly in the preparation of elections in spring 2006. Those three organizations within the developing world share the need for more effective, efficient and integrated institutions in order to produce positive results in security policy.

Greater institutionalization, according to Haftendorn *et al.* (1999), depends on three factors: commonality, specificity, and functional differentiation, which are interlinked. Commonality is the measure of how well actors share expectations of participatory behaviour and the world at large. Specificity is a consideration of institutional rules in terms of how precisely they are codified and how well they are enacted or ratified. Functional differentiation measures the degree to which an institution distributes functions and responsibilities amongst its participants. Greater commonality is more likely to result in the acceptance of and adherence to more specific institutional rules; more specific institutional rules will more likely be matched with a more complex differentiation of institutional tasks and functions; functional differentiation is more likely to occur when expectations are shared, embedded, and reciprocated by participants (Haftendorn *et al.* 1999: 24–5). However, these factors are affected by background conditions such as the existence or non-existence of state-to-state threats within the region in question, the interactive history of security actors (legacies of past wars or deeply engrained regional socialization procedures in which the sharing of norms and organized patterns of behaviour dominates) and limited defence capabilities among the constituent parts. These background features can be noted within the EU in both institutional and behavioural terms. Examples of institutional innovations at EU level can be observed in the establishment of the High Representative for the Common Foreign and Security Policy (HR), the Political and Security Committee, the Military Committee, the Military Staff Committee, Committee for Civilian Aspects of Crisis Management (CIVCOM), the Community Civil Protection Mechanism, the Monitoring and Information Centre (MIC), and the Centre for Information, Discussion and Exchange on the Crossing of Frontiers and Immigration (CIREFI). Through these means, the member states have invested the EU with incremental amounts of authority to play a role in the management of transnational threats. In behavioural terms, examples relate to the habit by national policy-makers to consider, consult or engage in joint actions before taking decisions in the field of security and defence (Nuttall 2000), the establishment of a European Security Strategy, and the willingness to introduce a 'solidarity clause',[11] as foreseen in the now stalled EU Constitutional Treaty. These institutional and behavioural patterns contribute to the rise of the post-Westphalian state within the EU. The latter phenomenon is suggestive of change from established patterns of world order and can be seen as contributing to a taming of anarchy in the international system and to a progression towards an international civil society. By contrast, Westphalian states of Eurasia are trapped by the logic of anarchy. Anarchy – and the state from which it derives its nature – precludes global or even regional government managing its attending liabilities. This expresses itself, in the first place, in 'weaker' forms of regional security collaboration and in more restrictive security functions by these organizations (Buzan and Wæver 2003). For example, the Association of Southeast Asian

Nations (ASEAN) and the ASEAN Regional Forum have been primarily concerned with conflict prevention and have held back from the collective use of force against one of their own members, as demonstrated during East Timor's struggle for independence (Williams 2005: 172). Security stability in the Asian-Pacific region is mainly achieved through a careful balancing of power among the main actors involved, namely China, Japan and the US. At the same time, however, all three actors pursue their very own security interests within specific cooperative frameworks. The meteoric rise of China very much shapes the security discussion about the region. But also the North Korean nuclear ambitions influence Asian-Pacific security policies.

China's main focus lies on economic development, but it also sees itself obliged to extend its military capabilities to be prepared against foreign assaults. The US tries to contain China's military development through military cooperation with countries in South, Southeast and Central Asia, exposing the prospect of an Asian-Pacific order dominated by the US alliance system. In a counter-reaction, China attempts to defend its interests by cooperating with states that have at least some affinity towards Chinese foreign policy goals, such as Russia and Kazakhstan. In addition, China safeguards its economic development by building up its influence at the expense of other states. The aim is clear: to become a great power. What makes this aspiration so problematic in security terms is the severe unpredictability in Beijing's policies. However, the international worries are somewhat eased by China's active involvement in the ASEAN Regional Forum and good relationships to its neighbours. Excluded from that are Sino–Japanese relations. They are a constant cause of security concerns, despite the fact that the two countries are each other's biggest trading partners. Taiwan is the other big hotspot of Chinese and international security, even though both China and the US are interested in preserving the status quo.

Japan and the US are very closely linked in their security policies. In fact, Japanese security policy has been formed in intimate cooperation with the US, at times even dictated by Washington. Chinese aspirations for a hegemonic position backed by military armament, including ballistic missiles, are seen to be a significant source of military threat. However, Tokyo is even more concerned about the North Korean capability to hit the Japanese mainland with missiles, perhaps equipped with nuclear warheads. As a member of the ASEAN Regional Forum, Japan has not actively used this platform to defend its security interests. Rather, it relies on the close bond to the US with its nuclear umbrella and its economic power as security instruments.

Pugh (2003) notes that regionalization does not offer a panacea for the problems of maintaining international peace and security. For Pugh, regionalization can undermine the UN's moral authority as the custodian of universal principles and entitlements by implying that people should receive only the level of peacekeeping their own region can provide.[12] Often also regional arrangements come with hegemons (e.g. the United States) attached. However, as Williams (2005: 174) points out 'successive US administrations have been less interested in regional organisations than in effective power projection – hence Washington's post-Cold War focus on "assertive multilateralism", "coalitions of the willing", and "pivotal" and "anchor" states'.

Global security governance

Although manifesting various degrees of cohesion and effectiveness, regional security governance efforts have become established features in the international system. The same cannot be said of global security governance. Jervis (2002) has provided five conditions for international security governance. Under these conditions, national elites must: eschew wars of conquest and war as an instrument of statecraft; accept that the cost of waging such a war is perceived as outweighing any conceivable benefits; embrace the principle of economic liberalism rather than conquest or empire; establish domestic democratic governance; and respect the territorial status quo. While these conditions are met in the Atlantic security community, they are lacking in the wider international context. Keohane (2002) has identified three barriers to global governance. The first is cultural, religious and civilizational heterogeneity on a global scale. The second and related barrier is the absence of a consensus on beliefs and norms at global level. The third barrier to global security governance is the absence of an institutional fabric that is thick enough to meet the challenge of governance.

A global system of collective security can only function if backed by a strong institutional basis with the coherent guidance of effectively working bodies that are equipped to respond opportunely and successfully to any breaches of international security. This institutional basis was created in 1945 with the United Nations, which also today remains the only organization with a global focus on security. In theory, the UN guarantees mutual security and peace through the cooperation of its members. National states are willing to give up parts of their sovereignty and power to this quasi-universal organization to obtain, in return, more security than in a purely anarchic system, since all UN members declare their renunciation of acts of aggression through their endorsement of the UN Charter. This stipulation is buttressed by the UN's military means to enforce it,[13] supplemented by mechanisms for the peaceful settlement of disputes (UN Charter: Ch. VII, Art. 42).

The UN Security Council's right to impose coercive measures against its members under Chapter VII of the UN Charter is at the heart of the collective system of international security. It is the only body in international law legitimized to 'determine the existence of any threat to the peace, breach of the peace, or act of aggression' and to respond accordingly (Article 39 UN Charter). However, in practice the Security Council has a rather mixed record to solve problems of global security. While its mechanisms proved to be effective for instance with regard to Afghanistan (2001), Ivory Coast (2003), and Haiti (2004), it was unable to take collective action against security threats from Serbia (1999), Iraq (2003), Iran (ongoing), and North Korea (ongoing), mainly due to differences among its permanent members. In addition, unilateralism by UN members, whenever supportive to their national interests, has undermined the Council's authority and ability to deter potential aggressors. And towards non-state actors the UN as a whole has remained largely ineffective.

Also the other UN bodies directly responsible for 'hard' security, namely the First Main Committee of the UN General Assembly, the UN Disarmament Commission and the Geneva Conference on Disarmament, are trapped in a constant impasse due to contradicting positions of UN member states. The global approach towards security led by the UN, however, has shown positive results in the field of peace-building and peacekeeping. The newly founded Peace-Building Commission will provide the UN with further possibilities.[14] Moreover, leaving aside the military dimension, the UN, together with its partners within the UN system, such as the Bretton Woods institutions, is the central global actor with regard to economic, social, cultural and environmental security. Its competence in those fields to set legal standards, to offer practicable solutions and to organize their realization is unrivalled and unquestioned by any other player. National states and regional organizations seem to have accepted the fact that only a global and multilateral approach can deliver results with respect to 'soft' security threats.[15] However, a comprehensive UN approach is needed, combining aspects of 'hard' and 'soft' security. Recent steps taken in that regard have not been encouraging, for example, the extremely modest results of the 2005 World Summit in September 2005, and the parallel failure of the crucial project of Security Council reform as well as the failure of the Nuclear Non-proliferation Treaty Review Conference in May 2005.

While future UN reforms remain uncertain, other forms of promoting global security governance can be envisaged. One such promotion could be through the role of the G8 and G20 networks. G8 meetings have dealt with conflict prevention measures in the areas of small arms and light weapons, conflict and development, illicit trade in diamonds, children in armed conflicts, international civilian police, the role of women and corporate social responsibility. Noteworthy, too, is the G8 Broader Middle East and North Africa Initiative. The G8 forum has widened its remit and involved issues of international terrorism as well as nuclear safety, for instance with the '10 plus 10 over 10' initiative, raising up to US$ 20 billion until 2012 to fund non-proliferation projects, principally in Russia.[16] There have been considerations of extending the G8 into the G20 in order to allow greater representation from the South (e.g. Brazil, China and India). For example, France has called for an upgrading of the G20 international forum on the economic and social governance of globalization from meetings involving finance ministers to those of heads of government.[17]

Another form of promoting global governance could be through greater interaction among regional organizations, and a concomitant closer cooperation by regional organizations with the UN.[18] In this respect, the role of the EU is instructive in three ways. First, the EU stresses the importance of regional organization and regional integration together with multilateralism in the task of promoting international security. In turn, many other regions look to the EU as an illustration of the benefits of regional integration. The EU also cooperates closely with such regional organizations as ASEAN, MERCOSUR, the Rio

Group, the Gulf Cooperation Council and the African Union. Second, the EU is involved in certain regions with specific tasks. For example, in the Asian region the EU supports the rebuilding of Afghanistan, assists the establishment of democratic governments in Cambodia and East Timor, and seeks a solution to the Korean Peninsula problem. Third, the EU engages in joint or mutually rein-forcing security functions with the UN as well as with NATO and the OSCE (Cameron 2005). Conflict prevention and crisis management are particularly important in that regard. Building on the successful 'bridging' peacekeeping operation in the Congo in 2003, the EU has sought to expand its cooperation with the UN and has announced the establishment of thirteen 'battle groups', 1,500 in strength, capable of being deployed within fifteen days and to operate under a UN mandate. Under the so-called Berlin-plus arrangement, the EU can borrow NATO military assets and planning facilities. This was the case with EU peacekeeping operations in Macedonia in 2003, and is now the case with a sim-ilar EU operation (Athena) in Bosnia and Herzegovina. The degree of cooperation reached among these three organizations will crucially impact on the division of labour these organizations can achieve with regard to the differ-ent security functions such as conflict prevention, peace enforcement, peacekeeping, and peace-building, and how effectively these functions can be carried out. There are also plans for EU–OSCE synergy in the fields of energy security, border management, good governance and institution building. In part, this could mean that the OSCE would play a supporting role in developing the EU's European Neighbourhood Policy. However, efforts must be made to mini-mize duplication of activities, as is, for example, the case with election monitoring, and the police missions in Bosnia and in Macedonia.

While the EU is perhaps the most active, if not effective, regional actor in promoting global security governance, other organizations make similar contri-butions to this end. Moreover, in some cases their roles involve linking adjacent regions as, for example, with NATO's Partnership for Peace (PfP), the Commonwealth of Independent States (CIS), the Shanghai Cooperation Organization (SCO), the Black Sea Economic Cooperation (BSEC) the Georgia, Ukraine, Uzbekistan, Azerbaijan and Moldova grouping (GUUAM), the ASEAN Regional Forum, and the Organization for European Security Co-operation (OSCE). The overlapping membership of these Eurasian security institutions may contribute to the creation of a single set of norms governing statecraft in the region. However, there is no guarantee that those norms will be consistent with those of the Atlantic community. The reason, as Sperling (2003) points out, is that many Asian states remain fixated with issues of territorial integrity and remain relatively unencumbered by the widespread norm against the use of military force to resolve outstanding territorial disputes among one another (e.g. India and Pakistan).

Moreover, there is a distinct possibility that, through changes in either mem-bership or organizational strategy, an inter-blocking rather than an interlocking of organizational activities could occur. This could happen with the SCO, which binds Russia, China and four former Soviet republics together to fight terrorism, boost border security and promote greater economic cooperation. In question is whether Russia and China see the SCO as a useful tool to fill the security vacuum in Central Asia or as an attempt to counter US interests. While the economic and especially military rise of China has become a growing worry for the US,[19] the growing influence of Russia in the region became also a concern both for Europe and for the non-proliferation treaty commitments in March 2006. The first involved a deal between Russia and China whereby Russia intends to supply China and the Asia-Pacific region with 60–80 billion cubic feet of gas, via two natural gas pipelines. This could potentially interfere with the amount of natural gas promised by Russia for Europe; Europe relies on Russia for 70 per cent of its gas.[20] The second was the announcement by Russia to supply India, which is not a member of the nuclear non-proliferation treaty, with 60 tonnes of nuclear fuel.[21]

Security culture

These different interests pose the question of what instrumental preferences does a country, or the EU, hold, if placed along a continuum of civilian and military instruments. Information on the difference between a preference for coercive and persuasive instruments in meeting security threats will help to differentiate 'civilian' powers[22] from 'normal' powers and to establish why certain countries prefer unilateral rather than multilateral responses, uphold preventive rather than pre-emptive measures, seek 'civilian outcomes' rather than military engagement, or adopt persuasive rather than coercive foreign policy tools. For example, according to Hyde-Price (2004) most Europeans since the end of the Cold War have a preference for deterrence, containment and soft power. As will be shown in the following chapters, history, geography, culture and limitations in capabilities are among the main reasons for the occurrence of different characteristics in the use of instruments. However, qualifications are necessary. While the legacy of 'failed' past regimes in Germany, Italy and Japan has contributed to the above characteristics, the legacy of an 'imperial' past together with the perceived special relationship with the US would, in the British case, point in the other direction. Yet what Britain shares with other European countries, though perhaps not to the same extent, is a perception of limited military capabilities. John Duffield (1998) and Thomas Berger (1996) provide overlapping definitions of security cultures. Both Duffield and Berger embed the concept of national security culture in the broader concept of political culture, which in turn focuses on how social belief systems determine how individuals think about the world and the type of world in which they wish to live. While they agree on the importance of security culture as an explanatory variable – a position endorsed in this study – they disagree on its essential components. Duffield identifies five variables: worldviews or the empirical understanding about the external environment; the content and form of national identity; the objectives defining the purposes of policy; the set of causal beliefs governing the assessment of alternative foreign policy outcomes; and the elite-shared norms that define the range of appropriate behaviours, objectives, and instruments (Duffield 1998: 24–5); Berger identifies four core elements of national security cultures: national identity, alliance relations, force structure, and civil–military relations (Berger 1996: 325–6). There is considerable overlap between the components of security culture developed by Duffield and Berger. Neither set of criteria, however, is sufficiently flexible or appropriate for cross-national comparison across states with different internal constitutional forms, historical experiences, or intellectual traditions.

We propose that four alternative variables not only capture the essential characteristics found in Berger and Duffield, but provide a better basis for cross-national comparison and economy of expression: worldviews of the external environment, national identity, instrumental preferences, and interaction preferences. Of these four variables, the worldview of the external environment overlaps perfectly with Duffield. The variable captures the underlying causal beliefs about the international system, the state's position in the system, and the definition and classification of the pertinent security actors. National identity, found in both Berger and Duffield, is central to the determination of a security culture. National identities, which establish the boundaries between 'us' and 'them', vary across national boundaries in terms of intensity, longevity, and consequence for defining the range of responses to external threats, if not their definition. The third element of security culture identifies the range of preferred instruments that a state avails itself of to meet the external challenges to its territorial integrity or way of life. Our focus on instrumental preferences is broader than Berger's concern with civil–military relations and force structure and is more economical than Duffield's unnecessary differentiation between the legitimacy and efficacy of foreign policy instruments. Berger's emphasis on alliance relationships is not misplaced, but it is too restrictive because it precludes entire categories of interaction patterns that are relevant to meeting contemporary security challenges. Interaction preferences capture the variety of formal and informal international institutions in which a state may participate to achieve its security goals, ranging from concerts to security communities with the traditional foreign policy goal of territorial integrity, to transnational or supranational arrangements facilitating the joint management of those elements of the new security agenda that resist a military solution, in particular.

While the content of the national security cultures of these nine countries as well as the points of convergence and divergence between them are of intrinsic interest, those security cultures also establish the limits of global and regional security cooperation. That the G8 countries plus China have responded differently to 11 September is a well-known fact: Canada's defence expenditure has remained more or less stagnant; France, Germany, Italy, the United Kingdom and Japan record slight increases in expenditure; China is simply continuing its modernization programme along its pre-11 September trajectory, and Russia and the US have increased their defence expenditures both in absolute terms and as a share of GDP. These divergent responses reflect not only disparate resource constraints, but national security cultures that favour a civilian response to a military one even where the risk and threat assessment are not dissimilar.

Conclusion

As will be shown in the following chapters, terrorism and proliferation of weapons of mass destruction (WMD) are seen as key threats by the nine countries plus the EU, though the agreement regarding the agencies of threat, the geographical sources of the threats and the targets of threat is far greater among the four EU members and the two North American countries. Less clear-cut are the responses envisaged by the nine countries as well as the EU to address the threats perceived. While all EU member states share the preference for a multilateral response, their institutional preferences (e.g. NATO, EU and UN) differ. Further differentiations emerge with regard to the other five countries, which seek to combine bilateral and multilateral instruments, and in the case of China and the US also stress the unilateral response option.

This points to the existence of considerable diversity in the characteristics of the nine countries. States that share the same threat perceptions do not necessarily have the same preferences in their threat responses. Dividing lines appear in nuances even within deep-rooted partnerships as the EU, but also between close allies such as the UK and the US. The result is different groupings on security culture. At the two opposing ends of security culture appear to be Canada, Germany, Italy and Japan, on the one hand, and the US, on the other. The former group seems to put the emphasis on conflict prevention, persuasion rather than the use of force, and multilateral engagement in the pursuit of security aims. The US, by contrast, seems to have adopted a policy of 'pre-emption' and to keep military means and unilateral engagements as important policy options in defence and security matters. Britain and France appear to fall between these two positions. Whilst emphasizing conflict prevention and multilateral engagement, they are more prepared than the other four to use military means. A position closer to that of the US than that of Britain and France appears to be the position adopted by Russia and China. It will be the task of the following chapters to determine the extent of these apparent similarities and differences in threat perception and institutional response and to assess to what extent different characteristics in security cultures expand or limit the prospects for security cooperation either among the nine countries in question, or security cooperation on a regional/global level.

Hence, emphasis will be placed on ensuring comparability between the following chapters. The substantive chapters on the security policies of the nine countries plus the EU (chapters 2–11) will follow the same structure and ask similar questions about each state's approach to the challenge of regional and global security governance. This approach will increase the opportunity for revealing insights into national differences and similarities that reflect different definitions of interest and different sets of threats that may be immune to multilateral solutions.

In each of these chapters, the introduction will place the security strategy of each country into its specific historical and geo-strategic context. It will also identify each country's 'exceptionalism' that makes it different from others (e.g. Britain's imperial legacy; Japan's peace constitution; Germany's preference for 'civilian outcomes'). Individual chapters will identify the critical security threats (including types, targets and sources) as defined by each national government or the EU and their probability of occurrence. They will further deal with the responses to threat, which will include an examination of the institutional preferences (e.g. regional, transatlantic, transpacific, or global), and the instrumental preferences (civilian versus military) for meeting threats. Information on threat perceptions and response to threats will be complemented with data on defence expenditures and public opinion.

In the conclusion of each chapter an assessment is sought as to whether the emphasis of a given country is more on security than defence. Two issues will be of particular relevance in this respect. First, whether the elites have a 'militarized', 'civilianized' or 'differentiated' understanding of security with respect to instruments relied upon to meet the security threat. Second, whether the dominant characteristics of national security cultures expand or limit the prospects for security cooperation.

Acknowledgement

The author wishes to thank Max Rasch for his valuable assistance in the research, Can Berk for his assistance with the bibliography, and Sven Biscop, Osvaldo Croci, Sten Reynning, Reimund Seidelmann and Wolfgang Wessels for helpful comments on a previous draft of this chapter.

Notes

1 There might be an argument for the inclusion of India and Brazil in such an investigation, as both are considered rising powers with growing influence in WTO and G20 affairs. However, unlike China, the only outside G8 country included, these two countries lack comparable global reach and power. Although India is a nuclear country, it is with the exception of the India–Pakistani conflict over Kashmir not much involved in the regional context. Neither India nor Brazil are permanent members of the UN Security Council.
2 This is basically a modified version of the definition provided by Webber *et al.* (2004: 4).
3 For an attempt at this see Kirchner and Sperling (2002).
4 This is not to deny that the legitimacy of the global order also requires that everybody's security concerns are taken into consideration at global level, as called for by the High-Level Panel of the UN.
5 For a more optimistic scenario see Buzan and Wæver (2003).
6 For details relating to governance and legitimacy issues see Keohane (2004) and Higgott (2005).
7 This section relies substantially on Kirchner and Sperling (2002).
8 This formulation embodies two assumptions. First, it assumes that states are constrained and dependent upon a network of norms, ideas and institutions that

shape state interests and behaviour. Second, the traditional definition of the national interest is too restrictive a concept for the post-Cold War European state system.

9   Notably, Buzan, Wæver and de Wilde's definition of a referent object *excludes* milieu goals and collapses state and societal security into an undifferentiated category. See Buzan *et al.* (1998): 21.

10   A biological/chemical attack; a nuclear attack; the criminalization of economies; narcotics trafficking; ethnic conflict; macroeconomic destabilization; general environmental threats; specific environmental threats; cyberwarfare against commercial structures; cyberwarfare against defence structures; terrorism against state structures; and migratory pressures.

11   However, this clause carries less in terms of solidarity implications than Article 5 of either NATO or WEU does.

12   The UN can of course sub-contract operations to regional organizations outside the specific region in question.

13   It needs to be stressed that of course the UN can act militarily only if member states provide the means.

14   UN Doc. A/59/565 (2004): 69–71; 80.

15   For a distinction between 'soft' and 'hard' threats see Nye (2003).

16   Statement by the Group of Eight Leaders (2002).

17   'For a lesson in combating political apathy, this is the place', *The Guardian,* 3 December 2004.

18   There is a platform that brings together the UN and regional organizations, but it is weak and brings together a diverse group of actors.

19   For example, US Secretary of State, Rice, warned on a trip to Indonesia in March 2006 that because of China's economic and military 'Beijing could become a negative power in the region'. Quoted in 'China remarks add edge to Rice trip to Sydney', *Financial Times,* 16 March 2006.

20   See 'Russia pledges gas pipelines to China', *Financial Times,* 22 March 2006.

21   See 'Non-Proliferation: Concern in west over Russian plan to sell nuclear rector fuel to India', *Financial Times,* 16 March 2006.

22   For a definition of civilian power see Duchêne (1972).

References

Alagappa, M. (1995) *Political Legitimacy in Southeast Asia: The Quest for Moral Authority,* Stanford, CA: Stanford University Press.

Berger, T. (1996) 'Norms, identity and national security in Germany and Japan', in P. Katzenstein (ed.) *The Culture of National Security: Norms and Identity in World Politics,* New York: Columbia University Press.

Bretheron, C. and Vogler, J. (1999) *The European Union as a Global Actor,* London: Routledge.

Buzan, B. (1991) *People. States and Fear,* London: Harvester Wheatsheaf.

Buzan, B. and Wæver, O. (2003) *Regions and Powers: The Structure of International Security,* Cambridge: Cambridge University Press.

Buzan, B., Wæver, O. and de Wilde, J. (1998) *Security: A New Framework for Analysis,* Boulder: Lynne Rienner.

Cameron, F. (2005) 'The EU and International Organisation: partners in crisis management', EPC Policy Paper.

Duchêne, F. (1972) 'Europe's role in world peace', in R. Mayne (ed.) *Europe Tomorrow: Sixteen Europeans Look Ahead,* London: Fontana.

Duffield, J.S. (1998) *World Power Forsaken: Political Culture, International Institutions, and German Security Policy after Unification,* Stanford, CA: Stanford University Press.

Ero, C. (2000) 'ECOMOG: A model for Africa?', in J. Cilliers and A. Hilding-Norberg (eds) *Building Stability in Africa: Challenges for the New Millennium,* ISS Monograph 46.

Graybow, C. and O'Brien, D. (2000) 'Review of Research: Regional Organisations and their Roles in Peace and Security, Humanitarian Assistance, Human Rights and Democracy Promotion', 1st draft, New York: Center on International Cooperation. Available online at: <http://www.cic.nyu.edu/archive/pdf/Review_of_Research.pdf> (accessed 10 May 2006).

Haftendorn, H., Keohane, R.O. and Wallander, C.A. (eds) (1999) *Imperfect Unions: Security Institutions over Time and Space,* Oxford: Oxford University Press.

Higgott, R. (2005) 'The theory and practice of global and regional governance: accommodating American exceptionalism and European pluralism', *European Foreign Affairs Review* 10: 1–20.

Hurrell, A. and Woods, N. (eds) (1999) *Inequality, Globalization, and World Politics,* Oxford: Oxford University Press.

Hyde-Price, A. (2004) 'European security culture, strategic culture, and the use of force', *European Security* 13 (4): 323–43.

Jervis, R. (2002) 'Theories of war in an era of leading power peace', *American Political Science Review* 96 (1): 1–14.

Keohane, R.O. (2002) *Power and Governance in a Partially Globalized World,* London: Routledge.

Keohane, R.O. (2004) 'Global governance and democratic accountability', in D. Held and M. Konig Archibugi (eds) *Taming Globalization: Frontiers of Governance,* Cambridge: Polity.

Kirchner, E. and Sperling, J. (2002) 'The new security threats in Europe: theory and evidence' in *European Foreign Affairs Review* 7 (4): 423–52.

Krahmann, E. (2003) 'Conceptualising security governance', *Cooperation and Conflict* 38 (1): 5–26.

Nuttall, S. (2000) *European Foreign Policy,* Oxford: Oxford University Press.

Nye. J. (2003) 'U.S. power and strategy After Iraq', *Foreign Affairs* 82 (4): 60–73.

Pugh, M. (2003) 'The world order politics of regionalisation', in M. Pugh and W.P.S. Sidhu (eds) (2003) *The United Nations and Regional Security: Europe and Beyond,* Boulder: Lynne Rienner.

Ruggie, J.G. (1986) 'Continuity and transformation in the world polity: toward a neo-realist synthesis', in R.O. Keohane (ed.) *Neorealism and its Critics,* New York: Columbia University Press.

Snyder, G.H. (1991) 'Alliances, balance, and stability', *International Organization* 45 (1): 126–7.

Sperling, J. (2003) 'Eurasian security governance: new threats, institutional adaptations', in J. Sperling, S. Kay and S.V. Papacosma (eds) *Limiting Institutions? The Challenge of Eurasian Security Governance,* Manchester: Manchester University Press.

Statement by the Group of Eight Leaders (2002) 'The G8 Global Partnership Against the Spread of Weapons and Materials of Mass Destruction', Kananaskis, Canada, 27 June 2002. Available online at: <http://www.state.gov/e/eb/rls/othr/11514.htm> (accessed 10 May 2006).

UN Doc. A/59/565 (2004) 'A More Secure World: Our Shared Responsibility'. Report of the High-Level Panel on Threats, Challenges and Change.

Webber, M., Croft, S., Howorth, J., Terriff, T. and Krahmann, E. (2004) 'The governance of European security', *Review of International Studies* 30 (1): 3–26.

Williams, P.D. (2005) 'Review article. International peacekeeping: the challenges of state-building and regionalization', *International Affairs* 81 (1): 163–74.

Part I
Europe

2 France

Between exceptionalism and orthodoxy

Thierry Tardy

Since the Second World War, France's security strategy has been the result of an unfailing anchorage in the West, its alliances and values, and a certain propensity to cultivate independence and non-alignment vis-à-vis the American superpower. France's foreign and defence policies lie at the junction of these two fundamental features.

The attachment to the West is unsurprising, as France has objectively been one of the main political, military, cultural and economic pillars of what constitutes the Western bloc and has therefore been logically involved in the security framework associated with it. The tendency towards non-alignment is more complex. It is an expression of France's political culture, inherited from the French Revolution and the subsequent role as a European power. This heritage has significantly shaped France's conception of its place on the international scene. It has led to the idea of a French 'exceptionalism', simultaneously reality and fiction, contained in the conviction that France has special responsibilities, that it has a rank to hold, a particular role to play. This, in turn, limits the extent to which French foreign and defence policies can be tied to its allies' respective policies, those of the US in particular. Insofar as French 'exceptionalism' implies a certain aspiration to universalism, it is inherently difficult to reconcile with another alleged source of universalism, namely the American (Hoffmann 2000).

In the broadly defined field of international security, the linkage between 'French exceptionalism' and the way France assesses the threats to its security is not yet clear. Throughout the Cold War, France was a genuine and reliable ally whenever the Alliance was being tested, as was the case during the Cuban Missile Crisis or during the INF (intermediate-range nuclear force) missile crisis in the early 1980s. In contrast, the 1956 Suez crisis and the 1966 French withdrawal from the NATO military structure did involve true differences in policy orientations, but did not reflect any fundamental difference in strategic threat assessment. For example, French particularism within NATO did not result in a different French analysis of the danger represented by the Soviet Union.

After the main factor of cohesion – the Soviet threat – disappeared, the very notion of 'the West' was shattered. In the new environment, the whole notion of threat is to be revisited, as are the policies aimed at tackling the so-called 'new threats'. In this process, France does not necessarily distance itself from its partners, but still aspires to be one of the driving forces in the changing environment.

The events of 11 September 2001 once again oblige Western states to look at their threat assessment and policy responses. The French approach is a mix of singularity and orthodoxy. France shares most of the concerns and policy orientations of its allies, but witnesses with increasing discomfort the emergence of unipolarity as one key feature of the international system. In this respect, the French peculiarity, if there is any, lies in the way policy should be conducted – that is in the way threats should be addressed – rather than in the threat assessment itself.

In this respect, even if France's threat assessment in the post-Cold War era can be seen as by and large accurate, it is not certain whether that assessment has been translated into policy. The shift from defence to security in theory and practice has not yet entirely taken place.

Security threat perceptions of a medium-sized power with a global vocation

As in every other Western country, the end of the Cold War had a direct impact on the definition of France's security threats. The threat against which French defence policy had been built for over forty years – the Soviet Union – was disappearing. Given its scale, such a threat had captured both attention and resources; it had heavily influenced French foreign policy, determined the format, budget and posture of the armed forces, and eclipsed almost any other kind of threat.

Yet the disappearance of the Soviet danger coincided with the emergence of new forms of threat. The Soviet threat – well identified, massive, state-based and of a primarily military nature – gave way to threats characterized by their diffuse nature, often originating from non-state actors, and containing an important non-military dimension: nationalism and identity-based conflicts, religious fundamentalism and terrorism, proliferation of weapons of mass destruction (WMD), and transnational organized crime among others. The 'novelty' of these threats is widely accepted: even if most of them were key features of the globalization process that came to be analysed in the 1970s, many were actually born out of it. However new, they augured for a new disorder in lieu of the short-lived New World Order proclaimed in 1990.

In France, this coming disorder was reflected both in the academic literature and the policy area. What was at stake was a fundamental reappraisal of the nature of the international system, and of the key concepts of security and threat. This was grasped in the first half of the 1990s in books by leading scholars such as *Le retournement du monde* (Badie and Smouts 1992) or *Appels d'empire* (Salamé 1996)[1] which challenged the realist paradigm. Both analysed the erosion of the state as the central actor of the international system and emphasized instead non-state actors and transnational issues. As the non-military nature of the 'new' threats was underlined, the term 'security' tended to replace the too narrowly defined term 'defence'. Taking heed of the new context, a significant part of the literature was also dedicated to the new form of wars, their causality and evolution (Delmas

1996; Murawiec 2000; Vennesson 1998). In this new environment, uncertainty characterizes the nature of the system, the roles and nature of its agents, and their relations.

After the short period of euphoria around the concept of a New World Order that had some resonance in France,[2] public discourse of the early 1990s was replete with references to the new security environment, its threats and, to a certain extent, the unpreparedness of the state when facing them. The dislocation of Yugoslavia and the wars that followed came as illustrations of the new context, while France became heavily involved at all levels in the managing of the Yugoslav crises (Tardy 1999b).

Those different evolutions were presented in a relatively comprehensive and coherent manner in the 1994 defence White Paper, written on the initiative of Prime Minister Édouard Balladur. The White Paper's first chapter takes note of the absence of an identified military threat to French territory, but also describes a European security environment that remained highly unstable. It presents the proliferation of WMD as one of the major challenges to international and French security, before identifying four sources of 'new vulnerabilities': terrorism; religious extremisms and nationalisms; drug trafficking; and the globalization of security and communication strategies (Ministère de la Défense 1994).

In the same vein, the White Paper defines three categories of national interests particularly threatened in the new environment (Ministère de la Défense 1994):

- vital interests: the integrity of national territory, including metropolitan France and overseas territories, and territorial airspace and waters; the free exercise of sovereignty and the protection of the population;
- strategic interests: although the White Paper states that there should not be a clear distinction between vital and strategic interests, it defines strategic interests as the maintenance of peace in Europe and in the areas bordering the European continent south and east; the Mediterranean and the Middle East as well as spaces essential to the French economic activity and to the freedom of trade and communication are also deemed to be of particular strategic importance;
- interests related to France's international responsibilities: these interests are linked to France's status as a permanent member of the UN Security Council and its 'particular vocation'.

By their nature, most of the new threats are not linked to a specific territorial base, which makes a geographical approach less relevant than during the Cold War. However, the strategic interests defined in the White Paper clearly identify Europe, the Mediterranean and the Middle East as the possible origin of threat. Similarly, the fact that no major threat to French territory is identified does not mean that France has necessarily become safer. On the contrary, the transnational nature of the evolving threats renders French territory unprotected by traditional means (such as nuclear deterrence and territorial defence). This also leads some decision-makers, such as Foreign Minister Hubert Védrine, to stigmatize the globalization process as being a fertile breeding ground for the development of the new threats (see Védrine 2000). A geographical approach retains pertinence when looking at particular categories of threat. Illegal immigration, for example, is an issue analysed differently in France, Italy or Spain as compared to Sweden or Ireland, largely because the geographical location of Mediterranean states renders the threat of refugee flows more immediate than in Northern Europe.

In the 1990s, the Iraqi invasion of Kuwait (with the associated threat to the oil supply), the wars in former Yugoslavia (which were provoked by or led to extreme nationalism, identity-based conflicts, ethnic cleansing, refugee flows, weapons smuggling and organized crime), the civil war in Algeria (and its impact on French internal security with the 1995–6 series of bomb attacks in France), the limited civil war in Albania (following the collapse of the Albanian economy in 1997 and subsequent refugee flows), or the development of Islamic fundamentalism in the Arab–Muslim world provide illustrations of what France identified as direct or indirect threats to its security. In this respect, the Iraqi invasion of Kuwait in 1990 is not seen as the most likely scenario of regional destabilization. In the post-Cold War era, conflicts are characterized by their intra-state nature, and instability is seen as coming from weak or 'failed' states rather than from powerful and aggressive ones.

Lastly, one threat that is identified in France and that distinguishes it from its partners is constituted by the unipolar international system centred on the United States. Drawing on an argument largely developed by structural realists (Waltz 1979), French public discourse is replete with references to the detrimental effects of one power dominating all the others and with advocacies for a multipolar world. This analysis led to the concept of 'hyperpower', coined by Védrine to describe the level of domination by the US on the international scene (Védrine 2003; 2000). By extension, this approach also insinuates that the United States itself can be a threat to international security – although not directly to French security. This concern became particularly acute in the context of the 2002/2003 Iraq crisis, when American policy was perceived in France as likely to make the world less safe. Such a threat is, however, in no way comparable with other threats to French security.

In this environment, French threat assessment, as laid down in public documents as well as the academic literature since the end of the Cold War, is a fair reflection of reality. The changing nature of the system is by and large understood, as is the non-military nature of the many so-called new threats.

It is interesting here to note the existence of a large consensus within political parties on foreign affairs and defence in general and on threat assessment in particular. The 1994 defence White Paper was written under the 'cohabitation' system and reflects the view of both the Socialists and the Right. With the exception of extremist parties, divisions on foreign policy issues lie within political parties rather than between them. The debates on the European Constitution or on the Iraq crisis in 2002/2003, or in the mid 1990s on the resumption of nuclear tests, provide illustrations of divergences that cannot be traced to a precise party affiliation. As an example, within the Gaullist *Union pour un Mouvement*

Populaire (UMP), there is a cleavage between the Atlanticists and the 'Gaullists', creating some tensions on issues such as French policy towards NATO or, more recently, the French position on Iraq.

11 September 2001: A confirmation of an already identified threat

The events of 11 September 2001 shed new light on the way France perceives security threats. In terms of threat assessment, the September 2001 attacks can be viewed from one of two separable perspectives. The first would treat the attacks as a brutal confirmation of a pre-existing threat rather than the discovery of a previously unknown one. The second would argue that the magnitude of the event fundamentally changed the nature of the threat as well as the assessment of the role that non-state actors now play in the international system. The French reaction to the events of 11 September would seem to demonstrate that France is leaning towards the first view, as is the case in Europe generally.

At the governmental level, the September 2001 attacks constitute a tragedy that should lead, in the first place, to an infallible demonstration of solidarity with the US at all possible levels and, in the longer term, to a reappraisal of threat assessment and of the ways this kind of threat can be addressed (Quilès *et al.* 2001). The attacks are, however, not interpreted as constituting an event that should lead to fundamental changes in French security policy. There is no significant push for a new defence White Paper that would take heed of the new situation. In January 2002, President Jacques Chirac expressed the view that the '11 September attacks force us to be more vigilant to ensure the safety of our peoples'. Chirac underlines the fact that terrorism is not a new phenomenon, while stating that what is new is the 'destructive capacity' of terrorist groups in the 'heart of our societies'.[3] In the same vein, Chirac states that 'terrorism is not the only threat' and that 'the world should not organize itself solely around the response to the challenge posed by 11 September'.[4] Such a position is central to the French policy and clearly distinguishes it from the American approach. While French policy-makers take terrorism seriously, it is understood that it should not be the only element to take into account.

Nonetheless, all documents dealing with security issues published by the executive or the legislative branch after September 2001 make constant reference to terrorism and related issues. The 2003–2008 'Military Programme Law' (MPL), which defines French defence priorities for the next five years, identifies four categories of threat: terrorism; intra-state conflicts; nuclear, radiological, biological, chemical and ballistic missile proliferation; and organized crime (Parlement français 2003). The document also mentions 'failing states' as sources of instability. Additionally, the text states that since France is a developed, urbanized and open society, it is particularly vulnerable to these new threats. Its involvement in the world makes it a potential target. In line with what was already observed, the 'Military Programme Law' underlines the 'blurring of the line between internal and external security' and the difficulty to tackle 'asymmetrical threats'.

French security experts have largely converged on the significance of the 11 September attacks for international relations and France. Some nuances exist as to their impact on world politics and the extent to which they represent a break with the previous configuration, but most analysts stigmatize the increasingly powerful (and destructive) role of non-state actors in the globalization process and see it as an enduring feature of the international arena. A general consensus also exists that 11 September represents an acceleration of already existing trends – observed at least since the end of the Cold War – rather than the emergence of totally new patterns. François Heisbourg, one of the most respected French experts on security issues and director of the Fondation pour la Recherche Stratégique, coined the expression 'hyper-terrorism' to reflect the combination of mass destruction and the apocalyptic nature of the perpetrators (Heisbourg 2001: 11–12). In the French leading journal *Politique étrangère,* Dominique David talks about a world that combines an accelerated process of globalization which makes it increasingly open, and the development of regional 'abscesses', both expressions of globalization and reactions to it (David 2001: 765–7).[5] One finds again here the reference to globalization as a possible fertile ground for the new threats.

In these different analyses, the French generally refuse to endorse Huntington's approach of the clash of civilizations to explain the September 2001 attacks or to describe the nature of the relationship between the 'West' and the Islamic World. The amalgamation of terrorism and Islam is rejected (see Kepel 2002 and 2004), while the very concept of 'terrorism', used with some reluctance, is analysed in security terms as well as in sociological terms (with the objective to understand its causes).

Public opinion and threat perception

French public opinion has largely embraced the evolution of the international security environment in the post-Cold War period. Throughout the 1990s, opinion polls show that the French population no longer fears a third world war or a territorial conflict involving France but increasingly worries about non-traditional threats such as terrorism or religious fundamentalism.[6] Along with these two phenomena, other issues such as WMD proliferation, inter-ethnic tensions in Europe or the Israel–Palestine conflict are also part of the threat spectrum. In geographical terms, the threat is perceived to come from the South; Algeria is mentioned first when people are asked to name a country from which a threat can originate (27 per cent in 2001), followed (until recently) by Iraq (between 12 and 30 per cent) (Mendras 2003: 138).

It is worth noting that terrorism was perceived as one of the key threats to French security before 2001. Thirty-six per cent of those questioned about the 'first danger for France' mentioned terrorism in 2000, compared to 41 per cent in 2002 (see Tables 2.1 and 2.2). Overall, threat perceptions and trends within the French population are more confirmed than modified or reversed post-September 2001.

Similarly, following the September 2001 attacks, beyond the expression of solidarity, encapsulated by a declaration in *Le Monde* that *'Nous sommes tous*

Table 2.1 French threat perceptions in 2002 (per cent)

Question: In the current international context, what is, according to you, the first danger for France?	
Mass terrorism, such as the 11 September attacks	41
Social, demographic inequalities or inter-ethnic tensions in France and in Europe	27
Opposition between civilizations or between systems (West versus Islam, or poor versus rich countries)	15
Spillover of regional conflicts (India/Pakistan or Israel/Palestine)	10
Development of mafias	4
Other/Don't know	3

Source: 'Les Français et les questions de défense, sécurité, civisme et forces armées', Opinion Poll conducted by the Institut BVA in May 2002, and published in *Ouest France*, 16 June 2002.

Table 2.2 French threat perceptions in 2003 (per cent)

Question: I am going to read you a list of possible international threats to Europe in the next 10 years. Please tell me if you think each one is an extremely important threat, an important threat or not an important threat at all.				
	Extremely important threat	*Important threat*	*Not important*	*Don't know/ refusal*
Economic competition from the US	18	63	18	1
Islamic fundamentalism	51	41	6	2
International terrorism	65	33	2	–
Large numbers of immigrants and refugees coming into Europe	22	50	26	2
Military conflict between Israel and its Arab neighbours	45	47	7	1
North Korea developing weapons of mass destruction	41	44	12	3
Iran developing weapons of mass destruction	36	46	14	4
US unilateralism	34	54	11	1

Source: TNS Sofres (2003) *Transatlantic Trends 2003 – Topline Data*, Montrouge: 19–21.

américains',[7] the French have not become overly concerned with their own vulnerability to terrorist attacks similar to those that occurred in New York or later in Madrid. Even less prevalent is the sentiment that France could be 'at war' against terrorist groups following the September 2001 attacks. Opinion polls show that terrorism is high on the list of threats to French security, yet remains an elusive threat. Finally, echoing what the leaders contend in a more or less clear-cut way, a significant portion of the French people see the US as possibly threatening French interests – though obviously not in a military way (see Mendras 2003; and TNS Sofres 2003).

Table 2.3 French threat perceptions in the post-11 September era

Type of key threats	Nuclear, radiological, biological, chemical and ballistic proliferation
	Terrorism
	Religious extremisms and nationalisms
	Organized crime/drug trafficking
	Regional and intra-state conflicts
	Failed states
Agency of threats	States and non-state actors
	Extremist groups
Target of threat	Population
	Military/Officials in France and abroad
	State structure
	Economic assets
	Official premises
Geographical source of threat	Global
	Balkans
	Eastern Europe
	Mediterranean
	Middle East

Institutional and instrumental response to threats

The very essence of a security policy is to respond to threats of whatever nature: 'traditional' or non-traditional, military or non-military. These responses depend on the nature of the threat and its degree of immediacy, the tools at the disposal of a state to address the threat, and other parameters such as the historical, geographical, political and cultural background of the state concerned. In any case, the perception of a threat is as important as its reality, if not more so.

Interaction preference

In the post-Cold War environment, French security policy has been characterized by an attempt to adapt to the new environment, combined with the asserted desire to maintain a certain degree of independence. In executing this policy, France has combined a 'realist' agenda, which pushes it to promote and defend narrowly defined national interests, and a 'liberal' approach to foreign and defence policies, whereby France advocates the development of international relations based on some agreed norms and values.

One important dimension of France's security culture is its approach to multilateralism as a way to regulate interstate relations. Multilateralism is for France simultaneously a framework of action, a way to promote French interests (multilateral bodies as forum), and a tool to constrain others. In the post-Cold War world, in which France is no longer a great power, multilateralism is not a policy option; it imposes itself on France.

This vision is partly linked to France's threat perception and to the interdependence between France's national interests and the interests of its closest allies. In 1995, in London, newly elected President Chirac and British Prime Minister John Major agreed on the fact that the 'vital interests of one country could not be threatened without also jeopardizing the vital interests of the other'.[8] Increasingly, the European integration process creates new solidarities, regardless of formal security guarantees. This phenomenon, together with the developments of the Common Foreign and Security Policy and European Security and Defence Policy (ESDP) in the second half of the 1990s and the evolving nature of the international system, makes it difficult to isolate the security policy of one particular European country. Yet the interdependence of European vital interests has not led France to launch an earnest debate on an 'enlarged sanctuary' for the French nuclear deterrent that would go beyond the protection of *French* vital interests (territory and population).

It follows that France views international cooperation and multilateralism as the only way to address contemporary security threats. A national response is necessary but cannot take place in isolation from what others are doing. This approach is valid for the so-called new threats that ignore borders as well as more traditional ones, such as conflicts in Africa. The need to promote international cooperation relates to the efficacy of the response, but it also concerns the legitimacy question, particularly when coercive action is contemplated. Consequently, organizations such as the EU and the UN, but also NATO, the Organization for Security and Co-operation in Europe or the Organisation Internationale de la Francophonie, are integral parts of the French foreign and defence policies. In many ways, they are the channels of elaboration and expression for these policies. International cooperation, however, faces formidable barriers: there is no doubt that a transnational threat cannot be effectively tackled at the national level; cooperation is nonetheless impeded by the extreme sensitivity of sharing intelligence with other states.

Though national in nature, French defence policy is tailored to support the ESDP (with the exception of nuclear deterrence). As noted previously, the EU has become for France the natural framework of action in the security field far beyond military action. The EU is perceived as the institution that should play the central role in coordinating states' security policies, including the fight against terrorism (Delebarre 2004), despite the extreme difficulties of developing joint European approaches. Because the EU has a holistic approach to security that combines military and civilian aspects and theoretically addresses both internal and external threats, it is seen as one of the key actors of the French response to the wide spectrum of security threats.

As a military alliance, NATO remains a central component of the transatlantic link for France. Even though NATO is perceived as an important forum for the French response to global threats, the deep-rooted French scepticism about the ability of the Alliance to adapt to the new environment limits its operational usefulness. NATO remains a key actor of crisis management, and France is the second largest contributor to the NATO Response Force. But the combination of

France's historic distrust vis-à-vis NATO, the decline of the collective defence leg of the organization, and the lasting doubts about future NATO missions have led France to view it as an organization that plays a subsidiary rather than primary role in threat management. All official documents dealing with foreign and defence issues make clear and recurrent references to the EU, which has become indissociable from French policy. By contrast, NATO is usually presented as one tool among others and neglected in most foreign policy papers. This attitude towards NATO enjoys broad support in France, but it is regularly criticized by the Atlanticist faction of the right favouring a rapprochement with NATO. France's approach is not always shared by its European partners, who often value NATO more than France does. France distinguishes itself from many of its partners in examining the channels to be favoured in responding to security threats. The French insistence on EU autonomy vis-à-vis NATO (i.e. vis-à-vis the US) is indicative of the French desire for Europeans to distance themselves from the Americans in addressing the threats to their security.

By the same token, working within multilateral frameworks to establish norms or to negotiate treaties and international legal instruments is also part of the French security policy. As always, this approach lies at the junction of the French realist and liberal agendas.

It is clear that the French position on the Non-Proliferation Treaty (NPT) and its role in limiting nuclear proliferation is not entirely driven by the will to promote a particular norm as an end, but to protect French security, rank and prestige in the international system. Similarly, France's support for key principles of the UN Charter is not always the result of a genuine adhesion to liberal values. The circumvention of the UN Security Council in the case of operation 'Allied Force' in Kosovo provides an illustration of the ambiguity of the French approach. Yet, the necessity for states to abide by internationally accepted rules in a highly deregulated world is part of French political culture. This means that responding to threats cannot be totally disconnected from the framework in which the response takes place.

In the case of Iraq in the 2002/2003 crisis, whatever the Anglo–American criticisms of the French position, it is a fact that the French policy discourse was, to a certain extent, genuinely motivated by the need to act in conformity with some widely accepted rules, such as the UN Charter and its provisions on the resort to force. Norms do matter to France, because France holds the view that norms help limit and contain various forms of instability.

Multilateral peace operations

France is deeply involved in the maintenance of peace and security in Europe and beyond through crisis management. French participation in peace operations, be it through coalitions of states, international organizations, or even on a national basis, is one of the key dimensions of the French response to security threats. Whatever the framework, as one of the top-ranking French officers put it, crisis management operations in the last fifteen years have been, and are most likely to remain, the 'daily job' of the military in the coming fifteen years.[9] By contributing to peace operations at the political and military levels, France is willing to tackle destabilizing factors such as regional conflicts, refugee flows, organized crime, humanitarian emergencies or violations of human rights, phenomena that often take place in failed or failing states. Through crisis management outside its borders, France intends to project security to areas where threats to its own security can emerge.

Beyond this contribution to regional or international stability, French policy also aims to guarantee that France is present on the international scene as a strategic actor. In many respects, the capacity to deploy forces in crisis management operations is a component of power, and France is concerned that its external action not only reflects its interests but also its power.

With the exception of African policy (which is less and less an exception), French policy of crisis management is channelled through multilateral bodies; the United Nations, the EU, NATO or the OSCE, but also the G8 or some ad hoc settings. In this respect, the UN and EU occupy a special place. Since the end of the Cold War, the UN Security Council has been a body of strategic importance for French foreign policy. The status of permanent member guarantees French centrality in the international security architecture; it maintains, somehow artificially, its position as one of the great powers. The 2002/2003 Iraq crisis illustrates well France's centrality in the international system despite its relatively modest (compared to the United States) economic and military power.

However, in the field of peacekeeping, if the UN retains its centrality as a political forum and an institution capable of shaping international norms and of legitimizing or legalizing interventions, France no longer views it as the most appropriate operational tool. In fact, following the difficulties encountered by the UN in Bosnia–Herzegovina and Somalia in the early 1990s and the subsequent discrediting of the organization, France ceased to contribute troops to UN-led peace operations and began to favour other channels (Tardy 1999a).

Indeed, NATO, ad hoc coalitions of states and, more recently, the EU have appeared as more appropriate vehicles for peacekeeping operations. The Balkans provide many examples of this reorientation, with NATO and the EU emerging as the pre-eminent actors in the stabilization processes. In this evolution, the EU has overtaken NATO (or any other institutional framework) as France's most favoured forum for crisis management, despite the shortcomings that the EU still has to overcome, and despite the fact that France is highly involved in NATO operations. The whole ESDP project was initiated and supported by France, at times at variance to some of its partners' ambitions for the EU. In this context, the French-led EU operation in the Democratic Republic of Congo further expanded the EU's role as peace implementer, in this case outside Europe and in close cooperation with the UN.

Instrumental preferences

In the last decade, the adaptation process has been defined in key moments, such as the release of the 1994 defence White Paper, the reform of the armed forces

and abolition of conscription announced in 1996, the MPL for 1997–2002, the
Saint Malo Declaration that launched the ESDP process in December 1998, and
the MPL for 2003–2008. Those different documents or decisions take stock of the
new environment and prescribe new approaches that employ military and non-
military instruments of statecraft.

French defence policy is oriented first and foremost to protecting France's
'vital interests' via its nuclear deterrence posture. The status of a nuclear state
remains a key element of France's place on the international scene and continues
to be of inestimable political value, comparable to the status of permanent member of the UN Security Council. Officially, nuclear deterrence is still a
cornerstone of French defence policy, its relevance as an ultimate guarantee is
regularly confirmed by President Chirac, notably in reference to WMD proliferation. The French doctrine remains one of non-use, framed by the concept of
suffisance (Tertrais 2000).

Militarily speaking, though, the nuclear capacity may appear unhelpful when
looking at the threats that confront France. The more diffuse, transnational, and
de-territorialized the threat, the slimmer the prospect that nuclear retaliation (or
the threat to retaliate) will deter. As a consequence, the French nuclear posture is
far less central than it was during the Cold War. Yet this lost centrality has not led
to a public debate on the relevance of the French deterrent and on its appropriate-
ness to the changing environment,[10] let alone the costs of modernizing the nuclear
arsenal.[11] By the same token, the idea that French nuclear policy could be
expanded to other states, or even 'Europeanized', has not been seriously discussed within France as a real policy option; it is also likely that its European
partners have yet to overcome their uneasiness vis-à-vis this issue.

The French will to retain its nuclear capacity coexists with its desire to retain an
independent military capability, capable of autonomous force projection outside
Europe. This preference reflects the independence leitmotif animating French foreign policy more generally, and is interesting in the European context as France is
also determined to 'go European' as often as possible. The French-led EU operation
in the Democratic Republic of Congo in the summer of 2003 illustrates this dual
approach: France is a strong supporter of ESDP but wants to retain the capacity to
'act on its own' (Ministère de la Défense 2003) whenever needed. As clearly stated
in the MPL for 2003–2008, France 'intends both to preserve its freedom of assessment and choice, and to diversify its capacity to act within coalitions – European,
allied or ad hoc – under less foreseeable circumstances' (Parlement français 2003).

France has sought to expand its military and non-military capabilities in order to
meet the various forms of threat to its security. Some French documents refer to this
effort as central to the task of 'global defence' (Parlement français 2003), though
the term 'defence' is certainly too narrow to embrace the diversity of the measures
considered. It is at this level that the adaptations have been the most demanding.

The French Armed Forces have undergone important changes in the last ten
years. The reform initiated by President Chirac in 1996 to end the military draft
is the central feature of the adaptation process. In a sense, this decision came as
a follow-on to the 1994 White Paper. The professionalization process was

accompanied by the definition of a new force structure that set as a target the completion of the so-called '2015 armed forces model'. The 2003–2008 MPL constitutes a key document in the analysis of French military responses to threats. While this MPL makes constant reference to terrorism and to 11 September 2001, it also addresses the means of French defence in their entirety. In the aftermath of 11 September, the four key functions of the French armed forces – deterrence, prevention, force projection and protection – were confirmed, yet theoretically adapted to the new needs.

Prevention is presented as a key component of the fight against asymmetrical threats. Through human as well as technical intelligence, which acquired a new dimension after 11 September, France had to possess a capacity to 'anticipate and assess any situation' (Parlement français 2003). With regards to force projection, one key objective is to have more mobile forces that are both capable of rapid deployment abroad and of operations along the entire conflict spectrum (protection of French citizens, humanitarian operations, peacekeeping or peace-enforcement operations, and high-intensity operations). For the army, the objective is a capability to deploy 50,000 troops, without relief, in a major operation within the Atlantic Alliance, or 'up to 20,000 men simultaneously and for an unlimited period in several theatres, whether in a national operation (1,000 to 5,000 men) or in a European one (12,000 to 15,000 men)' (Parlement français 2003; see also Parlement français 1996). The emphasis on mobile and sustainable forces reflects the judgement that the French armed forces must be capable of responding to threats with the highest degree of flexibility.

In this context, it is worth noting that the resort to force is part of French military doctrine. The Iraq episode and the American interpretation of the French posture should not lead to the perception that France has become, in principle, reluctant to use force to tackle an identified threat. As argued by President Chirac[12] at the time, France is neither a pacifist country nor has it 'stepped out of the Hobbesian world into the Kantian world' (cf. Kagan 2002). Such an evolution would contradict the idea France holds of itself. France has a preference for persuasive rather than coercive instruments in meeting security threats, but does not rule out the use of force in principle or practice; the use of force is part of France's political–military culture as defined by Thomas Berger (Berger 1996: 325–9). The essence of the Iraq case is that France and the US fundamentally disagreed on the threat assessment, and therefore on the appropriate response. Had France agreed with the US on the nature of the threat, it would have considered intervening along with its ally, as it did in Afghanistan. In such a case the question of France's willingness to intervene without a UN Security Council resolution would have arisen, but it is an option that has not been ruled out in principle.

As for the 'protection' function, the 2003–2008 MPL states that the 'emergence of diverse threats (terrorism, proliferation, trafficking and major crime) gives protection a renewed meaning' (Parlement français 2003). Outside the French territory, 'protection' covers the French population and the deployed armed forces. Inside, the challenge is for the armed forces to look at the protection of the country in a very different manner than during the Cold War. This is where the distinction between defence and security becomes irrelevant, hence the insistence of the Military Programme Law on strengthening the role of the Gendarmerie (which belong to the armed forces) and on the need to reinforce cooperation with civilian authorities. This awaited evolution is supposed to shape France's 'security culture' in the sense that security should increasingly be seen as a holistic concept, encompassing military and non-military issues, and also in the sense that a widened security approach should be conducive to civil–military relations. This process has indeed started, but there is still a long way to go before a culture of security fully replaces the culture of defence. As for the extent of interaction between the military and the civilian population, the end of conscription has had a negative impact on the 'army–nation link'. The French tend to hold their armed forces in high regard, but show little interest in who they are or what they do.[13] This creates some frustration for those in the military who, to a certain extent, feel they deserve more acknowledgment for the tremendous efforts they have made in facing the challenges associated with the metamorphosis of their missions over the last fifteen years. The relationship between the armed forces and the nation as a whole is also tested by the military's questionable ability to integrate into its ranks the French Muslim community and French citizens born of immigrants.[14]

At the inter-ministerial and non-military level, in line with the 'protection' dimension of French defence policy, the terrorist threat has also led to the creation of various mechanisms aimed at dealing with the consequences of terrorist attacks. The best-known mechanism is the 'Plan Vigipirate', created in 1978 but redefined in 2003, to take account of the implications of the 11 September attacks. The mandate of Vigipirate is to 'ensure the security of all activities of the State, of its agents, of the public and private companies, and of the French population' through the deployment of the military and gendarmes in sensitive areas.[15]

In addition to Vigipirate, the civil defence approach led to the creation of six civil defence action plans: 'Piratox', 'Biotox' and 'Piratome', to deal with chemical, biological and radiological threats, respectively; 'Pirate-mer', 'Piratair-Intrusair' and 'Piranet', to address the threats coming from the sea, the air and Internet. 'Vigipirate' has the role of coordinating these different programmes. These measures seem to reveal a broad effort to enable the French authorities to be better prepared to face various terrorist threats. Yet in practice, the mechanisms put in place are extremely limited in terms of budget and resources allocated to them. The very field of civil defence still suffers a lack of political support. In 2003, a report on the bio-terrorist threat in France was extremely critical of the level of unpreparedness of France in the face of infectious diseases, both in terms of the number of laboratories and the management of possible crises (Raoult 2003). By the same token, the death of approximately 15,000 people during the 2003 heatwave blatantly demonstrated that the French public services had only a limited ability to tackle health crises, be they the result of a terrorist attack or some other cause. Above all, a consistent and long-term inter-ministerial approach to the protection of French territory is still lacking,

Table 2.4 France's preferred responses to threats

Interaction patterns	Multilateral in principle, but unilateral response never ruled out
	Bilateral on intelligence sharing
Institutional preferences	European Union
	United Nations
	NATO
	OSCE
Instrumental preferences	All options possible
	Combination of civilian and military tools
	Crisis management/Peace operations
	Diplomacy
	Development aid
	Human intelligence
	Police
	Military intervention/use of force

while the management of a terrorist attack would inevitably involve several ministries (defence, interior, health, transport and others).[16] Here again, the evolution of the security environment and of France's security culture have not led to a significant restructuring of the agencies in charge of defining and implementing the French security policy.

Allocation of resources

One characteristic of the changing security environment is the difficulty of assessing the linkage between security threats and allocation of resources. During the Cold War, the nature of the Soviet threat meant that one needed to look primarily at the defence budget to have an idea about a country's effort in addressing the threat. Such an approach still has some relevance today, but is not sufficient to get a comprehensive view of resource allocation to threat management.

By the same token, if one assumes that many ministries should be involved in the elaboration and implementation of a security policy, it is difficult to distinguish between, on the one side, resources allocated to the 'traditional activities' of ministries such as the ministry of justice or the ministry of the interior and, on the other side, resources allocated (in the same ministries) to the management of the threats to (external) security. In the case of terrorism, to what extent can long-term development and cooperation policies in Afghanistan or the Middle East be considered as part of the overall fight against terrorism? Nonetheless, the assessment of the allocation of resources for the management of threats is consistent with the general approach throughout the 1990s, that is French policy has gone through a slow process of adaptation without fundamental change.

Table 2.5 French defence budget (without pensions)

Year	Defence Budget (without pensions, in million €)	% of GDP
1998	28,161	2.16
1999	28,959	2.14
2000	28,652	2.04
2001	28,804	1.97
2002	28,911	1.93
2003	31,070	1.98
2004	32,400 (estimate)	–
2005	32,920 (estimate)	2

Source: Ministry of Defence (2003) *La défense en chiffres*, Paris.

The most important changes can no doubt be observed in the ministry of defence, with the professionalization process and the development of EU capacities for crisis management, particularly the ESDP. Even though the MPL provides an overview over defence allocations and spending on a five-year basis with a Parliamentary imprimatur, these programme laws are known for not being respected. The MPL does provide a good indication of expenditure trends and defence priorities, but the prescribed budgetary allocations must be examined with some caution. Yet the current government and president seem intent on ensuring that the 2003–2008 MPL is respected, despite the need for budget cuts to bring France into conformity with the Stability Pact.

The 2003–2008 MPL details a French defence effort designed 'to ensure the security of French interests, to pursue the reform of our armies in the best way possible, and to strengthen France's place in the construction of European Defence and in the world' (Parlement français 2003). Accordingly, the Military Programme Law ranks equipment acquisitions according to where the shortcomings are the most critical: command and control; intelligence and communication; projection and force mobility; and the protection of deployed forces. Several projects, such as the A400M or the Helios II programme, are being confirmed. Equipment funds (Title V) receive an annual budgetary allocation of €14.64 billion during the 2003–2008 period, which represents a 10.5 per cent increase between 2002 and 2003 and a 9.2 per cent increase between 2003 and 2004 (see Table 2.6). Thus, the defence budget increased by 7.46 per cent between 2002 and 2003 and by an additional 4.3 per cent in 2004 (Faure 2003b). In terms of defence expenditure as a share of GDP, the defence budget will equal 2 per cent of the French GDP in 2005 and is planned to equal 2.2 per cent in 2008.

Defence policy priorities and budgetary allocations reveal a willingness to reinforce the French military capacities. For the current government, this willingness represents a breach with the previous policy of the Socialist-led government (but, Socialists point out, with a right-wing president). The Right

Table 2.6 Evolution of France's defence budget since 2001 (in billion €)

	2001	2002	2003	2004	2004/2003 (%)
Wages	12.9	13.4	14.0	14.0	+ 0.5
Operating budget	3.1	3.2	3.4	3.4	+ 0.1
Total (Title III)	16.0	16.6	17.4	17.5	+ 0.4
Equipment (Titles V and VI)	12.7	12.3	13.6	14.9	+ 9.2
Total	28.8	28.9	31.0	32.4	+ 4.3

Source: Report by Jean Faure (2003b) on the 2004 budget law ('defence, nuclear issues, space and common services'), document no. 76, French Senate, Paris, 20 November 2003: 11.

heavily criticized the previous government as too soft on defence, and for contradicting the MPL with budget cuts that fell largely on the acquisition budget. Beyond the controversy between political parties, the French armed forces have often been described in the last few years as overstretched, equipped with aging equipment, and unable to deploy significant numbers of troops for high-intensity operations. Interestingly enough, in its assessment of the shortcomings that France faces, the 2003–2008 MPL refers to the unfavourable gap between French and British military capabilities. As a matter of fact, during the Iraq episode, had the French decided to join the US–UK coalition in March 2003, it is very unlikely that they could have deployed 35,000 troops, as did the British.

As far as missions are concerned, the relatively high level of engagement in peace operations (at its peak in 2004, 15,000 troops were deployed), both in national and multilateral frameworks, will most likely be maintained. For the year 2003, the cost of French participation in peace operations was of €564.3 million (see Table 2.7). Regarding UN operations, the French contribution to the peacekeeping budget (which was €127.6 million in 2003 (Lamy 2003: 9)) must be added to the cost of contributing troops.

The 2003–2008 MPL is the second of three such Military Programme Laws that should lead to the '2015 armed forces model'. If the effort is sustained, France might catch up with the UK, but questions about French capacity remain in the meantime. Another point is the attention paid to civil protection in relation to terrorism, which lags far behind in terms of resources. After the release of the programme law, Pierre Lellouche, a member of the National Assembly, deplored

Table 2.7 Cost of France's participation in peace operations in 2003

	Troops deployed	*Cost (million €)*
Operations in coalition	9,280	393.8
UN-led Operations	347	13.6
National Operations	4,459	156.8
Total	14,086	564.3

Source: Report by François Lamy on the 2004 budget law, document no. 1114, National Assembly, Paris, 9 October 2003:15.

the fact that only €4.59 million were allocated to the inter-ministerial programme on the fight against nuclear, radiological, biological and chemical terrorism (Lellouche 2002).[17] He also deplored the absence of an inter-ministerial programme law on 'territorial defence' that would go beyond military issues.

Conclusion: the difficult transition from defence to security

Threats to French security are increasingly non-traditional, asymmetrical, diffuse, non-state in origin, and non-military in nature. The French authorities have by and large understood these characteristics. It is also widely accepted that the concept of 'defence' has become too narrow to reflect the complexity and diversity of the threats and that the term 'security', because it goes beyond strictly military issues, has become more appropriate. Those developments preceded the events of 11 September, but were tragically confirmed by them.

At the same time, the evolution of threat and the implications for the shift from defence to security may not have been totally identified and, most importantly, may not have been translated into policy. In other words, threat assessment is by and large accurate, but the instrumental responses are not always matched to the threats posed. This holds true for the military force structure, which remains heavily reliant on military units, and at the institutional and cultural levels; it is aggravated by the continued compartmentalization of the French ministries when they look at how to respond to the threats facing the country. Despite the diverse nature of threats and the consequent necessity for tackling them with an inter-agency approach, the key ministries continue to think about threats in a rather parochial way. The ministries of foreign affairs, defence, interior, justice and health remain absorbed by their own agenda, driven by their own culture, and ultimately ill-disposed to responses. In the same vein, while the state as a referent object has become less central for threat assessment, the French administration continues to think about international relations in terms of interstate relations, and has so far failed to integrate the non-state actor into its thinking about security issues. France still tends to think in terms of state diplomacy, alliances, and distribution of power among states rather than in terms of transnational actors operating independently of sovereign authority or control.

French foreign and defence policies have not undergone revolutionary changes in the post-Cold War era. In defence, a genuine adaptation process has started, but overall the general French approach to security has not been fundamentally altered. To a certain extent, the events of 11 September confirmed that the path France was taking in its foreign and defence policies was the way to tackle threats such as terrorism and WMD proliferation. No major changes, such as the ones that occurred in the United States, were therefore advocated. In a way, this can also be explained by the fact that the French have, to a certain extent, deliberately refused to look at security issues through the sole lens of the terrorist threat. Clearly, 11 September does not constitute the defining moment in France that it is in the US. While the terrorist threat must be taken seriously, it has not become the obsession of French policy-makers or fundamentally changed the French security culture (see Table 2.8).

Table 2.8 French national security culture

Worldview of external environment	Most important factor shaping interstate relations is the distribution of power among states; considerably less attention is paid to non-state or transnational actors. Transnational and non-state actors have not been integrated into the French understanding of security.
Identity	Though identity remains strongly national and Westphalian, it coexists with a 'European' identity and, to a lesser extent, with a Western identity. The European identity does shape security threat perception and responses.
Instrumental preferences	Emphasis is placed on military instruments as well as on the political power that France draws from its status; 'civilian' instruments of statecraft are not yet fully integrated into French security policy.
Interaction preferences	Primary approach shaped by requirements of interstate diplomacy. The EU rather than NATO is the preferred forum for fashioning a collective response to a common security threat. The United Nations is also an institution of strategic importance. Yet, unilateral response remains a politically and instrumentally viable option.

This approach reflects a security culture whose contours remain blurred. On the one hand, France has gone through a significant adaptation process affecting some of the core elements of its national security culture, such as alliance relationships, force structure and civil–military relations. On the other hand, the French national identity, as well as the way French policy-makers and public opinion think about security, tend to remain static and still largely influenced by the Westphalian state-centric system.

Notes

1 See also Badie 1995; Touraine 1995; and Laïdi 1993.
2 See Mitterrand's speech before the 45th session of the UN General Assembly, 24 September 1990.
3 Jacques Chirac's speech, Elysée Palace, Paris, 4 January 2002.
4 Jacques Chirac's speech, Conference of the Ambassadors, Elysée Palace, Paris, 29 August 2002.
5 See also David 2002; and Delpech 2002.
6 See 'Les Français et la Défense nationale', opinion polls conducted every year by the French Ministry of Defence Information Services (DICOD).
7 'Nous sommes tous Américains', *Le Monde,* 13 September 2001.
8 Joint Press Conference of Jacques Chirac and John Major, London, 30 October 1995.
9 Words of a high-ranking general at the Conference of the Ambassadors, Paris, 28 August 2004.
10 See the August–September 2004 issue of *Défense nationale,* in which General Bentegeat, Chief of Staff of the French armed forces, favours the opening of a debate on the French nuclear policy. See also Faure 2003a; and 'Revisiter la dissuasion nucléaire', *Le Monde,* 27 October 2004.
11 Bruno Tertrais (2000) says that 'between 1990 and 1999, the funds allocated to the

[French] nuclear capacity have been decreased by 55.9 per cent, while their share in the defence budget was reduced from 16.9 per cent to 8.75 per cent'.
12   'Interview: France is not a pacifist country', *Time,* 24 February 2003.
13   In June 2005, the French Ministry of Defence organized the first '*états généraux du lien armée–nation*', which looked at the evolution of the relationship between the French nation and its armed forces.
14   A recent survey conducted by the Paris-based Institut français des relations internationales (IFRI) severely criticizes the ability of the French armed forces to integrate these two communities effectively. See Bertossi and de Wenden 2005.
15   'Présentation du nouveau plan gouvernemental de vigilance, de prévention et de protection face aux menaces d'actions terroristes: Vigipirate', Paris, 26 March 2003: 7.
16   In his report on the 2003–2008 military programme law, Pierre Lellouche advocates the creation of an agency similar to the US Office of Homeland Security. See Lellouche 2002: 48.
17   See also 'La protection civile, grande oubliée', *L'Express,* 28 November 2002.

References

Badie, B. (1995) *La fin des territories. Essai sur le désordre international et sur l'utilité sociale du respect,* Paris: Fayard.
Badie, B. and Smouts, M.-C. (1992) *Le retournement du monde. Sociologie de la scène internationale,* Paris: Presses de la FNSP and Dalloz.
Berger, T. (1996) 'Norms, identity and national security in Germany and Japan', in P. Katzenstein (ed.) *The Culture of National Security: Norms and Identity in World Politics,* New York: Columbia University Press.
Bertossi, C. and de Wenden, C. (2005) 'Les militaires français issus de l'immigration', *Les documents du C2SD* 78, Paris: IFRI.
David, D. (2001) '11 septembre: premières leçons stratégiques', *Politique étrangère* 4: 765–75.
David, D. (2002) *Sécurité: L'Après-New York,* Paris: Presses de Science Po.
Delebarre, M. (2004) *Information report on international cooperation to fight terrorism,* document no. 1716, Paris: National Assembly, 6 July 2004.
Delmas, P. (1996) *Le bel avenir de la guerre,* Paris: Gallimard.
Delpech, T. (2002) *Politique du Chaos. L'autre face de la mondialisation,* Paris: Seuil.
Faure, J. (2003a) 'La dissuasion nucléaire', chapter II of the report on the 2004 budget law (defence, nuclear issues, space and common services), document no. 76, Paris: French Senate, 20 November 2003.
Faure, J. (2003b) *Report on the 2004 budget law (defence, nuclear issues, space and common services),* document no. 76, Paris: French Senate, 20 November 2003.
Heisbourg, F. (ed.) (2001) *Hyperterrorisme: la nouvelle guerre,* Paris: Odile Jacob.
Hoffmann, S. (2000) 'Deux universalismes en conflit', *The Tocqueville Review* 21 (1): 65–71.
Kagan, R. (2002) 'Power and weakness', *Policy Review* 113: 3–28.
Kepel, G. (2002) *Jihad: The Trail of Political Islam,* Cambridge, MA: Harvard University Press.
Kepel, G. (2004) *Fitna, Guerre au Cœur de l'Islam,* Paris: Gallimard.

Laïdi, Z. (ed.) (1993) *L'ordre mondial relâché. Sens et puissance après la guerre froide,* Paris: Presses de la FNSP.

Lamy, F. (2003) *Report by François Lamy on the 2004 budget law,* document no. 1114, Paris: National Assembly, 9 October 2003.

Lellouche, P. (2002) 'Avis relatif à la programmation militaire pour les années 2003 à 2008', no. 384, Paris: Assemblée nationale, 20 November 2002.

Mendras, H. (2003) 'Les Français et l'armée', *Revue de l'OFCE* 86: 134–69.

Ministère de la Défense (1994) *Livre Blanc sur la Defénse.* La documentation Française (sic).

Ministère de la Défense (2003) 'La défense en chiffres', Paris: Ministry of Defence.

Murawiec, L. (2000) *La guerre au XXIè siècle,* Paris: Odile Jacob.

Parlement français (1996) *1997–2002 military programme law.* La documentation Française (sic).

Parlement français (2003) *2003–2008 military programme law.* La documentation Française (sic).

Quilès, P., Galy-Dejean, R. and Grasset, B. (2001) 'Consequences for France of the attacks of 11 September 2001', document no. 3460, Paris: National Assembly, 12 December 2001.

Raoult, D. (2003) Report on Bioterrorism, Paris: Ministry of Health.

Salamé, G. (1996) *Appels d'empire. Ingérences et résistances à l'âge de la mondialisation,* Paris: Fayard.

Tardy, T. (1999a) 'French policy towards peace support operations', *International Peacekeeping* 6 (1): 55–78.

Tardy, T. (1999b) *La France et la gestion des conflits yougoslaves (1991–1995). Enjeux et leçons d'une opération de maintien de la paix de l'ONU,* Brussels: Bruylant.

Tertrais, B. (2000) 'La dissuasion nucléaire française après la guerre froide: continuité, ruptures, interrogations', Centre Thucydide, Brussels: Bruylant.

TNS Sofres (2003) *Transatlantic Trends 2003 – Topline Data,* Montrouge, TNS Sofres.

Touraine, M. (1995) *Le bouleversement du monde. Géopolitique du XXIè siècle,* Paris: Seuil.

Védrine, H. (2000) *Les cartes de la France à l'heure de la mondialisation (dialogue avec Dominique Moïsi),* Paris: Fayard.

Védrine, H. (2003) *Face à l'hyperpuissance: textes et discours, 1995–2003,* Paris: Fayard.

Vennesson, P. (1998) 'Renaissante ou obsolete? La guerre aujourd'hui', *Revue française de science politique* 48 (3/4): 515–34.

Waltz, K. (1979) *Theory of International Politics,* Reading, MA: Addison-Wesley.

3 Germany

From a reluctant power to a constructive power?

Alexander Siedschlag

Analyses of post-Cold War German foreign and security policy typically employ the leitmotif that everything remains different: they claim new sea-changing challenges to and changes in German policy, while concluding that these very alterations result from the constant of Germany's civil and self-restraining strategic culture (Berger 1998; Duffield 1998; Erb 2003; Rittberger 2001; Webber 2001). An example of this bias is the geo-strategic slant of many studies on united Germany's foreign and security policy. After the eradication of the Cold War borderlines in Europe, many authors continued to analyse German security strategy in terms of responses to structural pressure, to which Germany remained exposed as a power in the centre of Europe (Schlör 1993). Thus, the bulk of research came to focus on the 'normalization' of the 'new' Germany's foreign and security policy – a normalization, however, which extended over a broad spectrum, from an enlightened power in the service of Kantian democratic peace to a Waltzian power, choosing to seize any opportunity to safeguard, if not improve, its position in the international system.

Anglo-Saxon observers, judging united Germany's political and intellectual discourses about an appropriate place in the new security landscape, concluded early that the country was at best reluctant, if not unable, to take a position and define national interests in the post-Cold War international arena (Ash 1994; Gordon 1994; Sked 1991). Thus, Germany's self-proclaimed 'culture of restraint', which was primarily meant to alleviate anticipated fears in the neighbouring states about a new 'Greater Germany', instead provoked reproaches of irresponsibility and chequebook diplomacy. This discrepancy between self-image and outside perceptions was, to a considerable extent, nurtured by the then prevailing structural realist prediction that it would be a 'structural anomaly' if united Germany did not choose to become a great power (Waltz 1993: 66). In this vein, policy analyses initially expected united Germany to develop a security strategy portraying the country as a 'big power with many options' (Bergner 1993), free and able to choose the instruments that corresponded to its 'geopolitical ripening' (Asmus 1993; Sperling 1994).

Over the years it could, in fact, be observed that German politics were transformed from West Germany's perception of multilateralism as an end in itself into a notion of multilateralism as a strategic choice. Still, the latter also seems to produce a value-laden rather than interest-driven security policy. In equating a value-driven security policy with beliefs about the country's role in international affairs grounded in German society, constructivism can be said to have become the dominant strand for interpreting Germany's strategic choices over the last decade. An exemplar is Peter Katzenstein's (1996) contribution to strategic culture research, which investigates domestic–societal prerequisites for the formation of national security strategies. In his framework, a sociological concept of norms is central, describing collective external expectations of adequate behaviour that confront actors of a certain identity. In the German case, the leading constitutive norm, defining the country's security identity vis-à-vis others, is that of 'civilian power'. The leading regulative norm, setting the standard for adequate behaviour within this constitutive context, is multilateralism – the choice of institutions as a means of action.

However, another cultural aspect in security policy is often overlooked, namely ideational, normative and perceptive influences on the principles governing the choice of institutions. This is the aspect of 'culture in action' as Ann Swidler (1986) put it. Indeed, the remaining challenge to Germany's strategic culture is the need for a more pragmatic definition of the general principles guiding foreign policy decisions. The choice of institutionalism and multilateralism as contexts for national security policy is inadequate to define security interests or to develop practical security strategies. Germany's self-restraint and lack of clear intellectual foundations for its security strategy are mirrored in the fact that the country has had an elaborate, assertive action plan for civil crisis management and conflict prevention since 2004, while it updated the defence White Paper only in autumn 2006, that is, after more than twelve years.

This assertive peace policy may explain why the country's foreign policy orientation seems to be changing from multilateralism to multinationalism. Notably, thus, Germany's strategic culture does not owe this change to 11 September but rather to the experience of the Yugoslav wars of secession and their aftermath, especially the Kosovo conflict and intervention of 1999 (Hyde-Price 2001; Lantis 2002; Wood 2002). From 'Kosovo' emerged a new agreement within the then governing Red–Green coalition that peace policy needs to include military action as the ultimate instrument (Erb 2003). This emerging instrumental consensus also furthered the evolving public discussion of the spectrum of security threats the country was going to face.

Security threat perception

The German academic elite's views on impending security threats are most prominently articulated in *Internationale Politik,* a Foreign Ministry sponsored journal which identifies international security topics and then collects contributions that suggest how Germany should respond to outstanding policy problems. In its 2004 volume, *Internationale Politik* singled out seven security threats (not rank-ordered):

- Proliferation of nuclear weapons in rogue states as well as in the hands of terrorists (Harnisch 2004a and 2004b; Müller 2004; Riecke 2004). There is, however, a considerable tendency in the German academic elite to view nuclear proliferation as a proximate, not an ultimate source of insecurity. In this perspective, nuclear proliferation represents the cumulative impact of underlying societal and cultural disparities between the western and non-western world (Weihe 2004).
- Proliferation of nuclear, biological, chemical and radiological weapons of mass destruction (WMD) (Harnisch 2004b).
- The Middle East, a region of protracted conflict and authoritarian rule, as a breeding ground for geographically extending Islamist terrorism as well as the pivotal region for credible Euro-Atlantic politics of regional order-building, thus contributing to peaceful international relations (Hesse 2004; Perthes 2004).
- Political terrorism in and beyond the Middle East (Czempiel 2004).
- Terrorism as a strategy of asymmetric warfare, representing the contemporary variant of 'devastating war' (Münkler 2004).
- Continuing instability in Europe's peripheral regions, especially the Southern Balkans (Calic 2004).
- Obstacles to global and European energy supply (Umbach 2004a and 2004b).

The *Friedensgutachten* ('Peace Report'), a well-established yearbook focusing on threats to and strategies of peace, identifies four impending threats to German security as well as international peace (Weller *et al.* 2004): terrorism; WMD proliferation; failing states and bad government; and endangered peace processes in regions of protracted conflict. Political science analyses usually place the terrorist threat at the top of the security agenda (cf. Simon 2004; Weidenfeld 2004). Looking for a possible 11 September effect on the security perception of the academic elite, one could conclude that globalized threats had replaced regional destabilization at Europe's periphery as the primary threat to German security.

The threat perception of the Red–Green government (1998–2005) under Chancellor Schröder centred on international terrorism and asymmetric warfare, the risks of failing democratic transformations in Europe, environmental degradation (as a threat to human security), proliferation of WMD and the uncontrolled trafficking of conventional weapons to unstable regions of the world (Schröder 2003; Bundesministerium der Verteidigung (BMVg) 2003; Struck 2004a; Deutsche Bundesregierung 2004: 40–3). The latter, in the government's view, directly contributes to the privatization of violence and the reproduction of war as a type of business transaction undertaken by transnational criminal organizations. It was the Schröder government's strategy to confront this threat by promoting civil economic and social development, the prerequisite of which is the respective states' functioning monopoly over the use of force. Thus, security sector reform was seen as a key prerequisite for peace and sustainable development and centres on civilian control of the armed forces and democratic policing (see Table 3.1).

Table 3.1 Top threats identified by the German government

	Target: State	*Target: Society*
Agency: *State*	1 State-sponsored terrorism 2 Nuclear, chemical or biological attack as a consequence of WMD proliferation 3 Failing security sector reform in transformation countries, leading to amassing and proliferation of conventional weapons, also opening up new resources for organized crime 4 Failing democratic transformation in Greater Europe and new regional instability	1 State-sponsored terrorism 2 Nuclear, chemical or biological attack as a consequence of WMD proliferation 3 Failing security sector reform in transformation countries, leading to amassing and proliferation of conventional weapons, also opening up new resources for organized crime
Agency: *Non-state*	1 Transnational terrorist networks including WMD terrorism 2 Nuclear, chemical or biological attack as a consequence of WMD proliferation 3 Environmental degradation (also as a nurturing ground for 4 Asymmetric warfare 5 Small arms proliferation and privatization of violence	1 Transnational terrorist networks including WMD terrorism 2 Nuclear, chemical or biological attack as a consequence of WMD proliferation 3 Environmental degradation (also as a nurturing ground for terrorism)

Source: Adaptation of Figure 1 'Typology of threats to European security space', in Kirchner, E. and Sperling, J. (2002) 'The new security threats in Europe: theory and evidence', *European Foreign Affairs Review* 7: 434.

These priorities, however, were debated within the Red–Green coalition. For example, the Foreign Ministry followed the idea that a war economy and barriers to the benefits of globalization nurtures terrorism in the Middle East. It ranked failing states and underdevelopment as the most important underlying source of threat. Thus, the focus was on the danger of spillover effects from non-military threats into hard security threats. The Ministry of Defence, in contrast, had clearly ranked WMD proliferation and, since 11 September, terrorist attacks as the primary threat over the past few years. As for 11 September 2001 itself, it had changed the government's strategic orientation, which nevertheless continued to reflect the assessment of the academic elite: meeting a diverse set of security objectives on a global basis has displaced the stabilization of Europe's periphery as the primary security challenge facing Germany (BMVg 2003: para. 18).

All parties represented in the Bundestag rallied round the government's proclaimed unconditional solidarity with the US after 11 September. Yet when it came to discuss actual actions in response to international terrorism, deeply rooted differences in threat perception surfaced, not only between government and opposition, but also within the ranks of the ruling Red–Green coalition. The largest opposition party, the centre-right Christian Democrat Union (CDU/CSU),

Table 3.2 German governmental threat perceptions in the post-11 September era

Type of key threats	terrorism	WMD attack	failing security sector reform in transformation countries	failing democratic transforma-tion	environmental degradation
Agency of threats	state-sponsored or transna-tional/ network-based	proliferation	weak states, small arms proliferation and privatization of violence	weak states/weak societies	e.g. nurturing ground for terrorism
Target of threat	state, society	state, society	state, society	state	state/society
Geographical source of threat	no clear geographical concept, but tendency to see the Greater Middle East as a first-rank region of concern	no clear geographical concept, but tendency to see the Greater Middle East as a first-rank region of concern	not specified	Greater Europe	no clear geographical concept, but tendency to see the Greater Middle East and Africa as regions of concern

favoured Chancellor Gerhard Schröder's motion to take part in the US-led Operation Enduring Freedom in Afghanistan and elsewhere with Bundeswehr troops. In contrast, a minority of members of parliament of the coalition parties, the Social Democratic Party (SPD) and the Greens, were strictly opposed to any counter-terrorism strategy entailing military engagement. This minority within the coalition was large enough to present the Schröder government with the dis-comfiture of having to rely on opposition votes to pass the motion legitimizing the deployment of German troops. To avoid such an outcome, Schröder decided to link the vote on a Bundeswehr deployment with a constructive vote of no confi-dence. The result was that most of the ruling coalition members of the Bundestag finally voted in favour of the deployment, even if they opposed it, whereas a con-siderable number of opposition MPs rejected Schröder's motion though approving of a Bundeswehr deployment (see Oswald 2004: 92–4).

Conversely, looking at the level of general threat perception, there are no deep dividing lines. In her speech at the Munich Security Conference 2005, for exam-ple, Angela Merkel, the then-opposition leader of the CDU/CSU and now Federal Chancellor, mentioned terrorism, proliferation of WMD, and failing states as the security threats of the twenty-first century. Of these three, international terrorism tended and tends to be seen as the chief challenge by the CDU/CSU, because it requires common action by a European Union developing into a credible security actor within the transatlantic security community. This strategic orientation demonstrates that there is now a basic trans-partisan consensus on the necessity to consider a broad spectrum of risk factors when talking about security. Today, all parliamentary parties acknowledge that meeting asymmetric threats is a fundamental task for German security policy (IDS 2005).

Public interest in security and defence policy has steadily increased in the past three years, even if it has not yet reached its peak of autumn 2001 again. However, interest in the activities of the armed forces has not profited from this increased attention, which may be a sign of the public's differentiation between security and defence. According to an Emnid survey of 2002, combating terrorism was considered to be among the top ten general political tasks for Germany to accomplish on the verge of the twenty-first century, ranking it fifth (28 per cent) as compared to eighth in 2001 (AIK 2003: 13). However, the prime threats to Germany and its society continued, in the public perception, to stem from domestic factors, such as endangered workplaces (79 per cent) and the collapse of the welfare state (32 per cent). Organized crime as a borderline threat between domestic and transnational origin ranked second (34 per cent), whereas securing peace in Europe ranked ninth (14 per cent) on the security agenda, just after saving the environment.

Looking at the public perception of the biggest risks to European, as opposed to German, security leaves us with the following top five internationally based threats (AIK 2003: 19): international terrorism (32 per cent); transnational organized crime (11 per cent); violent conflict and general danger of war (8 per cent); immigration and too many foreigners (6 per cent); and WMD proliferation (5 per cent). A public opinion survey by the Konrad Adenauer Foundation conducted in late 2003 identified five national security threats (Neu 2004: 15): international terrorism (69 per cent); radical Muslims and Islamic fundamentalism (50 per cent); WMD proliferation (43 per cent); instability in the Middle East (32 per cent); and the consequences of environmental pollution and climate change (27 per cent). These figures show that, in contrast to the perceptions of the government and the academic and parliamentary elites, public perception in 2002–3 did not contain a geographic origin of threat and comprised both hard and soft security threats as well as threats to social security. Remarkably, the 2002 Emnid survey found that 12 per cent of the population believed that there was no existing threat to European security. An imminent danger based on the proliferation of WMD was ranked last in 2002, whereas academic and political elites had already identified it as a primary threat. This discrepancy is particularly interesting when compared to public opinion in the mid 1990s, where proliferation of all kinds of weapons came first, followed by environment-related threats, illegal immigration, collapsing export markets, scarcity of raw materials, and ethnic conflict.

Comparing the 2002 Emnid results to the Adenauer Foundation Study of 2003, it is tempting to draw the conclusion that, in many aspects, public threat perception seems to follow the government's lead. Public opinion, for example, immediately reflected the government's definition of the Middle East as a geographic origin of threats to German security and fundamentalism as the ideational origin of terrorism. Independently of this rally-round-the-flag effect, the public now identifies consistently international terrorism as the primary security threat of our times.

Sources of threat: global, transnational and oriental

The academic elite commonly perceives threats to emerge from transnational terrorist networks as well as from the Southern Balkans, the Middle East, Islamic countries, and North Korea. There are nevertheless some remarkable perceptual differences, for example, regarding the source of threats from WMD proliferation. Some authors clearly locate it in the Islamic countries of the Middle East (cf. Weihe 2004), some within President George W. Bush's 'axis of evil' (cf. Müller 2004; Umbach 2004c), whereas others classify the threat as transnational, terrorist-network based. There is also a view that identifies weak international institutions as the ultimate, structural source of the WMD proliferation threat (cf. Riecke 2004). As far as terrorist threats in general are concerned, there is the widespread belief that they are primarily non-state and arise from protracted conflicts as well as authoritarian social and political rule in the Middle East (cf. Hesse 2004). However, as German academics regard terrorism as a strategy of asymmetric warfare, they do not identify a geographic source of threat but rather attribute it to structural characteristics of the new century's 'new wars' (cf. Münkler 2002; 2004).

As a further example, the contributions in *Internationale Politik* centre on structural rather than regional sources of threat. They arise either from a combination of state and non-state rogue actors combined with faint international institutions, as in the case of proliferation of WMD, or from violence-laden structures of dependency, underdevelopment, and scarcity of economic resources. Concerning political reform as a regional security strategy, however, *Internationale Politik* focuses clearly on the Middle East. International terrorism as a source of threat, in this view, is not regionally concentrated in the Middle East or Islamist countries but, rather, constitutes a transnational, network-like phenomenon.[1] In contrast, the *Friedensgutachten* 2004 largely focuses on the Middle East as the nexus of terrorism, the proliferation of WMD, failing states and collapsing peace processes.

The Red–Green government's awareness (and now that of the grand coalition government after 2005) clearly differed from that of the academic elite. In the first place, Germany does not define the sources of perceived security threats in geographic terms nor in respect to certain regions. Rather, in identifying sources of threat, the government employs functional organizing principles. For example, the *Defence Policy Guidelines* (2003) maintained that German security policy needed to be formulated independently of territorial categories and be able to confront threats wherever they emerge. Moreover, the government typically considers crisis areas within a larger context rather than independently of each other. The Red–Green coalition, not unlike its predecessors, also believed that German security interests were shaped by the interweaving of structural and contextual factors. Moreover, the definition of threat is also partially dependent upon the perceptions and interests of allies and partner countries (Siedschlag 2003).

Nevertheless, the Schröder government had tended to focus on the Mediterranean Sea. The Mediterranean is Europe's connection to the regional sources of twenty-first century security threats, although the Middle East was generally regarded as the primary geographic source of threat to European security (Fischer 2003). The Ministry of Defence, in contrast, insisted on the globalized nature of threats and their sources; it maintained that these threats must be met with a strategically integrated set of domestic, foreign and security policies (Struck 2003).

Parliamentary opinion as a whole seems to converge on the view that, if the threats have a structural rather than geographic source, they need to be regarded as 'terrorist' or 'asymmetric' as such and not explicitly linked to geographic spheres of origin (cf. IDS 2005). In public opinion, the prevailing perception is that current security threats are 'de-territorialized' and global in origin. Therefore, the Red–Green government's preoccupation with the Middle East as the source of threat did not resonate with the public or a large number of MPs.

Institutional and instrumental responses to threats

For Germany, international institutions have traditionally provided constitutive, not just regulative norms: they are important building blocks of national identity in foreign and security affairs and serve as frame of reference for defining threats and deriving strategies to meet them. Accordingly, the 2003 *Defence Policy Guidelines* stated that the 'multinational integration of Germany and the Bundeswehr has become a constitutive characteristic of German security policy' (BMVg 2003). This constitutive multinational integration has led to the formation of a specific repertoire of action, typical of the post-war West German strategic culture that survived unification largely intact. This repertoire of action can be reduced to a single principle of action: do not provide clear-cut definitions of threat or national security interests but develop instead a manageable set of maxims that allow security and defence policies to correspond pragmatically and effectively with international developments (Banchoff 1999). Both the ideational and the strategic factors favour a continuation of the multilateral leitmotif, but under the conditions of newly emerging security challenges.

Interaction preferences

In academic deliberations, the appropriate strategies for German security policy are not usually linked to an analysis of threats and the functional imperatives to meet them but, rather, are embedded in a general exchange of views on German foreign policy as a whole. The debate has been defined by proponents and critics of more 'assertive' behaviour in the international arena (cf. Peters 2001). There is an academic consensus on two instruments (and their relation to the underlying cause of conflict) for meeting the threats posed to Germany's security. First, democratization, conceived as a bottom-up response that has both unilateral and multilateral components, is directed towards the elimination of the socio-economic sources for violent conflict. The democratization approach is broadly viewed as a suitable instrumental goal to meet security threats that have transnational and global roots or originate from comparatively distant regional sources such as the Middle East.[2]

Second, effective multilateralism, viewed as a top-down response, is directed against escalation and towards the promotion of conflict prevention or mitigation. As a rule, an effective multilateral approach is favoured as a response to the continuing instability in Europe's peripheral regions, especially the Southern Balkans (cf. Axt 2004; Bendiek 2004; Calic 2004).

Interestingly, critical left-wing academics, in particular, reprimanded Chancellor Schröder's proclamation of a 'new way' of national self-consciousness and multinationalism, rather than multilateralism in foreign and security policy. These academics reject the notion that Germany could contribute anything to the EU's envisaged 'effective multilateralism' in preventive diplomacy and peacemaking. Remarkably, and in a similar vein, academics subscribing to the realist school of foreign policy analysis criticized Germany's self-proclaimed role as a new 'promoter of peace' that assumed a moral responsibility for peace and development in just about any corner of the world (Siedschlag 2000).

On the part of the informed public, there has been a tendency over the past few years to place German foreign and security policy into question by asking for unilateral policy changes rather than effective multilateral contributions. The informed public seems to perceive the new security threats as an incentive to debate Germany's position in the world and weight in international politics. Particular examples of this trend are the contributions in the journal *WeltTrends*, discussing Germany's 'big power' status and 'ripeness for world politics' of the country (*WeltTrends* 28; *WeltTrends* 43).

The Red–Green government itself, notwithstanding its rhetoric of a 'German way', followed its preference for multilateral or multinational responses to threat. It also acknowledged – as does its successor – that when it comes to meeting hard security threats, the menu for strategic choice would need to include military action. In this context, there is not only an ideational but also a pragmatic foundation for Germany's preference for a multilateral response to threats: in its 1994 ruling, the Federal Constitutional Court maintained that the German constitution allows Bundeswehr troops to be sent abroad. This decision effectively ended the flaming domestic debate about the constitutional foundations of a German contribution to 'out of area' operations. However, at the same time, the Court made it clear that the constitution requires that any international mission be embedded in an international security system such as the United Nations, NATO or the EU. The Constitutional Court thus ruled out any German military engagement within a mere ad hoc coalition of states lacking a recognized institutional source of legitimacy.

In explicit responses to the challenges posed by the 'new' security threats, government leaders have promised a multilateral approach: at the Munich Security Conference 2004, for instance, Foreign Minister Joschka Fischer argued that the terrorist threat could not be met by a coalition of Western states. The increasing reliance on ad hoc coalitions within NATO led Fischer to assert that this development depreciated transatlantic security multilateralism. He then championed the development of an effective global multilateralism to 'positively design globalization' (Fischer 2004). At the Munich Security Conference 2005, Chancellor Schröder rejected the proposition that the new security threats redefined the transatlantic relationship and NATO, yet at the same time he called for a new, globally linked multilateralism as a response to global risks. One must not forget, however, that other members of the Red–Green government, such as Defence Minister Peter Struck, strongly favoured a continuation of transatlantic security multilateralism as the primary institutional locus for responding to threats and for projecting stability and power in order to manage the sources of threat emanating from the Middle East (cf. Struck 2004b).

In the field of crisis prevention, the Schröder government's *Action Plan 2004: Civil Crisis Prevention, Conflict Resolution and Peace Consolidation* (Auswärtiges Amt 2004) strongly called for multilateral approaches as well. However, a tendency towards unilateralism has been visible in the parliamentary realm. Interestingly, in the view of the CDU/CSU, the first response to the twenty-first century's security threats should be the immediate recovery of the German economy. As Chancellor Angela Merkel explained in her speech at the 2005 Munich Security Conference, only states with strong economic growth could exert influence in Europe. According to Merkel, meeting twenty-first century security threats requires a capacity for unilateral action with two aims: first, to bear the country's share in responsibility for European welfare; second, to meet the need of adequate military capabilities and well-defined national interests required for influential participation in the design of the international security order. Apart from its questionable voluntarism, such an approach seems to over-estimate the possible influence of one single country's policy in coming to terms with the global reach of this century's security challenges.

Even though the governing parties and opposition have accepted that eco-nomic factors generally shape the main security threat scenarios, their beliefs about the underlying causes are opposed. The SPD and Greens often regard a war economy as a source of violent conflict and believe that the European countries should exercise economic instruments to break cycles of violence and to reduce structural underdevelopment, the presumed breeding ground for terrorism. The CDU/CSU treat the economy as a tool for meeting security threats and for exer-cising German influence on the further development of the European security order, the classical approach the Christian Democrats applied to West German security policy of the 1950s (cf. Lider 1986). At a general level, however, there has been a consensus in the Bundestag that German defence and security policy should always be conducted multilaterally, though with somewhat diverging insti-tutional preferences (IDS 2005).

Institutional preferences

The academic literature defined security threats predominantly in terms of diffused global risks confronting states and recommended the urgent need for the adaptation of security policies to meet them. Although the focus has clearly been on the foreign and security policy challenges facing Germany and Europe, only in the pages of *Internationale Politik* are connections made between those challenges and the need for complementary institutional changes at the regional and global levels. There has not been a sound intellectual debate on institutional preferences in German security policy. Some authors have advocated an increased reliance on civil–military cooperation in post-conflict peace-building, but this concern reflects an assumption that the typical post-conflict environment does not permit an institutional separation of civil and military actions in the field (e.g. Heinemann-Grüder and Pietz 2004). These authors exhibit a clear institutional preference for non-governmental organizations (NGOs), with the military component, wherever possible, confined to providing a stable environment for NGO activities.

The Red–Green coalition, which formed a new government in autumn 1998 after 17 years of rule by Chancellor Kohl's Christian–Liberal coalition, introduced important changes in Germany's institutional preference for meeting threats to German security. During its first 100 days, the new governing coalition followed the footsteps of its predecessor in voicing its support for a European pillar within NATO (specifically, a European Security and Defence Identity (ESDI), functioning as the first institutional port of call within the Atlantic Alliance framework).[3] By the end of 1999, Chancellor Schröder had almost completely changed his view; he now argued for confining NATO to collective defence and critical military infrastructure (cf. Schröder 1999). Even though the NATO member states, naturally including Germany, had unanimously agreed on the Alliance's new strategic concept in April 1999, Schröder promptly devalued consultation, crisis management in flexible coalitions and partnership outreach – the very tasks redefined as NATO's new core functions. Instead, the Chancellor favoured a European Security and Defence Policy (ESDP) within the EU instead of ESDI within NATO as the institutional forum for meeting those security tasks (cf. Schröder 1999). At the 2005 Munich Security Conference, Schröder even maintained that NATO risked becoming outdated and was no longer the primary venue where transatlantic partners discuss and coordinate strategies.

In fact, the Schröder government seemed to regard the ESDP as the first-choice security institution and placed it in the normative context of a key project for European unification and a building block for the true political union of Europe (see BMVg 2003: para. 50). The central theme of German security multilateralism had thus shifted from a European NATO pillar to an independent ESDP merely 'compatible' with NATO (Siedschlag 2002: 305). Rooted in ESDP, the Red–Green coalition nevertheless advanced a civil–military approach to crisis management anchored to an EU-based security multilateralism that provided the nexus for security cooperation. This preference for a close combination of civil and military instruments to meet emergent security threats may explain the governing elite's shift from NATO to the EU as the preferred institution for coordinating responses to crises.

Notwithstanding this value-oriented instituitional choice, it must be pointed out that German security policy-making suffers now and then from elite myopia in the foreign policy establishment. This malady is especially true for the Ministry of Foreign Affairs, which has taken the position that ESDP should prepare to take over virtually all operational functions from NATO and regards NATO as a last resort security institution to cope with cases of 'genocide' and 'humanitarian catastrophes'

(Volmer 2000: 21). Such an institutional choice is typical of the Green party elite, which provided the leading personnel of the Foreign Ministry under the Schröder government. Greens typically failed to appreciate the political structures and functions of the Atlantic Alliance or the treaty-bound commitment of NATO member states to solve international disputes by peaceful means and to strengthen the institutions of democracy.

Corresponding with the Red–Green government's perception that considerable security threats result from the persistence of the underlying sources of conflict, the Schröder government lent the Organization for Security and Cooperation in Europe (OSCE) an important place among international security institutions, contributing 10 per cent of its staff (Deutsche Bundesregierung 2004: 28). Today as in the past, the OSCE is Germany's preferred institutional forum for creating a mechanism ensuring the transparency of small arms transfers and small arms control more generally. As failing democratic and economic transformations in greater Europe rank among the most immediate of security threats for the German government, it is natural that Germany also views the Council of Europe as a security institution in the stricter sense of the word (Deutsche Bundesregierung 2004: 29–30). Its added value is located in its ability to set normative standards, to build democratic institutions, and to further civil and human rights in order to safeguard human security in all parts of Europe.

Germany's institutional choices for meeting threats arising from instability in regions other than Europe or its immediate periphery are, so to speak, indigenous regional and subregional institutions. The Red–Green coalition strongly supported regional programmes – for example, within the framework of the G8 action plan on Africa (Deutsche Bundesregierung 2004: 31) – largely owing to superior operational capabilities and peace-building capacities. This preference also applies the action plan's goal of developing, until 2010, inner-African capabilities for crisis management and prevention of violent conflict by strengthening regional organizations such as the Economic Community of West African States (ECOWAS) as well as the African Union (AU). Germany also attaches great significance to domestic inter-ministerial activity in support of regional training centres for peacekeeping, such as the Kofi Annan International Peacekeeping Training Centre (KAIPTC) in Accra, Ghana, and the Peace Support Training Centre (PSTC) in Nairobi, Kenya.

The grand coalition government continues, as did the Red–Green coalition before it, to consider civil conflict prevention and peace consolidation as important strategies for meeting imminent threats, which constitute a broad field of action requiring the engagement of different types of actors (Deutsche Bundesregierung 2004: 10–35). In these tasks, the government emphasizes the role of the UN, which it regards as the central forum for discussing and coordinating ideas and objectives in international relations and security. From the German point of view, the UN's role in meeting global security threats should be expanded from conflict management to conflict prevention and the sustainable development of peace processes. In this context, the government places high hopes on an expansion of the United Nations Development Programme (UNDP), which could be more effectively employed as a means for preventing failed states or rescuing failing states. Also, the United Nations Environment Programme (UNEP), from the German point of view, could also take on a more prominent security role: the government recognizes the important role played by the UNEP in identifying and evaluating environmental degradation that could lead to violent conflict. However, the Red–Green coalition called for a stronger emphasis on societal capacity building as a critical contribution to stabilizing post-conflict settings, especially those where violent conflict has resulted in severe environmental damage.

Interestingly, the Red–Green coalition seemed to regard the proliferation of WMD as an issue that should be dealt with on the basis of interstate cooperation rather than within the UN. Only multilateral cooperation, in the view of the Schröder government, could tackle the core problems regarding an effective counter-proliferation regime, including the enforcement of legally binding commitments, the strengthening of multilateral agreements, the extension of export controls, and the deepening of political dialogue with third countries (Deutsche Bundesregierung 2004: 16). The Red–Green coalition was also sceptical of sanctions and placed high hopes on intergovernmental rather than institutional activity to refine this instrument and embed it in a comprehensive strategy of crisis prevention (Deutsche Bundesregierung 2004: 21).

A majority exists in the Bundestag that favours German military engagement in multinational frameworks. The Schröder government's motion to extend Bundeswehr participation in the International Security Assistance Force (ISAF) in Afghanistan and to take part in Provincial Reconstruction Teams was easily passed in September 2004; Germany now contributes the largest force contingent, with almost 2,000 troops deployed. The Bundestag has also passed a Forces Deployment Act in December 2004, which lays down procedures for deciding on Bundeswehr participation in international peace operations as well as military interventions.

Nevertheless, the predominant parliamentary views on the preferred institutional venue for meeting Germany's security requirements have not exactly paralleled those of the government (IDS 2005). The SPD puts the EU and NATO first, whereas its former coalition partner, the Greens, considers the UN as the prime framework for meeting Germany's security challenges. The Greens' axiom of action is that the 'coalition' should come to define 'mission', which, in their view, can best be put into practice within the UN system. The CDU/CSU, as Chancellor Angela Merkel pointed out in 2005, favours an EU-centred approach backed up by military capabilities, but insists on its continued embeddedness in the transatlantic framework. The CDU/CSU party elite view the UN as merely a framework for realizing human rights. Former Defence Minister Volker Rühe, a member of the CDU/CSU and chair of the Bundestag foreign affairs committee during the Red–Green coalition, defended NATO's capability to transform in order to meet the new categories of security threats and spoke out against Schröder's proposals at the Munich Security Conference. Yet Rühe joined Schröder in questioning the Alliance's core function of coming to common terms in defence and disarmament affairs. For example, he argued that NATO was not the perfect forum for addressing security threats arising from Iran's nuclear programme or reaching multilateral security policy decisions, such as lifting the arms embargo on China (EU Observer 2005).

Instrumental preferences for meeting threats: civilian rhetoric versus coercive impact?

German academics such as Herfried Münkler (2002) reject military action as a means to master security threats. In their 'new wars' paradigm, war as a means for reducing the complexity of conflict is replaced by negotiation and compromise as the painful process for managing territorial security threats in the twenty-first century. In a similar vein, the *Friedensgutachten* clearly advocates crisis prevention; namely, 'strategies of peace' such as nation building, human rights, including women's rights, and democratic security sector reform. These strategies are supported, in turn, by a strengthened UN system, comprehensive international arms control regimes, support of human security as a policy goal, and a deeper understanding of economic factors as a course of protracted ethno-national conflict and civil wars as well as the *sine qua non* of sustainable post-conflict peacemaking (*Friedensgutachten* 2004: 122–250).

In contrast to these strategies of peace which reject force as an instrument, political practice has revealed a growing German reliance on the deployment of coercive instruments to meet the tasks of threat management; this development is best illustrated by the Bundeswehr's participation in international military operations. Multilateralism here seems to have changed from a constraint (in the sense of Germany as a 'tamed power') to a 'strategic enabler' (Becher 2004: 404–5).

At the level of strategy and public diplomacy, however, the instrumental preference has clearly been civilian. Red–Green policy statements subsumed security and defence under the umbrella of foreign policy, with the main theme of 'German foreign policy is peace policy'. As noted above, the accompanying concept of security is a comprehensive one, including military as well as civilian means for preventing or settling conflicts (see Chrobog 2005). Yet, the emphasis has been unmistakably on a civilian approach and on conflict prevention. However, it is clear that little can be derived from the broadened definition of security and means to provide for it when it comes to defining threats to German national security. At the same time, there is little that does not constitute at least an indirect threat to the German idea of peace or a global cooperative security order. Germany's definition of its security interests – in terms of removing obstacles to world peace – has resulted in the old danger of overextension, thus risking a loss of credibility in international security affairs.

Nevertheless, the instrumental practice of German security policy continues to be multilateral. Multilateralism serves the German interest in finding common international approaches to managing transborder migration and in strengthening international institutions, not only as venues for voicing Germany's position and

Table 3.3 Development of international German force deployments

Name of country and operation	1999	2000	2001	2002	2003	2004	2005
Bosnia and Herzegovina (SFOR/EUFOR)	2,800	2,000	2,000	1,600	1,321	1,110	1,090
Georgia (UNOMIG)	9	9	9	11	11	12	11
Afghanistan/Uzbekistan (ISAF)			1,200	1,200	1,200	2,350	2,190
Eastern Mediterranean (Active Endeavour)			400	400	400	250	
Macedonia (Concordia)			450	600	40		
Djibouti/Horn of Africa (Enduring Freedom)				1,200	300	500	510
Kosovo (KFOR)				4,700	3,326	3,250	3,250
Kuwait (Enduring Freedom)				238	90		
Congo/Uganda (Artemis)					97		
Sudan (AMIS)						200	
Indonesia (post-Tsunami humanitarian assistance)						120	120
Ethiopia/Eritrea (UNMEE)						2	2
Total number of Bundeswehr troops deployed in the respective year	2,809	2,009	4,059	9,949	6,785	7,794	7,173

Sources:<http://www.einsatz.bundeswehr.de> (accessed 1 April 2005); <http://www.bundeswehr.de/C1256EF4002AED30/Docname/Einsaetze_Home> (accessed 1 April 2005).

defending its interests, but for defining and identifying common interests. This type of security multilateralism evolved from the Schröder government's conviction that civil conflict management should rank as the primary instrument for meeting security threats, but that coping with the global threat and security complexes would overtax the capabilities of any single nation or organization. Therefore, Germany advocated the idea of security multilateralism and a security 'multidimensionalism' – that is, cooperating within 'peace alliances' with 'peace-prepared' actors in the conflict regions themselves in order to facilitate a 'multi-track' approach to ameliorate the structural sources of violent conflict (Deutsche Bundesregierung 2004: 43–5). Thus, the Red–Green coalition hoped to help dismantle the concept of 'enemy' (*Feindbild*) and to promote intercultural dialogue.

Against this background, the *Action Plan 2004: Civil Crisis Prevention, Conflict Resolution and Peace Consolidation* defined civil conflict prevention and peace consolidation as the primary security policy objectives, and identified six policy instruments as the instruments of first choice (Deutsche Bundesregierung 2004: 1, 36–58):

- building reliable governmental structures including rule of law, human rights, gender equality, minority protection and freedom of religion;
- enforcing the rule of law in post-conflict situations as a means of sustainable conflict prevention with respect to failed states;

- building peace potential in civil society and the media, culture and education sectors;
- creating peace economies;
- strengthening the global level of international relations with the UN as the core institution; and
- strengthening the regional level in European politics with the EU as the core institution.

The *Action Plan* belies the gap that exists between Germany's growing military engagement on the one hand and an increasing programmatic impetus towards institution and nation-building endeavours on the other. This tension may tellingly illustrate how changes in strategic culture do not typically exchange one identity or self-image as a security actor with another, but instead how new identities are added on to and modify existing ones (see Barnett 1999; Weldes 1996).

Allocation of resources

The Red–Green coalition government's approach to combating terrorism and countering asymmetric threats after 11 September, which targeted development and economic transformation, did not exert a noticeable impact on budgetary allocations in absolute terms. Budgetary expenditures on economic cooperation and development have only enjoyed a noticeable relative increase as a share of the total federal budget after 2005. Second, military expenditure increased markedly in the wake of 11 September by 20.2 per cent from €23.3 to €28.0 billion (where it has since levelled out). Despite the aforementioned relative increase of the development budget, the share of the defence budget in the overall federal budget shrank from 9.0 per cent in 2004 to a target value of 7.5 per cent for 2005. Yet it

Table 3.4 Germany's preferred responses to threats

Interaction patterns	global	multilateral	multilateral	multilateral	multilateral
Institutional preferences for meeting threats	UN	flexible coalitions, partly within the CFSP framework	ESDP, OSCE, NATO	OSCE, CFSP	UN, empowerment of regional organizations such as ECOWAS
Instrumental preferences for meeting threats	sustainable development, conflict resolution, peace consolidation, peace economy	bargaining	democratization, civil crisis prevention	democratization, civil crisis prevention	sustainable development, development aid

Table 3.5 Development of annual budgetary allocations for the German Ministry of Economic Cooperation and Development

	1999	2000	2001	2002	2003	2004	2005
Billion €	3.9	3.6	3.7	3.7	3.7	3.7	3.8
Share in the total federal budget (in per cent)	1.6	1.5	1.5	1.5	1.4	1.5	2.2

Sources: Bundesministerium der Finanzen (2004) *Finanzplan des Bundes 2003–2007*, Berlin; Bundesministerium der Finanzen (2003) *Bundeshaushalt 2004: Tabellen und Übersichten*, Berlin; Bundesministerium der Finanzen *Monatsbericht des BMF Januar 2004*; Bundesministerium der Finanzen *Monatsbericht des BMF Februar 2005*.

Table 3.6 Development of annual budgetary allocations for the German Ministry of Defence

	1999	2000	2001	2002	2003	2004	2005
Billion €	24.6	23.3	28.0	28.4	28.3	28.1	27.9
Share in the total federal budget (in per cent)	9.2	9.5	11.5	11.4	11.0	9.0	7.5

Sources: Bundesministerium der Finanzen (2004) *Finanzplan des Bundes 2003–2007*, Berlin; Bundesministerium der Finanzen (2003) *Bundeshaushalt 2004: Tabellen und Übersichten*, Berlin; Bundesministerium der Finanzen *Monatsbericht des BMF Januar 2004*; Bundesministerium der Finanzen *Monatsbericht des BMF Februar 2005*.

must be noted that the Schröder government's understanding of Germany as a responsible, sometimes self-reliant security actor had been visible in budgetary allocations over its last year in office. Budgetary expenditures would support the conclusion that the government had reallocated resources from the defence budget to the budget for economic cooperation and development, but the expenditures are inconsistent with the government's security policy rhetoric (see Tables 3.5 and 3.6).

Conclusion

Germany's policy under the Red–Green government followed the notion that, in contemporary international politics, there is a sharp dichotomy between security and defence, and that this dichotomy must be overcome. Given the complex international security agenda at the onset of the twenty-first century as well as Germany's moral and political vow to deepen European integration in the defence and security sector, we should expect a continuously increasing impact of the country's strategic culture on its policy (see Table 3.7). Perhaps 'security is the best defence' captures best the essence of German security policy; it will undoubtedly remain the catchphrase of the grand coalition government. At the same time, Germany has tended to exaggerate the scope of security policy over the past few years, a development that allows neither for the development of criteria indicating success nor for gauging the reality-relatedness of the country's security policy. Moreover, it does not provide a frame of reference for systematically choosing

Table 3.7 German security culture

World view of external environment	Institution-based multilateral world order. Risks resulting from globalization and inequality should be met by a peace policy contributing to global governance; however, hard security threats may require military action and need to be met before they reach Europe's borders.
Identity	'Normalized', self-restraining but responsible power embedded in Europe.
Instrumental preferences	Institutions form building blocks of Germany's identity in foreign and security affairs and serve as frame of reference for devising interests, defining threats and deriving strategies to meet them. Military engagement must be embedded in an international security system such as the United Nations, NATO or the EU. OSCE and Council of Europe to play an important role in soft security issues and conflict prevention. EU's ESDP should be 'compatible' with NATO; empowerment of (sub)regional organizations in zones of concern (e.g. AU and ECOWAS).
Interaction preferences	Multilateralism and institution-based multinationalism; enforcement of democratic norms; focus on civilian preventive efforts; sometimes precarious mixture of ethics of responsibility and ethics of values.

policy instruments best suited to the policy challenge at hand; it also precludes any calculus for determining when and how a security shortage becomes a threat and requires reaction. In this context, the Germany governed by the Red–Green coalition indeed 'confound[ed] neorealism' (Duffield 1999) for it not only based its policy on the principle of ameliorating the state of the entire international system ('peace policy') rather than its own position, but also resisted international–structural pressure and instead placed itself under the aegis of ideas.

This aegis of ideas pushed the country into a policy that sought to link any perceived threat to an underlying evil in the world, which in turn reflects a prevalent injustice or asymmetrical opportunities for prosperity and development. In this respect, a united Germany undeniably has developed an art of declaring 'total peace' (Hellmann 1996). For the time being, this seems to be the major tenet of the country's strategic culture –rather than the general antimilitarism in Thomas Berger's sense (Berger 1998). Thus, Germany will, even under the present grand coalition government, continue to have a particular difficulty in finding 'the right mix between democratic norms, civic standards and historical consciousness on the one hand and a realistic perception of international politics' on the other (Seidelmann 1996).

According to John Duffield, we can expect national security culture to have a direct impact on policy in two settings (Duffield 1998: 27–8): first, in an international setting that is complex and in which strategy decisions are bound to be ambiguous, so that decision-makers need to rely heavily on a pre-existing worldview, styles of perception and standard operating procedures for decision-making; and second, in a domestic or institutional setting in which there are more than a small number of decision-makers and where long-term decisions with radiating effects are on the agenda. We should accordingly expect a widening gap between Germany's moral claims and promises on the one hand and its actual capacity for action on the other.

Notes

1   These topics were addressed in special issues of *Internationale Politik*: 'Proliferation' (59:1); 'Developmental policy' (59:11–12); 'Reforms for the Middle East' (59:7); and 'Terrorism' (59:2).
2   Cf. *Internationale Politik* 59 (7 and 11–12).
3   Cf. Gerhard Schröder's speech at the Munich Security Conference 1999, reprinted in Teltschik 1999.

References

AIK (Akademie der Bundeswehr für Information und Kommunikation) (2003) *Demoskopische Umfragen zur Sicherheits- und Verteidigungspolitik in Deutschland,* Strausberg: AIK.
Ash, T. (1994) 'Germany's choice', *Foreign Affairs* 73 (4): 65–81.
Asmus, R.D. (1993) 'The future of German strategic thinking', in G.L. Geipel (ed.) *Germany in a New Era,* Indianapolis, IN: Hudson Institute.
Auswärtiges Amt (2004) *Action Plan 2004 'Civilian Crisis Prevention, Conflict Resolution and Post-Conflict Peace-Building'.* Available online at: <http://www.auswaertiges-amt.de/www/en/infoservice/download/pdf/friedenspolitik/AP%20EN.pdf> (accessed 1 February 2006).
Axt, H.-J. (2004) 'Konflikte und Konfliktbearbeitung in Südosteuropa (2000–2004)', in Bundesakademie für Sicherheitspolitik (ed.) *Sicherheitspolitik in neuen Dimensionen Ergänzungsband,* Hamburg–Berlin–Bonn: BAKS.
Banchoff, T. (1999) *The German Problem Transformed. Institutions, Politics, and Foreign Policy, 1945–1995,* Ann Arbor, MI: University of Michigan Press.
Barnett, M. (1999) 'Culture, strategy and foreign policy change. Israel's road to Oslo', *European Journal of International Relations* 5 (1): 5–36.
Becher, K. (2004) 'German forces in international military operations', *Orbis* 48 (3): 397–408.
Bendiek, A. (2004) *Der Konflikt im ehemaligen Jugoslawien und die europäische Integration,* Wiesbaden: VS Verlag für Sozialwissenschaften.
Berger, T.U. (1998) *Cultures of Antimilitarism. National Security in Germany and Japan,* Baltimore, MD: Johns Hopkins University Press.
Bergner, J.T. (1993) 'Unified Germany: a great power with many options', in G.L. Geipel (ed.) *Germany in a New Era,* Indianapolis, IN: Hudson Institute.
Bundesministerium der Verteidigung (BMVg) (2003) *Defence Policy Guidelines.* Available online at: <http://www.bmvg.de/portal/PA_1_0_LT/PortalFiles/C1256F1200608B1B /W 268AHEH510 INFOEN/VPR _en.pdf?yw_ repository =youatweb > (accessed 27 October 2006).

Calic, M.-J. (2004) 'Herausforderung Kosovo. Die Europäer müssen sich noch stärker engagieren', *Internationale Politik* 59 (11–12): 95–102.

Chrobog, J. (2005) *Security Thinking in Comprehensive Terms: Challenges for Crisis Management in the 21st Century.* Keynote speech by State Secretary Jürgen Chrobog on the occasion of the opening of the conference on crisis management, Berlin, 6 April 2005. Available online at: <http://www.auswaertiges-amt.de/www/en/ausgabe_ archiv? archiv_id=7035> (accessed 1 August 2005).

Czempiel, E.-O. (2004) 'Der politische Terrorismus', *Internationale Politik* 59 (7): 74–81.

Deutsche Bundesregierung (ed.) (2004) *Aktionsplan 2004 'Zivile Krisenprävention, Konfliktlösung und Friedenskonsolidierung',* Berlin: Deutsche Bundesregierung.

Duffield, J.S. (1998) *World Power Forsaken. Political Culture, International Institutions, and German Security Policy After Unification,* Stanford, CA: Stanford University Press.

Duffield, J.S. (1999) 'Political culture and state behavior: why Germany confounds neo-realism', *International Organization* 53 (4): 765–803.

Erb, S. (2003) *German Foreign Policy. Navigating a New Era,* Boulder, CO: Rienner.

EU Observer (2005) *Schröder stands by NATO proposals.* Available online at: <http://euobserver.com/?aid=18420&rk=1> (accessed 16 February 2005).

Fischer, J. (2003) *The Near and Middle East – Considerations from a European Viewpoint.* Speech by the Federal Minister for Foreign Affairs Joschka Fischer at the Herzliya Conference, 17 December 2003. Available online at: <http://www.auswaertiges amt.de/www/en/ausgabe_archiv?archiv_id=5200> (accessed 16 February 2005).

Fischer, J. (2004) Speech on the 40th Munich Conference on Security Policy. Available online at: <http://www.securityconference.de/konferenzen/rede.php?menu_2004=& menu_konferenzen=&sprache=en&id=123&> (accessed 16 February 2005).

Gordon, P.H. (1994) 'Berlin's difficulties: the normalization of German foreign policy', *Orbis* 38 (2): 225–43.

Harnisch, S. (2004a) 'Transatlantische Kooperation tut Not. Europa, die USA und die Massenvernichtungswaffen', *Internationale Politik* 59 (1): 19–25.

Harnisch, S. (2004b) 'German non-proliferation policy and the Iraq conflict', *German Politics* 13 (1): 1–34.

Heinemann-Grüder, A. and Pietz, T. (2004) 'Zivil-militärische Intervention – Militärs als Entwicklungshelfer?', *Friedensgutachten 2004:* 200–8.

Hellmann, G. (1996) 'Goodbye Bismarck? The foreign policy of contemporary Germany', *Mershon International Studies Review* 40 (1): 1–39.

Hesse, R. (2004) 'Fliehkräfte des Fortschritts. Ausblicke auf den Nahen und Mittleren Osten der kommenden Jahrzehnte', *Internationale Politik* 59 (7): 1–9.

Hyde-Price, A. (2001) 'Germany and the Kosovo war: still a civilian power?', *German Politics* 10 (1): 19–35.

IDS (Info-Dienst Sicherheitspolitik) (2005) 'Sicherheitspolitische Positionen der Bundestagsparteien', in *IDS Info-Dienst Sicherheitspolitik* April 2005.

Katzenstein, P (ed.) (1996) *The Culture of National Security,* New York: Columbia University Press.

Kirchner, E and Sperling, J. (2002) 'The new sercurity threats in Europe: theory and evidence', *European Foreign Affairs Review* 7 (4): 423–52.

Lantis, J. (2002) 'The moral imperative of force: the evolution of German strategic culture in Kosovo', *Comparative Strategy* 21 (1): 21–46.

Lider, J. (1986) *Origins and Development of West German Military Thought. 1949–1966,* Aldershot: Gower.

Müller, H. (2004) 'Warum die Bombe? Die nuklearen Möchtegerne Iran und Nordkorea', *Internationale Politik* 59 (1): 12–18.

Münkler, H. (2002) *Die neuen Kriege,* 2nd edn, Reinbek bei Hamburg: Rowohlt Verlag.

Münkler, H. (2004) 'Terrorismus heute. Die Asymmetrisierung des Krieges', *Internationale Politik* 59 (2): 1–11.

Neu, V. (2004) *Die Deutschen und die Außen- und Europapolitik. Eine Umfrage der Konrad-Adenauer-Stiftung,* Berlin: Konrad-Adenauer-Stiftung. Available online at: <http://www.kas.de/db_files/dokumente/7_dokument_dok_pdf_4205_1.pdf> (accessed 16 February 2005).

Oswald, F. (2004) 'German security after 11 September', in P. Shearman and M. Sussex (eds) *European Security after 11 September,* Aldershot: Ashgate.

Perthes, V. (2004) 'Die neue Zentralität des Nahen und Mittleren Ostens. Konsequenzen für Wissenschaft und Politik', *Internationale Politik* 59 (7): 49–52.

Peters, D. (2001) 'The debate about a new German foreign policy after unification', in V. Rittberger (ed.) *German Foreign Policy Since Unification. Theories and Case Studies,* Manchester: Manchester University Press.

Riecke, H. (2004) 'Nichtverbreitungspolitik. Im Aufwind oder in der Krise', *Internationale Politik* 59 (1): 1–11.

Rittberger, V. (ed.) (2001) *German Foreign Policy Since Unification. Theories and Case Studies,* Manchester: Manchester University Press.

Schlör, W.F. (1993) *German Security Policy. An Examination of the Trends in German Security Policy in a New European and Global Context,* London: Brassey's.

Schröder, G. (1999) 'Regierungserklärung von Bundeskanzler Gerhard Schröder zum bevorstehenden Europäischen Rat in Helsinki am 10./11. Dezember 1999 vor dem Deutschen Bundestag am 3. Dezember 1999', in Presse- und Informationsamt der Bundesregierung (ed.): *Bulletin* 85: 805–8.

Schröder, G. (2003) *Rede vor der 58. Generalversammlung der Vereinten Nationen in New York am 24. September 2003.* Available online at: <http://www.international politik.de/archiv/jahrgang2003/november03/rede-des-deutschen-bundeskanzlers -- gerhard-schroder--vor-der-58--generalversammlung-der-vereinten-nationen-am-24-- september-2003-in-new-york--gekurzt-.html> (accessed 27 October 2006).

Seidelmann, R. (1996) 'German foreign policy and the European order', in R. Seidelmann (ed.) *Crisis Policies in Eastern Europe. Imperatives, Problems and Perspectives,* Baden-Baden: Nomos.

Siedschlag, A. (2000) 'Zwischen gezähmter Macht und gefordertem Engagement. Die Außen- und Sicherheitspolitik des vereinten Deutschland in ihrer ersten Dekade', *Gegenwartskunde* 49 (2): 143–56.

Siedschlag, A. (2002) 'Deutschlands Rolle in der europäischen Sicherheitspolitik', in R. Krämer and H. Arnold (eds) *Sicherheit für das größere Europa. Politische Optionen im globalen Spannungsfeld,* Bonn: Dietz.

Siedschlag, A. (2003) 'Allein und gemeinsam. Die Sicherheit Deutschlands und die Einigung Europas', *Y. - Magazin der Bundeswehr* 3 (12): 14–18.

Simon, C. (2004) 'International terrorism: the German response', in J. Sipilä *et al.* (eds) *Terrorism and Counter-Terrorism,* Helsinki: Maanpuolustuskorkeakoulu, Strategian Laitos.

Sked, A. (1991) 'Cheap excuses: Germany and the Gulf crisis', *The National Interest* 24: 51–60.

Sperling, J. (1994) 'German security policy in post-Yalta Europe', in M. Donald Hancock and H.A. Welsh (eds) *German Unification,* Boulder, CO: Westview Press.

Struck, P. (2003) 'Deutsche Sicherheitspolitik und die Bundeswehr vor neuen Herausforderungen', *Europäische Sicherheit* 52 (1): 18–25.

Struck, P. (2004a) Rede des Bundesministers der Verteidigung Dr. Peter Struck im Rahmen des 21st International Workshop on Global Security: A Broader Concept of Security for the 21st Century, 8 May 2004 in Berlin. Available online at: <http://www.bmvg.de/C1256F1200608B1B/CurrentBaseLink/N264X9PD152MMISDE (accessed 16 February 2005).

Struck, P. (2004b) *Future of NATO.* Speech at Munich Conference on Security Policy, 6–8 February, 2004. Available online at: <http://www.securityconference.de/konferen zen/rede.php?menu_2004=&menu_konferenzen=&sprache=en&id=125&> (accessed 16 February 2005).

Swidler, A. (1986) 'Culture in action: symbols and strategies', *American Sociological Review* 51 (2): 273–86.

Teltschik, H. (ed.) (1999) *German Security Policy on the Threshold of the 21st Century. Transatlantic Partnership at the Beginning of the Next Millennium – Development of the Asia Pacific Region – Requirements for Future Stability,* Berlin: Berlin-Verlag Spitz.

Umbach, F. (2004a) 'Internationale Energiesicherheit zu Beginn des 21. Jahrhunderts', in Bundesakademie für Sicherheitspolitik (ed.) *Sicherheitspolitik in neuen Dimensionen Ergänzungsband ,* Hamburg–Berlin–Bonn: BAKS.

Umbach, F. (2004b) 'Global energy supply and geopolitical challenges', in F. Godement, F. Nicolas and T. Yakushiji (eds) *Asia and Europe. Cooperating for Energy Security,* Paris: IFRI.

Umbach, F. (2004c) 'The North Korean nuclear state', *Transatlantic Internationale Politik* 5 (1): 79–83.

Volmer, L. (2000) 'Krisenprävention als Element deutscher Sicherheitspolitik', in Presse- und Informationsamt der Bundesregierung (ed.) *Stichworte zur Sicher heit- spolitik* 10.

Waltz, K.N. (1993) 'The emerging structure of international politics', *International Security* 18 (2): 44–79.

Webber, D. (ed.) (2001) *New Europe, New Germany, Old Foreign Policy? German Foreign Policy Since Unification,* London: Cass.

Weidenfeld, W. (ed.) (2004) *Herausforderung Terrorismus,* Wiesbaden: VS Verlag für Sozialwissenschaften.

Weihe, T. (2004) 'Iran: Der Atomkonflikt ist nur die Spitze des Eisbergs', *Internationale Politik* 59 (11–12): 25–6.

Weldes, J. (1996) 'Constructing national interests', *European Journal of International Relations,* 2 (3): 275–318.

Weller, C., Ratsch, U., Mutz, R., Schoch, B. and Hauswedell, C. (eds) (2004) *Friedensgutachten 2004,* Münster *et al.*: Lit.

WeltTrends. Zeitschrift für Internationale Politik und vergleichende Studien (various issues).

Wood, S. (2002) 'German foreign and security policy after Kohl and Kosovo', *Government and Opposition* 37 (2): 250–70.

4   Italy

New ambitions and old deficiencies

Paolo Foradori and Paolo Rosa

In the post-war period, Italian foreign policy has been characterized by some constants connected both to its particular geographic location – a peninsula jutting
down from the continental mainland and located at the centre of the Mediterranean
sea – and to its particular domestic political conditions which favoured a low profile security policy in order to avoid defence matters becoming a contentious
domestic policy issue.[1] Italy's geographic particularity pushed it into intervening in
different areas at the same time (Santoro 1991). As Ambassador Ludovico Incisa di
Camerana (pseudonym Ludovico Garruccio 1982) has written, Italian foreign policy unfolded during the post-war period in three concentric circles: the Atlantic,
the European and the Mediterranean. The Atlantic circle is characterized by the
adhesion to NATO and a passive position as regards the will of the American ally.
The European circle, marked by an immediate adhesion to the European
Community and by a strong integrationist attitude, took the form of rhetoric more
often than concrete actions, owing to Italy's economic and institutional backward-
ness (see also Coralluzzo 2000).[2] Finally, in the Mediterranean circle, considered
an area of great strategic importance derived from Italy's dependence on energy
imports from North Africa and the Middle East, Italy has exercised a high degree
of international autonomy, putting forward a pro-Arab policy, often in opposition
to the United States and the other European partners.

Aside from geopolitical location, Italian foreign and security policy had been
shaped by a domestic political system marked by deep cleavages between pro-
Atlantic parties and pro-Soviet parties. Once the big debates about the Atlantic
and European choices had taken place, the need to prevent the international cleavages from provoking excessive fractures in domestic politics pushed Italian
leaders to depoliticize the security issue, thereby removing it as a contentious
item vexing the domestic political agenda (Panebianco 1977; 1982).
Consequently, military policy was neglected for many years, with defence expenditures being considerably less than that of other medium powers with which Italy
could be compared. It was only in the 1970s with the passage of the so-called pro-
motional laws that the modernization of the armed forces began (Perani and
Pianta 1992). Finally, there is the weight of national history: the entire architecture of current defence structures and Italian security culture were subject to a
conditioning that originated in the desire of the first Republican Parliament and

Constitutional Assembly to put Italy's fascist heritage behind it once and for all (Dottori and Gasparini 2001: 51–2).

Geography, domestic politics, and a fascist past led Italy in the post-war period to refer most of its defence responsibilities and, to some extent, the definition of threat, to its American ally and the Atlantic Alliance. Italy was a security consumer. Being relieved of the burden of providing for its own defence left Italy militarily 'backward'; the armed forces in the post-Cold War period lacked the necessary military capabilities, R&D (Research and Development) base, and budgetary resources to undertake a thorough remodernization consistent with the evolution of modern warfare (Nones 2001). The end of the Cold War reopened the foreign policy and defence debate, made necessary a fundamental review of the Italian armed forces, and initiated a reconsideration of a defence policy based on territorial defence consistent with the static and unidirectional conception of security threats generated by the long post-war East–West conflict. The 11 September 2001 terrorist attack was a second crucial event in the reshaping of Italian defence and security policy, particularly the passing from the role of security consumer to a security producer. The risk of a terrorist attack, conventional or non-conventional, became the 'absolute danger'. Prior to September 2001, the threats to Italian security were largely defined as regional; after September 2001, the threats to Italian security were recognized as global and asymmetrical.

Security threat perception

There was a radical shift in the dynamics of threat perception after the fall of the Berlin Wall in 1989. The very notion of security was subject to significant conceptual revisions. The main change involved the passage from a monolithic and well identified security threat by the Soviet enemy to a more diffuse, unpredictable and multifaceted set of challenges that could put at risk national interests, values and welfare. This section is devoted to the analysis of security threats as perceived by the Italian academic elites, the informed public, and the Italian security and defence agencies as well as in public opinion surveys.

Academic debates

Even within the academic elites and the informed public there is a widespread awareness that the traditional definition of security – oriented towards the protection of the territory, state-centric and restricted exclusively to the military sector – offers a limited and distorted representation of the post-Cold War and post-11 September international system. Foreign policy analysts have progressively taken into consideration non-military threats to security, such as poverty, environmental decay, the spread of diseases, overpopulation, the uncontrolled inflows of refugees, nationalism, a nuclear catastrophe and, of course, terrorism. The 'referent objects' have expanded to include the security of individuals and groups in addition to states (Monteleone 2000). Thus:

security is understood in the broad sense and is based on a comprehensive approach which, in addition to military, also includes non-military factors. The attainment of security is thus regarded as dependent not only on disarmament and other measures of security cooperation but, more importantly, on the long-term achievement of structural stability in the societies and polities concerned.

(Aliboni 2002: 106)

A more in-depth analysis of the perception of threats held among the academic elite and informed public reveals that there has been a shift from an emphasis on threats to stability and regional order in the Balkans and broader Mediterranean prior to 2001 to an emphasis on diffused global threats thereafter. In the period between the end of the Cold War and 11 September 2001, regional instability was identified as the main risk to Italian security because of disorder, implosion and fragmentation on the regional geopolitical context (Jean 2003). Confronted with a progressive *regionalization* of threat and the indifference of key actors such as the United States, Italy has felt compelled to participate in stabilization interventions, particularly in the Balkan and Mediterranean area (Ammendola and Isernia 2000). Between 1995 and 2001, Italy committed a significant number of troops to five peacekeeping or peace-enforcement operations: 2,000 Italian troops were contributed to NATO missions (IFOR/SFOR) in Bosnia–Herzegovina (1995); 3,000 Italian troops of a 4,000-member multinational force were committed to a multinational force for Operation Alba (1997), for which Italy also assumed command; in 1999 Italy took part in the Allied Harbour mission in Albania sending 2,300 military personnel out of the total 8,000 of the coalition; in 1999 it had about 5,000 troops in Kosovo who were part of the NATO force of KFOR; and in 2001, 700 Italian soldiers participated in the NATO Essential Harvest mission in Macedonia (ISPI 2003: 17). These interventions clearly required the transformation of the Italian Armed Forces; that is making the transition from a standing army based on compulsory conscription and trained for a traditional conflict to a professional corps capable of rapid interventions in crisis situations and carrying out peacekeeping or peace-enforcing missions.

A recurring concern regards the role of Europe in general and of Italy in particular in the context of the new threats. The wars in Bosnia and Kosovo highlighted the capabilities–expectations gap in Europe (Hill 1993) and contributed to a strengthened interest in deeper European integration in the foreign policy and defence sectors. The possibility of growing American indifference towards the Old Continent's affairs intensified the debate over NATO's future, particularly its role 'out of area' as a guarantor of regional security supporting crisis management operations.[3]

Observers and analysts identify the Balkans as a critical area for Italian security interests. The main preoccupation is the linkage between terrorism and Islam, particularly the risk that the region could turn into a constellation of rogue states and provide an operational basis for the al-Qaeda network (Nava 2001; Carnimeo and Buturovic 2001). The risk that the region could fall prey to organized crime and that the Balkan mafia could spread into Italy is also viewed as a threat (Politi 1999). Balkan instability has also brought forward the Italian concern over unwanted and uncontrolled migratory flows. The 1990s witnessed a constant rise of migratory pressures on Italy precipitated by short-term 'migration crises' – acute and conjunctural flows of populations, often of a short duration but numerically significant and initiated by political crises as occurred in Albania (1991 and 1997) or Kosovo (1999) (ISPI 2003: 17). Together with the presence of about one million Muslim immigrants in Italy, migratory flows went from being a simple matter of maintaining public order to the more complex task of maintaining internal security and alleviating external disorder (Aliboni 2002: 104). The Italian government responded to this challenge by passing law 189/02 in August 2002. This law, which reformed Italian legislation regarding immigration controls arguably aligned 'Italian expulsion procedures to the most restrictive ones of European countries' (Sciortino 2002: 100). The other great area of crisis identified by professional analysts is the broader Mediterranean area. The Israeli–Palestinian conflict is considered a critical and primary source of instability for the entire Middle East region (Colombo 2000).[4] This conflict is of particular concern because of Italy's strategic dependence on energy resources supplied from the region (ISPI 2003: 17).

The terrorist attacks of 11 September were followed by a body of analysis regarding its causes and operational methods and strategies to fight it: coercive or persuasive instruments; a unilateral or multilateral response. The terrorism debate was sharpened by the unipolar evolution of the international system (Attinà 2003), unilateral American foreign policy initiatives on issues of common transatlantic concern, the capability–expectations gap of the European Union, and the domestic repercussions of the Berlusconi government's support of the Bush Administration's war against terrorism.

The globalization of the terrorist threat expanded the Italian foreign policy horizon (ISPI 2003: 17). As the Comitato Difesa Duemila reports (2003: 1):

> The globalisation of international relations spurs intervention in crisis areas which are even further away. The change increases commitments to support operations for peace and the stabilisation of 'failed states', linked not only to matters of ethics and principles, but also to a strong interest in constructing security in regions that would otherwise threaten regional and global stability.

The peculiarity of this new enemy is found in the fact that it is not clearly linked to a specific territory or a state, but is the '"perverse product" of the deterritorialization of international politics and thus, of globalisation and immaterial situations (for instance, in the case of attacks on computer systems)' (Ferraris 2003: 318). Global terrorists use non-conventional lethal weapons in unscrupulous ways and employ technologies that are widely available to civil society:

mobile phones for coordinating attacks; the internet for logistical organization; and civil aircraft for attacking 'soft' targets (Silvestri 2001: 6). The terrorist use of biological, chemical, nuclear or radiological weapons also constitutes a major security threat (Ferguson and Andreoni 2004). But fears are raised not only by the direct effects of such an attack on Italian territory or against Italian soldiers deployed in crisis areas, but also by the economic repercussions attending such attacks. Repeated terrorist attacks could create short-term panics, exacerbating the volatility of the financial markets or leading to liquidity crises. In the medium term, market pessimism could lead to drastic reductions in consumption and investment on a global scale (Bruni 2001). Moreover, if it is true that the globalization of the markets depends upon the operation of western 'open societies', then the onset of serious and repeated threats to internal security would inevitably lead to the closure of those open societies. Were that to happen, globalization would suffer as would the welfare of those least able to tolerate a global economic crisis (Panebianco 2001).

Italy is seen as a country that is particularly at risk, owing to three factors (Pelanda 2003: 209): the pro-American foreign policy pursued by the Berlusconi government; the participation of Italian contingents in military operations in Afghanistan and Iraq; the presence on Italian territory of targets of high symbolic value, particularly the symbols of Christianity located in Rome.[5] The new strategic scenario, represented by the terrorist threat, has broadened the concept of defence to include security more broadly conceived:

> The attention must be on the risks for the civil population. From this perspective, in the case of a conventional attack the critical nature of the transport sector emerges both as means and infrastructure, and in the case of an attack with nonconventional weapons, the critical nature of the water distribution sector.
>
> (Nones 2004: 72)

Government policy

In 2000, the Italian Ministry of Foreign Affairs (MAE) published its first White Paper (MAE 2000). It presented a fairly optimistic scenario of the international system. In examining the different geographical areas and the challenges that could emerge, no serious threats to Italian security were identified. The main geopolitical areas of concern centred on the Balkans, where Italy had intervened actively; the Caucasus and Central Asia, an area rich in natural resources of interest to Italy; and the Mediterranean and Middle East area, where Italy had interests in the normalization of relations with Libya, stabilizing the conflict in Algeria, and opening Iran. Attention was also devoted to sub-Saharan Africa, but the concerns revolved around the potential for northbound migratory flows triggered by inter-ethnic conflicts, demographic pressure, medical emergencies, and the collapse of state institutions (MAE 2000: 71).

The 2000 White Paper did not even mention terrorism. While analysing the risk of proliferation of weapons of mass destruction (WMD), it did not mention the possibility that they could fall into the hands of terrorist organizations or other non-state actors. The preoccupations were more of a traditional kind, connected to the possible impact of proliferation on interstate relations, as in the case of the atomic rivalry between India and Pakistan or the Iranian nuclear programme.

This foreign policy assessment changed after 11 September. The threat of international terrorism became a central priority of Italian foreign policy. In a speech to the Senate in January 2003 on the general direction of Italian foreign policy, then Minister of Foreign Affairs Franco Frattini listed the main preoccupations of the Italian government: the Balkans; the Korean peninsula, owing to the problem of nuclear proliferation; and the Middle East. Particular attention was paid to the matter of international terrorism, considered a global threat to society that required a military response as well as dialogue with various religious and cultural systems and interventions to support civil institutions in countries at risk. The Italian government viewed the EU as having a special role given its capacity to mobilize a wide range of instruments 'to assure the relaunch, the re-establishment and consolidation of difficult economic, social and political situations' (MAE 2003).

This change of perception can also been found in the 2002 defence White Paper. The Ministry of Defence underlined new factors of insecurity which required a rethink on defence policy (Ministero della Difesa 2002: 3):

> The terrorist attacks of 11 September have thrown the previous geo-strategic structures further into disorder and projected new risks on the international scene, particularly possible terrorist actions and organized crime. The traditional threat no longer exists. Regional risks have emerged and are based not only on armaments, but also on different and more sophisticated instruments such as money laundering or licit and illicit trade. These new instruments make possible the reaping of great profits that can be used for criminal intentions. These various asymmetrical activities, when combined and articulated among each other, multiply the future risks that the international community will have to face. Terrorism is the catalyst and multiplier of these risks. At present, security and defence policies can no longer be limited to the traditional sphere of war capabilities, but have to face a transversal enemy, often shifty and immaterial.

Minister of Defence Antonio Martino corroborated these positions during a hearing with the Defence Committee of the Camera dei Deputati on 19 March 2002. The Minister pointed out how security had assumed a varied and different dimension, including threats such as WMD proliferation, ethnic aggressions, low intensity conflicts, drug trafficking, migratory flows, ecological disasters, organized crime and terrorism. Terrorism was considered to be particularly dangerous, owing both to its extended breadth (global) and to the difficulty in recognizing the enemy. The transformation of the threats required remodulated responses that involved political, economic and diplomatic instruments, military and police forces, and redirected intelligence activities. The missions of the Italian Armed Forces required capabilities that would not only preserve the traditional task of territorial defence, but undertake missions contributing to 'stability and international security, the legitimate safeguard and protection of our interests and also the prevention of old and new risks, and the opposition to violations of rights and peace' (Ministero della Difesa 2002: 3). The Italian Armed Forces were placed into a well-defined multilateral context:

- active participation in NATO, which remains the main instrument for the collective defence of Europe and for Italian security, and in the EU, considered primarily as a regional organization guaranteeing security and stability, and facilitating transatlantic collaboration in the security field;
- participation in missions with UN or OSCE legitimization; and
- development of bilateral relations to strengthen common security.

For Italian policy-makers, the construction of a European Security and Defence Policy (ESDP) does not represent a first step towards the construction of a European army, but rather a project for a European rapid reaction force executing missions consistent with the so-called 'Petersberg tasks' (Rosa 2003). For the Ministry of Defence, and in a smaller measure for the Foreign Ministry, the EU is no substitute for NATO which remains at the heart of the European security architecture.[6]

Public opinion

In the period following 11 September, public opinion registered a considerable shift in perceptions regarding threats. At the end of the 1990s, the main preoccupation of Italians regarded dangers deriving from socio-economic inequalities in the world. In 1997, a third of the people interviewed indicated the differences between the northern and southern hemispheres as the underlying cause of threats to Italy (see Table 4.1). This generic preoccupation acquired a more concrete meaning if linked to other phenomena such as terrorism and immigration. The public made a connection between worldwide inequalities, migratory flows, and terrorist risks; it ascribed the terrorist threat to general factors and only indirectly to Islamic fundamentalism, which was actually losing salience among the Italian public in the 1990s. This shift is consistent with the waning perception of the Middle East threat, perhaps reflecting an apparent turning point in the peace process started by the Clinton Administration.

Public perceptions changed radically after 11 September. Ninety-one per cent of Italians now considered international terrorism to be either an extremely or rather important threat to Italy, even though Italy was not a direct object of attacks. In the same way, the perception of the threat connected to Islamic fundamentalism grew: 72 per cent of those polled identified it as an extremely or rather important threat. Parallel to this shift in threat perception is a growing preoccupation with the Middle East, connected in large part to the deterioration of the peace process after

Table 4.1 Threats to the security of Italy 1995–1997

In your opinion, in the future, what problems could become a threat to Italian security? Can you indicate the most important or worrying? (in percentage)

	Feb 95	Jul 95	Jan 96	Sep 96	Jun 97
Economic inequalities between the Northern and Southern hemispheres	27	29	33	33	33
Countries of the East and ex-USSR	4	6	4	2	2
Islamic fundamentalism	17	10	11	15	10
The Balkans	3	6	3	1	2
Immigration from the Third World	18	14	18	11	18
Terrorism	-	24	24	33	24
Middle East	-	-	-	-	2
Inadequacy of supranational institutions	13				
No threat for Italy	7	4	1	1	1
Other	6	3	3	2	4
Don't know / no answer	5	4	3	2	4
Total	100	100	100	100	100

Source: Archivio Disarmo-SWG, Difebarometro 1995-97. Reported in Battistelli, F. (2004) *Gli Italiani e la guerra*, Roma: Carocci: 143.

the outbreak of the second Intifada (see Table 4.2). It is remarkable that issues such as the greenhouse effect still occupy an important position among the security threats identified by the Italians, despite the active operation of al-Qaeda and other Islamic terrorist organizations (such as Salafita Preaching and Combat Group) on Italian soil. At the same time, immigration and (global) North–South inequalities have receded as priorities; indeed, they are indicated as extremely dangerous threats by only 13.9 and 15.1 per cent of the public, respectively.

If we pass from the perception of threats to the types of response that the Italians think are appropriate, two dimensions of comparison are useful. The first relates to the inclination to use force, with a continuum ranging from a preference for diplomatic negotiation in all circumstances to the automatic use of force in any contingency. The second dimension identifies the institutional location of the response, which ranges from the exclusively national to an exclusively multilateral response.

As regards the use of force, the data is very interesting, primarily because it refutes the notion of Italian reticence to rely on military solutions to security threats (see Table 4.3). Aside from the obvious case of a foreign attack against the homeland, where 85 per cent of those polled agree with the use of force, it is also interesting that 74 per cent of Italians favour the use of force in order to enforce

Table 4.2 Threats to the security of Italy in 2003 (percentage)

	Extremely important	*Rather important*	*Not so important*	*Not at all important*	*Don't know/n.a.*
International terrorism	55.8	35.3	7.8	1.2	0.0
Greenhouse effect	49.0	39.6	8.6	1.4	1.4
Islamic fundamentalism	31.1	41.0	18.7	5.6	3.6
The Israeli–Palestinian conflict	24.7	45.0	18.5	8.0	3.8
Economic inequalities between the Northern and Southern hemispheres	15.1	50.4	24.1	10.2	0.2
Immigration	13.9	38.2	29.9	16.9	1.0

Source: Archivio Disarmo-SWG, Difebarometro 2003. From Battistelli F. (2004) *Gli Italiani e la guerra*, Roma: Carocci: 144.

respect for international law; 72 per cent of Italians think that force must be used against terrorists, but a substantial minority – 26 per cent – disagree. What the poll cannot tell us, however, is whether this opposition is born from ideological aversion or from a negative evaluation of the efficiency of military force to ameliorate the terrorist threat.

What emerges from the data in Table 4.4 is that Italians, even though they do not dismiss the use of military force to combat terrorism, are less favourably inclined to rely upon it than their European partners (only the Germans have a greater aversion). As regards attacks with ground forces against weapons or terrorist camps, the number of Italians in favour is eight percentage points lower than the European average. Similar data emerges in relation to air strikes. A reliance on selective assassinations gained the support of 48 per cent of the Italians surveyed (3 percentage points beneath the European average). The Italians appear to be more favourable to a dependence upon political–diplomatic methods, such as economic aid to poor countries (97 per cent approval) and restrictions on migration (75 per cent approval). The methods of a 'civilian power' are thus in tune with Italian preferences.

Table 4.3 Attitude of Italians as regards the use of force (percentage)

	In favour	*Against*	*Don't know*	*Total*
Defend the national boundaries from terrorist attacks	85	14	1	100
Enforcing international law	74	23	3	100
Fight international terrorism	72	26	2	100
Control illegal immigration	69	30	1	100
Stop ethnic conflicts	56	39	5	100

Source: Survey Miur-Dies, January 2002. Cited in Battistelli, F. (2004) *Gli Italiani e la guerra*, Roma: Carocci: 148.

Table 4.4 Percentage of Italians favouring various measures to combat international terrorism

	Germany	France	Great Britain	Italy	Holland	Poland	Europe
Helping poor countries develop their economies	84	93	91	*97*	92	92	91
Attacks by ground troops against terrorist training camps and other facilities	58	80	78	*61*	77	75	69
Air strikes against terrorist training camps and other facilities	58	75	76	*60*	73	75	68
Restricting immigration into own country	44	62	74	*75*	57	69	63
Assassination of individual terrorist leaders	40	50	56	*48*	62	72	51

Source: EuropeanReport 2002. Available online at <http://www.worldviews.org> (accessed 23 November 2005).

From the data presented in Tables 4.3 and 4.4, we can claim that Italians, though with caution and some reservations, are not completely opposed to the use of force to combat new threats. It is significant that 69 per cent of those surveyed are in favour of using force to fight clandestine immigration and to resolve ethnic conflicts. These data probably reflect the growing Italian engagement in peace-keeping operations. In the fight against terrorism, however, there is a certain preference for addressing the structural sources of the problem.

If we turn to the decision-making locus for meeting these new security threats, the Italian public favours multilateralism rather than a national unilateralism. This preference is understandable if one considers the history of post-war Italian politics. Public opinion appears to opt for a European choice (see Table 4.5). During the decade after the signing of the Single European Act (1986), support for a European foreign policy increased a great deal. In 1987, only 37 per cent of Italians supported an integrated European foreign policy, six points below the EU average. In 1995, following the first post-Cold War enlargement, 79 per cent of Italians now favoured an integrated foreign policy, representing a 42-point increase compared to 1987. Even though there was a slight fluctuation in 1999, public support for the Common Foreign and Security Policy (CFSP) remained high at 70 per cent, eight points above the European average. Italian support for an integrated European foreign policy peaked at 80 per cent in favour after 11 September, a level of support corresponding to the high-water mark set in post-Maastricht euphoria of 1992.

Table 4.5 Percentage of Italians favouring integration of European foreign policy

	1987	1989	1990	1991	1992	1993	1994	1995	1998	1999	2002	2003	Var. 87 –03
Holland	48	68	66	79	74	78	76	79	79	75	69	71	23
Italy	*37*	*78*	*74*	*75*	*80*	*75*	*78*	*79*	*72*	*70*	*80*	*76*	*39*
France	42	73	63	72	73	70	74	76	71	67	67	64	22
Belgium	49	78	70	76	73	72	74	74	59	68	70	73	24
Germany	58	67	60	68	72	70	70	73	71	68	74	72	14
Spain	39	58	69	71	65	64	61	70	67	62	73	66	27
Ireland	36	64	62	60	67	64	66	66	60	59	61	61	25
Portugal	24	41	47	59	67	55	60	63	49	54	64	65	31
UK	53	61	64	68	65	61	61	62	52	43	38	35	–18
Denmark	50	47	47	56	57	58	60	62	59	56	74	72	22
Greece	33	36	42	54	55	50	49	61	81	70	79	75	42
Luxembg.									72	74	78	78	
Austria									65	62	70	65	
Sweden									47	46	53	48	
Finland									55	49	53	52	
EU	43	61	60	67	68	65	66	70	64	62	66	64	21

Source: Smith, M. E. (2000) 'Conforming to Europe: the domestic impact of EU foreign policy cooperation', *Journal of European Public Policy* 7: 627; Eurobarometer, 1999, report 51; 2002, report 58; 2003, report 60.

Even though Italian approval of an integrated foreign policy dipped slightly in 2003, support was only second to that recorded in Luxembourg.

Public support for a common European defence is largely consistent with the data on an integrated foreign policy. In 1999, 81 per cent of Italians supported the creation of a common European defence (Eurobarometer 1999: report 51); this support rose to 85 per cent of the population in 2002 (Eurobarometer 2002: report 58) and settled at 81 per cent in 2003 (Eurobarometer 2003: report 60). Ten years earlier, a mere 22 per cent of Italians favoured the prospect of a European defence independent of NATO (Isernia 1992: 232). This turn-around is even more significant when compared to Italian disillusionment with the euro, which is blamed, inter alia, for rising inflation. Between the spring and autumn of 2002, the number of Italians favouring the euro registered at around 71 per cent, an 11-point decline in support (Eurobarometer 2002: report 58).

From the Eurobarometer data, the multilateral vocation of Italians becomes clear. When asked who should be responsible for European defence, 64 per cent of Italians indicated EU institutions, the highest level of support within the EU. NATO followed the EU as the distant second most preferred security institution (16 per cent). The preference for a national response only found favour with 12 per cent of the Italian public (Eurobarometer 2002: report 58). Support for a significant UN role is also high, as data from Isernia and Everts shows: Italian support of the use of force increases by nearly 20 percentage points when it comes with a UN mandate (it rises from 40 per cent to 60 per cent) (Isernia and Everts 2004). In conclusion, the Italian public prefers to respond to threats to national security in unison with its European and Atlantic partners, and, if possible, with the formal authorization of the United Nations.

Institutional and instrumental responses to threats

During the period under consideration, a general Italian predisposition emerged towards facing the threats to security with an integrated approach of which military force was but one component. This method is considered a winning one even in the fight against global terrorism. Italy does rely on coercive tools and the use of force. At the end of 2003, 12,000 members of the Italian Armed Forces as well as police contingents were engaged in peacekeeping operations, in multilateral missions under the umbrella of the UN, NATO or the EU (e.g. interventions in the Balkan region, East Timor, Congo and the ISAF operation in Afghanistan) or in international coalitions led by the United States (operation Antica Babilonia in Iraq and the Alpine contingent in the Enduring Freedom Afghanistan campaign).

Interaction preference

Italian participation in military operations reflects an awareness that threats to regional instability, the increasing occurrence of 'new wars' (Kaldor 1999), and the collapse of failing states (for instance Afghanistan and Iraq) make necessary military interventions in order to guarantee the conditions necessary to bring forward peace and order, to aid stabilization and reconstruction and, even more ambitiously, to democratize the target country. Italian soldiers are involved not in simple peacekeeping, but rather in so-called operations of 'second generation peacekeeping' (Mackinlay and Chopra 1992; Cellamare 1999: 22–3): interventions with comprehensive mandates that encompass, in addition to narrowly defined security functions, the task of reconstructing the political and economic infrastructure damaged by conflict.

Notwithstanding the Berlusconi government's sudden bilateral turn-around in its support of Bush's war against terrorism, the Italian government's response to security threats has been traditionally characterized by a definite preference for a multilateral approach. Such a tendency is typical of a medium-sized power aware of its diplomatic, economic and military limitations and the need to realize its international ambitions within a multilateral framework. As the former Minister of Foreign Affairs Frattini stated: 'the pursuit of national interest is closely linked to that multilateral dimension whose ideal reference can and must be a renewed United Nations and which has to be concretely realized in the European Union and NATO' (Frattini 2004: 96). Renato Ruggiero, Frattini's predecessor, affirmed after the 11 September attacks, that 'the reaction to an attack striking universal values marked a renewed centrality of the UN. As the privileged centre embodying the consent of states and representing the principles shared by the entire international community, the United Nations represents the unique frame of reference in the global fight against international terrorism' (Ruggiero 2002: 55).[7]

Multilateralism and support of the main international organizations does not merely represent a juridical–ethical position for Italy. It is also a policy designed to reduce the risk of being excluded from formulating those decisions giving shape to international politics. This concern explains the activism within Italian diplomatic circles for the reform of the main international organizations; the Italian objective is to guarantee for itself a prominent role in any reformed international order. Towards that goal, the Italians view any reform of the Security Council of the UN as 'a matter of national interest' as is the persistent urge to deepen the political integration of the EU.[8]

Instrumental preferences

Italy's strategic tradition and its instrumental preferences for meeting security threats remain connected to an integrated approach that combines coercive methods, limited and proportional to the threat, with a multidimensional and comprehensive strategy. Central to this approach is the concept of soft power: the power of culture, of economy and commerce 'in pursuing its interests that are most of all interests of stability' (Toscano 2003: 222; Frattini 2004: 99). There is, in short, a complete awareness that soft and hard power go together and jointly produce more efficient outcomes. Italy has pursued this global and multidimensional approach in the Balkan context, where there has been a wide use of actions involving force (especially through military contingents), in combination with a vast range of instruments that could be described as examples of soft power. For these reasons, Italy supported the idea of a 'Stability Pact' for the Balkans, originally proposed by Germany. Italian support for a widening of the EU towards the East can also be interpreted as the exercise of soft power.

Even in the fight against terrorism, political and cultural dialogue, economic assistance and political reconstruction are considered very important elements of Italian security policy (Frattini 2004: 98). In Afghanistan, Italy has a key role in the humanitarian sector, providing about 35 million euro in aid (Ruggiero 2002: 58). As regards the Israeli–Palestinian conflict, the Italian government has proposed an integrated public–private sector plan for socio-economic development, conceived as a sort of Marshall Plan for the region (Ruggiero 2002: 60; Dini 2002: 67). As regards the Mediterranean area, the main instrument is the Barcelona Declaration and the institutions of the Euro–Mediterranean partnership, the aim of which is to build a '"region of peace and stability" on the basis of stronger economic, trade, social and human relations' (Spencer 1999).

Global terrorism has stimulated a rethink of national intelligence and law enforcement instruments. In 2004, there was a lively debate in parliament regarding reform of the intelligence services – which had been going on for several years – to face this new threat. The main suggestion regarded the unification of military intelligence (SISMI) and civil intelligence (SISDE). The services themselves obstructed this reform and asked for a review of the whole intelligence apparatus (*Corriere della Sera,* 31 July 2004: 9). On the police force level, activities of prevention and repression have been reinforced and a programme has been initiated involving the use of 4,000 soldiers to protect sensitive targets. The Ministry of Health has developed a plan to cope with possible bioterrorist attacks. At the Ministry of Finance, a committee has been established to coordinate actions cutting off the international finance channels of terrorism. Other institutions with similar duties, already in existence and dispersed within the Ministry of Interior, have been put into action. Legal instruments have been adopted to meet the novel challenge posed by the new form of terrorism. Law 438/2001, for example, establishes measures for the prevention and combating of international terrorism and introduces a new crime: association with the ends of international terrorism. Problems have emerged, however, with the introduction of the European arrest warrant, an EU policy initiative central to the collective fight against terrorism in Europe: the Berlusconi government has adopted obstructionist manoeuvres for domestic political considerations divorced from the task of combating terrorism.

There has been a major change in the perception of the threats to Italian security. The unidirectional preoccupation with survival and territorial defence typical of the Cold War period has been replaced by the threat of 'many possible wars' erupting in an unpredictable and fluid international environment (Romano 2002). In the post-Cold War period, a trend emerges which reflects the displacement of a regionally defined threat (1992–2001) to a more globally defined threat after 11 September 2001 (see Table 4.6).

For Italy, the period of regionalized threat corresponded with a preoccupation with the consequences of conflict and widespread instability 'on the

Table 4.6 Typology of perceived threats to Italian security 1999–2004

	1999–2001 regionalized threat	*2001–2004 globalized threat*
Type of threat	Regional instability Criminalization of economies Migratory pressure Indirect costs of conflict Environmental Narcotics trafficking	Global terrorism Asymmetric warfare Macroeconomic instability Conventional warfare WMD attack
Agency of threat	Ethnic factionalism Transnational criminal groups Migrants	Terrorists Guerrilla State actors
Target of threat	Civilian population Economic interests	State structure Civilian population and infrastructure Economic interests Italian contingents abroad Humanitarian personnel
Geographical source of threat	Regional: Balkans Greater Mediterranean	Global: Middle East Central Asia Islamic world Korea
Severity	Low–medium	High–extremely high
Type of response	Multilateral (NATO, UN, EU)	Multilateral Bilateral and within ad hoc coalition led by US
Tractability	Practicable/no great dangers	Uneasy/complex with great dangers

doorstep'. These threats were considered as low intensity rather than existential; they required actions of containment – through interventions in crisis management, stabilization or conflict prevention – in order to avoid a progressive deterioration and the spreading of conflict into neighbouring territories (Kirchner and Sperling 2002).

There are two key characteristics of the post-11 September threat environment: the source of threat is global rather than regional; the agent of threat is no longer states but an amorphous network of global terrorism. The probable threats to Italian security are defined as disruptive or catastrophic terrorist attacks, asymmetrical warfare, economic instability derived from an international environment in a constant state of alarm and turmoil, and the possible terrorist use of WMD. The primary source of threats emanates from a radicalized Islamic world projecting its grievances on a global scale. The severity of these threats is seen as extremely high for Italy, because it is highly exposed in the war against global terrorism and a potential target of attack. Given its complex and elusive nature, this menace is not easily tractable and implies taking great risks to counter it. As regards the type of response, Italy shows a clear propensity for multilateral solutions in order to combat both the regionalized and the globalized threat.

Allocation of resources

For the entire post-war period, Italian military expenditures were very low as a share of GDP and have always been close to NATO minimum levels. The share of the defence budget devoted to investment has always been small. This modest expenditure has caused, inter alia, the following consequences (Comitato Difesa Duemila 2002a: 4):

- the average age of equipment is higher when compared to Italy's partners; there has been a subsequent degradation of operational capabilities and rising maintenance costs; it has contributed to the technological and capabilities gaps within the alliance and has created a dependence on foreign sources of military equipment;
- efforts to redress these shortcomings have privileged expenditures on the most expensive weapons systems – airplanes, ships, and tanks – rather on those best contributing to the development of a leaner and more balanced force structure;
- the prolongation of research and development periods, caused in part by multiannual programmes, have created rigidities in the defence budget and obstructed participation in new activities;
- a strong linkage between development and acquisition programmes has made the reallocation of resources even more difficult, particularly as acquisition has been favoured over research and development; and
- a nearly twenty-year discussion regarding the need to modernize the Armed Forces and the elaboration of a new defence model, with little progress made towards either.

Bureaucratic resistances and a lack of resources have proved a formidable barrier to the timely adaptation of Italian defence and security policies. The terrorist attack of 11 September 2001 acted as a limited catalyst for reconfiguring the defence model. The first signs of change appeared in the fiscal year 2000 defence budget, presented immediately after the attacks. In the evaluation of the strategic frame of reference, the Ministry of Defence identified two fundamental changes in the defence policy context. The first acknowledged the 'extraordinary gravity and absolute novelty' represented by the terrorist attacks. The second regarded the necessary location of security within a multilateral framework that takes into consideration the profound transformations of the Atlantic Alliance in the preceding decade and the growing activism of the EU following the creation of the ESDP in 1999. To cope with these developments, five priorities were established:

- the adaptation of the Armed Forces to the new competencies which require local and regional crisis management rather than traditional defence;
- the improvement of the entire defence system through the provision of adequate funding and modernization;
- the improvement of capacity to handle anomalous situations, such as those deriving from the terrorist threat;
- the improvement of the Armed Forces' intervention capacity for assisting populations struck by natural disasters; and
- the harmonization of the defence system with the values and expectations of civil society.

(Nota aggiuntiva al bilancio della difesa 2002: 1-5)

In order to pursue these aims, the Ministry of Defence seeks a gradual rise in the level of military expenditure from the current 1 per cent of GDP to 1.5 per cent. Even then, defence expenditures are likely to be overstated: military expenditure routinely accounts for no more than 70 per cent of defence expenditure. The 'defence function' budgetary component is derived by subtracting from the defence budget expenditures earmarked for police forces, temporary pensions and external functions. This increase will be difficult to achieve in any event, given the sad state of Italy's public finances and the pressure to respect the Maastricht budget deficit criteria. There is, however, a commitment to rationalize expenditure, reduce the proportion spent on personnel and increase the budgetary share dedicated to investment. Since resources are scarce, respecting Italy's many international obligations – providing a 1,500-strong force available to UN missions and guaranteeing the availability of 22,000 military personnel for a NATO and EU rapid reaction force organized in ground, naval and air forces – requires Italy to draw upon the same military structure again and again under different hats (Nota aggiuntiva al bilancio della difesa 2002: 1–5).

The 2002 Defence budget witnessed a 7 per cent increase compared to 2001, rising from 17.777 to 19.025 billion euro. In particular, there has been an increase of 8.2 per cent in the expenditure destined for the 'defence function', that is to say the function most directly connected to the operational capabilities and strategic missions of the Armed Forces. Furthermore, expenditure destined for the *carabinieri* increased 9.1 per cent, attributable in part to its engagement in overseas peacekeeping missions. As regards the defence function, most of the increased expenditure was earmarked for the professionalization of the Armed Forces (with compulsory conscription coming to an end), whereas the second largest part was devoted to investment. The increase in military expenditure for the fiscal year 2002 represented the biggest increase in the defence budget over the entire 1999–2005 period (see Table 4.7).

Although there have been many attempts to modernize and increase military capabilities, inadequate progress has been made. In July 2004, the Ministry of Defence budget was cut by 875.5 million euro (the initially requested cut amounted to 1.8 billion euro) to keep the public deficit under control. And in 2005, for the first time, the defence budget suffered a decrease as compared to the previous fiscal

Table 4.7 Evolution of the financial appropriations for Italian defence 1999–2005 (million €)

	1999	2000	2001	2002	2003	2004	2005
Defence budget	15,935.1	16,963.4	17,777.0	19,025.1	19,375.9	19,811.0	19,021.7
Annual variation (%)		6.5	4.8	7.0	1.8	2.2	-1.2
Defence function (Armed Forces)	11,065.5	11,871.8	12,631.4	13,665.6	13,803.4	14,148.9	13,638.0
Annual variation (%)		7.3	6.4	8.2	1.0	2.5	-0.3
% of GDP	0.998	1.019	1.038	1.086	1.061	1.045	0.965
Law enforcement function (police force)	3,605.7	3,837.2	3,909.2	4,263.7	4,555.7	4,694.8	4,795.3
Annual variation (%)		6.4	1.9	9.1	6.6	3.1	13.2
External functions	127.7	112.9	234.7	216.9	245.9	238.4	222.5
Annual variation (%)		-11.6	108.0	-7.6	13.4	-3.1	-12.5
Temporary pensions	1,136,2	1,141.5	1,001.6	879.0	770.9	728.9	365.4
Annual variation (%)		0.5	-12.3	-12.2	-12.3	-5.4	-66.3

Source: *Note aggiuntive al bilancio della difesa* 2003, 2004, 2005.

year. According to the former French Minister of Defence Michel Richard, an adequate military capacity can only be guaranteed if at least 0.6 per cent of GDP is allocated to investment expenditures. If the current composition of the defence budget remains unchanged, Italian military expenditure would rise to 1.8 per cent of GDP or only 1.5 per cent with some optimization and rationalization of expenditure. Such an increase would imply a budgetary allocation of approximately 20 billion euro to the defence function, a figure significantly greater than planned and feasible owing to the poor state of public finances (Camporini 2003).

Conclusion

The culture of national security in Italy remains, even after 11 September, weak and inconsistent. In general terms, the country has had a rather positive view of the geopolitical dynamics, in which it has always aptly managed to protect its security, pursue its interests and find its specific role – although often in an incoherent, ambivalent, suboptimal and compromised fashion. This optimistic view seems, however, to have deteriorated significantly in the aftermath of the attacks on the Twin Towers and the Pentagon. In its essence, the international system is no longer seen as stable, but as volatile and fragile. There is now a need for a more proactive intervention to restore, enforce and guarantee order and stability. In this respect, Italy is ready and willing to contribute through participation in multidimensional and multilateral peace-support and peace-building operations.

As regards national identity, Italy considers itself to be both a loyal member of the community of Western nations and its main organizations, and a country which has repudiated the most extreme forms of nationalism and war as an instrument for regulating disputes. Owing to its past history, endowments and characteristics (lack of a significant imperial tradition, modest successes on the battlefield, the negative experience of interwar fascism, and defeat in the Second World War) and in consideration of its actual capabilities, the *Bel Paese* ('the Beautiful Country') maintains a comfortable stereotype of itself: Italy is a peaceful nation whose people (military included) are 'good chaps' and not 'pitiless soldiers', placid peacekeepers, not warriors.

When looking at its position on the international chessboard, Italy remains stuck between a perception of itself as the last of the great powers and the first of the small ones (Santoro 1991). Again, for very pragmatic reasons (insufficient relative power) and also genuine ethical–juridical considerations, Italy has developed a civilian and multinationalized security identity: a reflexive respect for international norms and the moral–political legitimacy of the main multilateral forums, particularly the United Nations. That said, and with specific regard to NATO, Italy has, over time, shed a passive acceptance of the military alliance with the United States and adopted more assertive forms of engagement. Italy's participation in ad hoc 'coalitions of the willing' has illuminated the limits and contradictions of Italian multilateralism.

As regards the instruments of intervention, the policy-makers, the academic elite, and public opinion prefer a multidimensional and integrated approach that

confronts the profound structural causes of instability through soft power interventions. Force, albeit as a last resort, is used in a limited way and is proportional
to the political objective sought. The public has generally accepted this formula
for the use of force in the aftermath of 11 September (see Table 4.8).

The change in threat perception has forced Italy to adapt aims and means
appropriate to the new security challenges, starting with the political–institutional reorganization of the defence system and a different hierarchy of foreign
policy goals. As regards force structure, Italy continues to renounce nuclear
ambitions. The Armed Forces have endured a profound change: its force structure has had to be transformed from one designed to meet the tasks of territorial
defence to one designed for the challenges presented by the tasks of peacekeeping, peace-enforcing and nation–building outside the NATO area. The lack of
available resources for defence remains problematic, will probably remain so
into the future, and will be exacerbated by waste and misallocation, particularly
with respect to the R&D and acquisitions budgets. As regards civil–military

Table 4.8 Italian national security culture

Worldview of external environment	Generally positive and not dramatically threatening the country's vital interests. This general perception significantly deteriorated after 11 September.
	Emphasis on the elements of fragility, disorder and weakness of international systems' units. This might necessitate the stabilization support/intervention of the international community.
National identity	Rejection of nationalism, militarism and force as instruments for pursuing national interests and regulating international disputes.
	Self-perception of Italians (military included) as 'good chaps', not warriors.
	Civilian and multinationalized identity (within regional and international organizations/alliances and in particular NATO, UN, EU).
	Respect for international law and the moral/political legitimacy of the United Nations.
Instrumental preferences	Comprehensive, integrated and multidimensional approach.
	General preference for civilian instruments and soft power, exceptionally backed by limited and proportional use of force.
	Multifunctional, 'second generation' peace-support and crisis management operations.
	Institution building and democratization.
	Economic aid and cooperation.
Interaction preferences	Preference for institutionalized multilateral frameworks at the regional (particularly NATO, EU, OSCE) or international level (particularly UN).

relations, Italy has passed from Armed Forces based on compulsory conscription – seen as a means for ensuring the democratization of the military – to a professional army. In this changeover, however, political–bureaucratic control of military policy has remained intact.

Notes

1 For a general view of Italian defence policy, see De Andreis and Miggiano (1987); Rallo (1989); Silvestri (1990); Caligaris and Santoro (1986); Caligaris (1990); Santoro (1992); Andreatta and Hill (1997); D'Amore (2001).
2 For a view of Italian European policy, see Ronzitti (1987); Bonvicini (1983; 1996); Ferraris (1996); Varsori (1998); Coralluzzo (2000); Soetendorp (1999); Foradori and Rosa (2004).
3 See *Limes* number 4, 1999, entitled 'A che serve la NATO?'.
4 A special themed issue by *Limes* entitled 'Israel/Palestine, the narrow land' is dedicated to this matter; also see Colombo (2000).
5 The 53rd biannual report of the Italian Secret Services presented to Parliament (first semester 2004) stated that Italy is a 'rewarding target' for Islamic radicalism (*Corriere della Sera,* 31 July 2004: 9).
6 According to the Minister of Defence Martino, it is necessary to head for the constitution of a rapid reaction force of NATO, to the detriment of a similar EU structure, which would only produce useless overlaps (Comitato Difesa Duemila 2002b).
7 Italy is the sixth major contributor to the UN (contributing about 5 per cent of the ordinary budget of the organization). Italy took part in 25 UN peacekeeping operations from 1950 to the present and currently has 9,000 troops involved (Permanent Mission of Italy to the United Nations. Available online at: <http://www.italyun.org/docs/peace/peacekeeping.pdf>(accessed 27 October 2006)).
8 Italy asked for the creation of 'new more frequently rotating seats for countries shouldering a heavier burden in the maintenance of international peace and security'. That is to say a 'new category of rotating non-permanent members, as opposed to a simple increase in the number of either of the existing categories, permanent or non-permanent' (Fulci 1999). On the importance to the Italian national interest, see Minister of Foreign Affairs Frattini in *Corriere della Sera,* 17 August 2004: 5; with respect to European integration, see Ignazi 2004: 272.

References

Aliboni, R. (2002) 'Upgrading political responses in the Mediterranean', *The International Spectator* 37 (2): 103–12.
Ammendola, T. and Isernia, P. (2000) 'Continuità e cambiamento nella politica estera italiana', in G. Di Palma, S. Fabbrini, G. Freddi (eds) *Condannata al successo? L'Italia nell'Europa integrata,* Bologna: Il Mulino.
Andreatta, F. and Hill, C. (1997) 'Italy', in J. Howorth and A. Mennon (eds) *The European Union and National Defence Policy,* London: Routledge.
Attinà, F. (2003) *La sicurezza degli stati nell'era dell'egemonia americana,* Milano: Giuffrè Editore.
Bonvicini, G. (1983) 'Italy: an integrationist perspective', in C. Hill (ed.) *National Foreign Policy and European Political Cooperation,* London: Allen and Unwin.

Bonvicini, G. (1996) 'Regional reassertion: the dilemmas of Italy', in C. Hill (ed.) *The Actors in Europe's Foreign Policy,* London: Routledge.

Bruni, F. (2001) 'Le conseguenze economiche del terrorismo', *Relazioni internazionali* 9 (8): 8.

Caligaris, L. (1990) 'La politica militare', in B. Dente (ed.) *Le politiche pubbliche in Italia,* Bologna: Il Mulino.

Caligaris, L. and Santoro, C.M. (1986) *Obiettivo difesa,* Bologna: Il Mulino.

Camporini, V. (2003) 'L'esercito europeo? Un'equivoco', *Liberal Risk* 3: 18–27.

Carnimeo, N. and Buturovic, A. (2001) 'L'Occidente "scopre" le cellule terroriste in Bosnia', *Limes,* Quaderno Speciale 4: 68–83.

Cellamare, G. (1999) *Le operazioni di peace-keeping multifunzionali,* Torino: Giappichelli.

Colombo, A. (2000) 'Quali prospettive di pace per il Medio Oriente?', *Relazioni internazionali* 8 (3): 5–7.

Comitato Difesa Duemila (2002a) 'Ci sentiamo in guerra?', in Comitato Difesa Duemila, *Rapporto 2002,* Roma: Fondazione Liberal.

Comitato Difesa Duemila (2002b) *Hearing of the Minister of Defence at the Defence Committee of the Camera dei Deputati, 19 March 2002.* Available online at: <http://www.difesa.it/Ministro/Compiti+e+Attivita/Dettaglio+audizione.htm?DetailID =46> (accessed 27 October 2006).

Comitato Difesa Duemila (2003) 'Per una nuova alleanza strategica tra Europa e Stati Uniti', in Comitato Difesa Duemila, *Rapporto 2003* Roma: Fondazione Liberal.

Coralluzzo, V. (2000) *La politica estera dell'Italia repubblicana (1946–1992): modello di analisi e studio dei casi,* Milano: Franco Angeli.

D'Amore, C. (2001) *Governare la difesa,* Milano: Franco Angeli.

De Andreis, M. and Miggiano, P. (1987) *L'Italia e la corsa agli armamenti,* Milano: Franco Angeli.

Dini, L. (2002) 'L'11 settembre e la società globale', *Affari Esteri* 34 (6): 64–71.

Dottori, G. and Gasparini, G. (2001) 'Italy's changing defence policy', *The International Spectator* 36 (4): 51–9.

Ferguson, C.D. and Andreoni, A. (2004) 'Le vie della "bomba sporca"', *Limes* 1: 93–101.

Ferraris, L.V. (ed.) (1996) *Manuale della politica estera italiana,* Bari: Laterza.

Ferraris, L.V (2003) 'Un nuovo sistema internazionale?', *Affari Esteri* 35: 316–26.

Foradori, P. and Rosa, P. (2004) 'Italy and the politics of European defence: playing by the logic of multilevel networks', *Modern Italy* 9: 217–31.

Fulci, P. (1999) 'Italy and the reform of the United Nations Security Council', *The International Spectator* 34 (2): 3–23.

Frattini, F. (2004) 'The fundamental directions of Italy's foreign policy', *The International Spectator* 39 (1): 95–9.

Garruccio, L. (1982) 'Le scelte di fondo e il retroterra culturale, *Politica Internazionale* 10 (2): 7–14.

Hill, C. (1993) 'The capability–expectations gap, or conceptualizing Europe's international role', *Journal of Common Market Studies* 31 (3): 305–28.

Ignazi, P. (2004) 'Al di là dell'Atlantico, al di qua dell'Europa: dove va la politica estera italiana', *il Mulino* 2: 267–76.

Isernia, P. (1992) 'Opinione pubblica e politica internazionale in Italia', in C. M. Santoro (ed.) *L'elmo di Scipio: studi sul modello di difesa italiano,* Bologna: Il Mulino.

Isernia, P. and Everts, P.P. (2004) 'Partners apart? The Foreign Policy attitude of the American and European Publics', *Japanese Journal of Political Science* 5(2): 229–58.

ISPI (2003) 'Geopolitica dell'Italia nel dopo guerra fredda', *Relazioni internazionali* 9 (13): 16–17.

Jean, C. (2003) *Manuale di geopolitica,* Bari: Laterza.

Kaldor, M. (1999) *New and Old Wars: Organised Violence in a Global Era,* Cambridge: Polity Press.

Kirchner, E. and Sperling, J. (2002) 'The new security threats in Europe: theory and evidence', *European Foreign Affairs Review* 7: 423–52.

Mackinlay, J. and Chopra, J. (1992) 'Second generation multinational operations', *Washington Quarterly* 15: 113–34.

MAE (Ministero degli Affari Esteri) (2000) *Libro bianco 2000,* Milano: Franco Angeli.

MAE (2003) *Communication of the Minister of Foreign Affairs regarding guidelines of Italian foreign policy,* Rome: Senato della Repubblica. Available online at: <http://www.esteri.it/ita/6_38_90.asp> (accessed 29 January 2003).

Ministero della Difesa (2002) *Libro bianco della Difesa 2002.* Available online at: <http://www.difesa.it/> (accessed 23 November 2005).

Monteleone, C. (2000) 'Sicurezza: una nuova agenda per un concetto in evoluzione', *Teoria Politica* 16 (2): 161–76.

Nava, M. (2001) 'Il nostro Afghanistan', *Limes,* Quaderno Speciale 3: 35–48.

Nones, M. (2001) 'L'Italia da capo: l'economia della difesa. Il nuovo contesto strategico impone la necessità di un adeguamento degli "affari militari"', *Liberal Risk* 2 (1): 27–36.

Nones, M. (2004) 'Strategie di difesa: fondi pubblici tecnologie private', *Liberal Risk* 4: 72–4.

Nota aggiuntiva al bilancio della difesa (varie annate). Available online at: <http://www.difesa.it/> (accessed 23 November 2005).

Panebianco, A. (1977) 'La politica estera italiana: un modello interpretativo', *il Mulino* 26 (2): 845–79.

Panebianco, A. (1982) 'Le cause interne del basso profilo', *Politica internazionale* 10: 15–21.

Panebianco, A. (2001) 'Di fronte alla guerra', *il Mulino* 6: 1000–6.

Pelanda, C. (2003) 'Difesa civile e antiterrorismo', in M. Dassù and C. Jean (eds) *L'Italia nel sistema globale. Interessi nazzionali e priorita europee,* Aspen Institute Italia.

Perani, G. and Pianta, M. (1992) 'L'acquisto di armamenti in Italia', in M. De Cecco and M. Pianta (eds) *Amministrazione militare e spesa per armamenti in Europa,* Bologna: Il Mulino.

Politi, A. (1999) 'The new dimensions of organised crime in Southern Europe', *The International Spectator* 34 (4): 49–59.

Rallo, J. (1989) 'Italy', in D.J. Murray and P.R. Viotti (eds) *The Defense Policies of Nations,* Baltimore: The Johns Hopkins University Press.

Romano, S. (2002) *Guida alla politica estera italiana. Da Badoglio a Berlusconi,* Milano: Rizzoli.

Ronzitti, N. (1987) 'European policy formulation in the Italian administrative system', *The International Spectator* 22: 207–14.

Rosa, P. (2003) 'L'europeizzazione della politica estera', in S. Fabbrini (ed.) *L'europeizzazione dell'Italia,* Bari-Roma: Laterza.

Ruggiero, R. (2002) 'La politica internazionale dopo l'11 settembre', *Affari Esteri* 34 (133): 54–63.

Santoro, C.M. (1991) *La politica estera di una media potenza: l'Italia dall'Unità a oggi,* Bologna: Il Mulino.

Santoro, C.M. (ed.) (1992) *L'elmo di Scipio: studi sul modello di difesa italiano,* Bologna: Il Mulino.

Sciortino, G. (2002) 'Le politiche di controllo migratorio in Europa e in Italia', in *Ottavo Rapporto sulle migrazioni 2002,* Milano: Franco Angeli.

Silvestri, S. (1990) 'L'Italia: partner fedele ma di basso profilo', in L. Caligaris (ed.) *La difesa europea: proposte e sfide,* Milano: Edizioni di Comunità.

Silvestri, S. (2001) 'Global security after 11 September', *The International Spectator* 36 (3): 5–9.

Soetendorp, B. (1999) *Foreign Policy in the European Union: Theory, History and Practice,* London: Longman.

Spencer, C. (1999) 'Partnership-building in the Mediterranean', *The International Spectator* 38 (4): 59–75.

Toscano, R. (2003) 'Sicurezza esterna: dimensioni non militari' in M. Dassù and C. Jean (eds) *L'Italia nel sistema globale. Interessi nazzionali e priorita europee,* Aspen Institute Italia.

Varsori, A. (1998) *L'Italia nelle relazioni internazionali dal 1943 al 1992,* Bari-Roma: Laterza.

5   United Kingdom

Punching above its weight

Elke Krahmann

Two events have transformed threat perception and national defence in the UK in the past few decades: the end of the Cold War and the terrorist attacks of 11 September 2001. The first brought the end of the superpower confrontation and the dissolution of the Warsaw Pact, but it also hailed in the break-up of Yugoslavia, the war in Chechnya, and a variety of conflicts in the Transcaucasus region. These new conflicts suggested that the end of bipolarity would not necessarily lead to a more peaceful 'new world order'. Greater international cooperation and integration across Western and Eastern Europe seemed possible for the first time since 1945 and have been achieved with the enlargement of NATO and the European Union. At the same time the fragmentation of established countries and alliances after the end of the Cold War has illustrated the complexities of the new international security environment.

In the UK, the government responded to these changes with a major Strategic Defence Review (SDR) published in 1998 (MoD 1998; McInnes 1998). The review reflected upon the changed nature of security after the end of the Cold War and suggested the modernization and reshaping of the British Armed Forces. Nevertheless, the review also maintained many of the basic tenets of British defence strategy. They included an essentially defensive and reactive approach towards global security.

The attacks of 11 September 2001 fundamentally changed the UK outlook. They appeared to suggest that the primary security concerns of the new millennium would not be civil war and ethnic conflict but transnational security threats such as global terrorism, organized crime, and the proliferation of weapons of mass destruction (WMD). While the former seemed to be essentially containable and potentially resolvable within a state-centric framework and the national and international security arrangements developed during the Cold War, the latter suggested the need for a radical reformulation of national and global security policy. It shifted the focus from national to social and individual threats and from deterrence and defence to security 'management' involving diplomatic, economic and military means. Moreover, it appeared to require proactive solutions, such as addressing the underlying causes of threat, but also pre-emptive interventions.

The UK government first expressed its changed understanding of the global security environment less than a year after the terrorist strikes against the US in

'A New Chapter' added to the SDR (MoD 2002a). The New Chapter, which specifically focused on terrorism, argued: 'Experience shows that it is better where possible, to engage an enemy at longer range, *before* they get the opportunity to mount an assault on the UK' (MoD 2002a: 9, italics added). The full scope of the transformation in the UK's threat perception and defence posture became apparent in the 2003 Defence White Paper *Delivering Security in a Changing World*. The White Paper confirmed the growing role of non-traditional security threats and further endorsed a proactive approach to national defence (MoD 2003).

Despite the reformulation of UK threat perception, strategy and capabilities after the end of the Cold War, some historical and geographical constants of British defence policy persist. The first constant, the UK's colonial legacy, is reflected in the specific interest in and responsibility the UK accepts for global security including its many business relations and its remaining thirteen overseas territories. The second constant is the special relationship with the United States. It involves the UK's role as the United States' main ally, both within international organizations such as NATO and in coalitions of the willing. The third is the UK's nuclear capability which it has retained as part of its national deterrent and in support of its special status as a major power.

Security threats

Threat perception in the UK

Taking account of the events following the end of the superpower confrontation, the 1998 SDR listed a broad range of new threats that replaced the relatively stable and predictable Cold War security environment with 'a complex mixture of uncertainty and instability' (MoD 1998: para. 2). This new strategic reality involved internal conflicts such as in Bosnia and Kosovo, rogue regimes with conventional weapons and the increasing threat of the proliferation of nuclear, biological and chemical WMD. The review also mentioned a growing range of asymmetric threats posed by non-state actors, ranging from drug trafficking, organized crime, terrorism, and environmental degradation to attacks on information technology (MoD 1998: ch.1, paras. 7–9).

Among these threats, the Ministry of Defence identified several priorities. Influenced by the break-up of Yugoslavia and the first Gulf War, it specifically emphasized two main threats. The foremost concern was instability in Central and Eastern Europe. The second was confrontation in the Gulf region and the Middle East. In particular, the regime of Saddam Hussein was singled out as a persistent threat owing to the size of its armed forces and its capability to develop and spread missile technology and WMD. In spite of the success of the first Gulf War and the imposition of United Nation and European sanctions on Iraq, the SDR argued that the threat from these sources was unlikely to wane, but had the potential to increase in the future (MoD 1998).

In sum, the SDR recognized the changed security environment after the end of the Cold War and made the first steps to broaden the focus of UK politicians and military planners to potential new security threats. In the short term, however, the UK's security priorities remained focused on more traditional state and intra-state conflicts. Only after 11 September 2001 did these priorities begin to shift.

The New Chapter, published nearly a year after the terrorist attacks in July 2002, made the threat from international terrorism a top UK priority. The SDR had recognized the growing presence of terrorism, yet it perceived the latter as a specific tactic rather than a threat in itself. The New Chapter pointed out the potential strategic impact of terrorism: terrorism was no longer interpreted as a means used by an enemy such as the IRA or a rogue state to limited effect, but it was considered an essential threat which could potentially shape and determine the outcome of a conflict.

The degree to which the events of 11 September had changed threat perception in the UK became fully apparent in the 2003 Defence White Paper. It practically reversed the order of the security threats as they had been presented in the SDR. International terrorism was the first security concern, followed by the proliferation of WMD, instability generated by failing states in Europe and Africa, and social and environmental tensions (MoD 2003: 4–5). Geographically, Europe remained central to UK national interest, but the Ministry of Defence (MoD) asserted that there was currently no major conventional threat to Europe. Conversely, 'asymmetric forms of attack, including from international terrorism, pose a very real threat to our homelands' (MoD 2003: 5).

The UK Parliament, represented by its Defence Committee, largely shared the perceptions of the government. In its commentary on the post-Cold War SDR, the Defence Committee had agreed that regional instability in Russia, the former Soviet Union as well as the Mediterranean, the Near East, North Africa and the Gulf were most likely to present new challenges (DC 1998: paras. 106–12). However, the Committee argued that the problems in Central and Eastern Europe would be of a diplomatic, political and economic nature rather than a military one. Even the military dangers presented by conflicts in North Africa, the Mediterranean, the Middle East and the Gulf were regarded as limited, and access to Gulf oil was considered a 'residual' security issue (DC 1998: paras. 114–15). Sub-state conflict, terrorism and organized crime were merely listed as 'further dimensions'. Unlike the government, however, the Committee identified environmental, developmental and population issues as increasingly important concerns for international security and urged the government to do more to integrate appropriate measures into its security strategy (DC 1998: para. 120).

The attacks of 11 September 2001 changed the parliamentary threat assessment as it had that of the government. It agreed that global terrorism was on the rise. But the Defence Committee disagreed with the government's approach to combating it. UK defence capabilities and strategies, it argued, tended to 'reflect the perceived level of threat rather than ... an assessment of the weak points of our society' (DC 2001). Instead, the Committee advocated a radically new form of defence planning based on identifying potential targets rather than threats.

Table 5.1 Popular threat perceptions in the UK after 11 September (in percentage of respondents)

Fears	October 2001	March 2002	October 2002	March 2003
International terrorism	83	72	85	80
WMD proliferation	83	66	82	77
Accident in a nuclear power station	79	60	74	65
Accidental launch of a nuclear missile	77	58	73	65
Organized crime	74	63	71	65
Nuclear conflict in Europe	73	55	69	59
World War	72	57	70	59
Epidemics	69	51	62	55
Ethnic conflict in Europe	67	53	63	53
Conventional war in Europe	62	47	60	47

Source: Author's compilation of various Eurobarometer polls from 2001 to 2003.

However, only in its subsequent 2002 report Defence and Security in the UK, the Defence Committee fully outlined its perceived gaps in UK homeland security and how they might be addressed (DC 2002).

The changing threat perceptions in the UK were widely reflected among the general public. After the end of the Cold War, public opinion had regarded the security threat to the nation as much reduced. New threats such as terrorism had not yet registered in the public mind, while the immediate security challenges such as the Gulf War and the ethnic conflict in the former Yugoslavia were too distant to pose any direct threat to the UK public. In the 1990s, typically less than 10 per cent of British adults considered defence an important issue, ranking it far behind concerns such as the EU, crime, education and the National Health Service (MORI 2005). After the events of 11 September, the numbers rose to 60 per cent and in the years that followed remained on average at 32 per cent. As for the type of threat, Eurobarometer surveys between October 2001 and March 2003 reported that the UK public ranked international terrorism as the top security concern followed by the proliferation of WMD, nuclear accidents and organized crime. The threat of a regional war in Europe, ethnic conflict, epidemics or even a world war were considered to be much less significant.

While there was significant agreement between the government and public opinion, academic experts assessed the threats facing the UK before and after 11 September differently. Leading scholars in the area of security studies specifically criticized the SDR's focus on regional instability and the shift towards an interventionist security strategy. They emphasized that, while direct threats to the UK mainland appeared to have been significantly reduced owing to the end of the Cold War, national defence should remain a priority for deterrence purposes and as an insurance against unforeseeable developments and new threats (Hill 1997). Academics highlighted the continued risks from the former Soviet bloc (Rogers and Mepham 1998; Sabin 1998) and pointed out the rise of transnational security threats such as crime and environmental degradation (Clarke 1998; Hodges 1997; Alexander and Garden 2001). Although the new threats might not pose a danger to the UK's territorial integrity, scholars argued that they could threaten the British 'way of life' (Clarke 1998; Hodges 1997). By 1998, academics were already mentioning the possibility of terrorist attacks on the UK homeland in response to interventions in regional conflicts (Sabin 1998). The proliferation of WMD was seen as an additional threat to national and international security (Rogers and Mepham 1998). Following 11 September, however, academics were careful to point out that terrorists were less likely to use WMD than conventional explosives or other less sophisticated tools (Pearson 2001; Pearson and Hay 2001). Moreover, the pre-emptive intervention in Iraq was criticized as having increased the threat of terrorism to the UK (Gregory and Wilkinson 2005), an assessment apparently vindicated by the London subway bombings on 8 July 2005.

Sources of threat

The 1998 SDR acknowledged the changing geography of the threat environment. Risks had shifted from the Warsaw Pact to instability *within* Europe. There was also a potential of new threats arising from conflicts in the Gulf or the Mediterranean. Beyond Europe, however, the risks to UK special interests were believed to be small. This, presumably, included Asia and Africa where the SDR argued the UK had only a 'wider interest in supporting international order' as part of its role as a Permanent Member of the UN Security Council (MoD 1998: para. 42).

This view was widely shared by UK parliamentarians. In its comments on the SDR, the Defence Committee reflected that Russia's military capabilities had been reduced to such a degree that they ruled out a major conventional attack against Western Europe and the UK. If there should be a breakdown of order within Russia, it was likely to give the UK a sufficiently long warning period (DC 1998: paras. 107–8). It also agreed that the Middle East and the Mediterranean would be of increasing importance, whereas events in the Asia-Pacific region could 'pose only indirect challenges to UK security interests' (DC 1998: paras. 112–8). Academic scholars, on the contrary, emphasized the broader geographic spread of risks to the UK. They warned not only that terrorist or chemical and biological attacks could be perpetrated on the UK homeland, but also that political and economic crises in Asia and Africa would increasingly have security repercussions in the UK.

Following the terrorist attacks of 11 September, the government soon adopted the academic assessment. The MoD and the Defence Committee admitted that the SDR's attention to regional conflicts in Europe had led to the neglect of homeland defence. The spread of global terrorism also appeared to require a reassessment of the geographical origins of threat including Central Asia, East Africa, the Indian

Table 5.2 UK governmental threat perceptions before and after 11 September

	1998–2001 *Regionalized threats*	*2001–2004* *Complex threats*
Type of key threat	1 Regional instability in Central and Eastern Europe 2 Conflicts in the Gulf and and Middle East 3 WMD proliferation to and from rogue regimes 4 Asymmetric threats from organized crime, terrorism, environmental degradation and attacks on IT	1 Global terrorism with strategic impact on UK homeland 2 WMD proliferation to rogue regimes and terrorists 3 Regional instability due to failed states in Europe and Africa 4 Social and environmental conflicts
Agency of threats	States Ethnic and nationalist factions Immigrants Transnational criminal groups Terrorists	Terrorists Rogue and failed states Transnational criminal groups Ethnic and nationalist factions
Target of threat	Neighbouring states Economic interests Overseas interests	UK homeland and infra-structure 'Way of life' Civilian population Economic interests Overseas interests
Geographical source of threat	Central and Eastern Europe Mediterranean Gulf region Middle East	Central and Eastern Europe Middle East Mediterranean Central Asia East Africa Indian subcontinent

subcontinent and other regions (DC 2001: para. 100). In its 2003 Defence White Paper, the government stated:

> since the SDR there has been a series of significant developments: More numerous crises of a wider range and a wider geographical area – Kosovo, Macedonia, Sierra Leone, East Timor, Afghanistan, Democratic Republic of Congo as well as Iraq – have demonstrated that the global security environment is more uncertain than it was five years ago and our Armed Forces face an even broader range, frequency, and often duration of tasks than envisaged in 1998.
>
> (MoD 2003: para. 1.4)

The rise of non-state sources of threat, such as ethnic conflict, transnational organized crime, terrorism, proliferation of conventional weapons and WMD, and trafficking in drugs and people, had already been noted in the aftermath of the Cold War. In fact, the changing nature of the sources threat was one of the reasons for the SDR in 1998. The attacks of 11 September merely changed the ranking of these threats; terrorism replaced regional conflict as the top priority, while the proliferation of WMD remained the second most important issue of concern for the UK.

Responses to threat

Since defence planning is based on long-term cycles of research, development and procurement, major changes in capabilities and operations can only be achieved over decades. UK military strategies and instruments, therefore, show significant continuity over the past two decades. Continuities include the transatlantic alliance, the special relationship with the United States, and the UK's independent nuclear deterrent which developed during the Cold War. However, terrorism and WMD proliferation clearly require different responses than the threat of superpower confrontation. The UK has therefore been faced with a considerable challenge to modify and modernize existing resources and strategies. Two changes in particular can be noted since the early 1990s. The first concerns a shift towards a more proactive 'management' of security threats, involving prevention and pre-emption. The second regards a greater emphasis on non-military tools and operations, such as diplomacy and development aid.

Interaction preference

The UK's preference for bi- and multilateral responses to perceived threats derived directly from the definition of British security interests within the context of Europe, the transatlantic community, and the world. During the Cold War, the UK's security perception was shaped by the confrontation between NATO and the Warsaw Pact. Its commitments within the Atlantic Alliance ensured that any threat against one of its members was understood as a threat to the UK itself.

Since the dissolution of the Warsaw Pact, increasing regional and global integration have taken the role of the glue that binds the UK to the security of Europe and overseas. As The Future Strategic Context for Defence pointed out in 2001, the UK is 'more dependent on international trade and investment than most' countries (MoD 2001). Exports make up a higher proportion of the UK's GDP than in France, Germany, Japan or the United States, and foreign investment accounts for more than 20 per cent of British manufacturing jobs. Disruptions in the global economy and the stability of financial markets are therefore likely to seriously affect the UK.

At the same time as globalization is increasing the UK's interdependence, it is limiting the effectiveness of autonomous action. On the one hand, the transnational nature of new security threats such as environmental degradation, immigration and proliferation undermines unilateral responses. On the other hand, the UK lacks the defence capabilities necessary to respond to 'each and every risk or crisis' that directly or indirectly affects UK interests (MoD 2003: para. 2.10). The UK government, therefore, believes that Britain's national and economic security is best supported by international collaboration.

Among its allies, the UK government has traditionally placed a strong premium on the 'special relationship' with the United States (Dumbrell 2004). This relationship has been strengthened by British support for American security policies after 11 September and during the intervention in Iraq (Dunne 2004). According to Defence Secretary Geoffrey Hoon, '11 September and its aftermath have underlined the importance of the transatlantic relationship. From the outset, we demonstrated by our actions our wish to work closely with our *most important* ally, the US' (in MoD 2002a: 5).

Despite the strong and long-standing tradition of bilateral and multilateral responses to contemporary security threats, however, the UK government has rejected the idea of increased role sharing with allied countries or the pooling of military capabilities in order to reduce defence spending and increase the level of specialized technologies for instance within the EU (DC 2001: para. 141). Although the UK government encourages such efforts by other countries, it believes that the UK's national defence and its ability to engage in coalitions of the willing require a broad range of capabilities.

Among parliamentarians and academic experts, there has been broad support for the special relationship and multilateral collaboration. But this did not prevent some academics from criticizing the government's undivided support for American policies in the 'war on terrorism' and the intervention in Afghanistan, suggesting that more multilateral responses could have been adopted, including 'the creation of a coalition and the participation of regional countries' (DC 2001: paras. 82–4).

Institutional preferences

Despite the transformations in UK threat assessment after the end of the Cold War and 11 September, the institutional preferences of the British government for dealing with contemporary security threats have changed very little. The dissolution of the Warsaw Pact and the break-up of the Soviet Union did not change the government's assessment in 1998 that NATO continued to be 'the cornerstone of our defence planning' (MoD 1998: para. 18). Similarly, the attacks of 11 September did not transform the UK's position that – with the exception of the pre-emptive interventions in Afghanistan and Iraq – defence against terrorism is primarily the responsibility of national and international intelligence and police forces rather than the military (Bamford 2004).

The UK government particularly believed in NATO as the vehicle for integrating the former members of the Warsaw Pact into the transatlantic security community and thus prevent further instability in Central and Eastern Europe. As part of this integration process, the UK has supported NATO's Partnership for Peace Programme, bilateral defence cooperation, and the enlargement of NATO from 12 to 26 members between 1999 and 2004.

The UK government has also been a strong advocate of NATO interventions in Europe and beyond. Following 11 September, the government made plans to enhance 'NATO's capacity to deal with new threats including terrorism and WMD from wherever the Alliance's members are threatened' (MoD 2002a: para. 71). And the 2003 Defence White Paper proposed NATO's 'evolution from large static forces to smaller response forces, able to undertake operations beyond the NATO area itself' (MoD 2003: para. 1.4).

Differences over the intervention in Iraq have since led to some disillusionment of the UK government with NATO. While the government argued that the divergences over Iraq did not undermine its commitment to the alliance, it argued that flexible coalitions of the willing might be necessary to deal with specific threats (MoD 2003: para. 2.16).

The second most important international institution for the UK is the United Nations. The UK's commitment to the UN rests on its permanent seat on the Security Council, a role simultaneously perceived by the government as an obligation to 'act as a force for good in the world' and an opportunity to 'play a leading role internationally' (MoD 1998: para. 21). Since the end of the Cold War, the UK government has supported the role that the UN Security Council has taken in an unprecedented number of international peacekeeping operations (MoD 1998: paras. 24, 53). After the terrorist attacks of 11 September, the UK government emphasized the role of the UN in the 'war on terrorism' as authorizing international interventions as in Afghanistan, promoting international consensus, imposing obligations to suppress terrorist financing, and addressing the breeding ground of terrorism through development initiatives (MoD 2002a: paras. 66–70).

As with NATO, the differences over the war in Iraq have since dampened British enthusiasm for the UN and the 2003 Defence White Paper announced that the UK had to be 'realistic about the limitations of the UN and the difficulties of translating broad consensus on goals into specific actions, particularly where proactive military intervention is concerned' (MoD 2003: para. 2.17).

Owing to its lack of military capabilities and consensus, the EU has so far ranked only third among British preferences for international organizations as a means of enhancing its national and international security (MoD 1998: introduction, para. 18). In 1998, the SDR merely included the EU among 'a wide range of other institutions' that had a role to play in *European* security (MoD 1998: para. 39). According to the MoD, the EU's primary capabilities were in 'helping to extend economic prosperity and political stability', presumably through enlargement, but also 'through the Common Foreign and Security Policy' (MoD 1998: para. 39).

The Saint Malo initiative of 1998 and the fight against terrorism have since improved the UK government's assessment of EU capabilities and utility for security and defence. The EU's 'ability to co-ordinate across all its areas of competence' ranging from civil protection to cooperation in border control and in dissolving terrorist finance networks has proved a particular asset. The New Chapter also praised the progress made on improving the EU's military capabilities as set out in the Helsinki Headline Goals (MoD 2002a: paras. 73–4). The UK government has strongly supported the development of these capabilities, first through the Saint Malo agreement with France and then at the Helsinki Council (Clarke 2000). However, the UK has always maintained that EU military capabilities were only 'to complement NATO' and to enhance the EU's role in the area of crisis management (MoD 2003: para. 2.19). The government has also promoted a European defence capabilities agency to coordinate acquisitions policies among the EU member states (MoD 2003: para. 2.19).

Nevertheless, the degree to which multilateral organizations can help improve national and international security has not been fully considered in UK government publications. The Defence Committee specifically noted that the 2003 'White Paper makes only limited reference to the United Nations in its two volumes' and asked that the government explain more fully how 'UK forces have supported the United Nations; how the UK expects to continue to do so; and how defence planners see the UK's military role within the UN system' in relation to its roles in NATO and EU (DC 2004: para. 25). A further omission concerns how the government intends to strengthen international regimes, particularly favoured in academic circles as key to controlling the proliferation of WMD among terrorists and rogue regimes (Pearson 2001: para. 27.i).

Instrumental preferences

While the UK's institutional preferences have remained relatively constant, the strategies and instruments advocated by the government and defence planners have changed radically since the end of the Cold War and the beginning of the 'war on terrorism'. The most important of these changes has been the shift from a defensive towards a proactive strategy. The second innovation has been the endorsement of defence diplomacy as part of the tasks of the Armed Forces. Both have required a considerable adaptation of UK defences. A notable exception from these transformations is the continued preference for the UK's nuclear submarines as a fundamental basis of its national deterrence.

The move from the defensive strategy of the Cold War towards a proactive security policy began in 1998 when the UK government observed: 'The challenge now is to move ... on to the active management of these risks, seeking to prevent conflicts rather than suppress them' (MoD 1998: para. 10). In the aftermath of the interventions in the former Yugoslavia, however, defence planners were ambiguous as to whether a proactive security policy should include pre-emptive interventions or merely conflict prevention. The SDR merely stated that the government's new policy would be supported by 'all instruments at our disposal, including diplomatic, developmental and military' (MoD 1998: para. 10).

Only after 11 September did the UK government fully endorse pre-emptive military operations. In the introduction to the New Chapter to the SDR, Defence Secretary Hoon argued: 'It is much better to engage our enemies in their backyard than ours, at a time and place of our choosing and not theirs' (MoD 2002a: 5). Although both the New Chapter and the 2003 Defence White Paper strictly avoided the term pre-emptive intervention, preferring instead the notion 'proactive prevention', the government acknowledged in answers to the Defence Committee that it was willing to consider pre-emptive military measures in the case of direct threats to the UK (DC 2001: para. 130). These measures included a growing range of security policy instruments and strategies such as prevention, deterrence, coercion, disruption and destruction of threats linked to terrorists or rogue regimes (MoD 2003: para. 1.5).

UK parliamentarians have been sceptical of the shift towards pre-emptive military operations. Although they have generally agreed that it is best to deal with threats before they reach the UK homeland, the Defence Committee in particular has doubted whether pre-emptive interventions would be suitable and effective against substate terrorist groups. In addition, the Defence Committee has identified two problems with pre-emptive interventions. The first regards the legal basis. The second concerns the UK's ability to pursue pre-emptive strikes either with missiles launched from aircraft or naval vessels or by close quarter ground action.

The Committee specifically pointed out that it was 'by no means confident that Article 51 of the UN charter would provide the necessary cover for pre-emptive action' unless there was a specific UN resolution authorizing the operation. The Committee therefore demanded that the UK government ensure that any military response would not lead to operations outside international law (DC 2001: para. 131). On the second point, the Committee suggested that British armed forces should acquire specialist agile ground forces for the effective implementation of pre-emptive strikes (DC 2001: para. 134).

Academic experts also raised questions about the UK government's shift towards a proactive defence posture. They stressed that prevention through efforts to address the root causes of conflict would be preferable to military involvement in regional crises (Hill 1997). Academics usually favoured instruments included in the government's second innovation in security planning: defence diplomacy.

The concept of defence diplomacy as a separate, but integrated, mission for the MoD and the Armed Forces was introduced by the SDR and elaborated in a separate MoD policy paper in 2000 (MoD 2000; Clarke 2000). According to the SDR, defence diplomacy covers 'arms control, non-proliferation and related security building measures; our Outreach programme in Eastern Europe; and wider military assistance and training for overseas countries' (MoD 1998: para. 49). The objective of the new mission has been to focus on the contribution that the military can make to conflict prevention. First positive results have been observed from its implementation in Central and Eastern Europe where UK bilateral and multilateral support for security sector reforms and civil–military relations contributed to improving the stability of the new governments and helped the accession of former Warsaw Pact members to NATO.

Since 11 September, the tasks of defence diplomacy have been further expanded to include addressing the origins and effects of global terrorism. The Armed Forces' contribution involves the provision of training and equipment to enhance regional counter-terrorism measures. However, neither the UK government nor security policy experts have explored possible further tasks of defence diplomacy. Limited resources for national and international defence and interdepartmental battles over budget allocations between the MoD, the Foreign and Commonwealth Office and the Department for International Development were already identified early on by the Defence Committee as possible obstacles to effective defence diplomacy (DC 1998: para. 150).

The final preference in British security policy is the government's continued commitment to an independent nuclear deterrent. Although the end of the Cold War has led to the reduction of nuclear weapons in Europe and North America, the UK government has maintained that a nuclear threat persists from other and emerging nuclear powers, and the possible use of WMD by terrorists. For the new millennium, the government therefore committed itself to a minimum deterrent based entirely on the Navy's Trident nuclear submarines which can be used for strategic as well as sub-strategic purposes (MoD 1998: para. 8). The sub-strategic role of the Trident had become necessary with the withdrawal of the Royal Air Force's freefall nuclear WE177 bombs in 1998 (MoD 1998: para. 62). As nuclear programmes in Iran and North Korea appear likely to continue, the 2003 Defence White Paper essentially reiterated this posture and argued that Trident remains the 'ultimate guarantor of the UK's national security' as long as there was a 'continuing risk from the proliferation of nuclear weapons, and the

Table 5.3 Preferred UK responses to threats

	1998–2001 *Regionalized threats*	*2001–2004* *Complex threats*
Interaction preference	1 Bilaterally with the US 2 Multilaterally through international organizations	1 Bilaterally with the US 2 Multilaterally through coalitions of the willing 3 Multilaterally through international organizations
Institutional preference	1 NATO 2 UN	1 NATO 2 EU 3 UN
Instrumental preferences	Defensive, but proactive strategy: – Nuclear deterrence – Conflict prevention – Peacekeeping – Regional cooperation and integration through NATO – Diplomacy, including military assistance and training, security building and non-proliferation measures	Proactive and pre-emptive strategy: – Pre-emptive interventions – Deterrence and coercion of rogue regimes – Disruption and destruction of terrorist networks – Diplomacy including enhancing regional counter-terrorism measures – Nuclear deterrence
Structure of UK Armed Forces	Small and flexible expeditionary forces (Rapid Reaction Forces)	Small and flexible expeditionary forces Improved air-lift High-tech and precision weapons Unmanned aircraft Network-enabled warfare capabilities

certainty that a number of other countries will retain substantial nuclear arsenals' (MoD 2003: para. 3.11).

Parliamentarians and academic experts in the UK have been doubtful about the continued utility of an independent nuclear deterrent. In particular Michael Clarke has argued that it is highly questionable whether 'other known nuclear powers such as India, Pakistan, Israel or North Korea, or for that matter a near-nuclear power such as Iran, could become a strategic threat to the UK homeland'. This would leave only China or Russia as potential strategic adversaries, but only if the UK is 'being drawn into a nuclear crisis' by its ally the United States (Clarke 2004: 56).

Allocation of resources

In reaction to the changing security environment, the allocation of UK government resources for national and international security has also undergone significant changes. The following examines three key trends which have increased the pressure on UK defence expenditure, the resulting spending priorities identified by the government and the trade-offs which have been made in order to sustain them.

Trends in defence expenditure

In international comparison, the UK is well equipped to pursue its perceived national and global security interests. Not only were UK Armed Forces better prepared for the post-Cold War security environment since they had smaller and more flexible expeditionary forces than most of the UK's continental European allies, they have also been able to secure a larger military budget despite popular pressures for a 'peace dividend' (Chalmers 2002; Hartley 2002a). In 2002, the UK ranked sixth behind the United States, Russia, China, France and Japan in terms of absolute defence expenditure, and third among its allies in terms of the percentage of GDP spent on defence.

A national analysis of UK defence spending since the Cold War, however, shows a significant and continuous reduction in the defence budget from its peak in 1985. Especially during the 1990s, the proportion of GDP spent on defence within the UK decreased steadily from 4.2 per cent in 1991 to 2.5 per cent in 1999. After 11 September, many countries including the UK have reversed the decline in order to support the fight against international terrorism. In July 2002, the UK government announced a commitment to increasing the defence budget by 1.2 per cent in real terms over the next three years (Hartley 2002b) and in 2004 plans were made for further increases of 1.4 per cent annually until 2007–08 (HM Treasury 2004: 74). Whether the increases can retain the ability of UK Armed Forces to modernize and meet the new security challenges is doubtful because of several simultaneous pressures on the defence budget.

First, independent of the security threats faced by the UK, the cost of military equipment has been increasing on average by 10 per cent per year in real terms

Table 5.4 UK defence spending in comparison (in percentage of GDP)

	1985	1990	1995	2000	2002
UK	5.2	4.0	3.0	2.5	2.4
USA	6.7	5.3	3.8	3.1	3.4
France	4.1	3.5	3.1	2.6	2.5
Germany	3.2	2.8	1.7	1.5	1.5
Italy	2.7	2.1	1.8	2.1	2.1
Japan		0.9	0.9	1.0	1.0
UK defence spending (£ million – 2002 prices)	33,559	30,384	25,169	23,591	23,997
UK number of military personnel (1,000s)	336.4	314.7	238.6	212.7	210.8

Source: SIPRI military expenditure database; MoD *UK Defence Statistics 1998*, and *UK Defence Statistics 2002*.

(Hartley 2004). A large proportion of the growth in expenditure can be attributed to the rising cost of military research and development. It is compounded by cost overruns and delays in delivery. In 1945 the UK government spent £1 million for each Lancaster bomber, whereas the government had to pay £20 million per aircraft for its successor, the Tornado, when it came into service in 1980 (Alexander and Garden 2001: 516). In comparison with the Eurofighter Typhoon these aircraft appear well priced. The Eurofighter cost the UK an estimated £20 billion in development, production and initial support by 2002, making it one of the most expensive aircraft at £92 million.

Second, military personnel are becoming more expensive (Hartley 2002c: 3). Partly, the increase reflects the growing need for specialist training as modern armed forces become more technically sophisticated. Partly, personnel costs are driven by competing employment opportunities in the private sector, in particular the proliferation of private security and military service companies which not only offer higher wages, but frequently also greater personal stability and fewer risks for their employees (Alexander and Garden 2001: 515).

Finally, significant financial pressure arises from the long-term demand for peacekeeping forces in the former Yugoslavia, Afghanistan and Iraq. In each of these countries, the military operations were completed relatively quickly, but peace maintenance has proven more protracted (Alexander and Garden 2001: 511). Between 2001 and 2004, the UK has spent an extra £4.4 billion on peace-keeping worldwide with simultaneous operations in Kosovo, Bosnia, the Gulf, Afghanistan and Iraq (HM Treasury 2004: 74).

To alleviate these pressures, the MoD has adopted a range of different measures over the past decades. The simplest, but also potentially the most controversial, is the reduction of Armed Forces personnel (Alexander and Garden 2001: 515). Following the end of the Cold War, the UK decreased its military personnel by more than 100,000 (Table 5.4).[1] During the 1990s, the diminished threat perception justified such cuts. Since 11 September further redundancies have been considerably more contested. As UK Armed Forces are overstretched with concurrent operations in several crisis regions ranging from Sierra Leone to Afghanistan, it appears irrational to propose additional cuts in personnel. In fact, the announcement in July 2004 that the government planned to disband four infantry regiments and merge up to 15 into larger units was greeted with harsh criticism by MPs across all parties,[2] and General Sir Mike Jackson admitted that the cuts would appear 'counterintuitive'.[3]

Additional cost reductions have been achieved through the closure of military bases overseas or the early retirement of military equipment, both of which are aimed at reducing the running expenses of the UK military (De Fraya and Hartley 1996). Each round of modernization proclaimed in the SDR and the 2003 Defence White Paper has thus gone hand in hand with further reductions. In the SDR, the government publicized that it would cut back the number of tanks and aircraft as part of its efforts to reform the Armed Forces. In July 2004, the government announced that the MoD's modernization and re-equipment programme required, amongst others, the closure of the Royal Air Force base Coltishall, the decommissioning of several Navy destroyers, frigates, minesweepers, submarines and patrol vessels, and the retirement of up to 90 Army Challenger tanks.[4]

Other cost-cutting mechanisms have included attempts to increase the efficiency and cost-effectiveness of the MoD through changes in procurement, management, maintenance and the provision of military services. These measures have focused on the use of private investors and contractors, and the introduction of market principles. Since the mid 1990s, the MoD has thus promoted the outsourcing of military and support services ranging from water sewage treatment to the training of fighter pilots to private companies (Krahmann 2005). Moreover, it has been encouraged to adopt Private Finance Initiatives 'where possible' to fund Royal Air Force Training Centres, the Joint Services Command and Staff College, and new equipment projects such as the Future Strategic Tanker Aircraft and the Roll-on/Roll-off Strategic Sealift.[5] In 1997, the MoD further introduced 'Smart Procurement' or 'Smart Acquisition' which attempted to decrease major cost overruns and delays in the delivery of new equipment programmes by adopting an incremental approach, creating integrated project teams with civil servants and industry representatives, and simplifying approval procedures (Hartley 2002b).

Spending priorities

Within the context of these budgetary pressures, successive defence reviews between 1998 and 2003 identified a number of spending priorities. The most important decision has been to put growing emphasis on expeditionary warfare – both in terms of international interventions in local crises abroad and to pre-empt emerging threats from global terrorism and rogue states. This decision has required a considerable modernization and transformation of British Armed Forces. In particular, new spending priorities have been set to create rapid reaction forces, improve air and sealift capacities, and invest in high-tech equipment such as precision attack weapons (MoD 2002b: 14).

The government has also dedicated further funds to upgrade the Armed Forces' emerging technologies in intelligence and communications. According to the MoD, these new technologies are essential for the UK's 'future ability to operate alongside our allies' in multilateral operations which will be necessary for most international interventions (MoD 2002b: 13). In particular, the technological advantage of the United States in network-enabled warfare requires extensive investments if the UK wants to continue partaking in bilateral operations with the world's military superpower. Finally, the UK is seeking to improve its capability to strike from a distance with precision-guided weapons and to develop unmanned air vehicles (MoD 2002b: 14, 16; Hartley 2002a: 204).

Trade-offs

The need to modernize the Armed Forces and to improve their technological capabilities in line with the revolution in military affairs that has swept the United States has required a range of trade-offs and led to a number of inconsistencies in UK security policy. The UK's growing preference for coalitions of the willing, rather than collaboration within NATO and the EU, has forced the UK to spend more on military equipment while achieving less than its full potential. In particular the government's refusal to consider role sharing or the pooling of military capabilities with allied states has increased its military burden and limited its ability to intervene globally.[6] Moreover, the UK's priority on bilateral cooperation with the US in the interventions in Afghanistan and Iraq has discounted the post-Cold War investments made into these multilateral security organizations.

The wish to maintain its close special relationship with the United States has also required the government to upgrade its military equipment and adopt network-centric technologies, thus widening the political and military gap between the UK and its European allies (Dunne 2004). Yet, given the size of the UK's military budget, any unilateral investments will be insufficient to close the technological gap with the United States and full cooperation is likely to become more difficult over time.

The priorities given to improving the UK's military technology and its expeditionary warfare capabilities would imply a trade-off between the UK's spending on strategic interventions and its investment in development aid and defence diplomacy. But the UK government is resisting this trade-off with plans to spend 0.35 per cent of its GNP on overseas development aid in 2004, a figure which is supposed to increase to 0.47 per cent by 2007 concurrent with simultaneous increases in the defence budget (HM Treasury 2004: 78). The MoD's Defence Assistance Fund, which supports defence diplomacy projects, such as security sector reform programmes in Central and Eastern Europe and the reintegration of former soldiers in African countries, was also increased from £7.2 million in 2001 to £10.4 million in 2003. Yet, these figures demonstrate that current UK development aid falls significantly short of the United Nations target of 0.7 per cent and is below the OECD average (OECD 2004). They also do not take into account that the Defence Assistance Fund was already £19.9 million in 2000 when parts of it were diverted to an interdepartmental Conflict Prevention Fund. Moreover, more than half of the Defence Assistance Fund is spent annually on support for defence exports.[7]

Altogether it is difficult to assess the degree to which major trade-offs have been made between coercive and civilian security instruments. So far, the indications are that the UK government is attempting to maintain both tasks by reducing defence spending through 'fudging' (Hartley 2002a). This approach includes reductions in military training and exercises, and delays in military base maintenance.[8] Most crucially, it involves cutting back numbers and investment in manpower although these are increasingly important in the face of non-state security threats and humanitarian operations (Alexander and Garden 2001).[9]

Conclusion

UK threat perceptions, strategies and capabilities have been transformed extensively since the end of the Cold War and the events of 11 September 2001. During this period, the UK government has shifted from a collective and defensive security approach to one of proactive threat 'management'. On one hand, change reflects the necessities of the new security environment. On the other hand UK policies continue to be defined by a security culture which was shaped by the UK's imperial past, transatlanticism, and its distancing from Europe following the two World Wars (Wallace 1991). This security culture explains the UK's commitment to playing a major role in global security, its special relationship with the US and its preference for NATO over the EU (see Table 5.5). It also helps to understand the

Table 5.5 UK national security culture

Worldview of external environment	Perception of Europe as a region of peace and stability that can be threatened by internal threats such as nationalism and terrorism or external threats such as proliferation, immigration and transnational crime. Era of national territorial defence is superseded by asymmetric threats to the British 'way of life'. Conflicts in other regions impact on UK security due to global economic interests and relations with former colonies.
National identity	Self-perception as a 'major power' with global security interests and responsibilities. A leader in international institutions such as the UN, the Commonwealth, NATO and the European Union. Special partner of the United States.
Instrumental preferences	Pragmatic mixture of diplomatic, economic and military means, as well as unilateral and multilateral instruments. New emphasis on 'defence diplomacy'. Shift from a preference for defensive and reactive to pre-emptive and proactive measures after 11 September.
Interaction patterns	Primacy of the special relationship with the United States. Commitment to, but realistic scepticism of, international organizations. Pragmatic use of coalitions of the willing where no international consensus can be reached.

inherent tensions within a UK security policy that attempts to punch above its weight by aligning itself with the US and refuses to embrace further European defence integration (Howorth 2004).

It is this difference between a security culture that was determined by the Cold War superpower confrontation and the new threat environment that puts increasing strain on the UK's security strategy and capabilities. In particular, it raises the question whether contemporary non-state threats can be effectively addressed through pre-emptive military action and whether the UK has the resources to remain the United States' junior partner.

The British government has appeared to recognize these limitations through its acknowledgement of the role that can be played by development aid and defence diplomacy. The 2003 Defence White Paper also indicated a more positive stance towards multilateral cooperation within the EU, for example, owing to its ability to deal with complex security problems involving transnational crime, immigration and terrorism. However, the divisions between the UK and its allies in NATO and the EU about how to deal with Iraq brought the UK government back to its closest ally, the United States.

The UK's special relationship with the United States and its wish to maintain a global role continue to define the UK's defence strategy. However, the UK's defence budget is increasingly under pressure and unlikely to allow the UK to keep up with the American-led revolution in military affairs. Recent increases in military spending helped alleviate some of the differences in military hardware, but British defence experts argue that, in the long term, the UK will only be able to implement its security plans and ambitions by joining Europe and pooling its resources.

Notes

1   See also De Fraya and Hartley 1996: 70–88.
2   'Defence shake-up to axe 12% of military posts', *Financial Times,* 21 July 2004; 'Fighting to strike a strategic balance', *Financial Times,* 21 July 2004; '20,000 jobs to go in big military shakeup', *Guardian,* 22 July 2004.
3   'RAF the big loser as forces modernise', *Guardian,* 22 July 2004.
4   'RAF the big loser as forces modernise', *Guardian,* 22 July 2004.
5   MoD *PFI Project Database.* Available online at: <http://www.mod.uk> (accessed 27 October 2006).
6   However, the MoD's review *The Future Strategic Context for Defence* of 2001 suggests: 'Pressures on defence budgets will continue ... These pressures are likely to encourage more serious consideration of role sharing and specialisation among allies.' MoD (2001).
7   House of Commons, Written Questions – Monday 14 June 2004, Hansard, Vol. 422, No.100, Column 637–8W.
8   'MoD cuts spending on soldiers and families as arms bill soars', *Guardian,* 6 September 2004.
9   'Military downsizing. Britain is planning to cut troops by 15,000', *New York Times,* 22 July 2004.

References

Alexander, M. and Garden, T. (2001) 'The arithmetic of defence policy', *International Affairs* 77 (3): 509–29.

Bamford, B.W.C. (2004) 'The United Kingdom's "War against terrorism"', *Terrorism and Political Violence* 16 (4): 737–56.

Chalmers, M. (2002) 'The New Activism. UK defence policy since 1997', *New Economy* 9 (4): 206–11.

Clarke, M. (1998) 'Memorandum submitted on the foreign and security policy aspects of the Strategic Defence Review', *Eighth Report: The Strategic Defence Review, Volume II – Minutes of Evidence & Memoranda,* 10 September 1998, HC 138-I.

Clarke, M. (2000) 'French and British security: mirror images in a globalized world', *International Affairs* 76 (4): 725–39.

Clarke, M. (2004) 'Does my bomb look big in this? Britain's nuclear choices after Trident', *International Affairs* 80 (1): 49–62.

DC (Defence Committee, House of Commons) (1998) *Eighth Report: The Strategic Defence Review*, Session 1997–1998, 10 September 1998, HC 138-I.

DC (2001) *Second Report: The Threat from Terrorism*, Session 2000–2001, 18 December 2001, HC 348-I.

DC (2002) *Seventh Report: Defence and Security in the UK*, Session 2001–2002, 24 July 2002, HC 518-I.

DC (2004) *Fifth Report: Defence White Paper 2003*, Session 2003–2004, 1 July 2004, HC 465-I.

De Fraya, G. and Hartley, K. (1996) 'Defence procurement: theory and UK policy', *Oxford Review of Economic Policy* 12 (4): 70–88.

Dumbrell, J. (2004) 'The US–UK "special relationship" in a world twice transformed', *Cambridge Review of International Affairs* 17 (3): 437–50.

Dunne, T. (2004) '"When the shooting starts": Atlanticism in British security strategy', *International Affairs* 80 (5): 893–909.

Gregory, F. and Wilkinson, P. (2005) 'Riding pillion for tackling terrorism is a high-risk policy', *Security, Terrorism and the UK,* ISP/NSC Briefing Paper 05/01, Chatham House. Available online at: <http://www.riia.org/pdf/research/niis/BPsecurity.pdf> (accessed 15 December 2005).

Hartley, K. (2002a) 'UK defence policy. A triumph of hope over experience?', *New Economy* 9 (4): 199–205.

Hartley, K. (2002b) *UK Defence Policy: An Economist's Perspective,* Research Paper, Centre for Defence Economics.

Hartley, K. (2002c) *UK Defence Spending,* Research Paper, Centre for Defence Economics.

Hartley, K. (2004) *The UK's Major Defence Projects: A Cause for Concern?* Research Paper, Centre for Defence Economics.

Hill, C. (1997) 'Examination of witnesses, Wednesday 12 November 1997', *Eighth Report: The Strategic Defence Review, Volume II – Minutes of Evidence & Memoranda,* HC 138-II.

HM Treasury (2004) *2004 Spending Review.* Available online at: <http://www.hm-treasury. gov.uk/spending_review/spend_sr04/spend_sr04_index.cfm> (accessed 7 September 2005).

Hodges, M. (1997) 'Examination of witnesses, Wednesday 12 November 1997', *Eighth Report: The Strategic Defence Review, Volume II – Minutes of Evidence & Memoranda,* HC 138-II.

Howorth, J. (2004) 'Discourse, ideas, and epistemic communities in European security and defence policy', *West European Politics* 27 (2): 211–34.

Krahmann, E. (2005) 'Controlling private military services in the UK and Germany: between partnership and regulation', *European Security* 13 (2): 277–95.

McInnes, C. (1998) 'Labour's Strategic Defence Review', *International Affairs* 74 (4): 823–45.

MoD (Ministry of Defence) (1998) Strategic Defence Review.

MoD (2000) *Policy Paper No. 1 – Defence Diplomacy.*

MoD (2001) *The Future Strategic Context for Defence.* Available online at: <http://www.mod.uk/NR/rdonlyres/7CC94DFB-839A-4029-8BDD-5E87AF5CDF45 /0/futurestrategiccontext.pdf> (accessed 26 October 2006).

MoD (2002a) 'The Strategic Defence Review: A New Chapter', Cm 5566-I.

MoD (2002b) 'The Defence Investment Strategy 2002', Spending Review 2002.

MoD (2003) *Delivering Security in a Changing World.* Defence White Paper, Cm 6041-I.

MORI (2005) *Most Important Issue.* Available online at: <http://www.mori.com/polls /trends/issues.shtml> (accessed 7 September 2005).

OECD (2004) *Modest Increase in Development Aid in 2003* – Tables and Graphs. Available online at: <http://www.oecd.org/dataoecd/42/61/31504039.pdf> (accessed 7 September 2005).

Pearson, G. (2001) *Memorandum, The Threat from Terrorism, Volume II – Minutes of Evidence and Appendices,* HC 348-II.

Pearson, G. and Hay, A. (2001) 'Examination of witnesses (Questions 96–119) Tuesday 13 November 2001', *The Threat from Terrorism, Volume II – Minutes of Evidence and Appendices,* HC 348-II.

Rogers, P. and Mepham, D. (1998) 'Examination of witnesses (Questions 1181–1199) Wednesday 25 March 1998', *Eighth Report: The Strategic Defence Review, Volume II – Minutes of Evidence & Memoranda,* HC 138-II.

Sabin, P. (1998) 'Memorandum submitted on the Strategic Defence Review', *Eighth Report: The Strategic Defence Review, Volume III – Minutes of Evidence & Memoranda,* HC 138-III.

Wallace, W. (1991) 'Foreign policy and national identity in the United Kingdom', *International Affairs* 67 (1): 65–80.

6 European Union

The European Security Strategy versus national preferences

Emil J. Kirchner

The arrival of the European Security Strategy (ESS) has raised questions about its collective nature, its capacity for autonomy, its capability to deliver and its ability to create a European security culture. Answers to these questions can be sought by exploring why and how the ESS arose, how its threat perception and means of institutional response compares with that of France, Germany, Italy and the UK and how it has performed or can potentially perform. Furthermore, such a comparison not only offers the possibility of examining the degree of convergence between national and EU perspectives on type of threats – for example, new security threats, or type of response such as non-military versus military – it also provides an indication of whether the ESS is closer to the British and French position, which is generally considered as more interventionist in military terms, than the German and Italian one. It is accepted that by only considering the leading countries, the scope and depth of all the EU member states is somewhat compromised. However, some of the cleavage dimensions found EU-wide[1] are nonetheless captured or reflected by the four leading countries. For example, the pacifist trends of the so-called non-aligned member states are explicated by Germany, the pro-NATO/US stance of the UK reflects that of many of the newer EU member states, and the pro-EU perspective of France and Germany is shared by some of the smaller EU countries and Spain. The four leading countries will therefore be considered as proxies for the entire EU.

Three multifaceted factors underlie the introduction of the ESS. These are external circumstances, the working of the internal market, and EU institutional development in the security field. Among the external factors were the changes brought about by the end of the Cold War and the emergence of new security threats, such as ethnic conflicts, particularly in South Eastern Europe, and the failure of the EU to deal with these conflicts. A further external factor was the impact of globalization via increasing international transactions, especially through the expansion of cyberspace. Whilst producing mostly positive benefits for international trade and communication, they also contribute to rising organized transnational crime and the spread of weapons of mass destruction. Perhaps the greatest external stimulant resulted from the fallout of disagreements among member states over how to relate to the Iraq conflict in the spring of 2003, the growing tensions in transatlantic relations, and the need to respond to the so-called Bush security doctrine of 2002. Similar security concerns to those arising from the external field can be noted with regard to those connected to the internal market operation. The free movement of goods, services, capital and people, whilst contributing to the economic and social benefits of EU integration, has also made borders within the EU more porous and subject to criminal and terrorist activities. Both the external factors and the need to safeguard the operations of the internal market against criminal activities have made EU member states realize that 'no single country is able to tackle today's complex problems on its own' (Solana 2003: 1), such as those arising from neighbours who have emerged from violent conflict, weak states where organized crime flourishes, and dysfunctional societies. It is in this context that the EU emerges as an actor capable of achieving a security goal that individual states and other international organizations could not attain. As Solana (2003: 13) asserts 'the point of CFSP and ESDP is that we are stronger when we act together'.

The absence of EU joint action was apparent in the early 1990s and became clearly visible in the Bosnian conflict (Edwards 1997). However, these failures were later recognized and contributed to a change in policy-making at EU level in security and defence. Heading these capacity and institution building efforts were agreements reached in the Amsterdam Treaty, the Saint Malo Accord between Britain and France, the Helsinki Headline Goals, and the decisions to establish the High Representative and Secretary General of the Council of Ministers (HR/SG), the Policy Unit and some high-powered committees in security and defence. Among the main aims were the promotion of an autonomous EU capacity in security and defence and the development of a common defence policy.[2]

It is in respect of a few of the external and internal security requirements, as well as the EU policy aims stipulated between 1999 and 2002, that 'the EU considers itself a collective of European countries ... committed to dealing peacefully with disputes and cooperation through common institutions' (Solana 2003: 1). As stressed in the European Council at Thessaloniki, the development of a European security culture under ESDP encompassing both civilian and military dimensions of ESDP is a priority. But it is precisely these claims that have divided both the policy-making and the academic community. For Lindley-French (2002) and Rynning (2003) the ESS is unable to overcome national differences. In contrast, Cornish and Edwards (2001, 2005), Howorth (2002) and Becher (2004) see the ESS as a sign that differences could be overcome and an EU strategic culture would be realizable. Such a strategic culture is defined by Cornish and Edwards as 'the institutional confidence and processes to manage and deploy military force as part of the accepted range of legitimate and effective policy instruments, together with general recognition of the EU's legitimacy as an international actor with military capabilities' (Cornish and Edwards 2001: 587). Such a definition reflects the thinking of traditional strategic studies. But strategic culture can also be understood in a looser sense and to refer to long-term objectives or the definition of broad categories of instruments on which to act resolutely and proactively in day-to-day policy-making. Hence the ESS is about more than how to 'react to and behave in security and defence situations', and represents a strategy for external action.[3]

To shed some light on the underlying assumptions of this debate requires an assessment of the commitment of the EU's leading constituents to the concerns, aims and declared capabilities of the ESS. The task is to compare national perspectives with ESS perspectives on security threat perceptions, the means (military or non-military) stipulated in response to these threats, and the capacity identified (self-reliance, the borrowing of NATO military assets, or other multilateral measures) to perform as an effective security actor. In other words, what are the points of convergence and divergence? Is the ESS basically the sum total of national perspectives or does the ESS provide distinct autonomous features in the field of security and defence? Do national strategic cultures converge towards 'higher preparedness to use coercive means and accept risks, lower thresholds for the authorization of force, and a higher acceptance of the European Union as the legitimate vehicle for conduct of defence policies' (Meyer 2005: 525–6)? It is the task of this chapter to explore these questions and to provide explanations. This will be done firstly by briefly reviewing the aims and collective aspirations of the ESS. This review will be followed by an attempt to assess points of convergence or divergence between the national perspectives of the four leading EU member states and the ESS with regard to security threat perceptions, means of response, resource allocations and public opinion. The final section of the chapter will deal with the issue of EU capabilities and performance as a security actor.

Form and aims of the European Security Strategy

The ESS provides a framework that indicates the form and means in which the EU as a collective actor should react to and behave in security and defence situations (van Ham 2004). It is yet another step since the introduction of European Political Cooperation in the early 1970s, which was primarily declaratory in character, and the provisions in the TEU, the Amsterdam Treaty and the stalled Constitutional Treaty, to bring about a genuine European Security and Defence Policy (ESDP). A primary motivation and goal of the ESS centres upon the construction of 'European values and visions of the world' (Osland 2004: 545). Subsequently, the rhetoric utilized in the ESS pays heed and submits to the rule of law and multilateralism that represents and promotes European norms and values (Quille 2004). One of its core functions is to express a European security identity (Becher 2004). The ESS also represents the EU's security agenda in combating the common threats (for a description of these see below) that threaten the internal and external security of the EU and its member states. In order to do so, the EU utilizes economic and political means, military operations and the mandate of multilateral institutions.

There is a certain duality manifested in the ESS. On the one hand, it is a confession of the Union's obligation to play a visible role in matters of international peace and security. On the other, the ESS remains quite imprecise and does not describe sufficiently when and how the EU intends to use force. Therefore many questions on the practical implications and the implementation of the ESS remain unanswered. But that is hardly surprising given that the formulation of the ESS touched upon the core of the individual strategic cultures of the Union's members, which came to the fore so prominently in the spring of 2003 with regard to the Iraq conflict, and which were a major factor for why the ESS was introduced. The 25 EU member states bring along very different historic and political experiences leading to a range of perceptions of the existing security environment. Jolyon Howorth (2003: 12) distinguishes six dichotomies showing the sources of differences in national security structures and cultures among European countries, namely allied/neutral, Atlanticists/Europeanists, power projection/territorial defence, nuclear/non-nuclear military/civilian instruments, large/small countries, weapons providers/consumers. Particularly important are the different attitudes among EU countries about the relationship with the US in situations where the EU would not use force (yet), but the US engages (or intends to engage) force. These differences surfaced with regard to the Iraq conflict in the spring of 2003, and demonstrated, in part, that the perception of the security threats in the post-11 September world and the appropriate response to them was not necessarily homogeneous among Union members. Moreover, while some EU countries, particularly Britain, responded quickly to the attacks in New York and Washington in September 2001, most of the 25 have not even adjusted their national security strategies to the new situation. Thus, not all of the current national differences are bridgeable at the moment and a convergence of strategic cultures is difficult to obtain. The secret of the ESS is therefore to maintain unity among the diverse national strategic needs, to bring closer together national security strategies and to promote the establishment of a distinct European security culture. While the success of these aims still seems uncertain, Longhurst and Zaborowski (2004: 390–1) already associate the ESS with the existence of a nascent European security culture.

If that were the case, what does such a culture look like? Hyde-Price's (2004) argument that the security strategies of European countries still reflect the realities of the second half of the twentieth century instead of the changed situation of the early twenty-first century might also be true for the EU's security culture. Today's thinking about security in Europe most often still 'revolves around soft power, containment, and deterrence' (Longhurst and Zaborowski 2004: 388). However, soft power should not be seen simply as a benign policy. Rather, as EU policy towards the Western Balkans indicates (conditionality under the Stability and Association process, the police missions and the peacekeeping force in Bosnia), it can intrude into the sovereign sphere of countries and effectively promote peace and stability. Consideration should therefore be given not only to the need of extending the role of the military, on the national as well as the EU level, but also on how to build up integrated military–civilian capabilities. The latter aim is espoused in the ESS (in contrast to the Bush doctrine), but despite some cases in operation needs to be strengthened in practice. There is also a need to widen the security horizon from a national to an international perspective. With the ESS the EU members have done just that: they take up the special responsibility deriving from their economic power and confront the special risks they are faced with as important global players by replacing their inward-looking perspective on security by an outward-looking one. At least on paper they are willing to exchange the national security policies with a European one.

Conflicting national interests and security cultures among EU members obstruct a well-functioning ESDP in many areas at the moment. They stand in the way of a coherent way forward and make the linkage of all forces difficult. In view of the resources, political sponsorship and consensus required for a successful ESDP, only concerted efforts by all 25 EU countries can produce positive outcomes. It is the task of this chapter to explore whether the ESS does contribute to the establishment of concerted efforts by comparing the points of convergence or divergence between France, Germany, Italy and the UK, with the ESS with regard to threat perceptions and the means of response to these threats.

Threat perceptions

The ESS characterizes the post-Cold War world as one of 'increasingly open borders in which the internal and external aspects of security are indissolubly linked' (European Council 2003: 4, hereafter 'ESS'). This also has consequences for the types of threats the EU is faced with. In the main, the EU's view on the current security situation consists of two very different aspects. On the one hand, 'large-scale aggression' against one of its members is not likely any more (ESS: 5). On the other hand, the threats the Union is faced with today 'are more diverse, less visible and less predictable' (ESS: 5). The concept of self-defence founded on the threat of invasion has been replaced by a concept in which defence of the EU has to begin abroad. Those new threats are also dynamic and often spread quickly. Therefore the Union pursues a strategy of conflict prevention and threat prevention through which potential crises can be contained before they reach uncontrollable scales.

Threats perceived by the EU as articulated in the ESS only partially concentrate on 'hard' security. Only one of the five key threats identified falls into this category, namely proliferation of WMD. Three of the other threats identified – terrorism, regional conflicts and state failure – have 'hard' security edges. But of course they also have significant 'soft' security implications as their roots, such as poverty and migratory movements, which cannot be tackled easily by military means. Organized crime is the fifth key threat given in the ESS. This dimension has a strong domestic political side to it and involves the third pillar of the EU (Police and Judicial Cooperation in Criminal Matters). Military force cannot usually cope in a sustainable manner with organized crime, making it a soft security threat. It is in this context that the ESS stresses that 'none of the new threats is purely military; nor can any be tackled by purely military means' (ESS: 9).

The identified targets in the ESS include factors that reflect civilian matters, economic interests, transport, energy supply and access to natural resources. But also the information infrastructure, especially that of the highly developed member states of the EU, is seen as vulnerable to attack. Another central target, particularly for terrorists, are the open and tolerant civil societies of the 25 Union members. Terrorists are seen to be 'willing to use unlimited violence to cause massive casualties' (ESS: 5) among civilians. However, the link between the 'dark side of globalization' and specific/immediate politico–military threat is not very well articulated in the ESS.

When looking at the geographical dimension of the threats, the Union acknowledges that in today's world 'distant threats may be as much a concern as those that are near at hand' (ESS: 8). However, despite the global scale of the threat perceived by all EU member states and incorporated in the ESS, they nevertheless identify certain hotspots. Clearly the EU sees itself particularly endangered from the same regions and countries as any other power operating globally. The Middle East, Asia (Kashmir, Korean Peninsula) and conflicts in Africa are to be mentioned in that regard. The ESS also perceives threats from the developing world: poverty, disease, conflict, criminality, competition for natural resources and problematic economic activity as giving rise to 'pressing security concerns' (ESS: 4). Specifically European are threat scenarios in connection with Central and Eastern Europe: the violent conflicts in the Balkans in the 1990s have shown that the (internal) security of the EU is at risk because of conflict in its immediate neighbourhood.

In every case it is important to emphasize that most conflicts that the EU perceives as touching upon its interests have been within rather than between states. Interventions in such conflicts involve peace enforcement or peacemaking activities, as well as humanitarian, peace-building or peacekeeping tasks. There is consensus among the EU member states about the need of interventions, including that of peace enforcement; what is lacking is agreement about the forum for implementation: NATO or EU.

Table 6.1 puts together the threat perceptions of the EU as described above and compares it with the perceptions of the most important EU member states France, Germany, Italy and the UK, as analysed in the preceding chapters of this book.

As Table 6.1 reveals, the ESS highlights similar threats to those of the leading member states. This is not surprising as the EU member states were involved in the drafting and finalizing of the ESS. In order to be agreeable to everyone, the document had to reflect the views of all governments of the EU member states. But it is nevertheless striking how similar the threat perceptions are among those four countries, despite the very different political preferences and traditions which exist. All countries see terrorism and proliferation of WMD as key threats. Also regarding the agencies of threat and the targets of threat the result is very congruent as is the analysis of the geographical source of the threats. Obviously the common denominator on which the ESS is based has not been a very low one. Rather, a common security perception or even culture seems to emerge among the large EU member states.

The public perception of threat

With regard to threat perceptions, the European public shares, to a large extent, the analysis given within the ESS and by EU member states: hard security threats

Table 6.1 EU threat perceptions in the post-11 September era

	EU	France (government)	Germany (government)	Italy (government)	UK (government)
Type of key threats	Terrorism; WMD proliferation; regional conflicts; state failure; organized crime	Terrorism; WMD proliferation; intra-state conflicts and state failure; organized crime; religious extremisms and nationalisms	Terrorism; WMD proliferation; asymmetric warfare; failing democratic transformations in Europe; environmental degradation; amassing of conventional weapons	Terrorism; WMD proliferation; ethnic aggressions; low intensity conflicts; drug trafficking; migrational flows; ecological disasters; organized crime	Terrorism; WMD proliferation; state failure; social and environmental tensions
Agency of threats	Terrorists; rogue/failing states; organized crime	Terrorists; extremist groups; failing states; organized crime	Terrorists; rogue/failing states; organized crime	Terrorists; rogue/failing states; organized crime	Terrorists; rogue/failing states
Target of threat	Civil society; economic interests; transport; energy; information	Population; military/officials in France and abroad; state structure; economic assets; official premises	Civil society	Civil society; economic interests	Civil society; economic interests
Geographical source of threat	Middle East; Asia (Kashmir, Korean Peninsula); Africa; Central and Eastern Europe	Global; Balkans; Eastern Europe; Mediterranean; Middle East	No official geographic delimitation, but tendency to see the Middle East and the Mediterranean as source of threat	Balkans; Korean Peninsula; Middle East	North Africa; Middle East; Persian Gulf; Central and Eastern Europe[a]

a   Analysis of the Defence Committee 1998.
Source: Content analysis of the European Security Strategy and information given in the country chapters of this book, reflecting the official governmental views.

such as terrorism and Islamic fundamentalism rank high in the four EU countries which are probably most affected by the new security environment, namely France, Germany, Italy and the UK (see Table 6.2). The publics of those four countries share a remarkable resemblance in their threat perceptions in the post-11 September period.

A broader perspective is taken by a survey carried out by the German Marshall Fund and other organizations, looking at threat perceptions in ten European countries,[4] conducted in May and June 2005 (German Marshall Fund 2005). Its figures are quite different from those of public opinion polls within the four major EU countries compared above (see Table 6.3). International terrorism and nuclear weapons also rank highly in this study, as both aspects of security are regarded by 53 and 55 per cent of the respondents respectively as being likely to personally affect their lives within the next ten years. However, economic downturn (74 per cent) and global warming (73 per cent) were perceived by the public as the most important threats. The different results in both studies should have methodological and statistical reasons, as the questions asked in relation to Table 6.2 took a *country perspective,* while the results shown in Table 6.3 represent the European public perceptions by security threats. And in general it is always problematic to compare polls undertaken independently from each other. That is true also for the results presented in Table 6.2, for which reason the individual country chapters in this book should be consulted to follow on the different approaches taken to collect the data.

Responses to threat

In its response to the threats posed, the EU is guided by the principle 'think globally and act locally' (ESS: 8). Also only a mixture of instruments is considered adequate to deal with the threats in all their complexity. In a sharp reminder of the multilateral concept forming the foundation of the EU and establishing its success so far, predominantly in the economic sphere, the ESS underlines that 'no single country is able to tackle today's complex problems on its own' (ESS: 3). In the Union's view, therefore, security substantially depends on an effective multilateral system. To that end a 'stronger international society, well functioning international institutions and a rule-based international order' have to be developed

Table 6.2 Public opinion: threat perceptions in the post-11 September era (in rank order)

	France (2003)	Germany (2004)	Italy (2003)	UK (2003)
Type of key	1 Terrorism	1 Terrorism	1 Terrorism	1 Terrorism
threats	2 Islamic fundamentalism	2 Islamic fundamentalism	2 Greenhouse effect	2 WMD proliferation
	3 Middle East conflict	3 WMD	3 Islamic fundamentalism	3 Nuclear accidents

Source: Information given in the country chapters of this book.

Table 6.3 European public threat perceptions (May/June 2005)

Question: *In the next ten years, are you likely to be personally affected by the following threat*	%
Economic downturn	74
Global warming	73
Nuclear weapons	55
International terrorism	53
Immigrants/Refugees	51
Diseases such as AIDS	41
Islamic fundamentalism	40

Source: German Marshall Fund of the United States, *Transatlantic Trends: Key Findings 2005*, 17–18.

(ESS: 11). The United Nations, and in particular the United Nations Security Council, are regarded as important elements in that approach. But other international organizations also have a prominent position in the Union's strategy against security threats, namely the WTO, NATO and regional organizations such as the OSCE and ASEAN. The EU sees itself obliged to defend the rules set up in the international system, if need be also through proactive engagement. But the Union also regards its close internal cooperation, mutual solidarity and 'increasing convergence of European interests' as crucial elements in its reaction to the threats it is faced with, making it a 'more credible and effective actor' on the international stage (ESS: 3).

Already, in the fight against terrorism, intelligence, police, judicial, military and other means are employed throughout Europe. Several important measures were put in place in the aftermath of 11 September 2001. Instruments are now available to freeze the financial resources of terrorists. A European Arrest Warrant when implemented by all member states will allow the extradition of alleged terrorists more easily. Mutual legal assistance in the fight against terrorism with other Western countries, including the US, has been implemented. The EU tries to undermine the proliferation of WMD by actively strengthening and supporting the International Atomic Energy Agency. Where it has the abilities to do so, it tries to influence export controls and to thwart illegal shipments and illicit procurement. Political and economic pressures complement those means while the 'underlying political causes are also tackled' (ESS: 9). Military intervention is the device proclaimed in the ESS to take care of failed states and to bring back order. Humanitarian means supplement such operations. The military is also needed to handle regional conflicts and short-term crisis management situations. However, political solutions are equally indispensable to disentangle them. In the post conflict phase the EU can offer support through economic means and civilian crisis management.

In a rather general and abstract way the EU wants to prevent the occurrence of all key threats mentioned in the first place. By creating a better world through the backing of social and political reform incorporating principles of good governance, by offering support in 'dealing with corruption and abuse of power, establishing the rule of law and protecting human rights' (ESS: 12), the breeding ground of those threats is to be undermined. This approach incorporates development, special trade cooperation and other assistance programmes. It can only show effects in the long run. But the European countries individually and the European Commission on behalf of the club have been active to that end since the early 1960s, longer than most other actors in the world. They have cooperated with whole regions in the world and supported them actively, in particular African, Caribbean and Pacific countries (Lomé and Cotonou conventions), generating tangible results. If exertion of influence of that kind bears no fruits, economic sanctions and political isolation as a pre-stage to military actions are seen as appropriate EU measures.

The comparison presented in Table 6.4 shows the clear multilateral orientation of the EU member states. However, not surprisingly, it also reveals the different institutional preferences of the leading member states. While France and Germany see the EU as best equipped to meet current security threats, Italy does not have such a clear preference. The UK emphasizes strong transatlantic ties and the special position of the UN and only gives third rank to the EU in the defence of its security interests. Given the strength of the British Army, this seems to pose a serious problem for the creation of a common EU security strategy and culture.

Differences also emerge with regard to the instrumental preferences. France and the UK still rely heavily on their nuclear weapons arsenals as a guarantor of security against threats from the outside. Of course, questions can be raised as to the relevance of such weapons in, for example, the fight against either international terrorism or organized crime. Despite significant changes in Germany's self-perception of its role in the world in recent years, the country and its government nevertheless have a strong preference for civilian means to solve conflicts, which could hamper effective European military action. However, as in the case of Kosovo, Germany has also shown a willingness to support military action. All four countries share the idea of an integrated approach against the threats the Union faces. The ESS can therefore be seen as reflecting such an approach, which will serve as the workable basis for a European security culture.

In general, the few areas of disparities between the ESS and national understandings of threats and threat response do not reveal underlying contradictions or inadequatenesses in the way the EU or its constituent parts cope with the new international environment. Rather they demonstrate that there is currently no security culture shared entirely by the four countries. Hence the ESS provides a blueprint of the common ground that exists at the moment among all EU members. In certain aspects, the views of the individual countries go beyond the ESS, as their historical experiences, relationships to third countries and resources generate other priorities. But as their threat perceptions and preferences in threat response stand not in contradiction to the policies conducted within the CFSP or ESDP, this fact is not necessarily a reason for concern. However, the incomplete congruency between ESS and EU member states policies in security matters

Table 6.4 Preferred responses to threat in the EU

	EU	France (government)	Germany (government)	Italy (government)	UK (government)
Interaction patterns	Predominantly multilateral responses	Predominantly multilateral responses, but unilateral response never ruled out	Predominantly multilateral responses	Predominantly multilateral responses	Bi- and multilateral responses with strong premium on special relationship with US
Institutional preferences for meeting threats	Mainly EU institutions from all three pillars; UN, WTO, NATO and regional organizations such as OSCE and ASEAN	EU is first-choice security institution; besides that important roles for UN, NATO, OSCE	EU is first-choice security institution; besides that important roles for NATO, OSCE and UN in specific areas	UN, EU, NATO (no clear preference)	Ranking of preferences: 1 NATO 2 UN 3 EU
Instrumental preferences for meeting threats	All instruments at its disposal, including diplomatic, economic, developmental and military	All options possible; combination of civilian and military tools; crisis management/peace operations; diplomacy; development aid; human intelligence; police; military intervention/use of force	Preference for civilian means; military engagement in crisis situations	Integrated approach of soft and hard powers	All instruments at its disposal, including diplomatic, developmental and military; nuclear deterrence is vital; proactive/pre-emptive military operations

Source: Content analysis of the European Security Strategy and information provided in the country chapters of this book, reflecting the respective official governmental views.

increase the likelihood of activities by EU countries outside the EU structures, guided by their national interests and their abilities.

Only two EU military intervention cases can so far be linked with the ESS and the potential development of European security culture, of which one is somewhat contested as to the way it was initiated and led, and the other takes the form of a peacekeeping operation rather than a crisis intervention or peace enforcement.[5] The deployment of EU-led forces in the summer of 2003 in the Democratic Republic of the Congo, 'Operation Artemis', was for the most part French inspired and led by French troops. What is important is that politically it was an EU operation and it opened the way for the EU to become an actor in Central Africa. In addition, the operation also preceded the formal adoption of the ESS by a few months, though the document as drafted by the High Representative of CFSP who is also the Secretary General of the Council of Ministers (HR/SG) had existed by the time of Operation Artemis. The replacement of NATO's SFOR by the 7,000 strong EUFOR in Bosnia and Herzogovina in December 2004 is strictly speaking a peacekeeping operation and supports the other peace-building measures – such as the Stability and Association process – the EU has taken in the Western Balkans region, involving Albania, Bosnia, Croatia, Serbia and Montenegro and Macedonia.

It will be interesting to see how the European Neighbourhood Policy (ENP), published by the European Commission in May 2004, will support the aims of the ESS and help to promote a European security culture. Through the ENP, the EU tries to stabilize 17 countries (including Palestine) in the east of the Union and around the Mediterranean. This echoes the ESS aim of 'promoting a ring of well governed countries' with which the EU can 'enjoy close and cooperative relations' (ESS: 10). The ENP constitutes, therefore, an important component of the ESS and emerges as a policy tool of the ESS. With the help of this new Policy the EU intends to prevent those countries from becoming hotspots of instability imperilling the EU, but also to guard itself against the spread of organized crime and exploding population growth. Financial aid, trade agreements, democratization measures and political dialogue are the main instruments to be used in the EU's armour. Agreements will be concluded with individual countries in the next few years, involving Association Agreements and Neighbourhood Policy Action Plans.

Public opinion on threat response

As progress in ESDP and a deep-rooted European security culture very much depend on public support for any institutionalized approach, it seems to be important also to look at public opinion concerning threat response.

Clear support for a role of the EU in security matters is illustrated in different public opinion surveys. For instance, the belief that the individual EU member states should refrain from solo efforts in security questions and rather act jointly under the EU umbrella or even through the EU institutions is highlighted in a Eurobarometer of 2005 (European Commission 2005b): 86 per cent of the respondents said that the fight against terrorism should be undertaken jointly within the EU instead of individually by national governments (see Table 6.5, left column). Similar high figures are reached in the field of organized crime, another of the key threats identified in the ESS, and humanitarian aid.

Thus it is not surprising that the public in the 25 EU member states sees a strong role for the EU in dealing with security related issues (see Table 6.5, right column). Noticeably, 'fighting terrorism' and 'defence' were the two issues mentioned by those interviewed as the ones in which the EU could play the most positive role (together with 'foreign affairs'); 57 per cent saw a positive role for the EU in 'fighting terrorism' and 52 per cent in 'defence'. Highly positive outcomes were recorded on the EU's role in addressing soft threats, such as 'protecting the environment' (52 per cent) and 'fighting crime' (44 per cent).

This expression in favour of the active involvement of the EU in strategic security questions is supported by another statistic: when choosing between national governments, NATO and the EU as the appropriate level of decision-making on European defence policy, a majority of 52 per cent opted for the EU, with only 22 per cent opting for national governments, and 15 per cent for NATO (European Commission 2005b: 120). In total, 81 per cent of respondents from the 15 'old' EU member states also said that the national governments should agree on a common position in case of an international crisis (European Commission 2004: B.86). A strong majority (70 per cent) is in favour of an EU Rapid Reaction Force to deal with such crises. Support for the ESDP among EU citizens oscillated since 1998 between 70 and 78 per cent, with only 13 to 19 per cent opposed to a common European defence policy in the same period (European Commission 2005c: 30).

All this shows a positive public response within the EU for a common EU security culture. However, the – already mentioned – study undertaken by the German Marshall Fund slightly qualifies those findings. While 70 per cent of Europeans believe that the EU should become a superpower like the United States, the way to that end is contested (German Marshall Fund 2005: 10); 26 per cent of Europeans see the EU as a civilian superpower, which should not increase its military strength but concentrate on economic means (German

Table 6.5 The EU as a medium and actor in threat response (October – November 2004) (per cent)

	Issues to be dealt with joint within the EU as opposed to individual national approaches	Areas in which the EU can play a positive role
Fighting terrorism	86	57
Fighting crime/Organized crime	76	44
Foreign policy/Affairs	68	53
Protection of the environment	67	52
Defence	57	52

Source: Eurobarometer 62, fieldwork: October – November 2004, publication: May 2005, pp. 26 and 35; includes respondents from all 25 EU member states.

Marshall Fund 2005). Conversely, 35 per cent believe that the EU should value both military and economic power, which should go along with an increase in defence spending.

The question is, however, whether the EU is really equipped to do justice to the expectations raised by the public, particularly as condensed in Table 6.5. Institutionally, most of the areas important for threat response fall into the second and third pillar of the EU, which are characterized by intergovernmental policy-making. Therefore it is the task of EU member states themselves to allow successful threat response under the EU umbrella, either by harmonizing their positions through employing the EU's institutional structures, or by asking the EU's institutions to act on their behalf, for instance through the EU Troika or the High Representative of CFSP. But currently the reality is rather that national governments are hesitant to revalue the EU in any way, and certainly not by giving it more competences. In some of the questions the public expects a strong EU in which the Commission has shared competences. Mainly in those areas an influential EU is possible from an institutional point of view. However, whether the resources and capabilities of the EU and its member states are sufficient to guarantee an adequate threat response, as expected by the public, is an entirely different matter. The next section will try to shed light on that aspect.

Allocation of resources

Despite the significant progress in ESDP over recent years, the expenses that result from the usage of the European mechanisms and capabilities, especially those falling under pillar two, are still dealt with to a large extent by national governments. Until now there has been no common budget for operational expenditures arising from military missions within ESDP. Activities and acquisitions are made, in contrast to the other expenditures for the EU Common Foreign and Security Policy, out of the budgets of the EU member states and not out of the regular budget of the EU. As a rule, expenditures are divided between the EU countries participating in an operation in accordance with the GNP ratio. It is clear, therefore, that the well-functioning of the ESDP – and with it the EU response to threats – depends directly on the budgetary allocations of its member states for their own military and defence structures. Since concerted responses on security threats, as outlined above, by EU members under the EU flag depend on the capabilities of each EU country, and particularly those of the three most important military players in the EU, the UK, France and Germany, their spending practice is crucial. Nevertheless, since the Seville European Council in 2002, common funding does apply to the incremental costs for headquarters and for costs incurred in providing support to the forces as a whole for EU-led operations. Other expenditures having an ESDP connection (e.g. non-proliferation and disarmament, conflict prevention and crisis management) are also covered by the general budget of the EU and amounted to 102 million euro in the year 2006 (EUR-Lex 2006: Chapter 19.03-CFSP).

In absolute numbers the defence budget of all 25 EU members combined has increased significantly from 2001 to 2004, from US$133.67 to US$186.28 billion.

Table 6.6 Defence expenditures and official development assistance

	Defence budget (billion of current US$)				Defence expenditure (percentage of GDP)			Official Development Assistance (ODA) (billion of current US$)			ODA (percentage of GNI)[c]		
	2001	2002	2003	2004	2001	2002	2003	2002	2003	2004	2002	2003	2004
United Kingdom	33.60	36.60	42.00	49.00	2.5	2.4	2.4	4.92	6.28	7.88	0.31	0.34	0.36
France	25.80	30.70	35.30	40.00	2.5	2.5	2.6	5.49	7.25	8.47	0.38	0.41	0.41
Germany	21.50	25.10	27.70	29.70	1.5	1.5	1.5	5.32	6.78	7.53	0.27	0.28	0.28
Italy	15.90	14.50	15.70	17.50	2.0	1.9	1.9	2.33	2.43	2.46	0.20	0.17	0.15
EU-15 Total	126.94	140.29	157.43	176.12	1.9	1.9	1.9	29.97	37.14[a]	42.89[b]	0.45	0.44	0.46
United States	329.00	362.10	456.20	460.50	3.0	3.3	3.7	13.29	16.25	19.71	0.13	0.15	0.17

Sources: Defence: Schmitt, B. (2005) *Defence Expenditure*, Institute for Security Studies document; ODA: own calculations based on Statistical Annex of the 2005 Development Co-operation Report by the OECD.

a In 2003, the European Commission contributed additional US$ 7.17 billion net ODA.
b In 2004, the European Commission contributed additional US$ 8.70 billion net ODA.
c gross national income.

Obviously the new security situation after 11 September 2001 resulted in an increase of military spending. Two other figures, however, modify this impressive increase by US$52.61 billion or 39 per cent in the annual defence expenditures. First, the total percentage of defence expenditure of the GDP of all 25 EU members remained unchanged between 2001 and 2003 at around 1.9 per cent. Only the percentage of the ten new members increased slightly from 1.9 to 2.0 per cent. Second, the scale of US spending on defence seen in comparison to the EU of 15 member states puts the European figures into a negative perspective. The 2004 US military allocations were nearly three times bigger than those of all EU member states taken together. Its increase between 2001 and 2004 amounted to US$131.5 billion or 40 per cent, while the percentage of defence expenditures increased between 2001 and 2003 from 3.0 to 3.7 per cent of US GDP.

Those figures show that on both sides of the Atlantic there was a shared perception after 11 September that defence expenditures had to be increased to meet the new threats. However, the Americans, in contrast to the Europeans, were willing to increase the military budget also in terms of their GDP. The US continued to play in a different league of military might from the EU. The Europeans were by no means able to catch up with the US, even though it has to be emphasized that it is still disputed among experts whether the EU really has to spend more money or whether it should spend the money more wisely (Howorth 2003: 14–15). But for the purpose of this study it is probably much more important to see that the very similar development of military spending of EU member states reflects their similar approach towards the new threats. Nearly all of the 25 have increased their allocations for defence since 2001 on a similar scale. But none of them was willing to do so by drastically increasing military expenditures in relation to their GDP.

However, in other areas it is important to address the security threats identified in the ESS. In comparison with the US, the EU's position seems to favour more the creation of 'soft' security. For instance, the EU is the largest contributor to the UN peacekeeping budget. In 2003, its share was 39 per cent compared to 27 per cent on the part of the US (European Commission 2004: 29). The EU is also the world's largest provider of official development assistance (ODA) (European Commission 2004: 15). Taking together the funding of the European Commission and the EU member states, the Europeans spent more than US$36.5 billion on ODA in 2002 alone. That was 56 per cent of the worldwide ODA flowing from industrial to developing countries. The US share was 20.7 per cent in the same period. In 2003, the EU reached an average of 0.34 per cent of ODA of its gross national income (GNI), a mark well above most other Western countries, including the US (0.15 per cent) (European Commission 2005a). Furthermore, the 25 EU member states decided to increase their financing for development considerably in the upcoming years: from €46 billion in 2006 (0.42 per cent ODA/GNI) to an estimated €66 billion in 2010 (0.56 per cent ODA/GNI), possibly achieving €84 billion by 2015 (0.7 per cent ODA/GNI) (European Commission 2005a).

Furthermore, humanitarian action occupies a key position in the EU's spending abroad. The Union is the world's main player in this field. The European Commission spends on average €604 million per year on humanitarian aid, which is 30 per cent of global humanitarian aid (European Community Humanitarian Office 2005). On top of that EU member states are separately responsible for 25 per cent of all official humanitarian assistance distributed worldwide.

These figures clearly reflect the quite different approaches of the US and the EU to post-11 September threats. The US sees the military as its main source of security and accordingly invests much more money than the Europeans into this sector. The EU member states, on the other hand, pursue an integrated approach where they spend proportionately significantly more money in those areas they deem useful rather than just simply on 'hard' security to defend their interests. Of course, the considerable investment of the Europeans in 'soft' security cannot compensate for the much higher US expenditures for 'hard' security. However, in the long run even relatively small amounts of money for development aid are likely to prevent instability and crisis in many developing countries. Spent wisely in the neighbourhood of the EU and in regions in which the EU has special interests and responsibilities, such as former colonies and ACP countries, the EU will probably be faced less with scenarios in which a military involvement is unavoidable, which can to a certain extent make up for their low defence expenditures.

Conclusion

Whilst the ESS has not yet developed a distinct identity or autonomy and still conceals important differences among the leading EU member states, it has nonetheless established sufficient foundation on which a common EU security strategy or security culture can build (Biscop 2005). As the data has shown, there is already considerable convergence among France, Germany, Italy and the UK with regard to the threat perceptions or on long-term policy: distinct identity, effective multilateralism and comprehensive security. Common views among Europeans can also be observed on budgetary allocations for military and defence. These convergence aspects promote the emerging EU security culture with regard to worldviews of the external environment and facilitate the group identity and group thinking among national officials in matters of security and defence. An overview of the nascent elements of security culture is provided in Table 6.7.

But obstacles remain. Differences among the four countries emerge primarily in terms of the responses to those threats or reaction to crises, especially

Table 6.7 Nascent elements of EU security culture

Worldview of external environment	UN is at the heart of the national policies
Identities	European norms and values
Instrumental preferences	Predominantly diplomatic, economic, developmental and military with multilateral slant
Interaction preferences	Decision-taking within EU institutions of second and third pillar

with respect to institutional and instrumental preferences (e.g. the use of force), which, incidentally, affect much of the EU internal discussions on security. Differences exist also on common identities where France and the UK try to conserve great power status (e.g. nuclear deterrence), while other EU member states want to pursue security mainly within CFSP and ESDP and are militarily self-constrained. Once again, this raises critical questions about the so-called autonomy of ESDP.

In terms of the realization of a European security culture, much will depend on the type and scale of the threat encountered and the capabilities of each individual EU member state to respond. A common reaction to a threat is more likely the less each individual state is able to respond to it on its own. In order to gain credibility as an effective actor on security issues, which carries greater political weight than hitherto, it is clear that the EU has to adjust its policies and structures. As the ESS states, the Union needs to be 'more active, more coherent and more capable' (ESS: 13). Besides the extension of military and civilian resources, the ESS suggests building up stronger diplomatic capabilities and the cooperation of EU member states in intelligence, in order to obtain common threat assessments as a shared basis for common actions. Institutions created within the EU giving support for third countries in combating terrorism and security sector reform could be an interesting part of the aim to attack threats abroad as the first line of defence. Emphasizing its multilateral stance, the EU acknowledges that only in cooperation with other actors will it be able to ward off the threats it faces. That includes employing international organizations as crucial means and bilateral cooperation with key actors, especially the US, Russia, Japan, China, Canada and India.

National security cultures of EU member states are still quite diverse on important points, but there is hope for a convergence of security cultures of the 25, as the findings presented above suggest. In general, the ESS has been an important first step in the direction towards a common European security strategy. But more detailed and concrete discussions among EU partners need to follow in order to give it a tangible impact and create a workable perspective for European security (Biscop 2005: 130). The development of a common European security culture is within the realms of possibility as the governments of the EU countries themselves state in the ESS. Very pragmatically they see the need to establish such a shared culture that 'fosters early, rapid, and when necessary, robust intervention' (ESS: 13). Such a shared culture will depend not just on the creation of the requisite military and civil capabilities, but also on a sufficiently shared pool of norms, beliefs and ideas regarding the means and ends of defence policy (Meyer 2005: 524). Particularly important in that regard is the 'group-identity and common thinking' among national officials dealing with ESDP issues in Brussels generated by the close daily cooperation described by Howorth (2003: 18–21) ('socialization effects'), spilling over even to new EU member states. The formation of high-powered committees, such as the Political and Security Committee, the creation of the Situation Centre (which monitors and analyses terrorist threats from intelligence supplied by member states) and the Policy Unit of the HR/SG are of particular significance in this respect. These innovations and mechanisms together with the role of the European Defence and Armaments Agency will help to make national solo efforts more seldom and to increase common political aims among the policy-makers of the 25 over time. Also, the range of means through which threats should be tackled is harmonized through cooperation within the ESDP frame-work, with a shift towards the acceptance of employing military measures even by pacifist societies such as Sweden or Germany. Furthermore, as Klaus Becher (2004: 354) pointed out, 'common vulnerabilities to threats and disruptions, the shared benefit of pooled resources' as well as the expectations directed towards the EU by the world community will inevitably lead to the gradual development of a shared European strategic culture by EU member states within the institutional framework of ESDP. However, doubts persist as to whether such a shared culture will be able to mobilize political forces in national capitals, increase defence expenditures and raise the level of military commitment in situations of international conflicts, including the use of force (Rynning 2003).

Hyde-Price (2004: 340–1) identified six key principles that should be the basis for a European strategic culture giving a sound response to the threats of the twenty-first century (primacy of expeditionary operations, coercion not brute force, 'just' use of force, imperative of force protection, imperative of limiting collateral damage, and short and sharp wars). All European governments should be able to support those principles as congruent with their own security strategies. Within political elites those ideas could be quickly internalized and result in coherent and effective common European actions. Strong convergence of EU policies and national security strategies would be the consequence. But it will take time and persuasion through successful activities by the Union to win the hearts and minds of the public in the 25 EU member states. The prerequisites for that are there, as has become clear in the analysis of the public's threat perception above.

Acknowledgement

The author wishes to thank Max Rasch for his valuable assistance in the research, Can Berk for his assistance with the bibliography, and Sven Biscop, Osvaldo Croci, Sten Reynning, Reimund Seidelmann and Wolfgang Wessels for helpful comments on a previous draft of this chapter.

Notes

1　For a description of these cleavages see Howorth (2003).
2　Uncertainties remain as to what the exact meaning of 'common defence' is, e.g. collective defence, mutual defence, etc.
3　I am grateful to Sven Biscop for suggesting this distinction to me.
4　France, Germany, Italy, Netherlands, Poland, Portugal, Slovakia, Spain, Turkey and the UK.

5   There is a third EU military intervention, but this happened before the drafting of the ESS. It concerns the takeover from NATO's 700-strong Task Force Fox in Macedonia between March and December 2003, known as Operation Concordia, and which marked the first EU-led peacekeeping mission

References

Becher, K. (2004) 'Has-been, wannabe, or leader: Europe's role in the world after the 2003 European Security Strategy', *European Security* 13 (4): 345–59.

Biscop, S. (2005) *The European Security Strategy: A Global Agenda for Positive Power,* Aldershot: Ashgate.

Cornish, P. and Edwards, G. (2001) 'Beyond the EU/NATO dichotomy: the beginnings of a European strategic culture', *International Affairs* 77 (3): 587–603.

Cornish, P. and Edwards, G. (2005) 'The strategic culture of the European Union: a progress report', *International Affairs* 81 (4): 801–20.

Edwards, G. (1997) 'The potential and limits of the CFSP: the Yugoslav example', in E. Regelsberger, P. de Schoutheete and W. Wessels (eds) *Foreign Policy of the European Union,* Boulder, CO: Lynn Rienner Publishers.

EUR-Lex – The portal to European Union law (2006) '2006 General Budget Volume 4 (section 3) – Commission'. Available online at: <http://europa.eu.int/eur-lex/budget/data/D2006_VOL4/EN/index.html> (accessed 8 May 2006).

European Commission (2004) *Eurobarometer 61, Public Opinion in the European Union, Spring 2004,* Brussels: requested and coordinated by the Directorate General Press and Communication.

European Commission (2005a) *Financing for Development. The Millennium Development Goals: Europe Cares,* Brussels: Publication by the Information Unit of the Directorate-General for Development of the European Commission.

European Commission (2005b) *Eurobarometer 62, Public Opinion in the European Union, Autumn 2004,* Brussels: requested and coordinated by the Directorate General Press and Communication.

European Commission (2005c) *Eurobarometer 63, Public Opinion in the European Union, Spring 2005, First Results,* Brussels: requested and coordinated by the Directorate General Press and Communication.

European Community Humanitarian Office (2005) *ECHO's finances.* Available online at: <http://europa.eu.int/comm/echo/finances/index_en.htm> (accessed 7 May 2006).

European Council (2003) *A Secure Europe in a Better World: European Security Strategy* (ESS). Available online at: <http://registerconsilium.europa.eu/ (accessed 7 May 2006).

German Marshall Fund of the United States (2005) *Transatlantic Trends: Key Findings 2005.*

Howorth, J. (2002) 'The CESDP and the forging of a European security culture', *Politique Européenne* 8: 88–108.

Howorth, J. (2003) 'Why ESDP is necessary and beneficial for the Alliance', in J. Howorth and J.T.S. Keeler (eds) *Defending Europe: the EU, NATO and the Quest for European Autonomy,* New York and London: Palgrave.

Hyde-Price, A. (2004) 'European security culture, strategic culture, and the use of force', *European Security* 13 (4): 323–43.

Lindley-French, J. (2002) 'In the shade of Locarno: Why European defence is failing', *International Affairs* 78 (4): 789–811.

Longhurst, K. and Zaborowski, M. (2004) 'The future of European security', *European Security* 13 (4): 381–91.

Meyer, C. (2005) 'Convergence towards a European strategic culture? A constructivist framework for explaining changing norms', *European Journal of International Relations* 11 (4): 523–49.

Osland, K. (2004) 'The police mission in Bosnia and Herzegovina', *International Peacekeeping* 11 (3): 544–60.

Quille, G. (2004) 'The European Security Strategy: A framework for EU security interests?', *International Peacekeeping* 11 (3): 422–38.

Rynning, S. (2003) 'The European Union: towards a strategic culture?', *Security Dialogue* 34 (4).

Solana, J. (2003) *A Secure Europe in a Better World: European Security Strategy,* Brussels: The European Union for Security Studies.

van Ham, P. (2004) *Europe Gets Real: The New Security Strategy Shows the EU's Geopolitical Maturity.* Available online at: <http://www.aicgs.org/analysis/c/vanham.aspx> (accessed 7 May 2006).

Part II
North America

7 Canada

Taking security seriously after 11 September?

Osvaldo Croci and Amy Verdun

Following the terrorist attacks of 11 September 2001, the American government ordered the quasi-closure of its borders. This precautionary measure almost brought to a halt the C$1.9 billion worth of daily trade between the United States and Canada. These two events led the Canadian government to take a series of security initiatives. The first was the setting up of an Ad Hoc Committee on Public Security and Anti-Terrorism chaired by John Manley, the Minister of Foreign Affairs. The committee was charged with examining 'all policies, legislation, regulations and programs across the Government to strengthen all aspects of Canada's approach to fighting terrorism and ensuring public security' (DFAIT n.d.). In mid October, the government unveiled an action plan on Canadian security, which led to the adoption, in short succession, of a number of policies. By the end of the year, the Canadian government had signed the Smart Border Agreement with the US, designed to increase security at the border while assuring the smooth flow of people. It had introduced the Anti-Terrorism and the Public Safety Acts, both designed to strengthen the capacity of the federal government to react to security threats. Finally, it had also made a direct military contribution to the US-led campaign against the terrorism-supporting regime of the Taliban in Afghanistan. The government then proceeded to modify the immigration and refugee legislation to curb its reported abuse by many claimants, and set up a number of new institutional bodies devoted to security, the most important of which was the Department of Public Safety and Emergency Preparedness (PSEP), created in December 2003. Finally, in April 2004, the government released its first ever paper on national security and announced a 'comprehensive international policy review' aimed at enabling Canada to reclaim its 'place and influence in the world' (Pratt 2004).

This chapter focuses on the changes in Canadian security policy since 11 September 2001. The first part offers a brief outline of the security environment faced by Canada after 11 September and examines the government's perception of security and threats. The second part analyses the policies and institutional changes the government has introduced as well as the resources it has allocated to security since that time. The chapter concludes that the post-11 September Canadian proactive approach to security is owed primarily to a heightened perceived need to reassure the US that Canada is taking security seriously.

Threat perception

The security environment

Canadian threat perception and responses to perceived threats after 11 September should be seen within the context of the Canadian security environment, the most important feature of which is Canada's geographic position. Canada shares the world's longest border with the US: 5,061km on land and 3,830km on water. Because of this strategic position, Canada could afford not to devote much attention or resources to security during the Cold War. Since the US considered Canadian security as its own, Canadian security needs were easily satisfied through membership of the North Atlantic Treaty Organization (NATO) and bilateral relationships with the US such as the North American Aerospace Defence Command (NORAD). With national security being assured, Canada's foreign policy could concentrate more on process than substance and came thus to be identified with 'multilateralism' understood both as 'the practice of multilateral diplomacy and ... policies supporting the establishment and maintenance of institutions and associations that facilitate and support the practice of multilateral diplomacy' (Keating 2002: 4).

If anything, the end of the Cold War reinforced Canada's relative ability to chart its own course in world affairs from under the protection offered by the ample US cloak. And indeed, in the 1990s, Canadian foreign policy took up the theme of 'human security', which implies a shift in emphasis from state-centric to individual security concerns, understood as the general improvement of the quality of life conditions experienced by individuals. Among these, Canadian foreign policy concentrated primarily on the banning of anti-personnel mines, rehabilitation of child soldiers, and the promotion of international human rights (Keating 2002: 223–4; Axworthy 2003).

After 11 September 2001, however, given the heightened concern on the part of the American government for its own territorial security, the Canadian government had little choice but to adopt some measures to reassure the US about the security of its northern border. Hence, it has privileged a state-centric understanding of security as well as policies undertaken at the national level or bilaterally, that is, in cooperation with the US. This is not surprising since failure to act would probably have led the US to permanently tighten entry into the US from Canada for both people and goods. This would have disrupted trade between the two countries and created serious economic difficulties for Canada since trade with the US accounts for 87 per cent of Canadian foreign trade in goods and services. This figure is even bigger for the industrial heartland of Canada: a staggering 94 per cent of Ontario exports, for instance, go to the US. By contrast, trade with Canada accounts for only 16.5 per cent of US foreign trade. This share of trade makes Canada the largest US trading partner but it does not make US economic prosperity as dependent on Canada as Canadian prosperity is on the US.[1]

The need to reassure the US was compounded by the perception south of the border that Canada was the North American gateway for terrorists. Contrary to early reports, none of the 11 September terrorists entered the US from Canada. Such a perception was, however, linked to a number of cases, the most important of which was that of Ahmed Ressam (aka. the Millennium bomber), the Montreal-based Arab terrorist who was fortuitously stopped by a US Customs inspector in Port Angeles (Washington) in December 1999 on his way to detonate a homemade bomb at the Los Angeles airport.[2] Perceptions do not have to be correct in order to influence action, especially when they are held not only by the American public[3] but also by the American counter-terrorist intelligence community (Federal Research Division 2003). In an article in which he imagines the future history of the war on terror, former US national coordinator for security and counter-terrorism, Richard Clarke, has more than one terrorist entering the US from Canada, some of them smuggling SA-14 and SA-16 missiles across the border and into Minnesota, Montana and Washington (Clarke 2005: 62, 71).[4] In a footnote (in his piece, footnotes provide evidence for his imagined future history), he writes that 'Canada's ethnically diverse population, liberal immigration and refugee policies, and long border with the US make it a good place for terrorists to raise funds, procure supplies and fake documents, and plan attacks'. He bases this statement on a report of the Canadian Security and Intelligence Service (CSIS), which acknowledged in 2003 that 'it considered more than 300 people in Canada to be members of various terrorist organizations, including al-Qaeda'. Clarke also imagines that, following a refusal by the Canadian government 'to allow US nuke squads to conduct warrantless searches at customs stations on the Canadian side of the border', the US would build a 'Northern Wall' and channel 'trucks and freight trains to a limited number of monitored border crossings' (Clarke 2005: 62–3, 75).

Finally, the post-11 September period has coincided with a public debate on Canada's diminishing status in the world and the general decline of its military force. This debate on Canada as a 'fading power' (Hillmer and Appel Molot 2002) was an additional spur for the government to act in the field of foreign, defence and security policies, areas which had been largely neglected by all previous Liberal governments.

Security interests and threats

In April 2004, the Canadian government published its first ever White Paper on national security, entitled: *Securing an Open Society: Canada's National Security Policy*. The paper identifies what the government regards as Canada's 'three core national security interests'. The first of these interests (protecting Canada and Canadians at home and abroad) is uncontroversial. The second (ensuring Canada is not a base for threats to its allies) is a signal sent to the US to counter the widespread perception that Canada is the North American point of entry for terrorists intending to strike at the US. The third (contributing to international security) is a reassuring message for those sectors of Canadian public opinion that regard 'multilateralism' not as a policy instrument but as a value in itself and a key component of the Canadian identity.

The White Paper does not provide clear insights into what the government regards as the most serious threats to Canadian security. It lists a number of threats but does not rank them in order of gravity or immediacy. Hence, it is not clear which ones, according to the government, demand more attention. Non-specific threats (e.g. natural disasters, foreign espionage, and critical infrastructure vulnerability) are mentioned together with others that could at worst create only a refugee emergency for Canada (e.g. failing states). Threats with which Canada has had some limited experience (e.g. violent secessionist movements, domestic extremism, organized crime, pandemics) are listed next to threats that have become prominent on the US security agenda since 11 September 2001 (e.g. religious extremism, state sponsored terrorism, proliferation of weapons of mass destruction), but which were hardly mentioned in Canadian public political discourse until then.

A clearer image of the type of threats perceived by the Canadian government is provided by the 2003 CSIS public report and summarized in Table 7.1. The CSIS report ranks terrorism as the greatest threat Canada faces. The threat is represented primarily by the activities of various terrorist groups operating in Canada. The CSIS report further subdivides terrorism into four categories, according to the gravity and immediacy of the threat. Religious extremism and particularly Sunni Islamic extremism is ranked first. It is followed by secessionist violence (e.g., Tamil secessionist groups extorting funds from Tamil communities in Canada), and by domestic extremism (e.g., white supremacist or anti-globalization groups). State-sponsored terrorism (e.g., Iranian sponsorship of Hizbullah) is the last to be mentioned. The CSIS report then mentions the danger posed by the proliferation of weapons of mass destruction, which poses an indirect threat to Canada by endangering international peace and stability. Other threats identified by CSIS, but deemed to be of a lower order, are espionage, especially economic espionage, the manipulation by foreign states of elements in the Canadian ethnic population, attacks on Canada's critical information infrastructure, and transnational organized crime (CSIS 2003).

The difference in the portraits painted by the White Paper and the CSIS report, the latter being much more precise, can probably be attributed to the fact that the White Paper is a political document which was expected to filter down to

Table 7.1 Threat perceptions in the post-11 September era

Type of key threats	Closure of US border as a result of a terrorist attack on the US Islamic terrorism and Sunni religious extremism in particular Secessionists extorting funds from immigrant communities
Agency of threats	US anti-terrorism initiatives which slow down border crossing Activities of terrorist and secessionist groups
Target of threats	Economic interests Civilian population, some immigrant communities in particular
Geographical source of threats	Domestic Islamic terrorist cells Domestic immigrant secessionist activists (e.g. Tamil)

the public at large. The CSIS report instead, even if public, was addressed to a very specialized audience and thus was expected to have limited political reper-cussions. Hence, it could afford to be starker and more precise. The impression given by the White Paper is that its list of threats, much like that of core national interests, has been crafted to reassure everyone and the US in particular. Indeed, as hinted at in the title and stated explicitly in the executive summary, the policy has been 'crafted to balance the needs for national security with the protection of core Canadian values of openness, diversity and respect for civil liberties' (Privy Council Office 2004: vii). Both in the White Paper and in its choice of security initiatives, the Canadian government has tried to reconcile two objectives, namely economic prosperity and what could be defined as 'Canadian distinc-tion'.[5] On the one hand, it has recognized the need to take security initiatives that would reassure the US of the safety of its northern border and thus ensure the smooth flow of goods and people across it, which in turn protects the inflow of direct investments into Canada. On the other hand, it has been careful not to characterize its new security measures as the beginning of a process of further integration with the US in order to uphold what it regards as Canadian core val-ues, in this case the protection of civil liberties. In fact the New Democratic Party (NDP), as well as some sections of Canadian public opinion, maintain that the US, in its search for increased security, has compromised civil liberties and that therefore the harmonization of US and Canadian security policies would have the same consequences in Canada.

The White Paper does not directly mention the threat that the government regards as the most serious, namely the possibility that Canadian access to the US market might be hampered or diminished. Such a threat is however mentioned explicitly in a more recent official document. The so-called 'international policy statement' released in April 2005 points out that 'a major terrorist incident within one of our continental partners could have direct and potential devastating conse-quences for the movement of people and commerce within the North American space' (Government of Canada 2005: 7). Even before this acknowledgement, however, various newspaper articles and academic papers on Canadian security discussed this issue. Historian Desmond Morton, for instance, put it starkly:

> Our priority ... is to do what we must do to make Americans feel secure on their northern frontier. Americans may remember 11 September; we must remember 12 September when American panic closed the US border and shook our prosperity to its very core.
>
> (Morton 2004)

Some Canadian economic and political elites advocate a foreign policy grounded in a conception of a national interest that explicitly recognizes the central role of the US in assuring Canadian national security and economic prosperity. The cen-tral objective of such a foreign policy would be the making of an economic and defence strategic agreement with the US aimed at creating what has been defined as a 'continental security perimeter' or an 'area of mutual confidence'. In the words of former Canadian ambassador to the US Allan Gotlieb (2003: 28), such an agreement should aim at 'establishing a common set of laws favouring the movement of people, services, and goods within a joint Canada–US space'.[6] Opposed to this project are nationalist intellectual elites, the Canadian Labour Congress (CLC) and the NDP as well as a good number of Liberal party members. Their view is that the major threat faced by Canadians in the wake of 11 September is the erosion of their civil liberties. According to them, the resoluteness of the Canadian government in adopting security measures designed to please the US has already begun to undermine them and the creation of a 'continental security perimeter' would make things even worse. As Jennifer Stoddart, Canada's Privacy Commissioner, has put it: 'Personal freedoms are becoming a casualty of the fight against terrorism'.[7] Any form of permanent integration with the US in the security field, moreover, would also undermine Canadian national distinction, or, as argued by another opponent of the project, pose an 'explicit threat ... to the expression of distinctive Canadian values on defence, international affairs, and immigration and refugees issues' (Jackson 2003: 26).[8] Under these circumstances, the Liberal government has chosen to take some steps to allay US concerns while, at the same time, taking care not to alienate that part of the Canadian electorate which believes that being Canadian means being different from Americans. This strategy has required semantic creativity, if not outright ambiguity, and steadfast denial that the new policies foreshadow a new round of continental integration.

Responses to threat

The Smart Border initiative

The rapidity with which the Canadian government was able to reach an agreement with its US counterpart on the simultaneous enhancing of border security and speed of crossing is deceptive. The two governments signed the so-called Smart Border Declaration on 12 December 2001, a mere three months after the terrorist attack on the Twin Towers. Yet, negotiations on border issues had been going on, albeit largely hidden from public view, since 1993, following an initiative taken by Congress to reform US immigration policy. Canada feared that a proposal known as Section 110, which aimed at developing an automated system capable of tracking all non-US citizens crossing US borders, might have an adverse effect on trading between the two countries. After failing to obtain an exemption for people entering the US from Canada, the two governments entered into a series of negotiations concerning the adoption of new technologies and procedures aimed at 'streamlining and harmonizing border policies and management, expanding cooperation at and beyond the border, and collaborating on common threats outside the United States and Canada'.[9] At first, negotiations were conducted by a committee of representatives from the main departments and agencies dealing with border issues. These were Citizenship and Immigration, Canada Customs and Revenue Agency, Foreign Affairs and International Trade, and their US counterparts. Other departments and agencies were involved on an ad hoc basis. In October 1999, moreover, the two governments signed the Canada–US Partnership Agreement, which provided for consultation with various stakeholders, especially border communities' leaders and business interest groups.

The Smart Border Declaration was not, therefore, a new policy initiative brought about by an increased concern for security. Rather, it reflected a new political will to work on an old dossier that had been languishing because of a lack of political urgency and inadequate funding on both sides of the border. The Smart Border Declaration, moreover, was not the announcement of a completed project but a 30-point action plan agreed upon after two months of intense negotiations. According to Christopher Waddell, the relative success of the negotiations after 11 September 2001 must be ascribed in no small part to the fact that they were centralized and became the responsibility of John Manley, the Chair of the Ad Hoc Committee on Public Security and Anti-Terrorism, and Tom Ridge, the Director of Homeland Security. The good personal relationship they quickly established and the fact that Ridge, as former governor of Pennsylvania, had direct experience with Canadian border issues were two other significant factors (Waddell 2003: 59).[10]

The Smart Border Declaration strikes a balance between enhancing border security (the US concern) and guaranteeing the quick movement of people and goods (the Canadian objective).[11] The plan provides for the implementation of a common, and in some cases also jointly managed, family of systems known as NEXUS, aimed at identifying high security risks while expediting the flow of low risk travellers. They include the sharing of basic air passenger information, the adoption of biometric identifiers, the issuance of permanent resident cards to all Canadian landed immigrants, the sharing of information relating to asylum seekers, the signing of a so-called 'safe third country agreement'[12] and the coordination of visa policy. Concerning the flow of goods, the two countries are developing approaches to move customs inspection activities away from the border both to improve security and relieve congestion. They have also established a programme, known as FAST (Free and Secure Trade), which expedites the movement across the border of shipments for low-risk companies. Funds have also been committed to the physical and technological improvement as well as the protection of border infrastructure (airports, ports, bridges, tunnels, pipelines and power lines).

As mentioned above, some of these systems are jointly managed. The two countries have set up joint units to assess information on incoming air passengers as well as joint Customs teams to inspect containers at the port of arrival in North America. They have also set up Integrated Border Enforcement Teams (IBETs) focusing on cross-border crime and bringing together agencies at all levels in both countries. Canada has also set up Integrated National Security Enforcement Teams (INSETs), which bring together representatives from federal enforcement and intelligence agencies and may also include US representatives, on an ad hoc basis, while some Canadian officials have been integrated into the US Foreign Terrorist Tracking Task Force.

The Anti-Terrorism Act

Introduced in the House of Commons on 15 October and proclaimed in force on 24 December 2001, the Anti-Terrorism Act (Bill C-36) attempts, according to the government, 'to create a balance between the need to protect the security of Canadians and the protection of their rights and freedom'. It provides 'new investigative tools' (mainly easier access to electronic surveillance) to law enforcement and national security agencies, makes it a crime to belong to, fund, or otherwise help a terrorist organization and strengthens existing provisions against hate crimes. Two provisions of Bill C-36 were, and continue to be, particularly controversial. The first is the so-called 'recognizance with conditions' (better known as 'preventive arrest'), which allows investigators and judges, with the consent of the Attorney General, to detain suspected terrorists without charges for up to 72 hours. The second concerns two amendments to the Canada Evidence Act and the Access to Information Act, which allow the non-disclosure of information in legal proceedings when disclosure 'would encroach on a specified public interest or be injurious to international relations or national defence or security'.[13]

To relieve the concerns of a vociferous minority, Parliament agreed on a five-year sunset clause for the most controversial provisions and provided for 'a comprehensive review of the ... Act' within three years of its passage. A subcommittee of the House of Commons Standing Committee on Justice, Human Rights, Public Safety and Emergency Preparedness and a Special Committee of the Senate began working on such a review in December 2004 and are yet to report to Parliament at the time of this writing. They are likely to endorse the view of PSEP Minister, Anne McLellan, who, at a February 2005 hearing, told them that the government had struck the right balance the first time and that no changes are needed.

Notwithstanding the doomsday scenario painted by its critics who depicted it as the first step towards a police state, the Anti-Terrorist Act has been used very sparingly. Most of its provisions have hardly been invoked, while the most controversial of all, 'recognizance with conditions', has never been used.[14] However, as Justice Minister Irwin Cotler told the reviewing committee, the government is considering the adoption of a number of 'control measures', such as house arrest, to deal with terror suspects who are deemed to represent a serious security threat but cannot be convicted because of insufficient evidence.[15]

The Immigration and Refugee Protection Act

Contrary to popular belief, Bill C-11, better known as the Immigration and Refugee Protection Act (IRPA), which became law on 28 June 2002, was not suddenly drafted because of 11 September 2001. IRPA had been in the pipeline for a long time. Its first draft, which served as the basis for discussion with the provinces and other stakeholders, was released in 1999. Its major objective moreover was to look for ways to reform the old 1976 Immigration Act in order to attract immigrants with the type of skills demanded by the current labour market. Most of the security related provisions of IRPA concern the attempt to curb abuse of the refugee system.[16] Canada is the most lax, or generous (depending on one's perspective), country as far as the determination system of 'in-country refugees'[17] as well as the treatment of failed claimants is concerned. As Stephen Gallagher has pointed out, this is largely due to a liberal interpretation of what constitutes a convention refugee.[18] Other factors are the influence of various interest groups (immigration lawyers and consultants, human rights groups, ethnic associations) all favouring a very open refugee policy, partisan electoral considerations (new Canadians vote overwhelmingly Liberal and make up the majority of electors in various urban ridings),[19] and the fact that Canada has a large and uncontroversial immigration programme. During the 1990s, for instance, refugees represented, on average, only around 15 per cent of the total number of newcomers into Canada (Gallagher 2002: 98–9 and 113–15).

One IRPA security provision in particular has been the object of much criticism. Known as the 'security certificate', it enables authorities to arrest, detain and eventually deport any non-citizen deemed to be a threat to national security. The evidence gathered must be sufficient to convince a Federal Court judge but can be withheld from the suspect and his/her lawyer.[20] Contrary to suggestions by its critics, however, this provision was not introduced by Bill C-11, and Canadian authorities have not resorted to it more often or more indiscriminately than before 11 September. Indeed, as with the Anti-Terrorism Act, they have used it very sparingly. Only five non-citizens have been held under such a provision since 11 September 2001. None of them, moreover, has yet been deported since all of them have chosen to argue that they would face torture in their countries of origin.[21] It should be noted that judges have begun to express their reluctance at having to perform the difficult task the Act assigns them, namely to decide whether an individual should be denied the most basic civil rights (i.e., not to be detained without precise charges, the right to know the evidence against them) on grounds of national security.[22] On the one hand, application of the provision might lead to the detention and deportation of some innocent people. On the other, however, since terrorists have no reluctance in exploiting every weakness in democratic societies, the price of letting one of them go free in the name of civil liberties could be very high. The use of 'security certificates' has been ruled constitutional (i.e., not in contradiction with the Charter of Rights) by the Federal Court of Appeal in December 2004. Adil Charkaoui's lawyers have since brought the issue before the Supreme Court which has accepted to hear the appeal.[23]

The Public Safety Act

The Public Safety Act provides for a series of initiatives designed to strengthen civil aviation and marine security as well as to facilitate the sharing of law enforcement and national security information between federal departments and agencies and between Canada and its partners internationally, particularly the US. Originally introduced in the House of Commons in November 2001, it went through three different versions before becoming law in May 2004. The controversy concerned a provision obliging air carriers to make basic information such as name, gender, date of birth, citizenship and a travel document number, as well as information related to the traveller's reservation, such as flight number and itinerary, available upon request to Transport Canada, the Royal Canadian Mounted Police (RCMP) and the CSIS. According to critics, such as then Privacy Commissioner George Radwanski, such a provision infringed upon the civil rights of Canadians. His main argument, which could be summarized as 'no by-catch allowed', is an example of the extremism occasionally exhibited by some civil rights defenders and deserves to be reproduced in its entirety:

> In Canada, it is well established that we are not required to identify ourselves to police unless we are being arrested or we are carrying out a licensed activity such as driving. The right to anonymity with regard to the state is a crucial privacy right. Since we are required to identify ourselves to airlines as a condition of air travel and since section 4.82 would give the RCMP unrestricted access to the passenger information obtained by airlines, this would set the extraordinarily privacy-invasive precedent of effectively requiring compulsory self-identification to the police. I am prepared, with some reluctance, to accept this as an exceptional measure that can be justified, in the wake of September 11, for the limited and specific purposes of aviation security and national security against terrorism. But I can find no reason why the use of this de facto self-identification to the police should be extended to searching for individuals who are of interest to the state because they are the subject of warrants for Criminal Code offences unrelated to terrorism. That has the same effect as requiring us to notify the police every time we travel, so that they can check whether we are wanted for something.[24]

It is not clear why the privacy rights of individuals who are the subjects of warrants for Criminal Code offences – and hence have already had at least part of their day in court – should trump the duty of the state to provide security to its citizens. The government, however, went back to the drawing board and after two years unveiled a rather peculiar compromise solution. In order to take into account the concerns of people such as Radwanski while providing for some degree of public security, the government decided that:

> The RCMP can only access passenger information for the purpose of transportation security. While screening passenger lists for transportation security, if the RCMP incidentally discovers a criminal wanted for a serious crime punishable by five years or more imprisonment and listed in regulations, the Force can disclose that information to a peace officer if there is reason to believe it would assist in the execution of a Canada-wide warrant. This aspect of the scheme is necessary for public safety because the RCMP needs to take appropriate action if it happens to find a passenger wanted for an outstanding warrant listed in the regulations which include serious offences such as murder or kidnapping.[25]

Afghanistan, Iraq, and the Ballistic Missile Defence Programme

Canada's attitude towards security can also be gauged by examining the government's position on three additional issues: the war against the Taliban regime in Afghanistan, the war against the Saddam Hussein regime in Iraq, and the question of the Ballistic Missile Defence Programme (BMDP). The Canadian government was eager to make a military contribution to the war against the Taliban. Operation Apollo, as the mission was called, made available a Canadian Naval Task Group (two frigates, a destroyer and a supply ship stationed in the Arabian Sea) while another frigate was integrated with a US Carrier Battle Group. It also provided 2,000 Canadian soldiers while a 1,000-strong light infantry unit was put on seven-day notice for deployment within an international stabilization force. The eagerness of the government to participate was not due solely to the perception that the Taliban regime had to be brought down because of the threat it posed to international security through its symbiotic relationship with fundamentalist Islamic terrorism. The fact that intervention was expected and supported by a majority of Canadians also played a very important role (Dawson 2003). Conversely, in the case of Iraq, the decision not to participate seems to be due primarily to a generally more divided public opinion on the issue and clear opposition in Quebec, where the incumbent Liberals were about to face a provincial election, rather than to the official explanation provided by the government, namely the lack of explicit UN support for the intervention (McGrath 2006).

The decision not to take part in the BMDP is even more revealing of the Canadian government's attitude towards security issues. The decision has little to do with the official justifications that the BMDP will not work with current technology and that it might lead to the weaponization of space. After having reassured the US, on more than one occasion, of Canada's support and intention to participate,[26] Prime Minister Martin announced at the end of February 2005 that Canada would not take part in the BMDP.[27] The decision was surprising for two reasons. First, Canada has participated in many joint defence arrangements with the US since the Second World War (Bercuson 2003; Mason 2003), the latest being the setting up of the Canada–US Planning Group. Created in the spring of 2003, the joint Planning Group has the task of examining land and maritime military cooperation and preparing contingency plans for deploying military forces within North America in the event of a crisis, terrorist attacks, or natural disasters (DND 2002). Second, since the Canadian government continues to be a member of NORAD, the main task of which is to detect incoming threats from the North, the decision not to be part of the BMDP results in Canada not participating in the decision of how to deal with an incoming missile. In other words, the decision not to be part of the BMDP does not change anything in terms of security, since Canada would still be protected against any missile threat. It does, however, build political capital with Canadian nationalists for the Liberal Party. Thus, ironically, the concern for Canadian sovereignty ends up making the North American defence partnership even more one-sided since the only practical implication of the refusal of the Canadian government to be part of the BMDP is its renunciation of a seat at the table and hence of 'voice'.

Institutions

In the wake of 11 September 2001, the Canadian government, besides adopting new security policies, has also set up new institutions concerned with security issues. The first was the Ad Hoc Cabinet Committee on Public Security and Anti-Terrorism, which was set up immediately after 11 September and chaired by Foreign Affairs Minister John Manley. When, in January 2002, Prime Minister Jean Chrétien reshuffled his government and Manley became Deputy Prime Minister, he retained the responsibility of chairing the Committee. In the government headed by Paul Martin, Anne McLellan replaced John Manley as Deputy Prime Minister and Chair of the Committee, which was renamed Cabinet Committee on Security, Public Health and Emergencies. McLellan also became head of the Department of Public Safety and Emergency Preparedness or PSEP, which was created in December 2003, to provide 'policy leadership' and deliver 'programs and services in the areas of national security, emergency management, policing, border security, corrections, and crime prevention'.[28] One of its responsibilities is to ensure 'policy cohesion among the six agencies that report to the Minister', namely the RCMP, CSIS, the Canada Border Services Agency (CBSA), the Canada Firearms Centre, the Correctional Service of Canada, and the National Parole Board.

In December 2003, the government announced the setting up of the Advisory Council on National Security (ACNS) within the Privy Council Office (PCO) as well as the creation of a National Security Committee of Parliamentarians. The mandate of the ACNS is to provide 'confidential expert advice on issues related to national security' as well as to suggest 'strategies, mechanisms and activities required to develop, implement, evaluate and improve a fully integrated security system'. ACNS reports to the Cabinet Committee on Security, Public Health and Emergencies and to the Government as a whole through the newly created position of National Security Advisor to the Prime Minister. ACNS is composed of 15 individuals selected and appointed by the Government on the basis of their security related expertise and experience. They serve a two-year renewable term in their individual capacities and not as representatives of specific entities or interest groups. The National Security Committee of Parliamentarians is supposed to foster a more informed dialogue on national security issues.[29] Because of its sensitivity to multicultural issues and because of the criticism with which Arab and Muslim spokespeople reacted to some of its security policy initiatives, the government has also set up within PSEP a Cross-Cultural Roundtable on Security. Its mandate is to engage Canada's ethnic groups and religious communities in a 'long-term dialogue on matters related to national security', and especially on 'the impact of security policies on a diverse and pluralistic society'.[30]

In early 2003, the government set up within CSIS an Integrated Threat Assessment Centre (ITAC), which draws personnel and input from the broader Canadian intelligence community. Its task is to prepare 'timely, client-focussed and value-added intelligence'.[31] Canada's intelligence capacity has traditionally been the responsibility of three main agencies. Security intelligence (i.e., intelligence related to the activities of domestic agents) was the responsibility of CSIS.[32] Foreign intelligence (i.e., intelligence related to the capabilities, activities, and intentions of foreign countries and agents) was the responsibility of the Communications Security Establishment, which dealt exclusively with signals intelligence (or SIGINT), and the Canadian Forces. For foreign intelligence, however, Canada mostly relied on its partners in the so-called UKUSA alliance, namely the US, the United Kingdom, Australia and New Zealand. Intelligence coordination among these different agencies was performed by the PCO through its Intelligence Assessment Secretariat. Such a role was relatively simple during the bipolar era given the primacy of the Soviet threat, but has become increasingly complicated since the end of the Cold War for two reasons. First, new threats have emerged and second, and consequently, the number of agencies responsible for intelligence gathering has increased with the addition, for instance, of PSEP, the Canadian Customs and Revenue Agency, the Financial Transactions and Reports Analysis Centre, Citizenship and Immigration, and Transport Canada. Under these conditions, the PCO, which worked primarily through periodic meetings, could hardly provide the necessary coordination, and hence this function has been assumed by ITAC.

As part of an overall policy of revitalization of the Canadian Forces, the Canadian government has also set up Canada Command, an integrated national operational command headquarters located in Ottawa which is supposed to make it easy for the Canadian Forces 'to bring the best available military resources from across Canada to bear on a crisis or threat, wherever it occurs, nation-wide'.[33]

Finally, the Martin government has set up a permanent Cabinet Committee on Canada–US relations chaired by the Prime Minister himself – an indication of the centrality of such relations for the Martin government. The Committee, in fact, allows the Prime Minister and his government to assess and evaluate all other policy initiatives in terms of their impact on the Canada–US relationship. The setting up of this committee should not be taken to signal a centralization of policy-making. Indeed, various authors, approaching security issues from different points of view, have emphasized the consolidation, even after 11 September, of a form of multi-level governance. Canadian–US border security, in particular, is developed and implemented by 'both traditional vertical intergovernmental networks in each nation, and of equal importance, newly formed horizontal networks that span a multitude of security agencies of both the local, county, state and provincial government levels, federal agencies and departments, and in some instances, the private sector as well' (Brunet-Jailly 2004: 124).[34] Table 7.2 summarizes Canadian institutional responses to threat after 11 September.

Allocation of resources

Immediately after 11 September, the government made available C$280 million to pay for measures designed to enhance policing and intelligence (e.g. the introduction of a 'smart' Permanent Resident Card for landed immigrants, the improvement of preliminary screening of refugee claimants and the hiring of new security personnel at ports of entry). The December 2001 budget provided C$7.7 billion over

Table 7.2 Canada's preferred responses to threats

Interaction patterns	Stated preference for multilateralism, but in essence bilateral (cooperation with US), especially on border management. Adoption and/or revision of a number of security-related public policies.
Institutional preferences for meeting threats	Establishment of a new Cabinet Committee, new Department (PSEP), and Integrated Threat Assessment Centre (ITAC) within CSIS and Command Canada. Increased and improved coordination among law enforcement and intelligence agencies.
Instrumental preferences for meeting threats	Increased intelligence capacity. New financial and logistical resources as well as new legal instruments for intelligence and law enforcement agencies and the Canadian Forces.

five years to enhance Canadian security. This amount included the money necessary to maintain existing public safety and policing programmes. Only part of it was designed to respond directly to the increased need for security after 11 September. The new funds were to be spent primarily to upgrade intelligence equipment, deploy more frontline investigative personnel, expand the anti-terrorism capacity of the military, improve critical infrastructure protection, enhance border and marine security, and create a new air security organization. It should be noted, however, that in the case of CSIS, for instance, the new funding simply restores operating budgets and number of employees to the mid-1990s levels (CSIS 2003: Fig. 1 and 2). Table 7.3 provides a summary and breakdown of the special security related budgetary allocations after 11 September.

The December 2001 budget disregarded the needs of the Canadian military despite repeated, undeniable demonstrations of its decline (Granatstein 2004). At the end of the Second World War, Canada had the fourth most powerful military in the world on which it spent 7.3 per cent of GDP (Gotlieb 2005: 23). In the year 2000, Canada ranked last (if one excludes tiny Luxembourg) among NATO countries in terms of defence expenditure as a percentage of GDP (1.2 per cent). As shown in Table 7.4, defence expenditures had basically remained the same (about C$13 billion per year) since the early 1990s.

The same was true for the number of armed forces (both military and civilian personnel) as a percentage of national labour force (King 2002). Inevitably, the role played by Canada in international peacekeeping had also become marginal. Having invented it, as it were, peacekeeping soon became part of Canada's international identity. For two decades – in the 1970s and 1980s – Canada participated in every UN peacekeeping mission and provided as much as 10 per cent of its military forces, which made it the largest contributor. Today, Canada provides only about 0.9 per cent of all UN peacekeeping forces, which places it 32nd in the ranks of contributors (Gotlieb 2005: 23). The Canadian military received a modest new allocation of C$270 million for Operation Apollo in Afghanistan in 2003

Table 7.3 Special budgetary allocations for security related functions 2001–2005 (C$ billion)

	2001	2002	2003	2004	2005
Military			0.27	0.8	12.8[a]
Peacekeeping				0.3	
Security (of which)	7.7[a]			0.6	
Border initiatives	1.3				
Intelligence and policing	1.6				
Screening of entrants	1.0				
Emergency preparedness	1.6				
Air security	2.2				
Coast Guard			0.95[b]		
Other allocations					
Trade promotion (in US)			0.11		
International assistance			1.4		3.4[a]
Peace/security initiatives					0.5
Diplomatic representation					0.042[a]
Embassies security					0.059

a over 5 years
b over 2 years
Sources: Compiled from data in Department of Finance Canada (2005) 'Budget Info by Year'.
Available online at: <http://www.fin.gc.ca/access/budinfoe.html#year> (accessed 16 November 2005).

Table 7.4 Canadian military expenditures 1990 and 2000–2005

Year	1990	2000	2001	2002	2003	2004	2005
C$ (billion)	13.4	12.3	13.1	13.3	14.1	14.9	15.5

Source: NATO (2005) 'Defence expenditures of NATO countries'. Available online at:
<http://www.nato.int/issues/defence_expenditures/index.html> (accessed 16 November 2005).

and another C$800 million in 2004, but had to wait until 2005 for a much-needed financial injection of C$12.8 billion, which will be spent, however, mainly between 2008 and 2010. At that time, the military budget will amount to C$19 billion against the current C$15.5 billion. Most of the money is designed to replace ageing equipment and increase the number of troops from the current level of 62,000 to 67,000.[35]

Notwithstanding the overhauling the Canadian security system has undergone, there is work that remains to be done. The March 2004 report of the Auditor General, for instance, observed that the government had yet 'to achieve improvements in the ability of security information systems to communicate with each other'. Deficiencies were also found 'in the way intelligence [was] managed across the government', the most glaring being the 'lack of co-ordination' which led to both 'gaps in intelligence coverage' and 'duplication'. Major problems (e.g. delays in the entry and quality of data) were also found in the 'watch lists used to screen visa applicants, refugee claimants and travellers seeking to enter Canada'. Problems also existed with stolen Canadian passports, which were not identifiable on the databases used by Customs officers at the ports of entry (Auditor General 2004: 1–2 and 31). The 2005 report pointed out that, because risk assessments to determine which areas were most in need of funding were not performed, some money has been spent ineffectively, or not at all (Auditor General 2005). Additional problems (e.g. the existence of 225 unguarded cross-border roads and that of 62 other cross-border points where agents do not have access to CBSA computer databases) were revealed in a brief submitted by the CBSA officers' union to the Standing Senate Committee on National Security and Defence.[36]

Conclusions

The events of 11 September have obliged the Canadian government to devote attention to its security policies and institutions, both of which had been neglected for a long time. Before 11 September, Canada, much like other US allies, could afford to pay little attention to security and privilege its 'distinction' from the US also in this field. After 11 September, however, the US administration has experienced a dramatic increase in threat perception. Under these conditions, the price Canada would pay to privilege its national 'distinction' over security could be high, namely the economic consequences of whatever measures the US would consider appropriate to adopt on its northern border. The Liberal government has therefore chosen to begin taking security seriously. It has done so, however, in its own 'distinctive' manner. On the one hand, it has taken some initiatives, mostly concerning border issues, aimed at convincing the US that it is indeed adopting counter-terrorist measures and improving Canadian domestic security. On the other hand, it has tried to minimize their significance, and eschewed choices having symbolic value, such as joining the BMDP, in an attempt to appease Canadian nationalists, a large contingent of whom find their home in the Liberal party.

Such a strategy does not represent a change in the core elements of Canada's 'security culture' (see Table 7.5), defined as the 'set of ideas relevant to security policy that are widely shared within a society or by its political elites' (Duffield 1998: 22). There has not been a general or even simple departure from the country's 'multilateralist' tradition even if some academics have chosen to denounce the government's recent security initiatives in these terms (Knight 2005; Drache

Table 7.5 Canadian security culture

View of external environment	Basic 'liberal–internationalist' view, i.e., belief that 'multilateralism' leads to a more orderly and peaceful world.
National identity	Defined primarily in opposition to the US perception of national role as 'helpful fixer', go-between.
Instrumental preferences	Preference for civilian instruments and soft power (diplomacy, economic aid and development, promotion of human rights) and peacekeeping when necessary.
Interaction preferences	Devotion to multilateral institutions but much attention also paid to bilateral relations with the US given the degree of economic dependence.

2005). As pointed out by Canada's foremost expert on the subject, Tom Keating, 'multilateralism' does not imply a pursuit of international community-wide interests to the detriment of national interests.

More often than not, especially in the case of medium-sized powers, national and multilateral interests simply tend to coincide (Keating 2002: 11). If, and when, the two diverge, national interests prevail. And indeed, Canadian relations with the US have always represented a 'noteworthy exception' to Canadian multilateralism (Keating 2002: 1) which means that Canada has always paid considerably more attention, usually on a bilateral basis, to relations with its southern neighbour. So much so that Keating (2002: 12–13) does not hesitate to characterize Canada's pursuit of multilateralism as a counterweight to its inescapably continentalist policy focus. The same was also suggested by former Canadian Foreign Minister Lester B. Pearson when he wrote that involvement in international organizations 'helped [Canada] to escape the dangers of a too exclusively continental relationship with [its] neighbour without forfeiting the political and economic advantages of that inevitable and vitally important association' (Pearson 1972: 32). It is precisely to defend economic interests that in the post-11 September period Canada has chosen to devote more attention to bilateral relations with the US than to 'multilateralism'. Protecting economic interests is after all an integral part of security policy. As pointed out by Duffield (1998: 17), 'although economic dependence is rarely if ever included in analyses of national security policy, it can nevertheless have an important bearing. In particular, highly dependent states will be more sensitive to how their actions are viewed by their economic partners'. It should also be pointed out that the 'human security' issue in which Canada has achieved some success, that is, the signing of a treaty banning anti-personnel land mines, was pursued outside the UN and other multilateral institutions (Keating 2002: 224).

The problem with the strategy adopted by the Canadian government is not that it betrays Canadian identity but that it might be interpreted south of the border as meaning that Canada does not yet take the terrorist threat seriously enough. In an interview given before leaving his post in March 2005, US Ambassador to Ottawa, Paul Cellucci, reiterated the American belief that 'it is inevitable that terrorists would look to Canada as a potential launching pad to get into the US' and that Canada could itself become a target if 'terrorists think that the US is too hard a target'. He also warned that another attack on the US would inevitably have repercussions on trade relations between the two countries because, in the US at least, 'security trumps trade'.[37] At home, however, the new security initiatives seem to have achieved one important goal, namely to convince Canadians that security must be taken seriously. In July 2002, a majority of Canadians – 77 per cent according to a Pollara survey[38] – believed that a terrorist attack could never happen in Canada, and if it did it would be because of Canadian eagerness to cooperate with the US. In its April 2005 international policy statement, the Canadian government pointed out that 'while some Canadians may feel relatively immune to such [terrorist] dangers, in truth we are not' and warned against the peril of 'complacency' (Government of Canada 2005: 7). By this time, however, the attitude of Canadians had already changed. An August 2005 *Globe and Mail* and a CTV poll revealed that 62 per cent of Canadians now believed that a terrorist act was likely to happen in Canada, 67 per cent believed that Canada was not well prepared to deal with a terrorist threat, 62 per cent supported giving the US information about Canadian citizens suspected of being terrorists, and 81 per cent favoured deporting or jailing anyone who publicly supports terrorists or suicide bombers.[39] Most Canadians, moreover, also disagreed with the opinion of the vociferous intellectual minority, which regards the Anti-Terrorism Act as undermining civil rights. In fact, an EKO public opinion poll taken in February 2005 revealed that 50 per cent of Canadians felt the Act had struck the right balance, 41 per cent believed the government should go even further, while only 7 per cent maintained that Ottawa had gone too far.[40]

Barring a 11 September type of event on US or Canadian soil, however, it is highly unlikely that the Canadian government will abandon its current pragmatic, low-key and low-visibility, step-by-step, sector-by-sector, approach in favour of a grand project such as the construction of a 'continental security perimeter', not least because the selling of such a project to Canadians would require a major public campaign on the part of the government, similar to the one that was necessary to sell the Free Trade Agreement. This is something that Canada's traditional brokerage parties would consider doing only when enjoying comfortable parliamentary majorities and forced by exceptional circumstances.

Acknowledgement

The authors would like to thank Rear-Admiral Ian Mack, Lt Colonel Jonathan Woodgate, Bill McGrath, Frank Harvey and Mark Rhinard for their comments on previous drafts of this chapter.

Notes

1   The importance of an open border for trade purposes can also be gauged by the fact that some 37,000 trucks cross the border between the two countries each day, most of them at five key border crossings – the Ambassador Bridge, Sarnia, Fort Erie (all in Ontario), Lacolle (Quebec) and the Pacific Highway (British Columbia). All trade figures come from the Canadian Department of Foreign Affairs and International Trade. Available online at: <http://geo.international.gc.ca/can-am/washington/trade_and_investment/default_139-en.asp> (accessed 15 November 2006).

2   On the Ressam case, see:<http://www.pbs.org/wgbh/pages/frontline/shows/trail/inside/> (accessed 20 March 2006). A second case is that that of the Khadr family, which has come to be known as 'Canada's al-Qaeda family'. The patriarch of the family, Egyptian-born Ahmed Said Khadr raised funds for al-Qaeda through Human Concern International, a Canadian non-governmental relief agency. Later, he and his sons fought with the Taliban in Afghanistan. Ironically, Pakistani authorities had arrested Ahmed Khadr in 1995 in connection with a bombing of the Egyptian embassy in Islamabad that killed 17 people, but Prime Minister Jean Chrétien pressed then-Pakistani Prime Minister Benazir Bhutto to release Khadr so that he could receive due process in Canada. Once back in Canada, however, Khadr never faced any charge (see <http://www.meforum.org/article/pipes/1639>, accessed 16 November 2005; and

Sands 2002: 55–56). A third case concerns Ghazi Ibrahim Abu Mezer, a Palestinian who received refugee status in Canada in 1994 and then illegally entered the US where he planned to place explosives in the New York subway system ('Plugging a very porous Northern border', *Washington Post,* 8 April 2002; Sands 2002: 57–60). Finally, there is Maher Arar, a Syrian and Canadian citizen arrested on a stopover in New York on his way back to Canada from Tunisia in September 2002. US officials detained him, claiming he had links to al-Qaeda, and then deported him to Syria (see <http://www.cbc.ca/news/background/arar/>, accessed 16 November 2005). The public debate in Canada has focused on the torture that Arar began claiming to have suffered in Syria some time after his return to Canada, but the Americans focus on the network of terrorists with whom he had contacts both in Canada and abroad (Jones 2004: 7). On Canada as a convenient base for terrorists, see Bell (2004).

3 'A majority of Americans polled said potential terrorists arrived from Canada', Canadian Press NewsWire, 11 May 2002.

4 Clarke is also the author of a book highly critical of President Bush's decision to topple Saddam Hussein, something he characterizes as a useless and counterproductive diversion from the most important security task, i.e., fighting al-Qaeda terrorism (Clarke 2004).

5 The term 'distinction' is used here not only to mean sovereignty, independence, and policy autonomy, but also in the sense of 'being different' and hence retaining one's identity. Many in fact argue that the Canadian identity is primarily defined in a negative manner, that is to say 'being Canadian' means primarily being other than American.

6 The proponents include economic elites (Canadian Council of Chief Executives 2004; George and d'Aquino 2003–2004), current (Haynal 2002) as well as former (Dymond and Hart 2003–2004) officials of the Department of Foreign Affairs and International Trade, policy analysts (Segal 2002) as well as some academics (Roussel 2002; Granatstein 2003). For a review of all these proposals, see Goldfarb (2003) and Barry (2003).

7 Quoted in 'Freedoms threatened, watchdog cautions. Canada's privacy commissioner warns anti-terror measures raise many concerns', *London Free Press,* 5 November 2004.

8 Critics of the security perimeter project do not define exactly what these values are, and how, and to what extent, they differ from those of the US. Their arguments simply imply that Canadian values are better than American ones and hence any form of integration with the US should be avoided.

9 These negotiations yielded various agreements such as the 1995 Canada–United States Accord on Our Shared Border, from which the citation in the text is taken. See <http://canada.usembassy.gov/content/can_usa/us_can_border_accord.pdf> (accessed 20 March 2006). They also led to other bilateral initiatives such as the USINS-CIC Border Vision (aimed at improving information sharing between Citizenship and Immigration Canada and the US Immigration and Naturalization Service), and the Cross-Border Crime Forum (aimed at improving cooperation in the fight against transnational crime). Various working groups were also formed, e.g. the 1997 Canadian Anti-Smuggling Working Group and Northeast Border Working Group, both concerned with human and contraband smuggling. For an analysis of the 1990s negotiations, see Sands (2002).

10 Waddell (2003) provides a detailed analysis of the negotiation process after 11 September 2001. He also reports that on 20 September 2001, at a meeting of the Organization of American States in Washington, Manley brushed off the suggestion made by Mexican Foreign Minister Jorge Castaneda that a trilateral approach to border issues be adopted and chose to work alone with the US (Waddell 2003: 58). This was probably the right choice since Canada did not stand to gain anything from merging its economic concerns with other issues affecting US–Mexican border relations. It is also evidence, however, that Canada – notwithstanding the public rhetoric surrounding this issue – does not have a multilateral gene in its national DNA and chooses to act

multilaterally, bilaterally or unilaterally according to its interests and capabilities, just like the US or any other country.

11   For more details, see *US–Canada Smart Border/30 Point Action Plan Update,* available online at: <http://www.whitehouse.gov/news/releases/2002/12/20021206-1.html> (accessed 16 November 2005).

12   The agreement impedes 'asylum shopping' because it obliges refugees to make the claim in the first safe country they reach.

13   For more information on the 'Anti-Terrorism Act', see <http://canada.justice. gc.ca/en/anti_terr/act.html> (accessed 16 November 2005).

14   See the Annual Reports of the Minister of Justice and Attorney General, and of the Solicitor General, available online at: <http://canada.justice.gc.ca/en/anti_terr /reports.html> (accessed 16 November 2005) as well as Roach (2003). Only one Canadian citizen, Pakistani-born and Ottawa resident Mohammad M. Khawaja has been arrested under the provisions of the Act ('Canada "terrorizing" citizens, suspect's father charges', *National Post,* 5 April 2005).

15   'Cotler seeks expanded anti-terror arsenal', *Globe and Mail,* 24 March 2005.

16   For more information about IRPA as well as the text of the Act, see <http://laws/justice.gc.ca/en/I-2.5/index.html> (accessed 27 October 2006).

17   An 'in-country refugee' is a person who submits a request for asylum to a country of his/her choice after travelling there as opposed to submitting a request from outside, usually from a camp operated by the United Nations High Commissioner for Refugees.

18   Gallagher (2002: 110), for instance, cites Immigration and Refugee Board documents on refugee case law arguing that 'economic deprivations may be components of persecution' and that 'education is a basic human right' and hence 'a nine year old claimant who could have avoided persecution only by refusing to go to school was deemed to be a Convention refugee'. He also reports that a woman with two children was granted refugee status because in their country they would have been 'subjected to Sharia law'. If applied consistently, these interpretations would make most Muslim women eligible for refugee status in Canada.

19   On this point, see also Sands (2002: 13) and 'Liberals complain that tougher rules could cost party its bedrock immigrant support', *National Post,* 14 January 2002.

20   Criticism of this provision has come not only from human rights and ethnic groups, immigration lawyers and consultants, and the NDP but also from libertarians usually on the right side of the political spectrum, such as *National Post* columnist George Jonas.

21   One of them, the Moroccan Adil Charkaoui, has been released on bail, a choice which even the liberal *Globe and Mail* characterized as a 'keep your fingers crossed decision' (19 February 2005).

22   'Terror suspect laws under scrutiny', *Globe and Mail,* 29 March 2005.

23   'Supreme Court reviews terror law', *Globe and Mail,* 25 August 2005.

24   Office of the Privacy Commissioner of Canada, News Release of 1 November 2002, available online at: <http://www.privcom.gc.ca/media/nr-c/02_05_b_021101_e.asp> (accessed 16 November 2005). Mr. Radwanski would later resign because of a series of scandals concerning his expense account, and was replaced by Ms Jennifer Stoddart.

25   *Backgrounder – Highlights of the Public Safety Act, 2002.* Available online at: <http://www.tc.gc.ca/mediaroom/releases/nat/2004/04-gc004ae.htm> (accessed 16 November 2005).

26   'Liberals back missile shield', *National Post,* 14 January 2005; 'PM reneged: Cellucci', *National Post,* 7 March 2005; see also Fergusson 2001.

27   In doing so, Martin was aligning the country with the preference of a very large majority of Quebeckers, a slim majority of Canadians as a whole ('Canadians open to missile plan: poll', *National Post* 28 February 2005), and a good number of Liberal party members while going against that of his Defence Minister and Canadian business leaders ('85% of CEOs say shield refusal bad for business', *National Post,* 7 March 2005).

28 Its website curiously claims that PSEP was created to fulfil 'the fundamental role of government to secure the public's safety and security'. Taken literally, the claim implies that the Canadian government did not fulfil one of the major functions of government until 12 December 2003, the date of inception of PSEP. See <http://www.psepc-sppcc.gc.ca/index_e.asp> (accessed 16 November 2005). In reality, until the creation of PSEP, Canada's security was the responsibility of various departments and related agencies (e.g. National Defence, Solicitor General, Foreign Affairs, Citizenship and Immigration, Customs and Revenue, Transport).
29 For a detailed analysis of the proposed National Security Committee of Parliamentarians see the Consultation Paper, available online at: <http://ww2.psepc-sppcc-gc.ca/publications/national_security/nat_sec_cmte_e.asp> (accessed 15 November 2006).
30 Online, available at: <http://www.psepc.gc.ca/prg/ns/ccrs/> (accessed 15 November 2006).
31 Online, available at: <http://www.csis-scrs.gc.ca/en/newsroom/backgrounders/backgrounder13.asp> (accessed 20 March 2006).
32 CSIS is a civilian agency, established in 1984. It took over the intelligence activities performed until then by the RCMP. This section relies on the overview of Canadian intelligence provided by Rudner (2002a and 2002b).
33 *Backgrounder – Canada Command,* available online at: <http://www.forces.gc.ca/site/newsroom/view_news_e.asp?id=1692> (accessed 27 October 2006).
34 See also Higginbotham and Heynen (2005) and Grieve (2003).
35 'Ailing Forces get big boost', *National Post,* 24 February 2005.
36 'Customs agents warn Senate that security gaps are critical' *National Post,* 11 April 2005.
37 'Wake up on terror, Cellucci warns Canada', *National Post,* 7 February 2005; Cellucci (2005); see also Harvey (2004).
38 Online, available at: <http://www.pollara.ca/Library/News/terrorsubsiding.html> (accessed 20 March 2006).
39 'Canadians want strict security, poll finds', *Globe and Mail,* 11 August 2005.
40 'Anti-terrorism law effective as it is, McLellan insists', *Globe and Mail,* 15 February 2005.

References

Auditor General (2004) *National Security in Canada – The 2001 Anti-Terrorism Initiative,* Report of the Auditor General of Canada to the House of Commons, Chapter 3. Available online at: <http://www.oag-bvg.gc.ca/domino/reports.nsf/html/20040303ce.html/$file/20040303ce.pdf> (accessed 16 November 2005).
Auditor General (2005) *National Security in Canada – The 2001 Anti-Terrorism Initiative – Air Transportation Security, Marine Security, and Emergency Preparedness,* Report of the Auditor General of Canada to the House of Commons, Chapter 2. Available online at: <http://www.oag-bvg.gc.ca/domino/reports.nsf/html/20050402ce.html/$file/20050402ce.pdf> (accessed 16 November 2005).
Axworthy, L. (2003) *Navigating a New World. Canada's Global Future,* Toronto: Alfred A. Knopf Canada.
Barry, D. (2003) 'Managing Canada–US relations in the post 11 September era. Do we need a big idea?', Washington DC: Center for Strategic and International Studies, Policy Paper on the Americas, Volume XIV, Study 11.

Bell, S. (2004) *Cold Terror: How Canada Nurtures and Exports Terrorism Around the World,* Toronto: John Wiley & Sons Canada Ltd.

Bercuson, D. (2003) 'Canada–US defence relations post-11 September', in D. Carment, F.O. Hampson and N. Hillmer (eds) *Canada Among Nations 2003: Coping with the American Colossus,* Don Mills: Oxford University Press.

Brunet-Jailly, E. (2004) 'NAFTA, economic integration, and the Canadian–American security regime in the post-September 11, 2001 era: multi-level governance and transparent border?', *Journal of Borderland Studies* 19 (1): 123–42.

Canadian Council of Chief Executives (2004) *New Frontiers: Building a 21st Century Canada–United States Partnership in North America,* North American Security and Prosperity Initiative discussion paper, Ottawa. Available online at: <http://www.ceo-council.ca/publications/pdf/8502a13cf417d09eab13468e2a7c9f65/New_Frontiers_NASPI_Discussion_Paper_April_2004.pdf> (accessed 16 November 2005).

Cellucci, P. (2005) *Unquiet Diplomacy,* Toronto: Key Porter Books.

Clarke, R.A. (2004) *Against All Enemies: Inside America's War on Terror,* New York: The Free Press.

Clarke, R.A. (2005) 'Ten years later', *The Atlantic* 295 (1): 61–77.

CSIS (Canadian Security Intelligence Service) (2003) *Public Report.* Available online at: <http://www.csis-scrs.gc.ca/en/publications/annual_report/2003/report2003.asp> (accessed 27 October 2006).

Dawson, G. (2003) 'A special case: Canada, Operation Apollo, and Multilateralism', in D. Carment, F.O. Hampson and N. Hillmer (eds) *Canada Among Nations 2003: Coping with the American Colossus,* Don Mills: Oxford University Press.

DFAIT (Department of Foreign Affairs and International Trade – Canada) (n.d.) *Canada's actions against terrorism since September 11th.* Available online at: <http://www.duke.edu/web/northamer/program/Canadactions.html> (accessed 16 November 2005).

DND (Department of National Defence – Canada) (2002) *Enhanced Canada–US Security Cooperation.* Available online at: <http://www.forces.gc.ca/site/newsroom/view_news_e.asp?id=509> (accessed 27 October 2006).

Drache, D. (2005) '"Friends at a distance": reframing Canada's strategic priorities after the Bush revolution in foreign policy', in A.F. Cooper and D. Rowlands (eds) *Canada Among Nations 2005: Split Images,* Montréal-Kingston: McGill-Queen's University Press.

Duffield, J.S. (1998) *World Power Forsaken. Political Culture, International Institutions and German Security Policy after Unification,* Stanford: Stanford University Press.

Dymond, B. and Hart, M. (2003–2004) 'The Potemkin village of Canadian foreign policy', *Policy Options* 25 (1): 39–45.

Federal Research Division (2003) *Nations Hospitable to Organized Crime and Terrorism,* Washington DC: Library of Congress, October.

Fergusson, J. (2001) 'National missile defense, homeland defense, and outer space: policy dilemmas in the Canada–U.S. relationship', in F.O. Hampson, N. Hillmer and M. Appel Molot (eds) *Canada Among Nations 2001: The Axworthy Legacy,* Don Mills: Oxford University Press.

Gallagher, S. (2002) 'The open door beyond the moat: Canadian refugee policy from a comparative perspective', in N. Hillmer and M. Appel Molot (eds) *Canada Among Nations, 2002: A Fading Power?,* Toronto: Oxford University Press.

George, R.L. and d'Aquino, T.P. (2003–2004) 'Memo to the Prime Minister: building our country, and shaping Canada's role in the world', *Policy Options* 25 (1): 68–73.

Goldfarb, D. (2003) 'Beyond labels: comparing proposals for closer Canada–US economic relations', *C. D. Howe Institute Backgrounder* 76.

Gotlieb, A. (2003) 'Foremost partner: the conduct of Canada–US relations', in D. Carment, F.O. Hampson and N. Hillmer (eds) *Canada Among Nations 2003: Coping with the American Colossus,* Don Mills: Oxford University Press.

Gotlieb, A. (2005) 'Romanticism and realism in Canada's foreign policy', *Policy Options* 26 (2): 16–27.

Government of Canada (2005) *Canada's International Policy Statement: A Role of Pride and Influence in the World.* Available online at: <http://www.dfait-maeci.gc.ca/cip-pic/IPS/IPS-Overview.pdf> (accessed 16 November 2005).

Granatstein, J.L. (2003) *The Importance of Being Less Earnest: Promoting Canada's National Interests through Tighter Ties with the U.S,* Toronto: C. D. Howe Institute.

Granatstein, J.L. (2004) *Who Killed the Canadian Military?,* Toronto: Harper Flamingo.

Grieve, M. (2003) 'Downloading security: defence and emergency preparedness before and after 11 September', paper presented to the Atlantic Provinces Political Studies Association, St. John's.

Harvey, F.P. (2004) *Smoke and Mirrors. Globalized Terrorism and the Illusion of Multilateral Security,* Toronto: University of Toronto Press.

Haynal, G. (2002) 'Interdependence, globalization and North-American borders', *Policy Options* 23 (6): 20–6.

Higginbotham, J. and Heynen, J. (2005) 'Managing through networks: the state of Canada–US Relations', in D. Carment, F.O. Hampson and N. Hillmer (eds) *Canada Among Nations 2004: Setting Priorities Straight,* Montreal and Kingston: McGill-Queen's University Press.

Hillmer, N. and Appel Molot, M. (eds) (2002) *Canada Among Nations, 2002: A Fading Power?,* Toronto: Oxford University Press.

Jackson, A. (2003) 'Why the "Big Idea" is a bad idea', *Policy Options* 24 (4): 26–8.

Jones, D.T. (2004) 'When security trumps economics: the new template of Canada–US relations', *Policy Options* 25 (6): 3–8.

Keating, T. (2002) *Canada and World Order. The Multilateralist Tradition in Canadian Foreign Policy,* 2nd edn, Oxford: Oxford University Press.

King, D.L. (2002) 'We need a Romanow Commission for defence and foreign policy', *Policy Options* 23 (3): 7–14.

Knight, W.A. (2005) 'Plurilateral multilateralism: Canada's emerging international policy?', in A.F. Cooper and D. Rowlands (eds) *Canada Among Nations 2005: Split Images,* Montréal-Kingston: McGill-Queen's University Press.

Mason, D.N. (2003) 'US–Canada defence relations: a view from Washington', in D. Carment, F.O. Hampson and N. Hillmer (eds) *Canada Among Nations 2003: Coping with the American Colossus,* Don Mills: Oxford University Press.

McGrath, B. (2006) 'A change of road: Canadian foreign policy from Kosovo to Iraq', in O. Croci and A. Verdun (eds) *The Transatlantic Divide. Foreign and Security Policies in the Atlantic Alliance from Kosovo to Iraq,* Manchester: Manchester University Press.

Morton, D. (2004) 'Keynote address to the Inter-University Seminar on Armed Forces and Society', Toronto, 1 October 2004.

Pearson, L.B. (1972) *Mike: The Memoirs of the Right Honourable Lester B. Pearson,* vol. 2, Toronto: University of Toronto Press.

Pratt, D. (2004) *Speaking notes for The Honourable David Pratt, P.C., M.P. Minister of National Defence for an appearance before the Standing Committee on National Defence and Veterans Affairs (SCONDVA), 1 April.* Available online at: <http://www.forces.gc.ca/site/newsroom/view_news_e.asp?id=1340> (accessed 16 November 2005).

Privy Council Office (2004) *Securing an Open Society: Canada's National Security Policy,* Ottawa. Available online at: <www.pco-bcp.gc.ca> (accessed 16 November 2005).

Roach, K. (2003) *September 11: Consequences for Canada,* Montréal-Kingston: McGill-Queen's University Press.

Roussel, S. (2002) 'Le Canada et le périmètre de sécurité nord-américain: sécurité, souveraineté ou prospérité?' *Policy Options* 23 (3): 15–22.

Rudner, M. (2002a) 'Contemporary threats, future tasks: Canadian intelligence and the challenges of global security', in N. Hillmer and M. Appel Molot (eds) *Canada Among Nations, 2002: A Fading Power?,* Toronto: Oxford University Press.

Rudner, M. (2002b) 'The globalization of terrorism: Canada's intelligence response to the post-September 11 threat environment', *Canadian Issues,* September 2002.

Sands, C. (2002) 'Fading power or rising power: 11 September and lessons from the Section 110 experience', in N. Hillmer and M. Appel Molot (eds) *Canada Among Nations, 2002: A Fading Power?,* Toronto: Oxford University Press.

Segal, H. (2002) 'The Canadian–American defence relationship: nostalgia ain't what it used to be', *Policy Options* 23 (3): 23–6.

Waddel, C. (2003) 'Erasing the line: rebuilding economic and trade relations after 11 September', in D. Carment, F.O. Hampson and N. Hillmer (eds) *Canada Among Nations 2003: Coping with the American Colossus,* Don Mills: Oxford University Press.

8 United States

The unrelenting search for an existential threat in the twenty-first century

James Sperling

The end of the Cold War and the eventual dissolution of the Soviet Union left the United States bereft of an existential threat. The administrations of George H.W. Bush and William Clinton struggled with the intellectual challenge and policy task of substituting the containment of the Soviet Union with a positive security strategy facilitating the political and economic transitions of the former Warsaw Pact states and the successor republics of the former Soviet Union (FSU). The terrorist attacks on the World Trade Center and the Pentagon on 11 September 2001 accelerated the reorientation of the American security strategy and the reconceptualization of security. Just as in the past communism and the Soviet Union posed an existential threat to the American way of life, 'radical Islam' and Muslim terrorists pose one today. The simplicity of the struggle between capitalism and communism has been largely reduced to a simplistically conceived clash between Christendom and Islam, despite public protests to the contrary. The ambiguities of the immediate post-Cold War world have given way to the certainties of an Islamic 'other' at war with the West.

This new Manichean worldview comports well with the historical trajectory of American foreign policy, particularly its rise to great power status in the late nineteenth century and the consolidation of its position as the dominant power over the course of the twentieth century. The American self-image has been that of a state acting as an agent, if not God's agent, for good in the world and for righting geopolitical wrongs. The Wilsonian compulsion conflates a high-blown universalistic rhetoric with the national interest; the legitimizing rhetoric of American foreign policy substitutes the defence of national interests with the selfless task of building a just world order, spreading democracy, and ensuring global prosperity. This American exceptionalism – the pursuit of an other regarding foreign policy implementing and protecting universal values on a global scale – reflects both Christianity's proselytizing imperative and functions as a legitimizing salve for the pursuit of narrow national interests. Moreover, the fascist and communist threats confronting the United States between 1931 and 1989 encouraged a reflexive reliance upon a universalistic rhetoric. America's adversaries were repeatedly treated as outsized threats to the United States and the American way of life. This foreign policy tradition has continued into the twenty-first century, but an intractable clash of civilizations has substituted for the ideological struggles of the twentieth century.

Security threat perceptions

The geopolitical ambiguity of the post-1989 world posed a considerable challenge for the American foreign policy establishment, particularly the crafting of a
coherent strategy akin to containment that could provide a common frame of reference for the conduct of foreign policy by Democrats and Republicans alike.
While the goal of stability remains a constant and provides an element of continuity between the three post-1989 administrations, the nature and sources of threats
evolved from a general preoccupation with the necessity of democratizing and
stabilizing Central and Eastern Europe to alarm over the emergence of China as a
peer competitor in the Asia–Pacific and the activities of malevolent non-state
actors, particularly Muslim terrorists, and rogue states subverting the nuclear non-
proliferation regime.[1] These later concerns emerged during the second Clinton
administration and have dominated the security agenda since 11 September.

Academic debate

The academic debate in the United States has two distinct but interdependent trajec-
tories. The first revolves around the theory that best defines the content of American
foreign policy and America's role in the international system. This theoretical
debate, which some would no doubt dismiss as relatively harmless in consequence,
has had important policy implications, particularly when scholars and public intel-
lectuals become policy-makers.[2] The second, more prosaic debate centres on the
definition of what constitutes a threat and where those threats originate.

The policy debate on the source and nature of the threats to the United States
anticipates and reflects upon untoward developments in the international system.
Articles published between 1995 and 2005 in *Foreign Affairs*, the publication of
the non-partisan Council on Foreign Relations, and *International Security*, one of
the leading academic journals on security affairs, provide a rough approximation
of how the vetted foreign policy elite perceives the most pressing categories and
sources of post-Cold War threats facing the United States. Five dominant categories of security threat emerge in these journals (measured in terms of the
number of dedicated articles appearing in both journals): international terrorism
(29 articles); nuclear proliferation (26 articles); energy insecurity (15 articles);
ethnic conflict (12 articles); and national missile defence and missile proliferation
(9 articles). Ten other categories of threat – primarily those associated with the
new security agenda – received episodic or epiphenomenal treatment. All of the
major geopolitical regions of the world are portrayed as posing some kind of
security challenge to the United States, particularly the Middle East as it pertains
to the Arab–Israeli conflict. Europe, which no longer presents the security pathology it once did, no longer enjoys the attention lavished on it during the Cold War.
Instead, attention has been redirected to the Indian subcontinent and East Asia (19
articles each), Eurasia (9 articles), the Korean Peninsula (8 articles), and the
Persian Gulf (7 articles). China emerges as the most important potential adversary
of the United States: 55 articles were devoted to the implications of China's rise as

a global power or peer competitor. Iran and Iraq are the only two other countries meriting sustained attention, although the bulk of the articles on Iraq were published in the run-up to and after the American-led invasion in 2003.

The longest-lived foreign debate in the Anglo-Saxon foreign policy community has been between 'realists' and 'utopians' (Carr 1938). That debate continues today, albeit in a different guise. At one level, scholars have been mired in sorting out and testing the competing claims of neorealism (Waltz 1979; Gilpin 1981; Mearsheimer 2001), neoliberal institutionalism (Martin and Simmons 1998; March and Olsen 1998), and constructivism (Wendt 1994; Jepperson *et al.* 1996; Finnemore and Sikkink 1998). Like much else in American public life, these debates have generated as much heat as light. The most critical policy relevant debate, however, is between the realists and neoconservatives. Realists favour a foreign policy that judiciously blends American power with a respect for international law and participation in international institutions – even if they are sceptical about the effectiveness of either – as substantive as well as instrumental foreign policy objectives (Carr 1938; Wolfers 1962; Osgood 1953). The neoconservatives, however, have captured the key foreign policy posts in the current Bush administration (Mann 2004). Their foreign policy philosophy evinces a millennial fatalism that democracy will triumph and that America has a duty to ensure that it does.

Francis Fukuyama (2006) identifies the three core principles of the neoconservative worldview: domestic constitutional orders are projected externally and therefore matter; states have a positive obligation to intervene in the affairs of others to create the conditions for the emergence of democratic states or to effect regime change allowing democracies to flourish; and international law and institutions are weak reeds on which to rest the edifice of American foreign policy or to sustain world order. Charles Krauthammer, a prominent neoconservative journalist, has summarized the neoconservative vision of America's appropriate role in the world: the United States should support 'democracy everywhere, but we will commit blood and treasure only in places ... central to the larger war against the existential enemy, the enemy that poses a global moral threat to freedom', namely an 'Arab–Islamic totalitarianism' akin to Nazi Germany in content and ambition.[3] Just as the proponents of the democratic peace hypothesis, who accept Immanuel Kant's early assertion that democratic states are unlikely to go to war with one another, conclude that more democracy means more peace, neoconservatives hold as an article of faith that the imposition of democracy by the force of arms spontaneously generates peace and order without the supporting infrastructure of binding international law and robust institutions mediating inevitable conflicts of interest. Neoconservatives strongly believe in the transformative power, resiliency and desirability of democracy in every corner of the world regardless of pre-existing political traditions or historical experience. The neoconservative worldview overestimates the reach of American power and has created a racial and theological 'other' that legitimizes the transgression of established international law. Like the liberal foreign policy establishment that mired the United States in Vietnam, the neoconservative worldview has produced an unnecessary and costly war.

The executive branch

The post-Cold War international system has produced a remarkable degree of continuity in American security and defence policies, particularly with respect to definition and origin of threat. Changes have occurred, however, in administration perceptions of the primary agents of threat, the perceived utility of force in meeting those threats, and the pattern of interaction with allies and adversaries alike. With the end of the Cold War, the Bush administration announced that the United States needed to move beyond containment. Yet the administration remained committed to preventing 'any hostile power or group of powers from dominating the Eurasian land mass' (White House 1990: 1). American interests were conceived within an intellectual framework that retained a traditional geo-strategic understanding of security while acknowledging the interdependence of national security and economic power. Even under the aegis of fostering democracy and the market economy, the security strategy emphasized the desire to 'maintain stable regional military balances to deter those powers that might seek regional dominance' (White House 1990: 2–3). As the Bush administration focused on the requirements of facilitating the transition to democracy in Central and Eastern Europe (CEE), the American security strategy increasingly appreciated the importance of the non-military instruments. This appreciation was linked to the idea that market-oriented democracies were more likely to share the values and interests of the United States.

The Clinton administration, which downgraded further the reliance on military force to meet the security threats facing the United States, predicated its strategy of engagement and enlargement upon the assumption that the future security of the Euro–Atlantic region depended upon the successful transitions to democracy and the market economy in the CEE states as well as the republics of the FSU, particularly the Russian Federation. This strategy modified the Bush administration's strategy of engagement and leadership. The change was more than cosmetic, but it obscured as much as it revealed. The Clinton administration went much further than the Bush administration in demonstrating a greater willingness to employ the non-military instruments of diplomacy to achieve American security objectives. It also recognized that the security threats facing the United States had changed qualitatively; security threats were no longer solely military in nature and were increasingly transnational phenomena, particularly terrorism and organized crime. These new threats were expected to dominate the future security agenda.

The Bush administration's final National Security Strategy (1993) identified four major threats to the United States: nuclear proliferation stemming from unsecured nuclear materials in the FSU, particularly in Ukraine and Kazakhstan; a generic concern with terrorism; the nexus between narcotics and transnational organized crime; and an undefined challenge to American military–strategic dominance (see Table 8.1). The Clinton administration published two national security strategies, the first in 1995 and the second in 1999. Both identified a relatively stable number of traditional security threats: the acquisition of nuclear weapons by Iran, Iraq, North Korea and other rogue states; the proliferation of nuclear weapons

Table 8.1 Threat perception in the National Security Strategy 1993–2006

	1993	1995	1999	2002	2006
Nuclear Proliferation		+	+	+	+
– FSU	+	+	+	+	
– Iran		+	+	+	+
– Iraq		+	+	+	
– North Korea			+	+	+
– Rogue states			+	+	+
– Terrorists				+	+
Biological weapons proliferation				+	+
Chemical weapons proliferation			+	+	+
Missile technology proliferation		+	+	+	+
– Iran			+		
– North Korea		+	+	+	
Terrorism	+	+	+	+	+
– Radical Islam/al-Qaeda			+	+	+
– WMD				+	+
Drugs	+	+	+		
Disease (HIV/AIDS)			+	+	+
Energy supply		+	+	+	
Environment		+	+		
Failed states			+		
Infrastructure			+	+	+
Imbalance of power	+			+	
Tyranny and repression					+

Sources: White House 1993, 1995, 1999, 2002a and 2006.

owing to the continuing problem of securing nuclear materials and sites in the Russian Federation; missile technology proliferation, particularly its acquisition by Iran and North Korea; terrorism, including specific references to al-Qaeda and Osama bin Laden. By 1999, the Clinton administration turned its attention to a number of security threats often best addressed with the 'soft' elements of power: cyber-vandalism and information warfare; the proliferation of dangerous technologies; environmental and health threats (irreparable damage to regional ecosystems or epidemics); and the flow of narcotics into the United States.[4]

President George W. Bush issued his first National Security Strategy (NSS) in 2002 and updated it in 2006 (White House 2002a; 2006). His administration has focused upon Islamic terrorist groups and their acquisition of chemical, biological, radiological and nuclear (CBRN) devices, and upon the acquisition of nuclear, chemical and biological weapons by the three states constituting the 'Axis of Evil' – Iran, Iraq and North Korea. While many of these concerns were held in common with the previous Clinton administration, the 2002 NSS was clearly preoccupied with the threat posed by 'radical Islam', which eventually mutated into a Sunni jihadist or extremist movement (Tenet 2003; Loy 2005). In the 2006 iteration of the NSS, the administration employed inflammatory rhetoric describing the 'War on Terror' as a fight 'against terrorists and against their murderous ideology' and claimed that al-Qaeda sought 'a totalitarian empire that denies all political and religious freedom' (White House 2006: 1, 9). The administration also adopted and then modified the Cold War syllogism, substituting terrorism for communism: democracy was 'the opposite of terrorist tyranny' and that terrorism presents a threat to democracy everywhere (White House 2006: 11). Unsurprisingly, the foreign policy corollary equates the presence of tyranny or repression anywhere in the world as a direct threat to the United States. A second change emerged in the strategic objectives of the United States between 1995 and 1999. In 1995, the Clinton administration echoed the previous Bush administration's concern about preventing another hegemon from emerging on the European continent (White House 1995: 25; cf. Hamilton 1997: 91). At century's end, it nonetheless adopted two assumptions of a 'civilian power': first, that peace in Europe was contingent upon continent-wide political and economic stability; second, direct and indirect security threats were diffused throughout the international system and were best addressed in multilateral forums (White House 1999: 29).

The Clinton administration's NSS identified three categories of interest that justified the calibrated use of American armed force: vital interests, important interests, and humanitarian interests. Vital interests were defined generally as the defence of American territorial integrity, national survival, and defence of allies. Important interests were defined as interests that do not affect national survival, but 'affect importantly our national well-being and the character of the world in which we live.' Humanitarian interests only called for the use of American armed forces where military capabilities are necessary to alleviate human suffering and when 'the risk to American troops is minimal' (White House 1995: 12). This threat hierarchy, however, is specific to American security interests and does not appear to be readily generalizeable for America's allies in Europe or Asia. European and Asian security officials and experts are unlikely to be persuaded that either Somalia, Rwanda or, especially, Haiti meet even the slack criteria of an important threat justifying the deployment of force; Europeans are likely to consider the civil conflicts in Kosovo and Bosnia as having transgressed the boundary demarcating a vital interest from an important one – an assessment not shared by either Asians or Americans (Carter and Perry 1999; Carter 1999–2000). The American approach to security remains narrowly national in the definition of interest and threat, was largely state-centric prior to 11 September, and only slowly appreciated the security implications of malevolent non-state actors, a failing no doubt corrected in the recent past.

Correspondingly, the Department of Defense (DoD) has produced a fairly tightly defined set of security threats, most of which either threaten US combat forces (biological and chemical warfare particularly) or target the acquisition of nuclear weapons by rogue states and proliferation more generally (see Table 8.2). The war against terror has become *the* preoccupation of the DoD, although combating terrorism has become virtually indistinguishable from concerns with rogue regimes, particularly North Korea, Iraq, Iran and Syria. Notably, China has emerged as America's most likely, if not certain, competitor for geo-strategic dominance in Central Asia and the Asia–Pacific. While views of China's ambitions do vary widely within the current administration, the DoD has long been

Table 8.2 Threat perception of the Department of Defense 1992–2005

	1992	1994	2000	2002	2004	2005
Nuclear proliferation	+	+	+	+	+	+
– Rogue states				+	+	
Chemical and biological weapons proliferation				+		
Missile technology proliferation				+		
Peer competitor						
– China			+			+[a]
– India			+			
– Russian Federation			+			
Collapse of Russian Federation	+	+				
Terrorism			+	+	+	+
Infrastructure			+			
Loss of dominance					+	
Energy security			+			
Rogue states				+	+	
Sovereign free territory						+

a   Department of Defense 2005a.
Sources: Department of Defense 1992, 1994, 2000, 2004, 2005b and 2005d.

wary of Chinese military power and its ability to degrade the dominance the United States currently enjoys in Asia (DoD 2005a).

The 2002 National Strategy for Homeland Security (NSHS) identified a biological, chemical, nuclear or radiological attack on the homeland as the major threat facing the United States (Office of Homeland Security 2002: vii; cf. Fingar 2005). America's vulnerability to CBRN terrorism was ascribed to the liabilities facing any open society, long and difficult-to-control borders, unsecured key infrastructures, and an extraordinarily large number of soft, valuable targets (Office of Homeland Security 2002: 7–10). Yet, the preoccupation with homeland security preceded both 11 September and the Bush administration. Presidential Decision Directive-63 (PDD-63), issued in 1998, had already recognized the problem of protecting critical infrastructures in the United States and led to the creation of the National Infrastructure Protection Center housed in the FBI. The primary menaces to the American infrastructure were identified as an attack on information networks by vandals, organized crime and terrorists, as a form of foreign espionage, or as a component of an adversary's strategic attack. Cyberspace presented a double-edged threat to the United States: first, information warfare could erase the battlefield advantages of net-centric warfare which was key to the modernization of the American forces; second, the government and public rely upon cyberspace for every aspect of daily life and that dependence left society and the state vulnerable to threats ranging from cyber-vandalism to cyber-terrorism (Freeh 1998; Vatis 2000: 5; cf. Goslin 2000; Department of Justice 2003; Federal Bureau of Investigation 2004). The concern with protecting cyberspace only accelerated after 11 September. The Bush administration also understood that protecting cyberspace was particularly problematic owing to the absence of defensible boundaries and the relatively low barrier to carrying out a successful attack (White House 2003b: 6–7).

The Clinton administration also implemented a Key Asset Program targeting potential attacks on critical infrastructures. The catalogue of critical infrastructures identified in 1998 included government and private sector telecommunications and information systems, critical sectors of the economy highly dependent upon information technologies (banking and finance), energy distribution networks, and transportation systems (Vatis 1999: 1). The Bush administration's national strategy for the protection of critical infrastructures responded to the dramatic demonstration on 11 September that the United States was not only vulnerable to terrorist attacks, but that the American (and global) financial system could have come unglued had the terrorists targeted the New York Stock Exchange or the New York Federal Reserve. In the USA Patriot Act, the Bush administration not only expanded the number of categories constituting critical infrastructures, but added to the list national monuments and icons, both considered 'symbolically equated with traditional values and institutions or US political and economic power' (White House 2003a: viii).[5]

Public and elite threat perception

Public and elite threat perceptions have not diverged markedly since 1990. Prior to 1989, the Soviet Union and communism were viewed as *the* threats to the United States. In fact, this threat was treated as virtually self-evident in the public opinion polls conducted by the Chicago Council on Foreign Relations (CCFR). The public's perception of threat, like that of the elite, has undergone fundamental changes since 1990 (see Tables 8.3 and 8.4). At the end of the Cold War, economic competition from Japan emerged as the only threat to the United States mentioned by over 60 per cent of the respondents. As the 1990s progressed, Japan experienced its 'lost decade' of economic stagnation and the public fully discounted Japan as a threat. The only persistent post-Cold War threat of importance has been the potential emergence of China as a world power threatening either American prerogatives or American interests in the Asia–Pacific. Between 1994 and 11 September 2001, the public identified the critical threats to the United States as international terrorism (84 per cent), unfriendly countries acquiring nuclear weapons (75 per cent), chemical and biological weapons proliferation (76 per cent), pandemics (72 per cent) and uncontrolled immigration (55 per cent). These threats and 11 September produced a threat complex that elevated the importance of international terrorism and diminished the purchase of traditional threats (e.g. the emergence of China as a peer competitor). The post-11 September threat complex contracted to matters directly threatening personal security or serving as a potential *casus belli:* international terrorism (81 per cent), chemical and biological weapons proliferation (70 per cent), unfriendly countries acquiring nuclear weapons (66 per cent), and the Israeli–Arab conflict (43 per cent). Perhaps surprisingly, the public did not accept that Islamic fundamentalism threatened the United States, perhaps revealing the public's assumption that the criminal acts of individuals do not necessarily reflect the tenets of a confession.

The elite surveys conducted over the post-Cold War period do not differ significantly from the public perception of threat, although that conclusion requires some qualification. While the elites, like the public, viewed Japan, and to a lesser extent Europe, as the primary threats to the United States in 1990, Japan's economic reversal of fortune and Europe's stagnant growth immediately led to the downgrading of both as threats to the United States. The elite lagged behind the public in their perception of China as a potential threat to American interests in the Asia–Pacific despite the considerable and escalating interest in China's economic and military capabilities found in the academic and policy literature. Foreign policy elites have also developed a post-11 September threat complex, but slightly different weights are given to its constituent elements; they view the militarization of the Arab–Israeli conflict as the second greatest threat to American interests (73 per cent) and Islamic fundamentalism as a critical threat (61 per cent).[6] The most glaring differences between elite and public threat perception, however, are located in the different assessments of low wage countries (7 per cent versus 31 per cent) and uncontrolled immigration (14 per cent versus 51 per cent). These divergences are easily explained: the public, rather than the elite, suffers the downward pressure on wages and loss of jobs attending globalization and contends with the difficult process of social integration and dislocation attending uncontrolled immigration.

The perception of threat – as well as responses to those threats – can also be inferred from the public and elite views of 'important foreign policy goals'.

Table 8.3 Public post-Cold War threat perceptions 1990–2004[a]

	1990	1994	1998	2002	2004
Economic power of Japan	60	62	45		
Military power of Soviet Union/Russia	33	32	34		
China as world power	40	57	57	56	40
Economic competition from Europe	30	27	24	13	20
International terrorism		69	84	91	81
Unfriendly power becoming nuclear power		72	75	85	66
Large numbers of immigrants and refugees		72	55	60	51
Islamic fundamentalism		33	38	61	38
Chemical and biological weapons			76	86	70
AIDS, Ebola virus and other potential epidemics			72	68	55
Global warming			43	46	37
Economic competition from low wage countries			40	31	35
Military conflict between Israel and Arab neighbours				67	43
World population growth				44	30

a Empty cells indicate that question was not asked.
Source: Chicago Council on Foreign Relations 2004b: 6–12.

Table 8.4 Elite threat perception post-Cold War 1990–2002[a]

	1990	1994	1998	2002
China as world power	15	46	56	47
Economic competition from Europe	41	11	16	9
Military power of Soviet Union/Russia	20	16	19	7
Economic power of Japan	63	21	14	5
International terrorism		33	61	83
Unfriendly power becoming nuclear power		61	67	72
Islamic fundamentalism		39	31	61
Large numbers of immigrants and refugees		31	18	14
Chemical and biological weapons			64	67
AIDS, Ebola virus and other potential epidemics			34	48
Global warming			27	28
Economic competition from low wage countries			16	7
Military conflict between Israel and Arab neighbours				73
World population growth				25

a   Empty cells indicate that question not asked.
Source: CCFR and German Marshall Fund 2002: 20–7.

Neither the elite nor public is particularly concerned with maintaining global military superiority, despite the DoD's desire to ensure the United States full spectrum dominance (DoD 2001), an attitude that may reflect a common assumption that dominance is a foregone conclusion or that military dominance is of limited utility in the new security environment.[7] The only foreign policy goal that persistently preoccupied both elites and public was nuclear proliferation. The public and elite have been in general concordance in terms of the hierarchy of foreign policy goals: they agree on the need to combat international terrorism (71 per cent and 84 per cent) and to secure a stable supply of energy (69 per cent and 57 per cent); they also agree on the unimportance of spreading democracy throughout the world (14 per cent and 29 per cent). They do diverge, however, on the relative importance of those foreign policy goals connected to the new security agenda (Reilly 1987: 12; 1991: 15; CCFR 2004a: 13–20; 2004b: 13–20).

Sources of threat

The sources of threat have remained fairly constant in the post-Cold War period. Two critical sources of threat assessment are found in the NSS (see Table 8.5) as well as the global threat assessments presented by the Director of Central Intelligence (DCI) in annual hearings before the Senate Armed Services and Intelligence Committees. Surprisingly, the executive branch and intelligence community did not share identical assessments, primarily because the executive branch initially took a broader view of security. Between 1990 and 2002, the executive branch was extremely concerned with the failure of the economic and political transitions in the CEE states as well as the republics of the FSU, while the intelligence community (and DoD) remained concerned with regions and states presenting traditional security threats, particularly the proliferation of WMD to potential adversaries. Between 1998 and 2005, the DCI identified the Persian Gulf as the single most important geographic source of threat to the United States, an orientation that the Bush and Clinton administrations shared between 1993 and 1999. In making this assessment, both pointed to its role as the major transit point of the world's oil, its role as an incubator of terrorism, and the existence of unstable authoritarian regimes aligned with (Saudi Arabia, Oman) and opposed to (Iran, Iraq and Syria) American interests in the region. Prior to 11 September, South and Central American narcoterrorism and drug trafficking were identified as prominent regional threats (US Senate 1999); thereafter, the Korean peninsula and Central Asia emerged as foci of attention, primarily owing to the increased bellicosity of the North Korean regime towards its northeast Asian neighbours as well as its aggressive development of intermediate range missiles and a nuclear capability. Central Asia's growing importance is owed to the preoccupation with Muslim terrorism and separatist movements conjoined to the importance of the Caspian Sea region as a significant alternative source of oil and natural gas (Tenet 1998, 2000, 2003, 2004; Goss 2005; cf. Jacoby 2000, 2003, 2004, 2005).

After 1989, North Korea, the Russian Federation, Indonesia, Iran, Iraq and China were identified as the states representing the greatest threats to American security. Even before President Bush bestowed the moniker 'Axis of Evil' on Iran, Iraq and North Korea in his 2002 State of the Union Address, the Clinton administration viewed these states as presenting the greatest risks to regional stability and the nuclear non-proliferation regime. Iraq was cited for its call to overthrow moderate Arab regimes in the Gulf region and its 'hidden weapons of mass destruction', while Iranian nuclear ambitions were considered unlikely to evaporate, even in the presence of a moderate government.[8] Iran and Iraq, as state sponsors of terrorism, were also presumed to be willing purveyors of WMD to terrorist groups, particularly al-Qaeda. North Korea was designated a greater threat than either Iraq or Iran in 1999 and has been persistently identified as the major threat to northeast Asian stability and American interests there. North Korea, a fragile regime led by a mentally unstable individual and overly fond of brinksmanship in its dealings with the outside world, also posed a credible military threat to South Korea and American forces stationed there (Tenet 1999; Jacoby 2003). After 11 September, Iran, North Korea and al-Qaeda (and Iraq until 2003) were considered as the actors most likely to acquire or possess and use biological weapons.

Each post-Cold War administration identified India, Russia and China as global powers posing quite different threats to the United States. The Indian (and then Pakistani) acquisition of nuclear weapons threatened the non-proliferation regime and placed nuclear weapons in the arsenals of two countries that have been at intermittent war since the 1947 partition. The Russian threat mutated and conformed to that country's ongoing political and economic progress and regress. The Russian Federation's integration into the Western security and economic systems, central to removing Russia as a geopolitical threat to the United States and

Table 8.5 Source of threats, National Security Strategy 1993–2006

	1993	*1995*	*1999*	*2002*	*2006*
States					
North Korea	+	+	+	+	+
FSU/NIS	+	+	+		
Russian Federation				+	+
India–Pakistan		+	+	+	
Iran		+	+	+	+
Iraq			+	+	+
Syria					+
China			+	+	+
Regions					
Indian subcontinent		+	+	+	
Korean peninsula			+		+
Gulf	+	+	+		
South America	+		+	+	
Central and Eastern Europe	+	+	+		
Central Asia			+	+	

Source: White House 1993, 1995, 1999, 2002a and 2006.

its European allies, remains vulnerable to domestic political upheaval, corruption, and organized crime. Economic privation has also sustained concerns that nuclear technologies and material would be sold directly to states such as Iran in order to generate hard currency or to enrich individual Russians. More pressing was the task of securing nuclear weapons, research and material that could otherwise fall into the hands of criminal organizations or Muslim terrorists. China poses the more traditional threat of a rising, revisionist power. China's sustained weapons modernization programme, particularly the development of a power projection capability, and the oft-expressed desire to reclaim its historical role in Southeast and Central Asia will inevitably constrain America's unfettered military presence in the Asia–Pacific and place into question the American commitment to Taiwan at a time when relations between the two Chinas are deteriorating (Tenet 1998, 2000, 2003, 2004; Jacoby 2003; Goss 2005; DoD 2005a).

The public and elite have had different rank-orderings of the states posing a threat to the United States. The public has only remained wary of China and Iraq over the entire post-Cold War period. North Korea, Russia, Japan and the United States itself figured as prominent threats in the early 1990s, but in 2005 the public only considered North Korea and Iran as substantial threats to the United States.[9] The elite has been preoccupied with China and Iran over the entire post-Cold War period, while North Korea re-emerged as an acute threat after the invasion of Iraq. Two remarkable gaps exist in the elite and public perception: first, a not insignificant share of the elite (12 per cent) views the United States as a threat to itself, while only a negligible share of the public shares a similar position; second, 18 per cent of the general public (as compared to 4 per cent of the elite) still consider Iraq a threat despite the US occupation (Pew 2005).

Agency of threat

States were identified as the most likely source of threat to the United States in the immediate post-Cold War period, a condition that lasted well into the late 1990s. Non-state actors nonetheless grew in importance by the mid 1990s as a specific source of threat, particularly as terrorist groups and transnational criminal organizations began to demonstrate their reach as well as the liability they represented. Despite the first bombing of the World Trade Center in the early 1990s, states remained the predominant focus of administration threat assessment. What had changed, however, were the kinds of threat states presented. The initial concern with a militarily renascent Russian Federation seeking to re-establish the Soviet imperium in Central or Eastern Europe ebbed as the 1990s progressed, only to be replaced with concerns over a militarily assertive China that would seek a similar position in the Asia–Pacific. The failed or failing state was also an agent of insecurity, particularly as sanctuaries or havens for non-state actors and more generally as a generic source of regional disorder. Rogue states also posed a direct threat to American security, particularly their efforts to acquire WMD for use against the United States or an ally and their willing support or abetting of terrorist groups targeting American assets or citizens.

Although the Bush administration defined Muslim terrorists and al-Qaeda, in particular, as the existential threat confronting the United States after 11 September, the administration did not ignore the continuing importance of states in the international system. The Department of Defense identified 'key states' and 'problem states' as the two categories of states threatening American security (DoD 2005b: 5; cf. DoD 2005c: 7). Key states covered likely geo-strategic peer competitors; China and Russia were the usual referents in this context. Problem states included regional states seeking to upend the existing status quo and 'rogue states' seeking WMD capabilities or supporting terrorism. While rogue states and peer competitors constituted longer-term and more dire threats to American security, terrorists 'represent the most immediate challenge to the nation's security' (DoD 2005c: 7, 9). This preoccupation with terrorism reflects not only the consequences of 11 September – materially as well as psychologically – but the willingness and inevitable capability of terrorists (and rogue states) to inflict catastrophic damage on the critical infrastructures of American society and economy (White House 2003a: xii; White House 2003b: vii-ix).[10]

Institutional and instrumental responses to threat

The range of actors posing putative or acute threats to American interests or the American homeland changed how the United States interacts with the rest of the world and, since 11 September, led to the remilitarization of American security policy. The Bush administration continued the security multilateralism characterizing post-war American foreign policy, notably the building of the global coalition evicting Iraq from Kuwait. The Clinton administration continued in a similar vein, particularly in response to the disintegration of Yugoslavia and the collapse of civil order there. Both administrations relied not only on military force to achieve American security goals, but also supported policy initiatives that relied upon the 'civilian' instruments of security policy. The post-11 September Bush administrations, however, effectively jettisoned the formal multilateralism of the post-war period for ad hoc coalitions where allies supply expeditionary forces without strings. There has been an increasing proclivity to substitute military force for diplomacy and negotiation and a willingness to violate established international law (Urquhart 2006; Sands 2005; Byers 2006). Despite his administration's heavy reliance upon military force to protect American interests after 11 September and pronounced preference for unilateral solutions to global problems, President Bush has devoted considerable financial and diplomatic resources, including the selective strengthening of multilateral mechanisms, to protect the homeland (particularly measures to defend against CBRN attacks) and to secure nuclear facilities and material in the Russian Federation.

Interaction pattern

The current Bush administration – despite its proclamation that 'the mission defines the coalition' and stated preference for coalitions of the willing – is merely continuing the long-standing American foreign policy principle that the United States will act unilaterally when American interests are threatened (White House 1993, 1995, 1999 and 2002a). The pronounced disregard of America's closest European allies on matters affecting European as well as American security, however, does represent a significant departure in terms of style, although it is doubtful that multilateralism has ever meant much more for any administration than European obeisance to American policy proclamations.

The international and regional security institutions created and sponsored by the United States in the post-war period still play important roles in the definition and execution of American policy. The WMD threat and the non-proliferation regime provide a window on the multilateral commitment of each post-Cold War administration. The Bush administration's 1993 NSS placed greater value on the institutions, treaties and conventions defining the non-proliferation regime than had the Clinton administration (see Table 8.6). More striking, however, is the total disregard for each component of the non-proliferation regime in the 2002 and 2006 NSS. Not only do both documents ignore non-proliferation treaties and conventions as integral components of American policy, but downgrade the critical watchdog role played by the International Atomic Energy Agency.[11]

All three administrations have treated regional security institutions similarly. Whereas Clinton and his predecessor favoured NATO as a collective defence organization with a primary responsibility for maintaining the balance of power in the European political space and providing order along its periphery, the current Bush administration has treated NATO as a pool from which to draw 'mission-based coalitions' (White House 2002a) and expeditionary forces standing ready to support or substitute for American troops deployed abroad (Sperling 2004).

Table 8.6 Interaction patterns, National Security Strategies 1993–2006

	1993	1995	1999	2002	2006
Non-proliferation regime					
– NPT	+	+	+		
– CTBT	+		+		
– MTCR	+	+			
– Chemical Weapons Convention	+	+	+		
– Biological Weapons Convention	+				
– IAEA	+	+	+		
– UN		+			+
– Australia Group	+				+
– G7				+	
– Six-Party Talks				+	+
Regional Security Institutions					
– NATO	+	+	+	+	+
– ASEAN Regional Forum		+	+		+
– C/OSCE (democratization)	+	+	+		+
– OAS (democratization)	+				+
HIV/AIDS					
– UN				+	+
– G8			+		
Bilateral Security Relationships					
– Japan	+	+	+		+
– FSU (nuclear legacy)	+				
– Russian Federation	+	+	+	+	+
– North Korea			+		
– South Korea			+	+	+
– China				+	+

Source: White House 1993, 1995, 1999, 2002a and 2006

The Clinton administration considered the ASEAN Regional Forum (ARF) to be a worthwhile pan-Pacific security arrangement facilitating security cooperation among the major Pacific powers and their smaller neighbours. His successor ignored the ARF as an institutional mechanism for enhancing American security after 11 September, although it did merit brief mention in the 2006 NSS. The other major regional security institutions, the Organization for Security and Cooperation in Europe and the Organization of American States, were viewed as institutional mechanisms facilitating the global democratization strategy presented in the 2006 NSS.[12]

An important assumption underpinning the Clinton administration's approach to security policy reflected the varieties of threat and the rising vulnerability of the United States and its partners: 'international cooperation will be critical for building security in the next century because many of the challenges we face cannot be addressed by a single nation' (White House 1999: 3). This sentiment was replaced soon after 11 September with a national strategy that welcomed international cooperation, but only on American terms in the service of American interests. Another major departure has been the cavalier treatment of international laws uncongenial to the administration (e.g. the redefinition of prisoners of war as enemy combatants in an effort to place them outside the Geneva Conventions, which the administration considers 'quaint' in any event) and the selective use of international law to justify American foreign policy, particularly the invasion of Iraq (Urquhart 2006; Byers 2006). The administration has claimed that its assertive policies towards Iran and North Korea represent efforts to defend international law, particularly breaches of the Non-Proliferation Treaty – even though the NPT permits the production of low-enriched uranium – and North Korea, once it withdraws from the NPT, will no longer be subject to its provisions.

There are marked differences in the public and elite views of America's world role, America's allies, and the role of international institutions as constraints on American foreign policy. The public is much less certain than the elite that the United States should maintain an active role in international politics, although the sizeable gap between the public and the elite has been remarkably stable between 1986 and 2004 (see Tables 8.7 and 8.8). Correspondingly, the public is considerably more wary of committing US troops to defend its *allies* than the elite. The CCFR surveys reveal that neither the public nor the elite supports the proposition that the United States should act as the world's policeman. A recent Pew public opinion survey shows, however, that as the public taste for world leadership has waned (from 81 per cent in 1993 to 42 per cent in 2005), that of the elite has waxed (58 per cent in 1993 to 88 per cent in 2005). Elite support for leadership does not translate into a

Table 8.7 Public interaction preferences 1986–2004

	1986	1990	1994	1998	2002	2004
Role perception						
– Active role in world politics	64	62	65	61	71	67
– Use of force to defend allies	52	59	47	35	39	40
– Act as world policeman					34	20
– Remain sole superpower					7	8
Interaction preference						
– Act in concert with allies				72	61	
– Should act alone				21	31	
– Use force only with UN mandate						73
– Right to use force without UN mandate						56
Institutional preferences						
– Keep present commitment to NATO	62	56	56	59	57	
– Strengthen UN role	46	44	51	45	68	58
– Participate in UN peacekeeping missions			51	57	78	78
– Support for stronger EU		48	49	45		
– Support for international treaties:						
Comprehensive nuclear test ban					84	87
Banning of land mines					76	80
Kyoto					69	71
International Criminal Court					77	76
Comply with adverse WTO decisions					64	69

Sources: Reilly 1987, 1991;CCFR and German Marshall Fund 2002; CCFR 2004a.

Table 8.8 Elite interaction preferences 1986–2004 (per cent)

	1986	1990	1994	1998	2002	2004
Role perception						
– Active role in world politics	98	97	98	96	96	97
– Use force to defend allies	74	72	79	74	80	
– Maintain military superiority			54	58	52	37
– Act as world policeman						18
Unilateral impulse						
– Act in concert with allies				48		
– Should act alone (unilateralism)				44	43	
– Use of force requires UN mandate						75[a]
– Use force without UN mandate						51[a]
Institutional preferences						
– Keep present commitment to NATO	77	35	57	64	69	66
– Strengthen UN role	22	39	33	32	28	40
– Take part in UN peacekeeping missions					79	84
– Support for stronger EU		79	85	63		
– Support for international treaties:						
Kyoto					63	62
Land mine ban					74	80
Comprehensive nuclear test ban					82	85
International Criminal Court					65	70
Comply with adverse WTO decisions						78

a   Average of responses based on alternative scenarios.
Source: Reilly 1987,1991; CCFR and German Marshall Fund 2002; CCFR 2004a.

preference for unilateralism, however. The public is not only less willing to countenance unilateral action than is the elite, but greatly prefers that the United States act in concert with its allies (72 per cent vs. 48 per cent). The public and elite also accept by a substantial margin that the use of force requires a UN mandate, although under certain circumstances both agree that a mandate is not necessary (Pew 2005).

The public and elite also favourably view international institutions and treaties. Both agree that the United States should maintain its existing commitment to NATO, although the public level of support is markedly lower than the elite's support. A stronger Europe – an important post-war American foreign policy objective – does not now enjoy the support of the American public and, more remarkably, support among the elite has declined over the 1990s and into the new century. The source of elite disenchantment with a stronger EU is not explored in the CCFR surveys, but as the EU consolidates its foreign policy profile, Europeans have become more capable and willing to challenge the United States – an unintended and undesirable policy outcome from the American perspective. More surprising is the public's sustained support for the UN, despite the low level of elite support and the palpable contempt with which it is held by the current administration. Finally, the elite and public deviate from the Congress and administration in supporting American ratification of the Kyoto Treaty on global warming and the jurisdiction of the International Criminal Court – both firmly rejected at either end of Pennsylvania Avenue.

James Sperling

Instrumental preferences

The United States increasingly relied upon the exercise of 'soft power' to ameliorate the underlying sources of threat between 1990 and 2000. The rapidly changing geo-strategic context prompted a change in American thinking about the utility of force. Even though the Bush and the Clinton administrations recognized that after 1989 many of the threats to American security could not be adequately remedied or deterred by an over-reliance upon military force, each NSS produced after 1989 continued to place a relatively greater emphasis on the military rather than the economic or diplomatic elements of power. Each administration has sought military preponderance to ensure favourable regional milieu conditions providing the United States with the greatest degree of freedom in executing the security strategy of the day. The Bush administration had also concluded as early as 1992 that American force would be used 'often in concert with the United Nations, to mediate economic and social strife and to deter regional aggressors' (DoD 1992: 4).

The Clinton administration established two principles guiding the use of military force: its use would serve the national interest 'first and foremost'; and it would only be employed unilaterally if necessary (DoD 2000: 4). The American military was assigned traditional geopolitical objectives: protecting territorial integrity; maintaining balance; open markets for raw materials; freedom of the seas; and deterring aggression against the US or its allies. The administration also established a hierarchy of policy instruments which left the military instrument as the option of last choice. The Clinton defence strategy also relied heavily upon diplomatic measures promoting regional stability via participation in multilateral alliances or sponsoring confidence-building measures between regional antagonists, supporting the democratization process where possible, particularly with regard to civilian control of the military, and enhancing military cooperation and transparency with potential adversaries. Clinton accepted his predecessor's operating assumption that security was contingent upon eliminating nuclear, biological and chemical capabilities in the former republics of the FSU, securing nuclear material and weapons in the Russian Federation, supporting international non-proliferation treaties – the Chemical Weapons Convention, the NPT, and Missile Technology Control Regime – and participating in bilateral and multilateral programmes, particularly the Cooperative Threat Reduction Program, the Expanded Threat Reduction Initiative, the 1994 Agreed Framework between the United States and North Korea, and the 1999 G8 initiative to take measures inhibiting WMD proliferation (White House 1993: 16; White House 1999: 13–15; cf. US Senate 1998).

President Clinton also continued his predecessor's emphasis on global prosperity as a critical component of the American security strategy. Global prosperity was made contingent upon creating a multilateral framework for the management of integrated financial markets, promoting an open trading system and strengthening the World Trade Organization, and providing an international context that facilitated global economic growth and the emergence of democratic government where none existed. These economic objectives would inhibit the persistence of 'repression, corruption and instability [that] could engulf a number of countries and threaten the stability of entire regions' (White House 1999: 25).

The 2006 NSS pushed the promotion of democracy to the top of the security policy agenda. The Bush administration asserted that 'the fundamental character of regimes matters as much as the distribution of power among them' and that the creation of democratic regimes would eradicate terrorism, remove an important source of regional instability, and prevent the proliferation (and use) of WMD against the United States and its allies (White House 2006: 10). The administration made an unvarying causal connection between the eradication of terrorism and the appearance of democracy and the rule of law. Democracy functioned as a panacea eradicating the underlying sources of terrorism – alienation, misattribution or external projection of grievances, 'sub-cultures of conspiracy', and an 'ideology that justifies murder' (White House 2006: 10).[13] The structural sources of terrorism identified – economic deprivation and poor governance – did not figure into the Bush administration's policy calculus, a major departure from previous administrations.

The 2002 NSS was issued against the backdrop of the terrorist attacks on the Twin Towers and the Pentagon. By the time of publication, President Bush had declared that the United States was a country at war. Policy-makers fastened upon the traditional and asymmetrical military threats that rogue states and terrorists present; there emerged a corresponding infatuation with the military instrument combined with an impatience with diplomacy. The administration 'unveiled' a comprehensive strategy to meet the threat of WMD proliferation, but that strategy merely replicated the Clinton administration's emphasis on counter-proliferation, non-proliferation, and consequence management (White House 1999; White House 2002b: 2). The Bush doctrine, which took aim at rogue states and terrorist groups seeking WMD, invoked the principle of pre-emptive attack in response to an imminent threat to the United States or simply to forestall or prevent 'hostile acts' (White House 2002a: 15; White House 2006: 18). The doctrine also downgraded the importance of formal alliances and emphasized the administration's intention to rely upon coalitions of states 'able and willing to promote a balance of power that favors freedom' (White House 2002a: 25; cf. Jervis 2003).

The 2005 National Military Strategy concluded that the United States military required a force structure capable of defeating 'a wide range of adversaries – from states to non-state actors'. The Strategy formulated a new form of deterrence tailored to the WMD threat that rogue states and terrorists posed. It called for a 'diverse portfolio of capabilities' enabling the United States to destroy terrorist networks, effect regime change, 'swiftly defeat' an adversary or undertake a prolonged occupation that entailed a 'significant investment' of blood and treasure (DoD 2005b: 3 and 12; cf. DoD 2005b: 7–8). Pre-emption was a central feature of the new deterrence strategy, but the deterrent also included a non-military component that consisted of policies protecting the homeland (improved collection and analysis of data as well as R&D expenditures improving responses to WMD threats), deepening bilateral and multilateral cooperation, particularly with respect to intelligence sharing, countering ideological support for terrorism (thereby delegitimizing terrorism and its state sponsors), supporting 'models of moderation in the Muslim world', and implementing 'targeted strategies against hostile states and terrorists' (DoD 2005d: 5; White House 2002b: 2). The administration also relied upon interdiction strategies (Proliferation Security Initiative), the use of sanctions against state or non-state actors threatening to use or acquire WMD, and the belated recognition that American support of the multilateral non-proliferation regimes served American interests.

Nuclear weapons guaranteed American security during the Cold War. The specific function of the American nuclear arsenal was put into play as Russian–American confidence-building measures accelerated, the mutual reduction of strategic nuclear weapons within the START framework took effect, and Russia participated in the NATO security system. Despite these positive developments, nuclear weapons retain their strategic importance as the primary means for deterring the use of WMD and serving as 'a hedge against the emergence of an overwhelming conventional threat' (DoD, Joint Chiefs of Staff 1995: v, ix). The Clinton administration also noted that, while the law of nations did not prohibit the use of nuclear weapons, their use would be subject to the principle of proportionality: the collateral damage attending the use of nuclear weapons could not outweigh the military benefit of their use (DoD, Joint Chiefs of Staff 1995: ix). The Bush administration amended the Clinton era nuclear doctrine to account for the use of nuclear weapons against rogue states and terrorist groups. The contingencies legitimizing the use of theatre nuclear weapons included cases where an adversary intended to use WMD against the United States or its allies, an adversary's 'imminent attack' with biological weapons, or the need to disable an adversary's WMD infrastructure to forestall an attack (DoD, Joint Chiefs of Staff 2005: III-2). The Joint Chiefs identified the likely targets as 'numerous nonstate organizations (terrorist, criminal) and about thirty nations with WMD programs' (DoD, Joint Chiefs of Staff 2005: III-1). Over the course of the post-war period, nuclear doctrine had been an elaborate and potentially deadly form of shadowboxing that deterred war between the United States and the Soviet Union. The contingencies identified in the most recent statement on nuclear doctrine, however, are not inconsistent with the alleged plans to use tactical nuclear weapons to destroy Iran's uranium enrichment facilities.[14]

Homeland security policies, which have targeted borders, critical infrastructures and key assets, have become progressively militarized. In its 2005 Strategy for Homeland Defense and Civil Support (SHDCS), the DoD seized a domestic role for itself in the war against terrorism on American soil. This domestication of the DoD's role in the war against terrorism reflects an assessment that terrorists considered US territory 'an integral part of a global theatre of combat' (DoD 2005c: 1). While the SHDCS makes a distinction between homeland security (the bailiwick of the Departments of Homeland Security and Justice), and homeland defence (the responsibility of the DoD), the wall separating the two is a thin one. The DoD, for example, claimed the right to conduct homeland defence missions whenever the President exercises his 'constitutional authority as Commander-in-

Chief' – an authority that the Justice Department has so broadly interpreted that it amounts to a presidential blank cheque (DoD 2005c: 26). Many homeland security challenges do require a military component, particularly interdiction on the high seas as well as patrolling American air space. The administration has initiated a number of multilateral programs, including the Container Security Initiative and the Proliferation Security Initiative, to manage the security vulnerabilities arising from the high volume of global shipping; the protection of American airspace, particularly the defence against cruise or ballistic missiles, remains a national responsibility (DoD 2005c: 25).

Unlike the high seas and US airspace, cyberspace is one operating theatre in the new security context that cannot be easily defended. The Clinton and Bush administrations acknowledged that defending cyberspace is largely immune to a military solution and beyond the capabilities of government. To meet the threat to information systems and cyberspace more generally, the Bush administration has effectively adopted subsidiarity as a governing principle. Responsibility for monitoring and protecting much of cyberspace and information systems has been delegated to the private sector as well as state and local levels of government. This privatization and devolution of cyber security are creatures of necessity, yet the current policy amounts to little more than rhetorical platitudes devoid of legislative obligations or guidance (White House 2003b: 11).

The instrumental preferences of the elite fall into one of three categories: the use of military force, the use of diplomacy, and the use of civilian instruments addressing the sources of threat in the international system. Elites support the retention of permanent military bases in Turkey, Germany, Japan and South Korea, although they do not support as strongly bases located in the Middle East (see Table 8.9). The use of force remains a viable policy option: majorities support the use of force in the event of a war on the Korean peninsula, the Taiwan straits, or between Israel and any of its Arab neighbours. Prior to 2003, there was also a large margin of support for aiding Saudi Arabia in the event of an Iraqi invasion. These contingencies for the use of force are consistent with the post-war consensus demarcating the zones of critical geo-strategic importance to the United States. The elite response to terrorism is more nuanced. While elites are generally in agreement that low-intensity engagements against terrorists are necessary and advisable, a majority no longer supports regime change, even in states supporting terrorism – a change no doubt reflecting the botched occupation of Iraq. The elite acceptance of military force as a necessary and viable instrument of statecraft should not overshadow, however, an equally strong support for diplomacy and civilian instruments of statecraft. They are virtually unanimous in their assessment that the UN and international law have important roles to play in the suppression of terrorism and that the root cause of terrorism is located in economic deprivation – a rationale that the Bush administration largely rejects. Unlike the architects of the Bush foreign policy and their neoconservative allies, the mainstream foreign policy elite also questions whether spreading democracy is a cure-all for what ails the United States (CCFR 2004c; 2005).[15]

Table 8.9 Elite instrumental preferences 1986–2004 (percentage)

	1986	1990	1994	1998	2002	2004
Use of force if:						
– Soviets invade Japan	83	73				
– Soviets/Russians invade W. Europe	93	87	91			
– North Korea invades South Korea	67	57	82	74	82	82
– Arabs invade Israel	60	70	72	69	77	64
– Iraq invades Saudi Arabia		89	84	79		
– China invades Taiwan				51	52	51
Use of force against terrorism						
– Air strikes against terrorist facilities				77	87	83
– Attacks by US ground troops				58	81	74
– Topple states supporting terrorism					61	38
Use of diplomacy against terrorism						
– Strengthen international law and role of UN in enforcing it					91	94
– Develop economies of poor countries					92	94
– Try suspected terrorists in ICC				89	74	80
Bringing democracy to others ('very important')	29	26	21	27	33	29
Expand economic aid		43	20	38	58	61
Reduce military aid to other countries		75	67	51	40	40
Expand intelligence gathering capabilities			16	34	63	58
Should US have permanent military bases in:						
– South Korea					78	71
– Turkey					77	63
– Japan					64	56
– Germany					67	54
– Afghanistan					46	53
– Saudi Arabia					46	33

Source: Reilly 1987, 1991;CCFR and German Marshall Fund 2002 CCFR 2004a.

The constituent elements of the pre- and post-11 September security environments evince elements of continuity as well as fundamental change (see Table 8.10). The elements of continuity include similar perceptions of threat, the agents of threat, and the targets of threat, although there has been a notable shift in the rank-ordering within each category. The fundamental differences that have emerged are located in the severity of threat and the type of response: the post-11 September environment has produced a new existential threat to American security, downgraded multilateralism as a substantive goal of American foreign policy, and legitimized military force as an instrument of first rather than last resort. Moreover, where the Bush and Clinton administrations promoted democracy through diplomatic and economic incentives, the current Bush administration has opted for the forced democratization attending regime change. Elements of continuity and change coexist with respect to the geographic source of threat: while China has remained a constant source of concern, the Middle East now presents the chief security pathology vexing American foreign policy.

Table 8.10 Summary characteristics of US security orientation

	Post-Cold War	Post-11 September 2001
Type of threat	a) failure of transitions to democracy and the market regionally and globally b) spread of nuclear weapons, materials, and human capital c) rise of peer competitors d) integrity of international law and international institutions	a) international terrorism, particularly that posed by radical Islam in Persian Gulf region b) The rise of China as a peer competitor and threat to existing status quo c) Axis of Evil: reflects preoccupation with nuclear proliferation programmes that pose (in)direct threats to US interests
Agency of threat	a) primarily states, both established, new and failing b) rogue states c) secondary threat by non-state actors, particularly terrorist groups	a) rogue states that support terrorism to further national ends b) terrorist networks symbolised by al-Qaeda and Osama bin Laden. c) States remain critical actors in terms of strategic threat
Target of threat	a) stability of the American supported international system b) state viability and concurrent disorder	a) terrorist threat to American way of life, its economic and social institutions b) threat to broader US foreign policy goals in Middle East (Israeli security, a secure supply of oil and democratic regimes) c) American hegemony
Geographical source of threat	Threats were generally linked to specific geographic areas: a) failed transitions in eastern and south-eastern Europe and FSU b) loss of control over nuclear weapons and material primarily in Russia, but concern at end of decade with Pakistan, India, North Korea and Iraq c) China peer competitor of US in Pacific. More generally, the US had a global rather than a regionally demarcated set of security concerns	The geographical source of threat contracted to: a) Middle East, particularly Afghanistan, Iraq and Iran b) North Korea and China c) Pakistan and India More generally, US security policy has several regional foci that are embedded in a global frame of reference.
Severity of threat	No single threat was viewed as an existential threat to the United States. Rather, threat posed to US order and potentially to allies across the globe.	The threat posed by terrorism and rogue states seen as an immediate and existential threat to US; the threat posed by potential peer competitors is longer-term concern.

	Post-Cold War	*Post-11 September 2001*
Types of response	Primarily one of democratic engagement; the use of civilian instruments, but willingness to employ military instrument when appropriate and as a last resort. Multilateral approach to security matters when possible, unilateral or bilateral if necessary.	The response to these threats has been largely militarized. Even where diplomatic efforts are made, the shadow of preventive war makes US policy coercive rather than persuasive. Unilateralism when possible, multilateralism when necessary.
Tractability	Most of the threats were considered susceptible to negotiation, although amelioration of most threats viewed as amenable to military solution.	Threats posed by terrorism and non-state actors are seen as relatively intractable and long-term. Threats posed by state actors are seen as resolvable either by negotiation or force.

Allocation of resources

The American security agenda was in a state of flux after 1989. There was no longer a palpable enemy threatening the United States or its closest allies in Europe and Asia. The most pressing security tasks required the application of military force for peacekeeping and peacemaking tasks (as in the case of the Balkans) and expenditures facilitating the transitions from authoritarian rule to competitive market economies and liberal democracies in the CEE states. Accordingly, American expenditures on defence fell from 6.1 per cent of GDP in the 1980s to 3.5 per cent of GDP prior to 11 September. European defence spending also fell sharply from 3.3 per cent to 2 per cent of GDP in the same period. The Europeans, in particular, seized the peace dividend promised with the end of the Cold War. The United States protected its position as the only state possessing a global reach commensurate with its global responsibilities and ambitions. The transformation of the American military, the so-called Revolution in Military Affairs, represented an effort to create highly mobile and agile expeditionary forces capable of defending core US interests as well as maintaining global order, particularly in areas adjudged as critical to American interests. Yet the United States also devoted considerable financial resources to meeting the challenges of the new security agenda, ranging from nuclear safety to supporting fledgling constitutional democracies. The Bush administration's 'War on Terrorism', the considerable energy devoted to strategies for protecting the homeland, the desire for regime change in the countries constituting the 'Axis of Evil', and the potential threat of nuclear proliferation remilitarized American foreign policy. Effective statecraft requires the rank-ordering of threats, the matching of capabilities with threats, and the allocation of national resources consistent with that threat assessment. Has the Bush administration met that test of effective statecraft since 11 September?

American defence expenditures account for 47 per cent of world defence expenditures and 61 per cent of the defence expenditures of the ten countries with the highest military expenditures (SIPRI 2005: Appendix 8A). American defence expenditures experienced a very sharp rise after 2002. Total defence expenditures almost doubled between 1999 and 2005, from US$274.9 billion to $465.9 billion. Total non-defence security expenditures increased almost six-fold in the same time frame, from $11.2 billion to $61.2 billion (see Table 8.11).[16] Federal expenditures on homeland security have fluctuated between $26.5 billion and $35.4 billion between 2002 and 2005, although border and transportation security account for roughly half the total homeland security budget. The Coast Guard and three major components of border and transportation security – customs and border control, INS and customs enforcement, and the Transportation Safety Administration – have experienced steep increases in expenditures, although it is difficult to assess whether the money has been spent wisely or to what effect (see Table 8.12).

The expenditures on security reveal six major security policy objectives: preventing the proliferation of nuclear and biological weapons, enhancing health security, inhibiting drug trafficking, providing a secure supply of energy, enhancing counter-terrorism capabilities, and fighting organized crime. All three post-Cold War administrations ranked the proliferation of CBRN weapons as the most likely threat to America's long-term security interests. This threat was the rationale presented to the international community that justified the American invasion of Iraq; it remains the rationale justifying the hard line taken against Iran over its enrichment activities and against North Korea's nuclear programme. As important has been the far-sighted policy of securing Russian nuclear weapons,

Table 8.11   Budgetary allocations for security functions (defence and non-defence) 1999–2005 (million US$)

	1999	2000	2001	2002	2003	2004	2005
Defence	274,873	294,495	304,882	248,555	404,908	455,908	465,871
Homeland Security				35,373	31,182	26,537	33,259
WMD, of which:	1,357	1,816	1,558	3,822	3,265	7,286	10,568
Nuclear							
non-proliferation	1,233	1,593	1,325	1,344	2,051	2,361	3,940
Biological warfare	124	223	233	2,478	1,214	4,925	6,628
Health security	2,831	3,191	3,586	4,115	4,232	5,072	5,721
Drug trafficking	2,196	2,764	2,405	3,019	3,411	4,048	3,973
Energy security	2,249	1,979	1,726	2,023	2,052	2,822	3,197
Counter-terrorism	362	357	364	1,729	2,669	2,497	2,843
Organized crime	2,087	2,121	2,225	2,224	2,313	2,739	2,681
Total non-defence	*11,182*	*11,906*	*11,854*	*52,305*	*49,124*	*51,001*	*61,242*
Gross interest on							
national debt	*353,511*	*361,998*	*359,508*	*332,537*	*318,149*	*321,566*	*347,890*

Sources: National Institute of Allergy and Infectious Diseases/National Institute for Health 2005; Center for Disease Control 2005; Executive Office of the President of the United States 2001, 2005a and 2005b.

Table 8.12 Border and transportation security budget before and after 11 September (million US$)

	1999	2000	2001	2002	2003	2004	2005	2006
Border and transportation security	5,743	6,835	5,667	10,816	12,160	13,508	14,642	16,099
US Customs and border control	3,440	3,913	3,211	4,933	5,294	5,997	6,416	6,725
INS and Customs enforcement	2,201	2,922	2,306	2,206	2,218	3,669	3,854	5,364
Transportation safety admin[a]	120	0	150	3,677	4,648	4,578	5,405	5,561
Coast Guard	2,929	3,114	3,555	4,129	4,376	5,084	5,166	5,642

a   Figures for 1999–2001 reflect FAA civilian aviation security budgetary outlays.
Sources: Executive Office of the United States President 2001, 2005a and 2005b; Department of Homeland Security 2004 and 2006.

material and facilities. Department of Defense non-proliferation programmes have targeted this goal since the inception of the Nunn–Lugar Cooperative Threat Reduction Program. The goals of the Nunn–Lugar programme remain far from accomplished; unsecured Russian nuclear materials remain the most likely source of highly enriched uranium for non-state actors seeking a nuclear capability. Total expenditures on non-proliferation programmes grew from $1.2 billion in 1999 to almost $4 billion in 2005 (US Senate 2000; 2001; 2004).

The budgetary allocations for biological warfare and defence have risen from a mere $124 million in 1999 to over $6.6 billion in 2005, despite protests from the medical research community (NIA/NIH 2005). To these expenditures can be added the $5.7 billion devoted in 2005 to health security, although research on sexually transmitted diseases (STD), particularly HIV, is the primary research target. Nonetheless, basic research on viral or bacteriological STDs serve the broader objective of developing effective vaccines and antibiotics mitigating the consequences of biological or viral warfare; just as research dollars are fungible so too are the results from basic research.

Expenditures on counter-terrorism have risen from $362 million in 1999 to $2.8 billion in 2005. These expenditures do not include the unpublished National Security Agency or Central Intelligence Agency counter terrorism budgets or the budget for the FBI, which has grown from $3.5 billion in 1999 to over $5.7 billion in 2005. Budgetary allocations for combating criminal organizations, which are linked to terrorist organizations, particularly as financiers and purveyors of weapons, have remained relatively flat compared to the other non-defence security-related expenditures since 11 September. Total non-defence security expenditures (including Homeland Security) amounted to 5 per cent of defence expenditures in 1999 and 13 per cent in 2005. The trajectory of these expenditures since 11 September, particularly as compared with the Clinton administration, demonstrates (on a sympathetic reading) that the Bush administration has matched its homeland security and 'War on Terrorism' rhetoric with increased federal expenditures. A less sympathetic reading would question those expenditures on at least three counts: first, it is not at all clear that the funds allocated to border and transportation security have markedly increased the security of American borders – the absence of an effective monitoring mechanism for container shipping, the inability to control migration across the Mexican–American border, and the questionable effectiveness of airport screening are three cases on point; second, the relative share of the federal budget devoted to those threats that are the most probable – terrorism, organized crime, nuclear proliferation, epidemics (natural or man-made) and drug trafficking – is too low as compared to the share devoted to traditional defence; and third, rising expenditures on defence modernization not only limit the resources available for those other security threats, but leave future administrations dependent upon military force to meet threats that may very well resist a military solution.

The final dimension of resource allocation is the interrelationship between the total costs of the invasion, occupation and reconstruction of Iraq and the debt service obligations attending a national debt of at least $9 trillion. In 2006, the current cost of the Iraq invasion and occupation approached $250 million and the final costs have been estimated to fall between $410 billion and $1.9 trillion.[17] The demonstrated aversion to taxation in the Republican controlled Congress, the unwillingness to eliminate questionable expenditures (e.g. the red-lining of Senator Ted Steven's [R-Alaska] bridge to nowhere), and the debt incurred to cover the gap between Federal tax receipts and expenditures foreshadow a future constraint on American security expenditures; namely, as interest rates rise in response to a weakening dollar caused by structural budget and balance of payments deficits, the gross debt service burden will almost certainly rise and absorb an even greater share of the Federal outlays. Government debt service not only dwarfs current non-defence security expenditures and is almost three-quarters the size of the defence budget, but could eventually crowd out government investment in the nation's security infrastructure.

Conclusion

The circumstances of the post-1989 world led to a fundamental reassessment of the relationship between security and defence. Arguably, the United States came full circle between 1945 and 1989 in its security policy: in the immediate postwar period those 'present at the creation' understood the importance of providing the prerequisites of a stable international system, including international institutions and law to manage conflict. The strategy of containment blurred the line between security and defence; the Clinton administration strategy of democratic engagement conceptually separated security and defence, a development that reflected the challenges of the post-1989 international system. The collective trauma experienced on and after 11 September in conjunction with the positive predisposition within the Bush administration to rely on force collapsed security and defence into virtually indistinguishable categories.

The American security culture encourages the confluence of security and defence. Kantian optimism about the possibility of perpetual peace and prosperity is wedded to a Hobbesian pessimism about human nature and the dynamics of the international system. For any number of plausible reasons – cultural, theological or sociological – Americans require a palpable existential threat to conduct a purposeful security policy; there appear to be no permanent interests independent of the threat posed by a malevolent 'other'. This worldview largely explains the often parochial definition of interest and unwillingness to treat differences of interest as just that, a difference of interest rather than as evidence of an ally's (or adversary's) moral or ethical failing. Likewise, placing the United States in mortal combat with a well-defined enemy limits the electorate's tolerance of an American foreign policy presented in shades of grey rather than in black and white. Finally, the American preference for multilateralism has been episodic and generally valued instrumentally rather than substantively. The preference for multilateral, bilateral or unilateral responses to international crises or challenges varies from administration to administration, although multilateralism enjoys less support within the Bush administration than in any other post-dating America's entry into the Second World War.

The Bush administration has been slow to recognize the limits on American power or the American ability to shape the world in its own image. Arguably, the administration and the neoconservative movement informing it have drawn the wrong lessons from Kant. While it may be true that democracies are more pacific and less likely to go to war with one another, the emergence of democratic governments will not spontaneously produce a stable international system; Kant and the Abbé de St. Pierre recognized that republican states also required binding international law to produce the advertised perpetual peace. Moreover, the emergence of democratic government is an organic process; it requires the presence of certain

Table 8.13 US national security culture

Worldview of external environment	Paradox of Kantian optimism combined with Hobbesian expectations. See world as hostile and threatening. Threats are always existential: first communism, now 'radical Islam'. Or threat posed by a great power with interests inimical to the United States (Soviet Union prior to 1989 and China since then on a sporadic basis). US requires a hostile 'other' to frame its understanding of the external world.
National identity	National and parochial. Largely free from cosmopolitanism.
Instrumental preferences	US administrations have relied on military as well as civilian instruments. There is an embedded assumption that military instruments are the most efficacious and appropriate. Arguably, the most recent administration has fully remilitarized American foreign policy.
Interaction preferences	Interaction pattern dependent upon the threat faced. Has been a greater willingness to avoid institutionalized multilateral frameworks and operate either unilaterally or in ad hoc coalitions of the willing which allow the US the greatest freedom of action.

preconditions, sociological and economic, and is helped along by a historical experience and a supportive intellectual tradition. It cannot be easily or dependably imposed from without. The neoconservative movement bears a remarkable likeness to South Sea cargo cults. Just as indigenous peoples waited on ritualistic runways in the expectation that Europeans would deliver the bounty of the industrial world without its attending evils, neoconservatives have assumed that the 'natives' *are* waiting at the airport to be liberated by the United States, to have democracy bestowed upon them, and to have their spirits lifted by an enlightened West. Unfortunately, this cargo-cult Kantianism has only delivered a Mesopotamian folly undercutting the American instinct to harness force to justice.

Notes

1 I refer to 'Muslim terrorists' rather than radical Islam, jihadists, or any of the other variations that causally link Islam and terrorism.

2 As Kenneth Waltz (1959) pointed out almost 50 years ago, bad theory leads to bad policy.

3 Cited in 'Breaking away: Francis Fukuyama and the neoconservatives', *New Yorker,* 27 March 2006: 82.

4 See also the testimony of Phyllis E. Oakley (1998) which identifies the chief threats to US security as proliferation (CBN), terrorism, organized crime, and the drug trade.

5 The critical infrastructures identified were: agriculture and food supply, water, public health, emergency services, defence industrial base, telecommunications, energy, transportation, banking and finance, chemicals and hazardous materials, and shipping. The key assets included national monuments and icons, nuclear power plants, dams, and commercial key assets (White House 2003a: xii).

6 The 9/11 Report drew a similar assessment (National Commission 2004).

7 In the 2006 *Quadrennial Defense Review Report*, the DoD's specific goal of full spectrum dominance was dropped in favour of military predominance and in recognition of the changed strategic environment, particularly the war against terrorism (DoD 2006: 3).

8 According to DCI George Tenet, the Iranian political classes regarded the acquisition of WMD as an essential component of Iran's long-term security. The intelligence communities also pointed to the nuclear ambitions of other rogue states, particularly Syria and Libya. While Libya has voluntarily forgone its WMD ambitions, Syria remains a preoccupation for the current Bush administration (Tenet 1999).

9 In 1986, for example, an elite survey found that Russia was the primary source of concern (46 per cent), while in 2002 only the Middle East constituted a geographic source of threat (CCFR and German Marshall Fund 2002: 1).

10 The Clinton administration previously identified a set of non-state actors most likely to threaten critical infrastructures. Cyber-security, in particular, identified the widest array of malevolent actors and underscored the protean nature of contemporary security policy, not only in terms of content but agency (US Senate 2000). In 2000, Michael Vatis, Director of the National Infrastructure Protection Center, identified five major categories of actor that threatened cyberspace: hackers, criminal groups, terrorists, foreign intelligence agencies, and foreign militaries (Vatis 2000: 3–4; cf. Ashley 2003).

11 *The National Strategy to Combat Weapons of Mass Destruction* (White House 2002b) did note the important conventions and treaties of the non-proliferation regime. The strategy also underscored the monitoring role of the IAEA and the diplomatic role of the G8 in meeting the proliferation challenge (See also Department of State 2001; US Senate 2000, 2001 and 2004).

12 In the 1990s, the OSCE and OAS were assigned a similar role as agents of democratization, but the assigned writ was regional rather than global.
13 While the promotion of democracy suffuses the entire NSS as the solution to the security dilemmas facing the United States, the administration also acknowledged that the United States would have to cooperate with 'other main centers of global power' (White House 2006: 1).
14 'The Iran Plan. Would President Bush go to war to stop Tehran from getting the bomb?', *New Yorker,* 17 April 2006: 30–37.
15 The general public is not only quite sceptical about the benefits of spreading democracy for American security (Chicago Council on Foreign Relations 2005: 3–7), but the Congress appears unaware of their constituents' foreign policy preferences on this matter (CCFR 2004c; cf. Kohut and Stokes 2006).
16 The non-defence security expenditures are all expenditures which are explicitly defined in the budget line as defence or security related, broadly defined. These figures do not include the budgets of the Central Intelligence Agency or the National Security Agency.
17 'Paying for Iraq: blood and treasure', *The Economist,* 6 April 2006: 33.

References

Ashley, G.D. (2003) 'Statement' before US Senate Committee on Foreign Relations, Subcommittee on European Affairs, *Transnational Organized Crime,* 30 October.
Byers, M. (2006) *War Law: Understanding International Law and Armed Conflict,* New York: Grove Press.
Carr, E.H. (1938) *The Twenty Years' Crisis, 1919–1939: An Introduction to the Study of International Relations,* London: Macmillan.
Carter, A.B. (1999–2000) 'Adapting US defence to future needs', *Survival* 41 (4): 101–23.
Carter, A.B. and Perry, W.J. (1999) *Preventive Defense: A New Security Strategy for America,* Washington, DC: Brookings Institution.
Center for Disease Control (2005) *CDC and Prevention. Budget Report Summary. Fiscal Year 2006,* Washington, DC: CDC.
Chicago Council on Foreign Relations (CCFR) (2004a) *Global Views 2004. U.S. Leaders Topline Report,* Chicago: CCFR.
CCFR (2004b) *Global Views 2004. U.S. Public Topline Report,* Chicago: CCFR.
CCFR (2004c) *The Hall of Mirrors: Perceptions and Misperceptions in the Congressional Foreign Policy Process,* Chicago: CCFR.
CCFR (2005), Americans on Promoting Democracy, Chicago: CCFR.
CCFR and German Marshall Fund (2002) *Worldviews 2002. U.S. Leaders Topline Report,* Chicago: CCFR.
Department of Defense (DoD) (1992) *National Military Strategy,* Washington, DC: DoD.
DoD (1994) *Report of the Secretary of Defense to the President and the Congress,* Washington, DC: GPO.
DoD (2000) *Annual Report to the President and the Congress,* Washington, DC: DoD.
DoD (2001) *Quadrennial Defense Review Report,* Washington, DC: DoD.
DoD (2005a) *Annual Report to Congress: The Military Power of the People's Republic of China, 2005,* Washington, DC: Office of the Secretary of Defense.
DoD (2005b) *The National Defense Strategy of the United States of America,* Washington, DC: DoD.

DoD (2005c) *Strategy for Homeland Defense and Civil Support,* Washington, DC: DoD.

DoD (2005d) *National Military Strategy of the United States of America,* Washington, DC: DoD.

DoD (2006) *Quadrennial Defense Review Report,* Washington, DC: DoD.

DoD, Joint Chiefs of Staff (1995) *Doctrine for Joint Nuclear Operations. Joint Publication 3–12,* Washington, DC: DoD.

DoD, Joint Chiefs of Staff (2005) *Doctrine for Joint Nuclear Options. Final Coordination (2),* Washington, DC: DoD.

Department of Homeland Security (2004) *The Budget for Fiscal Year 2004,* Washington, DC: GPO.

Department of Homeland Security (2006) *The Budget for Fiscal Year 2006,* Washington, DC: GPO.

Department of Justice (2003) *FY 2003–2008 Strategic Plan, U.S. Department of Justice.* Available online at: <http://www.justice.gov/jmd/mps/strategic2003–2008/pdf.html> (accessed 28 October 2004).

Department of State (2001) *New Ways to Strengthen the International Regime Against Biological Weapons.* Available online at: <http://www.state.gov/t/isn/bw/fs/2001/7909.htm> (accessed 27 October 2006).

Executive Office of the President of the United States (2001) *Appendix: Budget of the U.S. Government, Fiscal Years 1999–2001,* Washington, DC: GPO.

Executive Office of the President of the United States (2005a) *Appendix: Budget of the U.S. Government, Fiscal Years 2002–2005,* Washington, DC: GPO.

Executive Office of the President of the United States (2005b) *Budget of U.S. Government. Fiscal Year 2006,* Washington, DC: GPO.

Federal Bureau of Investigation (2004) *Strategic Plan, 2004–2009,* Washington, DC: Federal Bureau of Investigation.

Fingar, T. (2005) 'Statement of Thomas Fingar, Assistant Secretary of State for Intelligence and Research' before US Senate Select Committee on Intelligence, *Security Threats to the United States,* 16 February.

Finnemore, M. and Sikkink, K. (1998) 'International norm dynamics and political change', *International Organization* 52 (4): 887–917.

Freeh, L.J. (1998) 'Testimony of Louis J. Freeh, Director, Federal Bureau of Investigation' before Senate Select Committee on Intelligence, *World Wide Threats to National Security,* 28 January. Available online at: <http://www.fas.org/irp/congress/1998_hr/s980128f.htm > (accessed 27 October 2006).

Fukuyama, F. (2006) *America at the Cross-Roads: Democracy, Peace and the Neoconservative Legacy,* New Haven: Yale University Press.

Gilpin, R. (1981) *War and Change in International Politics,* Cambridge: Cambridge University Press.

Goslin, T.B. (2000) 'Statement of Major General Thomas B. Goslin, Jr., USAF, Director of Operations, U.S. Space Command' before United States Senate Committee on Armed Services, Subcommittee on Emerging Threats and Capabilities, 1 March. Available online at: <http://www.armed-services.senate.gov/hearings/2000/e000301.htm> (accessed 30 November 2004).

Goss, P. (2005) 'Global intelligence challenges 2005: meeting long-term challenges with a long-term strategy' in US Senate Select Committee on Intelligence, 16 February.

Hamilton, D. (1997) 'Creating the new Atlantic community', in J. Gedmin (ed.) *European Integration and American Interests,* Washington, DC: AEI Press.

Jacoby, L.E. (2000) 'Statement' before US Senate Committee on Armed Services, *Anthrax and Biological Warfare Threat,* 13 April. Available online at: <http://armed-services.senate.gov/statement/2000/0004131lj.pdf> (accessed 20 September 2004).

Jacoby, L.E. (2003) 'Current and projected national security threats to the United States', before US Senate Select Committee on Intelligence, *Worldwide Threats to the Security Community,* 11 February. Available online at: <http://intelligence.senate.gov/0302hrg/030211/jacoby.pdf> (accessed 27 October 2006).

Jacoby, L.E. (2004) 'Current and projected national security threats to the United States', before US Senate Select Committee on Intelligence, *Security Threats to the United States,* 24 February. Available online at: <http://intelligence.senate.gov/0402hrg/040224/jacoby.pdf> (accessed 27 October 2006).

Jacoby, L.E. (2005) 'Current and projected national security threats to the United States' before US Senate Select Committee on Intelligence, *The World Wide Threat,* 16 February. Available online at: <http://intelligence.senate.gov/0502hrg/050216/jacoby.pdf> (accessed 27 October 2006).

Jepperson, R.L., Wendt, A., and Katzenstein, P.J. (1996) 'Norms, identity, culture and national security', in P.J. Katzenstein (ed.) *The Culture of National Security: Norms and Identity in World Politics,* New York: Columbia University Press.

Jervis, R. J. (2003) 'Understanding the Bush doctrine', *Political Science Quarterly,* 118 (3): 365–88.

Kohut, A. and Stokes, B. (2006) 'The problem of American exceptionalism', 9 May. Available online at: <http://pewresearch.org/obdeck/?ObDeckID=23> (accessed 16 May 2006).

Loy, J. (2005) 'Statement of Jim Loy, Deputy Secretary of Homeland Security' before US Senate Select Committee on Intelligence, *The World Wide Threat,* 16 February.

Mann, J. (2004) *Rise of the Vulcans: The History of Bush's War Cabinet,* New York: Penguin.

March, J.G. and Olsen, J.P. (1998) 'The institutional dynamics of international political orders', *International Organization* 52 (4): 943–69.

Martin, L.L. and Simmons, B.A. (1998) 'Theories and empirical studies of international institutions', *International Organization* 52 (4): 729–57.

Mearsheimer, J. (2001) *Tragedy of Great Power Politics,* New York: W.W. Norton.

National Commission on Terrorist Attacks (2004) *The 9/11 Commission Report: Final Report of the National Commission on Terrorist Attacks upon the United States,* New York: Norton.

National Institute of Allergy and Infectious Diseases/National Institute for Health (2005) *Open Letter in Science Regarding NIH Biodefense Funding: Questions and Answers,* 17 March. Available online at: <http://www3.niaid.nih.gov/news/newsreleases/2005/scienceletter.htm> (accessed 27 October 2006).

Oakley, P.E. (1998) 'Statement by Assistant Secretary of State for Intelligence and Research, Phyllis E. Oakley', before the Senate Select Committee on Intelligence, hearing on *Current and Projected National Security Threats to the United States,* 28 January.

Available online at: <http://www.state.gov/www/policy_remarks/1998/980128_oakley_security.html> (accessed 27 October 2006).

Office of Homeland Security (2002) *National Strategy for Homeland Security,* Washington, DC: White House.

Osgood, R.E. (1953) *Ideals and Self-Interest in American Foreign Policy: The Great Transformation of the Twentieth Century,* Chicago: Chicago University Press.

Pew Research Center for the People and the Press and the Council of Foreign Relations (2005) *America's Place in the World 2005. Opinion Leaders Turn Cautious, Public Looks Homeward,* Washington, DC: Pew Research Center.

Reilly, J. (ed.) (1987) *American Public Opinion and U.S. Foreign Policy 1987,* Chicago: CCFR.

Reilly, J. (ed.) (1991) *American Public Opinion and U.S. Foreign Policy 1991,* Chicago: CCFR.

Sands, P. (2005) *Lawless World: America and the Making and Breaking of Global Rules from FDR's Atlantic Charter to George W. Bush's Illegal War,* New York: Viking.

SIPRI (2005), *SIPRI Yearbook 2005. Armaments, Disarmament and International Security,* Stockholm:SIPRI.

Sperling, J. (2004) 'Capability traps and gaps: symptoms or cause of a troubled transatlantic relationship?', *Contemporary Security Policy* 25 (3): 452–78.

Tenet, G.J. (1998) 'World wide threats to national security' before US Senate Select Committee on Intelligence, *Hearing on Current and Projected National Security Threats,* 28 January. Available online at: <https://www.cia.gov/cia/public_affairs/speeches/1998/dci_speech_012898.html> (accessed 27 October 2006).

Tenet, G.J. (1999) 'Statement' before US Senate Armed Services Committee, *Current and Projected National Security Threats,* 2 February. Available online at: <http://www.senate.gov/comm/armed_services/general/statemnt/1999/990202gt.pdf> (accessed 27 October 2006).

Tenet, G.J. (2000) 'Testimony' before US Senate Select Intelligence Committee, *Annual Assessment of Security Threats Against the United States,* 2 February. Available online at: <http://www.iranwatch.org/government/US/Congress/Hearings/sic-020200/us-sic-tenet-020200.htm> (accessed 27 October 2006).

Tenet, G.J. (2003) 'Testimony of George J. Tenet, Director, Central Intelligence Agency' before US Senate Select Committee on Intelligence, *Worldwide Threats to the Intelligence Community,* 11 February. Available online at: <http://www.fas.org/irp/congress/2003_hr/021103tenet.html> (accessed 27 October 2004).

Tenet, G.J. (2004) *DCI's Worldwide Threat Briefing. The Worldwide Threat 2004: Challenges in a Changing Global Context,* 24 February. Available online at: <http://www.fas.org/irp/congress/2004_hr/030904tenet.pdf> (accessed 27 October 2006).

Urquhart, B. (2006) 'The outlaw world', *New York Review of Books* 53 (8): 25–8.

US Senate (1998) *Department of Energy's Fiscal Year 1999 Authorization Request for Environmental Management, Non-Proliferation, and Fissile Materials Disposition,* hearings before US Senate Committee on Armed Services, Subcommittee on Emerging Threats and Capabilities, 105th Congress (2nd session), 12 March. Available online at: <http://www.armed-services .senate.gov/hearings/1999/f980312.htm> (accessed 30 November 2004).

US Senate (1999) *Threat of International Narcotics Trafficking and the Role of the Department of Defense in the Nation's War on Drugs,* US Senate Committee on Armed Services, Subcommittee on Emerging Threats and Capabilities, 106th Congress (1st session), 27 April. Available online at: <http://armed-services.senate.gov/hearings/1999/e990427.htm > (accessed 27 October 2006).

US Senate (2000) *Department of Defense's Cooperative Threat Reduction Program and the Department of Energy's Russian Nonproliferation Programs,* US Senate Committee on Armed Services, Subcommittee on Emerging Threats and Capabilities, 106th Congress (2nd session), 6 March. Available online at: <http://www.armed-services.senate.gov/hearings/2000/e000306.htm> (accessed 30 November 2004).

US Senate (2001) *Cooperative Threat Reduction, Chemical Weapons Demilitarization, Defense Threat Reduction Agency, Nonproliferation Research and Engineering, and Related Programs,* US Senate Committee on Armed Services, Subcommittee on Emerging Threats and Capabilities, 107th Congress (1st session), 6 March. Available online at: <http://www.senate.gov/comm/armed_services/general/hearings/2001/e010712.htm> (accessed 27 October 2006).

US Senate (2004) *Nonproliferation and Arms Control: Strategic Choices,* Hearing before the Committee on Foreign Relations of the United States Senate, 108th Congress (2nd session), 10 March. Available online at: <http://www.senate.gov/~foreign/hearings/2004/hrg040310a.html> (accessed 27 October 2006).

Vatis, M.A. (1999) 'Statement of Michael A. Vatis, Director, National Infrastructure Protection Center, Federal Bureau of Investigation' before US Senate Committee on Armed Services, Subcommittee on Emerging Threats and Capabilities, 16 March. Available online at: <http://www.armed-services.senate.gov/statmnt/1999/990316mv.pdf> (accessed 27 October 2006).

Vatis, M.A. (2000) 'Statement of Michael A. Vatis, Deputy Assistant Director and Chief, National Infrastructure Protection Center, Federal Bureau of Investigation', US Senate Committee on Armed Services, Subcommittee on Emerging Threats and Capabilities.

Waltz, K. (1959) *Man, the State and War,* New York: Columbia University Press.

Waltz, K. (1979) *Theory of International Politics,* New York: Random House.

Wendt, A. (1994) 'Collective identity formation and the international state', *American Political Science Review* 46 (2): 391–425.

White House (1990) *National Security Strategy of the United States, 1990,* Washington, DC: White House.

White House (1993) *The National Security Strategy of the United States, 1993,* Washington, DC: White House.

White House (1995) *A National Security Strategy of Engagement and Enlargement,* Washington, DC: White House.

White House (1999) *A National Security Strategy for a New Century,* Washington, DC: White House.

White House (2002a) *The National Security Strategy of the United States of America,* Washington, DC: White House.

White House (2002b) *National Strategy to Combat Weapons of Mass Destruction,* Washington, DC: White House.

White House (2003a) *The National Strategy for the Physical Protection of Critical Infrastructures and Key Assets,* Washington, DC: White House.

White House (2003b) *The National Strategy to Secure Cyberspace,* Washington, DC: White House.

White House (2006) *The National Security Strategy of the United States of America,* Washington, DC: White House.

Wolfers, A. (1962) *Discord and Collaboration: Essays on International Politics,* Baltimore: Johns Hopkins University Press.

Part III
Eurasia

9 China

Security cooperation with reservations

Liselotte Odgaard

Chinese perceptions of security threats are grounded to a great extent in the theme of foreign humiliation dating back to the late Qing dynasty in the nineteenth century. At this time, Western and Japanese influence began to encroach on Chinese authority by using force to protect interests such as opium imports. The trading war from 1839 to 1842 between Britain and China ended with the Treaty of Nanjing which forced China to cede Hong Kong to Britain, pay war reparations, and which introduced the unequal treaty system placing British citizens under British jurisdiction. The weakening of China's central government allowed for internal uprisings that left the Qing dynasty without any means to control Chinese territory. Towards the end of the nineteenth century, Sino–Japanese hostilities broke out. Japan won the 1894–5 war over Korea and forced China to cede Taiwan, revealing China's weakness in the face of a rising power. Japan's attack on Chinese troops in Manchuria in 1931 resulted in the creation of the Japanese state Manchukuo and Japan's invasion of northern China in 1937. Manchurian soldiers, armed civilians and Chinese communists formed the core of Chinese resistance, allowing Mao Zedong to consolidate himself as the leader of the communists. Japan's defeat in 1945 was followed by civil war in China. Kuomingtan fled to Taiwan and the communists proclaimed the People's Republic of China in 1949. Mao Zedong's rise to power signified the end of foreign encroachments on Chinese territory.

The theme of foreign humiliation was to continue to affect Chinese threat perceptions (Callahan 2001). China has been determined not to ignore even minor violations of its alleged territorial rights and to prevent the expansion of potential opponents on the Asian continent, presumably because expansion is seen as a slippery slope towards creeping encroachment on its territorial integrity and its freedom of action. In the post-Second World War era, China therefore combined the use of force to defend what it perceived as inalienable rights with diplomatic instruments designed to allow China a level of political influence disproportionate to its economic and military capabilities. This foreign policy priority implied that, once the Sino–Soviet alliance began to fall apart in 1956, China developed a policy of non-alignment, with the exception of its alliance with North Korea.

With some adjustments, Beijing has maintained this basic scheme of foreign policy after the Cold War. Chinese foreign policy focuses on limiting the possibilities of violent conflict in its neighbourhood without compromising on the right to use force against entities defined by China as separatists or as aggressors threatening Chinese sovereignty. The policy aims at allowing Beijing to concentrate resources on internal economic development and is pursued by cooperating with states that are at least partially supportive of Chinese foreign policy goals. US military and economic superiority and the prospects of an Asia–Pacific order dominated by the US alliance system encourage Beijing to prioritize diplomatic as well as military instruments. The view that China must guard itself against foreign assaults on what it defines as its historical rights thus continues to determine Chinese threat perceptions.

Perceptions of security threats and their sources

Academic threat perceptions

The realist school of thought prevails in academic opinion on security issues, arguing that power balancing continues to play the most important role for stability in the Asia–Pacific. Academic sources indicate that Washington wants to strengthen its military alliance system, but cooperative security dominates Asia–Pacific diplomacy, which prevents the US and Japan from unilateral pursuits of their security goals (Interview 7). The United States treats China as a great power, but does not, in the view of Chinese academic opinion, seem to recognize that this involves non-interference in Beijing's sphere of influence. This ambiguous policy is caused by US insecurity as to what kind of China it is facing; is it a China determined to challenge US interests or will China remain committed to peaceful coexistence? US doubts about Beijing's intentions are reflected in its policy towards China. On the one hand, compared to the 1990s, Washington is less hostile. On the other, Washington's vow to adopt sanctions against the EU if it lifts its arms embargo against China, its enhanced military cooperation with partners and allies in South, Southeast and Central Asia, and continued US arms sales to Taiwan imply to Chinese academics that containment of China remains an important element in Washington's policy (Interview 2).

China may be its own worst enemy if it continues to conduct what may be called an enigmatic foreign policy, leaving the impression that its decisions are motivated by the realist dictum of amassing power at the expense of other states. Beijing's policy entails a high level of unpredictability. To a large extent, this is a deliberate strategy designed to safeguard it against foreign encroachments on its sovereignty. China now aspires to the position of a great power with global rights and responsibilities. It is difficult to do so under conditions of high unpredictability.

The liberally oriented part of China's academic community, in particular, highlights the benefits to be gained from increasing China's international commitments and lowering the element of unpredictability in its foreign policy through adherence to international agreements on state conduct. This group emphasizes that focusing on economic development requires a more benign international environment than during the Cold War, and China's neighbours are important to create this environment. There is a perception that Beijing's accession in 2003 to the Association of Southeast Asian Nations (ASEAN), established in 1976 by the Treaty of Amity and Cooperation, demonstrates that China uses multilateral diplomatic means to alleviate fears that China has aggressive intensions (Interview 12).

China's improved relations with neighbouring states after the Cold War exclude Japan. Despite growing levels of economic interdependence and cultural exchange, an animosity at the popular and political levels continues to mar Sino–Japanese relations. Those parts of China's academia subscribing to a constructivist approach depict Japan as a nation characterized by a crisis mentality that encourages thinking in terms of national interest before thinking in terms of the common interests of states, to the detriment of the international community (Interview 3). The realist part of academic opinion argues that Japan's principal foreign policy priority is to reap individual benefits from its alliance with the US (Interview 4). Even the more liberal parts of Chinese academia consider the ball to be in Japanese hands when discussing the prospects of improved Sino–Japanese relations. Most importantly, Japan has to face the reality that it is a declining power whereas China is a rising power. As such, it is in Tokyo's interest to recognize China's integration into the international community as a responsible great power. Instead, during Prime Minister Koizumi's reign, Japan has increasingly concentrated on individual goals such as insisting on permanent membership of the UN Security Council and planning to extend its military role in the Asia–Pacific (Interview 6).

Historical enmities are at the heart of adversarial Sino–Japanese relations. The most important of these are the repeated visits of Japanese politicians to the Yasukuni Shrine, which is dedicated to Japanese war casualties since 1868, the question of Japanese history textbooks, which in China's view gloss over wartime atrocities, and Japanese Second World War chemical weapons leftovers. These issues are seen to fuel Chinese and Japanese nationalism to an extent which does not encourage optimism about the prospects of Sino–Japanese relations (Interview 16).

The Taiwan issue gives rise to security threats, principally stemming from separatist forces in Taiwan and from the Taiwanese diaspora, particularly in Washington (Interview 1). Regarding the question of whether Taiwan might generate war, there are two lines of thought: one which considers violent conflict in the Taiwan Strait to be a Chinese security concern, and another that considers the Taiwan issue an unlikely source of war because both the US and China go to great lengths to avoid it and because the majority of the Taiwanese population does not support independence (Interviews 11 and 16). The second group appears to be in the majority, emphasizing that both Washington and Beijing are keen to maintain the status quo. By implication, Japan seems to be perceived as the principal geographic source of threat.

Crime, infectious diseases such as AIDS and SARS, environmental problems, cyberspace,[1] the proliferation of weapons of mass destruction and drug trafficking are also perceived as threats (Interview 13). However, the main non-geographic threats, according to Chinese academics, are insufficient energy resources, economic dissatisfaction in the Chinese lower classes and terrorism. These are all considered potential threats to the survival of the communist regime. China is comfortable with the globalization process, as witnessed by annual growth rates of 7 to 8 per cent and its status as the second largest economy in the world after the US, measured on a purchasing power parity basis (Interview 1). China's neighbours may not doubt that it is already an established economic great power, but China still defines itself as a developing country that needs to focus on strengthening its domestic economy to expand its wealth (Interview 1).

One precondition of China's ability to keep the economy growing is energy resources. China has attempted to reduce its dependence on deliveries from the Middle East by diversifying its sources of oil and gas, partly because the Middle East is politically unstable, partly because the influence of the US in this region is much greater than China's. Important sources of energy supplies are Russia and Kazakhstan (Interview 2). China's dependence on energy deliveries from abroad is connected to the protection of sea lanes, such as the Malacca Strait, against piracy, and to jurisdictional conflicts over maritime areas encompassing sea lanes and energy and gas resources (Interview 2).

China's concern about scarce energy resources in large part stems from the most immediate threat to continued Communist Party rule, namely the possibility of economic dissatisfaction among the Chinese lower classes. Therefore, the most immediate non-geographic security concern is to sustain economic development and ensure growing social equality (Interview 10). A scenario similar to Argentina in 2000 is considered possible in China if the government fails to deliver on the promises of rising living standards as rewards for economic entrepreneurship and if it does not address growing concerns about the asymmetrical distribution of wealth (Interview 13).

Muslim radicalism is perceived as a threat to Chinese unity. One key source of Islamic terrorism is Central Asia. From here, militant Islam spreads to western China, particularly the Xinjiang province which encompasses a large Muslim Uighur population that is ethnically related to the Turkish part of the Central Asian population. However, Muslims inhabit many parts of China. According to one interviewee, this generates the impression that extremism, terrorism and separatism are the three evil forces threatening civilians and the coherence of the mainland (Interview 5). Muslim radicalism encourages Beijing to secure political stability in Central Asia where incumbent governments have a weak hold on power. Beijing shares this concern with Russia and the US. However, China is more comfortable with Russia's support since both countries prioritize stability. By contrast, Washington's democratic priorities imply that the US may support political opposition groups in Kazakhstan, Uzbekistan, Turkmenistan and Tajikistan planning to oust incumbent governments. China cooperates with Russia to actively discourage this development in Central Asia (Interview 2).[2]

The potential for Sino–US conflict on the grounds of US commitment to the spread of liberal democracy is not confined to Central Asia but is perceived as another potential threat to the People's Republic of China. However, in recent years, the US has demonstrated an understanding that the relationship between economic development and civil and political rights is complex. Therefore, stability is in some instances seen as more important than liberal democratization measures. Hence, according to one leading academic, disagreements with George W. Bush's administration over the democracy issue are not viewed as a major threat by China (Interview 5).

Governmental threat perceptions

The Chinese government realizes that geographic and non-geographic sources of threat are intertwined and need to be addressed simultaneously. Thus, the Department of Policy Planning in the Ministry of Foreign Affairs has noted that, although threats might be 'hard' or 'soft', measures to counter them allow no such division and they require attention of the same intensity (Department of Policy Planning 2004: 6). Nevertheless, geographic sources of threat remain at the heart of governmental security concerns: the abrupt rise of the 'Taiwan independence' forces is listed as the biggest immediate threat to peace and stability. The political establishment notes that the US contributes to the gravity of the threat by continuing to increase its arms sales to Taiwan (The State Council Information Office 2004).

The government has emphasized its unwillingness to compromise on the Taiwan issue with the adoption of an anti-secession law on 14 March 2005 which legitimizes the use of non-peaceful means to stop any incidents entailing Taiwan's secession from China (BBC News 2005). Officially, the government attaches more importance to the Taiwanese security threat than Chinese academia does. Off the record, however, Chinese government officials recognize that the Sino–American prioritization of stability in the Taiwan Strait alleviates the risk of violent conflict (Interview 14). The difference between official and unofficial assessments of the Taiwan issue is due to Beijing's need to take action against President Chen Shui Bian's calls for Taiwanese independence, and to demonstrate to mainland nationalists and the population at large that Beijing does not tolerate Taiwanese moves towards independence. Forceful Chinese rhetoric also forms part of the standard policy of the mainland intended to preserve the status quo. It involves responding to separatist Taiwanese tendencies by the same means and intensity as Taiwan. The anti-secession law, thus, can be seen as a response to Chen Shui Bian's 2004 referendum which asked the population whether, if China refuses to redeploy missiles currently pointed at Taiwan, the island should bolster its missile defences. The referendum failed because the voter turnout was too low, but Chen Shui Bian was re-elected president and allegedly plans to hold a second referendum, the subject of which is as yet unknown.

The Chinese government also lists the 2002 nuclear arms standoff on the Korean peninsula and Japanese defence policy as geographic sources of threat. The foundation of the six-party talks on the Korean peninsula is not considered sufficiently solid, as uncertainties linger in the settlement of the nuclear issue (The State Council Information Office 2004). This elusive statement conceals Chinese concerns that Washington's policy prevents conflict resolution. Hence, the nuclear standoff forms part of a general problem of Sino–US relations: they are marred by an ambiguity that surfaces in the reinforced US containment of China whilst simultaneously strengthening the Sino–US security dialogue (Interview 14).

Although the government does not make much of the Japanese threat in its defence White Paper, Chinese government officials mention that poor Sino–Japanese political relations, unresolved historical issues and anti-Japanese sentiment in the Chinese population, combined with the prevalence of the US alliance system, renders bleak the prospects of confidence-building between the two states (Interview 14). Hence, governmental perceptions of geographic security threats seem in large part to correspond to academic views on Chinese security concerns.

Non-geographic security threats are considered to play an increasingly important role. However, the most important, namely the technological gap resulting from the Revolution in Military Affairs (RMA) which has enhanced war fighting capabilities through information technology, is useful for countering geographic security threats. The defence White Paper mentions that US, Japanese and Taiwanese military capabilities have been reinforced and that the United States is leading in RMA, partly because it can afford to invest substantially in military technology, nuclear arsenals and information warfare. These developments underscore Beijing's concern about the asymmetrical military balance produced by RMA (Interview 14; The State Council Information Office 2004).

The risks and challenges caused by economic globalization constitute another important non-geographic source of threat. Economic globalization is perceived as an opportunity, but it has also aggravated the imbalance in world economic development (The State Council Information Office 2004). A minority in the Chinese government argues that economic integration alleviates geographic security threats because enhanced interaction levels produce better understanding and more ideas on how to solve security threats. Economic globalization implies that a resort to force is not useful for solving problems (Interview 15). However, the majority sees China's successful integration into the world economy as a means to restore China's great power status, allowing for a modernization of its armed forces so as to be able to defend the nation against continual geographic threats to its territorial integrity. Since the US is a likely future strategic rival, economic development is necessary for military reform. Moreover, access to markets and energy resources are considered imperative to contain domestic, social and political unrest (Interview 9).

Finally, the continuation of global unipolarity, which looks set to be challenged by an emerging multipolar structure in the Asia–Pacific, will have a major impact on Chinese security. In the official Chinese view, hegemonism and unilateralism have gained new ground, as struggles for strategic points, resources and dominance crop up occasionally. While cooperating with and seeking support from each other, the world's major countries are checking on and competing with one another as well (The State Council Information Office 2004). In particular, the US decision to bypass the UN and wage a preventive war against Iraq is seen as an assault on the majority of countries that are in favour of bilateral negotiations and multilateral coordination when handling international disputes (Department of Policy Planning 2004: 1–2). A discrepancy has arisen between the only remaining superpower relying increasingly on military capabilities and the majority of countries relying on multilateral institutions and diplomacy to obtain strategic stability. The American preference for imposing its demands by military means creates incentives for China and other states to counterbalance the US (Interview 14). In other words, US foreign policy gives rise to a security dilemma that may prevent the consolidation of an international community focusing on the joint interests of states.

Parliamentary threat perceptions

China's parliament, the National People's Congress (NPC), tends to focus on domestic rather than foreign policy issues. The NPC convenes in an annual session. The NPC Standing Committee serves as the executive body when the top legislature is not in session, meeting approximately six times per year. The Chair Committee carries out the day-to-day conduct of NPC affairs. The NPC is usually regarded as a 'rubber stamp' for the Chinese Communist Party (CCP) since it follows the CCP on virtually all occasions. However, since the 1950s, there have been exceptions to this pattern. In particular, the reform period beginning in 1978 was followed by an increased willingness in the NPC to resist the party leadership. The NPC may hence ask for amendments, but it stops short of reversing a policy decision made by the CCP or its leadership (Mackerras *et al.* 1998: 159–60).

In general, Chinese parliamentary views on threat perceptions and their sources closely correspond to those of the CCP. This is particularly the case on issues that are considered central Chinese security concerns. An obvious example is the NPC's ratification of China's Anti-Secession Law on 14 March 2005 with a vote of 2,896 to nil (Xinhua Online 2005a). The NPC fully endorses governmental views on the secessionist activities of the 'Taiwan independence' forces posing a grave threat to China's sovereignty and territorial integrity (Xinhua Online 2005b). The NPC also agrees with the government's criticism of continued US support for Taiwan. China's top legislature has expressed strong dissatisfaction and opposition over a resolution adopted by the American House of Representatives on 16 March 2005, which criticized China's Anti-Secession Law (Xinhua Online 2005c). Governmental and parliamentary views can be expected to be in unison on the Taiwan issue; it is not unusual for the NPC to serve as a public display and confirmation of the leadership's views on Chinese security concerns.

Public opinion

Governmental control of public opinion in China is strict, as indicated by the fact that bodies such as party and government organizations effectively control or influence the media that hence primarily function as the mouthpiece of the Chinese Communist Party. If publication of investigative reporting occurs, it has been instigated or backed by influential political leaders. The official media also must be aware of the CCP's expectation that they will assist in maintaining national stability and unity and promote economic development. In addition, the risk of libel suits and the lack of legal protection for journalists continue to put a brake on critical reporting, although political interference has decreased considerably (Mackerras *et al.* 1998: 154–5). Public opinion polls are therefore not a reliable source of information. Nevertheless, polling was introduced in China in the 1990s and has rendered information increasingly transparent (Xinhua Online 2005d).

The internet is another indicator of public opinion although there is still no evidence of its role in the formation of public opinion. Nor is it yet a major factor in the organization of pro-democracy campaigns, in dissident activities by non-Han ethnic groups, and in the organization of religious movements such as the Falun Gong inside China. Nationalist internet activity, however, is growing, posing a potential threat to governmental surveillance and control of public opinion in the long run (Hughes 2002: 220).

Academics working in the social sciences are a good information source on public opinion because they operate relatively independently of governmental control and are well positioned to establish a wide network of societal contacts allowing them to obtain an impression of public opinion, though not verifiable in scientific terms. Although governmental control remains tight, public opinion sets constraints on the Chinese government (Interview 8). The present leaders are concerned about the continued legitimacy of Communist Party rule. The government is not inclined to change foreign policy positions as a result of public opinion, but rather tries to accommodate people's demands at least rhetorically to avoid domestic uprisings. The present leadership is aware that Chinese nationalism must be taken into account when responding to security threats (Hughes 2006: 151–6). On the issue of Taiwan, the public feels, China can afford to be more proactive and assertive, calling for reunification even if it involves war with the US (Interview 8).

Table 9.1 summarizes results from public opinion polls on perceived security threats. Public opinion polls such as those referred to here are problematic because the inquiry technique used is usually characterized by leading rather than by open-ended questions. For example, in the opinion poll on relations with Taiwan the respondents are, in practice, encouraged to endorse the mainland government's efforts at improving relations with Taiwan by peaceful means. In addition, respondents are residents of major Chinese cities, implying that the results have an inherent geographic bias. The results should therefore be interpreted with some caution. For example, unbalanced regional development is likely to be perceived as more of a threat in the Chinese countryside. Nevertheless, polling gives some indication of perceived security threats in the wider population.

A public opinion poll conducted by the Social Survey Institute of China shows that as many as 43 per cent of mainland Chinese think Taiwan should be reclaimed by force; 55 per cent said it should be reclaimed peacefully, while only 20 per cent of respondents said they were not interested in the matter (*The Economist* 2004).

Table 9.1 Chinese public perceptions of geographic and non-geographic security threats

Opinion poll, question (approximation)	Percentage of respondents answering in the affirmative (rounded)
Taiwan should be reclaimed by force	43
Taiwan should be brought back peacefully	55
Not interested in the Taiwan issue	20
A fresh version of middle school history textbooks approved by the Japanese government distorted history gravely	93
A fresh version of middle school history textbooks approved by the Japanese government constitutes an insult to the Chinese people	96
A fresh version of middle school history textbooks approved by the Japanese government constitutes an open provocation and a crime committed against world peace and harmony	81
The Japanese government must make a thorough retrospection of the country's aggressive past and apologize	97
Corruption is a concern	84
Unbalanced regional development and the growing income gap is a concern	57
Education fees are a concern	54

Source: Author's compilation of various opinion polls.

Public opinion also considers Japan a threat to China's international standing that is to be met by increasing governmental assertiveness. According to a telephone survey conducted by the Social Survey Institute of China with 1,000 respondents, about 93 per cent think that a fresh version of middle school history textbooks approved by the Japanese government on 5 April 2005 'distorted history gravely', while 96 per cent thought such action constituted an insult to the Chinese people. About 81 per cent of the respondents said that Japan's action was an 'open provocation' and 'a crime committed against world peace and harmony'; 97 per cent of respondents demanded the Japanese government 'make a thorough retrospection' of the country's aggressive past and apologize (Xinhua Online 2005e). The issue of Japan is similar to that of Taiwan in the sense that the public tends to favour assertive responses to what is perceived as Japanese provocation – in contrast to the more moderate long-term governmental view (Interview 13).

Non-geographic threats are most important because they affect people's daily livelihood and quality of life. An opinion poll of 40,000 respondents launched by the Chinese internet forum www.xinhua.net attempted to reflect these concerns. The poll showed that 84 per cent were concerned about 'corruption', 57 per cent about 'unbalanced regional development and the growing income gap', and 54 per cent about 'education fees'. Other security concerns mentioned by respondents included monopolies in telecommunications and railways, farmers' incomes, social security, the social welfare system, the environment and employment. Hence, the progress and drawbacks of modernization, corruption, and solutions to the growing gap between rich and poor are perceived as the most serious non-geographic security threats by the Chinese population (Xinhua Online 2004).

Table 9.2 summarizes perceptions of security threats to China. Strategic and economic threats remain at the centre of Chinese threat perceptions. State actors as well as domestic and transnational groups are perceived as main sources of threats, targeting the political, economic and military structures of China. Geographically, the main sources of threat to mainland China are located in its immediate environment in Northeast and Central Asia as well as the only remaining global great power, the United States. The severity of the threats is generally perceived as high, whereas their tractability is seen as low. China's Cold War preference for responses of a unilateral type supplemented with bilateral measures has been adjusted to include multilateral instruments.

Responses to threats

Interaction preference

Determined not to risk a repetition of the discriminatory practices of foreign powers, Beijing has avoided entering alliance commitments except for the Sino–North Korean Mutual Aid and Cooperation Friendship Treaty. China's reluctance to accept binding long-term commitments to other states has invested

Table 9.2 Typology of perceived security threats to China post-Cold War

Type of threat	Macroeconomic instability
	Domestic social and political instability
	Regional instability
	Conventional warfare
	Asymmetric warfare
	Oil and gas resources
	Global terrorism
	The environment
Agency of threat	State actors
	Domestic lower classes
	Terrorists
Target of threat	State structure
	State leadership
	Strategic interests
	Economic interests
	Civilian population
Geographical source of threat	Northeast Asia
	Central Asia
	The United States
Severity	High
Type of response	Unilateral, bilateral and multilateral
Tractability	Low

it with an autonomy allowing for swift unilateral responses to security threats. These responses often involved using force to counter threats to China's territorial integrity or to its claim to great power status. Thus, China used force against Chiang Kai-shek's Nationalist forces over the offshore island of Quemoy in 1958, in border conflicts with India in 1962, with the Soviet Union in 1969, and with Vietnam over the Paracels in 1974. In addition, China relied on bilateral responses to threats. For example, Beijing's approval of the 1972 Shanghai Communiqué meant that China accepted a continued US diplomatic and military presence on Taiwan in return for US agreement to 'one China but not now' (Yahuda 2004: 174). Beijing's tilt towards Washington allowed it to counter Soviet encirclement. For example, the Chinese invasion of Vietnam in 1979 was accompanied by US reassurances that it would not penalize China for the intervention. During the Cold War, China was not completely averse to multilateral responses to threats. The most conspicuous example is China's permanent membership of the UN Security Council, giving it a veto on decisions at odds with Beijing's security interests. The dominant tendency in Chinese foreign policy was, however, to supplement unilateral responses with bilateral responses to threats.

After the Cold War, China embraced multilateralism. According to academic opinion, China takes a proactive attitude towards Western forms of multilateralism while simultaneously supporting the development of an Asian alternative that prioritizes consensus over outcome (Interview 3). China has opted for multilateralism as a tactical response to threats because it is imperative for China to improve relations with neighbouring states to secure a regional environment conducive to economic development and to consolidate China's relative position of power.

Post-Cold War Chinese foreign policy involves a proactive attitude in consolidating and transforming multilateral responses to threats (Interview 6). For example, Beijing advocates supplementing intergovernmental 'track-one' multilateralism by transnational 'track-two' multilateralism. 'Track-two' diplomacy is an informal dialogue between people participating in their private capacities. 'Track-two' diplomacy allows for informal dialogue on conflictual issues without risking engendering violent conflict, but with the potential to establish a basis for formal intergovernmental 'track-one' dialogue. 'Track-two' diplomacy has proven useful to reduce tensions and establish consensus on sensitive issues prior to the initiation of intergovernmental dialogue. For China, multilateralism is an attractive means to convince the surroundings that its foreign policy concept of cooperative security is a genuine attempt to act as a responsible power that takes into account the common interests of states (Interview 6). Multilateralism is important to reduce not only geographic sources of threat, but also issues such as piracy, viruses, environmental problems and similar transnational security threats (Interview 4).

Bilateralism remains an important tactical means of responding to security threats. China is proactive in building bilateral partnerships. It maintains a bilateral dialogue with the US to alleviate the potential for conflict between the two powers over issues such as Taiwan and North Korea. At the same time, China establishes bilateral partnerships with entities that oppose US hegemony such as

Russia, the EU and ASEAN to protect Beijing from US demands at odds with Chinese interests (Interview 4). Additionally, the settlement of outstanding border conflicts, access to arms, energy supplies and new markets, and counter-terrorist operations are important benefits of China's bilateral partnerships with countries such as Russia, Kazakhstan and Kyrgyzstan (Interview 1).

Public opinion is more sceptical of the government's management of China's growing economic power. There are concerns that China is too keen to sell out its national interests to accommodate foreign interests, hence parting company with China's commitment not to compromise central foreign policy demands even when faced with far superior powers. The public therefore demands that what is perceived as economic great power status is translated into political and strategic great power status to resurrect China's standing as a civilization second to none. The call for economic resources to be used for a more assertive foreign policy ties in with the expectation that the US is a prospective strategic rival. Beijing cannot afford a conciliatory attitude towards its future opponent, but instead needs to adopt unilateral measures whenever Chinese interests are threatened by US foreign policy (Interview 8).

The government's response to threats lies somewhere in between academic and public opinion. The principal bilateral and multilateral strategies are strategic consultation and dialogues, regional security cooperation, cooperation in non-traditional security fields, participation in peacekeeping operations, military exchanges, contributions to the non-proliferation of weapons of mass destruction, advocacy of the international arms control and disarmament process, the fulfilment of international obligations, and participation in humanitarian efforts in the area of international arms control (The State Council Information Office 2004).

One main purpose of these strategies is to convince the outside world that China's rise will be peaceful, hence repudiating the fear of future Chinese aggression. The government does not want to convey an image of China as already a great power. It stopped speaking of China's peaceful rise in 2004 because the term implies that it might pose challenges to the interests of other states. Instead, the government now speaks of China's peaceful development (Interview 4). The term is designed to convey an image of China as a secondary power like Russia and India and that its ascendance to the position of a great power is not predetermined. China's embrace of multilateralism in recent years has been accompanied by an American preference for unilateral strategies. China can therefore not afford to rely solely on cooperation with other states, but still has to prioritize unilateral strategies of national defence. This is another reason for the government not to use the term 'China's peaceful rise' anymore. Potentially, it has a negative implication for defence modernization, encouraging the government to allocate less funding to the armed forces. Insufficient military modernization makes the country vulnerable to future security challenges and impedes China's ability to deter Taiwanese independence (Interview 10). Although, rhetorically, the government advocates multilateralism, in practice, it has second thoughts about this concept because a balance of power is thought to remain the basic dynamic of the international environment and because military force is needed to maintain domestic stability. Consequently, a central part of China's foreign policy strategy, of necessity, is defence modernization (Interview 7).

Institutional preferences

According to academic opinion, the UN forms the basis of Chinese post-Cold War multilateralism because Beijing wishes to demonstrate that its pursuit of national interests is embedded in globally accepted principles of state conduct centred on non-interference and respect for state sovereignty (Interview 6). In addition, Chinese academics emphasize the importance of sub-regional Asian institutions such as ASEAN and the Shanghai Cooperation Organization (SCO). Those academics adopting a positive view on the impact of institutions on state conduct consider ASEAN to be necessary because it is the principal driving force in providing institutional settings for dialogue between indigenous and external powers, maintaining regional peace and stability (Interview 3). Similarly, the SCO is seen as a leading institution in securing stability in Central Asia; it is important for addressing non-geographic threats such as piracy, drug trafficking and terrorism (Interview 5). However, Chinese academics also emphasize that existing institutions are unlikely to provide any assistance on the most important Chinese security concerns, namely Taiwan, Japan and US Northeast Asia policies. Forums such as ASEAN and SCO are therefore important mainly to counter secondary security threats outside China's sub-regional environment (Interview 8).

An important element in the government's foreign policy is to play a proactive role in regional security institutions such as the SCO and the ASEAN Regional Forum (ARF) (The State Council Information Office 2004). These institutions are thought to help maintain stability in Asia without subjecting local powers to US leadership (Interview 14). The Asian countries have looked to Europe's positive experiences with security cooperation, but do not emulate the European security mechanisms. Due to differences in stages of development and in security environments, Asia progresses at a slower pace and focuses on confidence building and dialogue rather than conflict resolution and treaties (Interview 15). To counter non-geographic threats, such as terrorism, infectious diseases, piracy, drug production and trafficking, Chinese cooperation with institutions such as ASEAN and ASEAN+3, also involving Japan and South Korea, has been strengthened (The State Council Information Office 2004). These forums are considered useful platforms for Asian cooperation on security threats. However, the government prioritizes the UN as a leading institution in counter-terrorist operations and participates with increasing frequency in UN peacekeeping operations (The State Council Information Office 2004). The UN is the principal platform for China to demonstrate its commitment to universal principles of state conduct and to show that China is a responsible power fulfilling its obligations towards the international community.

In the economic field, China's membership of the World Trade Organization (WTO) from 2001 is worth noting as an example of a proactive attitude towards integration into the world economy (Department of Policy Planning 2004: 371). Instead of trying to oppose overseas demands for reforms, as is the case with Russia, Beijing embraces existing rules of world trade with the purpose of transforming the rules to better match Chinese needs. In contrast, despite Chinese membership of the World Health Organization (WHO), Beijing proved very reluctant to share information and allow assistance from this organization to contain SARS in 2003. This case indicates that China has yet to accept the consequences of membership of international institutions for the handling of non-geographic threats because such institutions attempt to interfere with governmental policies affecting the Chinese population. Nevertheless, overall, the government's view of institutional responses is similar to academic opinion in that these are seen as beneficial to China's image as a benevolent power and as useful for developing an Asian foundation for countering geographic and non-geographic security threats.

Instrumental preferences

The mainstream of Chinese academia emphasizes the continued importance of military responses to security threats. However, soft power such as economic and diplomatic instruments will become more important in the future, implying that China will increasingly rely on consensus building, cooperation and consultation (Interview 12). The relative importance of hard and soft power depends on the issue. In case of a war in the Taiwan Strait, hard power would be necessary, but its usefulness for reaching political goals and for countering non-geographic threats is decreasing (Interview 11). Contemporary Chinese foreign policy is based on the principle that if you have the moral high ground, you have the support of the majority, but this position can only be achieved through the use of soft power (Interview 10). Since China is a much weaker military power than the United States, multilateral economic and diplomatic instruments are also imperative to keep US power in check (Johnston 2003: 32). For example, China is economically very important to the US, creating incentives for a more cautious US policy towards Taiwan.

The government adopts a two-pronged strategy of prioritizing economic and political cooperation and dialogue as well as military power. The importance of soft power is not only reflected in China's participation in international organizations at the formal and informal level, but is also noticeable in its determination to enhance cultural and educational exchanges as a confidence-building measure at the people-to-people level and as a means of increasing the educational level of the Chinese people. Beijing has also started to use its growing economic leverage to demonstrate its benevolent intentions towards neighbouring states. During the Asian financial crisis, China refrained from devaluing its currency to promote stability, and it contributed US$2 billion to the financial bailout of Thailand, Indonesia and South Korea, the countries most adversely affected by the crisis (Yahuda 2004: 320).

In the military sector, a principal concern is to update the armed forces to meet the requirements of the Revolution in Military Affairs. To realize this goal, the People's Liberation Army (PLA) gives priority to the navy and the air force, to a reduction of the PLA by 200,000, to accelerating the modernization of weaponry and equipment, to intensifying joint training among services and arms to enhance joint fighting capabilities, and to deepening logistical reforms to provide fast, efficient and integrated support (The State Council Information Office 2004). International military cooperation is an important element in Beijing's anti-terrorist activities, in its efforts to learn from the armed forces of other countries, and in its plans to keep in check the US military presence in Asia. Beijing puts particular emphasis on joint exercises with countries that are critical of Washington such as India, France and the Central Asian states. China also allocates considerable resources to strengthening its relatively weak military–industrial complex to increase its independence from foreign sources of arms supplies (IISS 2004: 161). The government's continued efforts to modernize the armed forces indicate that geographic threats remain at the centre of threat perceptions in the political establishment and that the use of force remains an option in a region with unstable relations between the major powers.

China also uses military power to convince the international community that China is a non-aggressive and responsible power acting in accordance with global standards of state conduct. Hence, China has become active in UN peacekeeping activities. As of January 2006, China contributed a total number of 1,060 military observers, civilian police and troops to UN peacekeeping operations, participating in Afghanistan, Burundi, Côte d'Ivoire, Liberia, the Democratic Republic of the Congo, Ethiopia and Eritrea, Kosovo, Sierra Leone, Sudan, Timor-Leste, Western Sahara, Haiti and the Middle East (United Nations 2006). It has become a substantial contributor to human security operations that have been authorized by the UN Security Council and have been accepted by the receiving governments. This development demonstrates China's commitment to protect world society from gross human rights violations without compromising its respect for the principles of non-interference and absolute sovereignty.

Allocation of resources

Threat perceptions vs. budgetary allocations

China ranks among the countries with the largest defence budgets in the world, only surpassed by the United States, Russia and the EU-15 combined. According to the International Institute for Strategic Studies (IISS), China spent US$43.55 billion in 2001, 51.16 billion in 2002 and 55.95 billion in 2003. China's defence expenditure as a proportion of GDP was 3.7 per cent in 2001, 4.1 per cent in 2002 and 3.9 per cent in 2003. This amounts to a larger proportion than for the United States, but a smaller proportion than in the Russian case. In March 2004, US$2.6 billion were added to the defence budget to boost progress in the reforms of the armed forces (IISS 2004: 355). These figures reflect the continuing growth of China's military capabilities due to Beijing's focus on military modernization and transformation for the next 10 to 15 years.

China's own estimate of its defence expenditure is considerably lower. According to the 2004 defence White Paper, China's annual defence expenditure as a proportion of its GDP was 1.48 per cent in 2001, 1.62 per cent in 2002, and 1.63 per cent in 2003 (The State Council Information Office 2004). China's budgetary allocations for defence purposes have become increasingly transparent with the publication of defence White Papers for the past decade. Hence, according to official data, China increased its defence budget by 11.9 per cent in 2003. Nevertheless, the figures released by the government are inadequate. According to IISS, the publicly reported defence budget only represents part of actual military expenditure: proceeds from defence sales are not included, and procurement, research and development as well as most pensions for retired personnel are funded from elsewhere within the state budget (IISS 2004: 319). IISS estimates are therefore considered the most reliable information source.

Government information on spending items in the defence budget is also limited, although China does not make a secret of its priorities, namely RMA-driven reforms, having fewer but better troops, and stepping up its military posture across the Taiwan Strait. Chinese arms deliveries amounted to US$500 million in 2003, but China received US$1 billion worth of arms deliveries in 2003. Substantial amounts of the PLA's budget allocated to the procurement of weaponry are used to buy arms and defence-related technology from Russia. In 2003, China spent US$1 billion alone on 24 advanced Russian Su-27 and Su-30 fighter aircraft. Chinese arms procurements reflect the fact that Beijing continues to be heavily dependent on outside sources of arms supplies.

China is strengthening its naval capabilities, which involves the allocation of resources to the construction of an aircraft carrier on the basis of Russian designs and the development of modernized long-range, anti-ship missiles. China's space programme is also an important item on defence budgets. In 2003, China became the third country to achieve a manned space mission, and China spends heavily on military communication satellites (IISS 2004: 161, 253, 327–8). Despite the scant information on Chinese defence expenditures, there is no doubt that China expends considerable resources in transforming its armed forces from self-sufficiency in manpower to self-sufficiency in military technology to be able to adopt swift and flexible defence responses to geographic and non-geographic threats. Defence allocations on the state budget hence reflect government perceptions of threats and the military responses appropriate to counter those threats.

Conclusion

Security/defence dichotomy

Chinese worldviews follow the perception that, in international relations, the dichotomy between security and defence is weak. Consequently, a strong national defence is seen as the safest path to security. Phenomena such as economic interdependence and transnational security threats produce an increased focus on

Table 9.3 Security culture of China

Worldview of external environment	Weak dichotomy between security and defence
National identity	Humiliation Motherland Freedom of action
Strategic purpose	Long term: great power status Intermediate: peaceful coexistence
Instrumental preferences	Hard power Soft power
Interaction preferences	Freedom from alliances Temporary cooperation
Civil–military relations	Top-down

multilateral security cooperation and soft power. However, zero-sum power games remain the fundamental dynamics of international relations, implying that national defence remains an important means of responding to threats.

Chinese national identity is moulded on the theme of humiliation following from foreign encroachments on Chinese territorial unity and political autonomy in past centuries. This experience forms the basis of China's uncompromising attitude towards the legitimacy of its claim to territory defined as its motherland and its concern to maintain its freedom of action. Loyalty is directed towards the Chinese nation and its territorial rights, sustaining focus on geographic threats in contemporary international relations.

China's strategic purpose is hence to defend Chinese interests and demands, not only by amassing economic and political power, but also by convincing the international community that China's foreign policy decisions have a sound moral basis. Thus, Beijing advocates peaceful coexistence, requiring that states' pursuit of national interests should be a combination of individual foreign policy choices and extensive multilateral dialogue to prevent violent conflict. Multilateralism, diplomacy and soft power are means to allow states to concentrate on fulfilling their individual goals rather than ends in themselves.

The combination of power and morality in Chinese foreign policy implies that China cannot merely rely on military instruments to protect its interests. The post-Cold War concept of cooperative security is designed to show that China's foreign policy goals are not driven by a desire for world dominance, but are founded in legitimate claims compatible with the national interests of other states. To demonstrate the sincerity of Chinese intentions, Beijing takes a proactive attitude towards international cooperation. China's participation in international activities such as UN peacekeeping operations is a means of demonstrating that China is also willing to defend the fundamental rights of other nations, even if these activities have no immediate bearing on its national interests. China's force structure is nuclear and aggressive. Beijing is transforming it from a force structure based on territorial defence into a structure allowing China to fight a limited war with the United States. China hence adheres to the principle that coexistence is best promoted by preparing to defend vital Chinese interests. This defence culture reveals that, although China supports international cooperation, it does not trade in its right to use force. Interests and threats such as China's claim to Taiwan, its growing need for energy resources, Washington's continued containment of China and militant Islamic separatism create incentives for China to strengthen its nuclear force posture and to acquire and develop offensive weaponry such as fighter aircraft, destroyers and submarines. Such priorities are aimed at allowing Beijing a capability to perform military strikes against a probably US-protected Taiwan when necessary, to defend its ocean frontier and ultimately to exert control over central shipping lanes (Interview 8).

Chinese interaction patterns are determined by the theme of humiliation. The concern with safeguarding China against threats against the unity of nation and territory thus inform the tangible expressions of national security culture. China remains averse to alliance relations because it sees rigid commitments to collective defence as an impediment to its ability to adopt swift responses to changes in the international realm. Beijing has retained its aversion to alliances since it fell out with the Soviet Union in the 1950s, subsequently following the rationale that to maximize the realization of its national interests, China would have to adopt a foreign policy characterized by flexibility and temporary strategic cooperation so long as China's economic and military capabilities did not qualify it for the position of a global great power.

Chinese civil–military relations form a top-down system aimed at sustaining Communist Party rule. At the same time, the armed forces form an inherent part of Chinese nationalism. The military is perceived as the utmost expression of the autonomy and greatness of the Chinese nation because it constitutes the principal insurance against China's submission to foreign demands. At present, Beijing is concerned to promote an image of China as a peaceful, cooperative and responsible country. The identification of the armed forces with the Chinese nation and its entitlement to great power status works at cross purposes with this priority since it encourages popular demands for a more assertive foreign policy towards Taiwan and Japan.

The upside to Chinese security culture is its flexibility, which allows for swift adjustments to a changing international environment, resulting in a level of international political influence far beyond that justified by China's capabilities. The downside is its conservatism. It suggests no viable alternative to the Cold War structure of international relations based on absolute sovereignty, non-interference and traditional power balancing. As international demands increase for institutional structures based on a world society of people-to-people relations, China may not be able to continue to base its foreign policy on yesterday's understanding of international relations.

Interviews

1   Research Professor Jin Canrong, Institute of American Studies, Renmin University, 4 November 2004.
2   Professor Zhu Feng, Director of International Security Programme, School of International Studies, Peking University, 7 November 2004.
3   Qin Yaqing, Professor of International Studies, Vice President, China Foreign Affairs University, 9 November 2004.
4   Anonymous Professor of International Studies, Peking University, 10 November 2004.
5   Associate Professor Su Hao, Deputy Director, Centre for International Security, China's Foreign Affairs College, 10 November 2004.
6   Associate Research Professor Yuan Peng, Deputy Director of Division for American Studies, China Institute of Contemporary International Relations, 12 November 2004.
7   Niu Jun, Research Professor, Director of Division of the US Diplomacy, School of International Studies, Peking University, 13 November 2004.
8   Professor Shi Yinhong, Director, Centre for American Studies, School of International Studies, Renmin University of China, 15 November 2005.
9   Anonymous former Chinese military official, 15 November 2004.
10 Professor and Associate Dean Jia Qingguo, School of International Studies, Peking University, 16 November 2004.
11 Chu Shulong, Director, Institute of Strategic Studies, Professor, School of Public Policy and Management, Tsinghua University, 17 November 2004.
12 Vice President and Senior Research Fellow Ruan Zongze, the China Institute of International Studies, 18 November 2004.
13 Professor Zhu Liqun, Director, Institute of International Relations, China Foreign Affairs University, 19 November 2004.
14 Anonymous high-ranking Chinese military official, expert in defence and national policy studies, 20 November 2004.
15 Anonymous Chinese military official, 20 November 2004.
16 Senior Fellow Tao Wenzhao, Institute of American Studies, Chinese Academy of Social Sciences, 22 November 2004.

Notes

1   Cyberspace is a potential threat since opponents of the regime can use it to distribute information that is critical of the Communist regime. Internet cafés have proliferated in the major Chinese cities, making the internet easily accessible. In principle, the internet is easy to control through central servers that are programmed to prevent users from accessing websites using vocabulary such as the Falun Gong, but in practice websites on issues such as terrorism are not easy to block because of the vast possibilities of describing the phenomenon without using words that are known to be singled out as offensive by the Chinese government.
2   According to anonymous Russian sources, the US supported the overthrow of President Akaev in Kyrgyzstan in March 2005.

References

BBC News (2005) *Text of China's Anti-Secession Law.* Available online at: <http://news.bbc.co.uk/2/hi/asia-pacific/4347555.stm> (accessed 27 October 2006).
Callahan, W.A. (2001) *National Humiliation, National Salvation and Chinese Foreign Relations,* Paper presented at the International Studies Association Conference in Hong Kong, Panel: Chinese Political Culture, 26–28 September 2001.

Department of Policy Planning, Ministry of Foreign Affairs, People's Republic of China (2004) *China's Foreign Affairs: 2004 Edition,* Beijing: World Affairs Press.

Hughes, C.R. (2002) 'China and the globalization of ICTs: implications for international relations', *New Media and Society,* 4 (2): 205–24.

Hughes, C.R. (2006) *Chinese Nationalism in the Global Era,* London: Routledge.

Johnston, A.I. (2003) 'Is China a status quo power?', *International Security* 27 (4): 5–56.

Mackerras C., McMillen, D.H. and Watson, A. (1998) *Dictionary of the Politics of the People's Republic of China,* London: Routledge.

The Economist (2004) *Chen Survives Again.* Available online at: <http://www.economist.com/agenda/displaystory.cfm?story_id=2516204> (accessed 23 March 2004).

The International Institute for Strategic Studies (IISS) (2004) *The Military Balance 2004–2005,* London: Oxford University Press.

The State Council Information Office (2004) *China's National Defense in 2004.* Available online at: <http://www.fas.org/nuke/guide/china/doctrine/natdef2004.html> (accessed 27 October 2006).

United Nations (2006) *Peacekeeping.* Available online at: <http://www.un.org/Depts/dpko/dpko/index.asp> (accessed 16 March 2006).

Xinhua Online (2004) *Public Airs Issues for China's Upcoming 'Two Sessions'.* Available online at: <http://news.xinhuanet.com/english/2004-02/27/content_1339081.htm> (accessed 27 February 2004).

Xinhua Online (2005a) *Full Text of Anti-Secession Law.* Available online at: <http://news.xinhuanet.com/english/2005-03/14/content_2694180.htm> (accessed 14 March 2005).

Xinhua Online (2005b) *Top Legislature Adopts Anti-Secession Law.* Available online at: <http://news.xinhuanet.com/english/2005-03/14/content_2694645.htm> (accessed 14 March 2005).

Xinhua Online (2005c) *Chinese Top Legislature Expresses Strong Dissatisfaction, Opposition over US Resolution on China's Anti-Secession Law.* Available online at: <http://news.xinhuanet.com/english/2005-03/19/content_2715985.htm> (accessed 19 March 2005).

Xinhua Online (2005d) *Polling Makes China's Information More Transparent.* Available online at: <http://news.xinhuanet.com/english/2005-05/16/content_2964040.htm> (accessed 16 May 2005).

Xinhua Online (2005e) *Japan's Textbook 'an Insult to Chinese People'.* Available online at: <http://news.xinhuanet.com/english/2005-04/11/content_ 2816987.htm> (accessed 11 April 2005).

Yahuda, M. (2004) *The International Politics of the Asia-Pacific,* 2nd edn, London: Routledge.

10 Japan

Recasting the post-war security consensus

Haruhiro Fukui

Modern Japan was born in the mid nineteenth century after a nearly bloodless revolution that toppled a 250-year-old feudal regime. It then fought and won a war with China and another with Russia, respectively, in the last decade of the nineteenth century and the first decade of the twentieth century and participated in the First World War as an ally of the victorious European powers. In the Second World War, however, the nation met its first and crushing defeat and was occupied by the victorious, American-dominated Allied Powers. In its effort to democratize and demilitarize Japan, the occupation authorities undertook sweeping reforms of its political, economic, social and cultural institutions and practices.

By far the most significant of these reforms was the replacement of the autocratic and militaristic constitution of the Japanese Empire that had been promulgated in 1889 by a new constitution designed and drafted by a group of US lawyers (Masumi 1988: 45–7; 54–60). The most unusual, and arguably the most important, of the 103 articles of this new constitution, which came into effect in May 1947, was Article 9, popularly known as the 'peace clause'. It reads:

1   Aspiring sincerely to an international peace based on justice and order, the Japanese people forever renounce war as a sovereign right of the nation and the threat or use of force as means of settling international disputes.
2   In order to accomplish the aim of the preceding paragraph, land, sea, and air forces, as well as other war potential, will never be maintained. The right of belligerency of the state will not be recognized.

From the beginning, however, the peace clause was controversial not only among Japanese leaders and people but even among leaders of the Allied Powers. Even while the nation was still under occupation, the article was interpreted in such a way that it would permit the nation's de facto rearmament. Following the outbreak of the Korean War in 1950, a 'Police Reserve Force' was created at Washington's instigation. This was not a military force but a police force concerned solely with the maintenance of domestic peace, according to Prime Minister Shigeru Yoshida defending the constitutionality of the government action in the House of Representatives (lower house) plenary session at that time (Maeda and Iijima 2003: 37). In 1952, however, the force was reorganized, a naval complement added, and the combined force was renamed Security Force and, in 1954, further reorganized and renamed the Self-Defence Force (SDF).

For the next three and a half decades, the SDF's mission remained confined to the territorial defence of the Japanese archipelago. By the early 1980s, however, the Japanese government had begun to suggest that it would not be unconstitutional to send SDF troops abroad for purposes other than the use of military force. Following the outbreak of the Gulf War in January 1991, half a dozen Maritime Self-Defence Force minesweepers were actually dispatched to the Persian Gulf and a new law was enacted that made it explicitly legal for SDF troops to participate in UN-sponsored peacekeeping operations outside Japanese territory. Thereafter, it became increasingly commonplace and uncontroversial for SDF troops to be sent abroad on peacekeeping missions (Maeda and Iijima 2003: 173; *Asahi Shimbun* 1 May 2004: 26).

As the spatial scope of SDF activities expanded beyond Japan's borders, it became increasingly difficult for the Japanese government to defend its insistence on the SDF's strictly non-military character and mission. In November 1991, for example, a senior Ministry of Foreign Affairs (MOFA) official told the lower house special committee on international cooperation for peace that the SDF was treated as a military force under international law (*Asahi Shimbun* 1 May 2004: 26). A debate on the constitutionality of the SDF ensued, giving rise to a campaign – originally largely clandestine among a handful of conservative politicians but increasingly open, public and effective – for a formal revision of the constitution, including Article 9.

In a February 1983 public opinion poll published by the *Asahi Shimbun,* only about a quarter of the respondents approved and nearly half disapproved of a revision of the constitution. But, in an April 2004 poll, more than half of the respondents approved and only about a third disapproved (*Asahi Shimbun* 20 January 2000: 7; 1 May 2004: 1, 26).[1] When they were asked in the 2004 poll specifically whether Article 9 should be amended, about one-third of the respondents said yes and about two-thirds said no (*Asahi Shimbun* 1 May 2004: 1). As of early 2004, Japan thus remained constitutionally a uniquely pacifist state, but there was a movement afoot in the nation for a potentially sweeping change in the text of the document, including its best-known signature provision.

Security threat perceptions

As is probably true for most other peoples, there is no single, well-defined national perception of threat among the Japanese. Like opinions about threat, perceptions of threat vary among Japanese scholars according to their ideological persuasions, as well as their cognitive orientations, and among Japanese politicians according to their partisan affiliations. Japanese government leaders and policy-makers have tended deliberately to be inarticulate, even obscurantist, about their perceptions of the types and sources of threat, while the Japanese public sees the threats to security in a broad range of domestic and international problems.

Academic debate

Japanese academic opinion is divided on nearly every major security and foreign policy issue. On one side are the conservative nationalists who subscribe to the standard realist view of international politics and support a substantial expansion of Japan's military power and role. Terumasa Nakanishi (2003: 25), for example, writes: 'Needless to say, international politics is inherently governed by its basic determinants, i.e., power and national interests. International cooperation is but an epiphenomenon that materializes only sporadically'. He then comments on the current structure of the international system and its consequences for Japan: 'For a fairly long period in the twenty-first century, international politics will revolve around rivalries between the US and Europe across the Atlantic and between the US and China in East Asia', and Japan ought to decide to arm itself with nuclear weapons.

On the other side are the liberal internationalists who espouse the standard liberal view. Ikuo Kabashima (2004: 8), a University of Tokyo political scientist, approvingly cites Dalchoong Kim's keynote address to the 2003 International Political Science Association World Congress, in which Kim urged Japan and its neighbours in East Asia to develop a regional, as opposed to national, vision of security based on a culture of cooperation. In the same article, Kabashima warns that a Japan with offensive conventional weapons, not to mention nuclear weapons, would be a serious obstacle to the birth and growth of such a culture and vision of regional security. These two divergent schools of thought – the Japanese realists and multilateralists – have set the boundaries of a relatively circumscribed academic debate.[2]

Government policy

Conservatives, represented by today's Liberal-Democratic Party (LDP), have dominated post-war Japanese politics and monopolized government power except for two and a half years from mid-1993 to early 1996, when multiparty coalitions, initially excluding but later including the LDP, ruled. Since June 1994, the LDP has been in power in coalitions with another, and much smaller, party or parties, most recently the Clean Government Party (CGP).

A notable aspect of the security policy debates in the succession of LDP-led governments during the Cold War was a nearly complete silence on the nature, magnitude and source of security threats the country faced, with the exception of the Soviet Union, which was explicitly and officially identified in the 1980s as a serious military threat to Japan. Given Japan's highly circumscribed defence capability, successive governments were understandably anxious to avoid antagonizing any foreign state or group, particularly one in close proximity to Japan, and provoking a hostile action or even attitude. Japanese governments in the post-Cold War period have been somewhat more forthcoming, explicitly referring to both China and North Korea as potential military threats to Japanese security.

The terrorist attacks on the United States on 11 September 2001 suddenly and vastly expanded the range of phenomena perceived as security threats by the Japanese government. While the pre-11 September Japanese Defence Agency's annual White Paper mentioned only conventional military threats to the nation's sovereignty and territorial integrity, the post-11 September JDA White Papers discuss in considerable detail the threats of terrorism and actions Japan must and will take not only to defend itself from potential terrorist attacks but also to contribute to the international war on terrorism (Boeicho 2000; 2001–2005).

The SDF Law was revised and several new laws were enacted in the wake of 11 September to enable SDF troops to participate in a variety of operations beyond the limits previously imposed on its mission and activities, including operations around Diego Garcia in the Indian Ocean and in the area around Guam. For the first time, terrorist attacks with nuclear, biological and chemical weapons as well as cyberwarfare were identified as realistic threats to Japan's security (Boeicho 2002). Also for the first time, domestic terrorism, exemplified by the sarin gas attacks on a suburban neighbourhood in Matsumoto City in 1994 and on subway trains in Tokyo the following year, was mentioned. So were such natural disasters as earthquakes, typhoons and volcanic eruptions, as well as potential accidents at nuclear power plants.

Parliamentary debate

Virtually all Japanese legislators are affiliated with particular national parties and their views of security-related issues vary with their party affiliation, roughly along a right–left axis. On the constitutional revision issue, for example, an overwhelming majority of LDP lower house members favoured a revision in the wake of the 2000 general election, while about half of CGP, about a quarter of Democratic Party of Japan (DPJ), a negligible number of Social Democratic Party (SDP) and none of Japan Communist Party (JCP) members did so (*Asahi Shimbun* 27 June 2000: 5). When asked about a year later whether they agreed or disagreed with the view that Japan should claim and exercise its right to participate in collective self-defence actions in cooperation with other nations, all of SDP, nearly all of JCP and over three-quarters of CGP lower house members categorically disagreed, as compared to a little less than two-thirds of DPJ and virtually all of LDP members who agreed (*Asahi Shimbun* 13 July 2001: 5). On core security issues such as whether Japan's defence capability should be substantially expanded, whether the Japanese–US military alliance should be strengthened, and whether a pre-emptive attack could be justified against a foreign state that poses an imminent threat to Japan, there is a consistent pattern of variation among the members of parliament affiliated with the several parties: LDP members are overwhelmingly positive, JCP and SDP members overwhelmingly negative, and CGP and DPJ members neutral in their collective orientations (Ampo yori shakaikozo 2003).

The right–left division is more blurred on the question of whether Japan should seek to possess nuclear weapons: whereas JCP, SDP and CGP lower house members were unanimously opposed to Japan's nuclear armament, so were the overwhelming majorities of those affiliated with the other parties, as of mid 2003 (Ampo yori shakaikozo 2003). What is worth noting about the politicians' opinions about this particular issue, however, is the slow but steady erosion of principled opposition to the SDF's acquisition of nuclear weapons. Whereas only about 10 per cent of the lower house members were in favour of such a move in August 2003, this percentage was actually more than twice as high as it had been in 1998, when only about 4 per cent of all Diet members had supported the move (Kabashima 2004: 8). The erosion of the anti-nuclear sentiment among Diet members resulted largely from a steady decline in the number of SDP and JCP members. The SDP's fall has been particularly dramatic: its predecessor, the Japan Socialist Party (JSP), was a major parliamentary party in the late 1950s through the early 1990s, winning, for example, 166 of the 467 lower house seats in the 1958 general election and 136 of the 512 seats in the 1990 general election. In the series of general elections that followed, however, the number of SDP members elected to the Diet plummeted to 70 in 1993, 15 in 1996, and 6 in 2003. The JCP's fall has not been as spectacular as the SDP's, mainly because it began at a much lower level: it won only one seat in the 1958 general election, but 16 in 1990, 15 in 1993 and 26 in 1996, before its ranks were reduced to nine seats in the 2003 election (*Asahi Shimbun* 14 November 2003: 5).

Public opinion

Public perceptions of security threat or threats that Japan faces have been unfocused and blurry. In the wake of 11 September, the attention of the Japanese public was clearly drawn to the threat of terrorism. In a *Yomiuri Shimbun* poll, for example, as many respondents listed terrorism as their most serious security concern as any other issue. However, nearly as many mentioned global warming, while only slightly fewer respondents mentioned Japan's relations with other Asian countries and the general state of the world economy (see Table 10.1). Moreover, and as will be discussed in the following section, the average Japanese is less concerned about threats posed by foreign states or terrorists and more concerned about a number of domestic problems, such as increasing crimes and violence, potential accidents at nuclear power plants, and natural disasters.

Sources of threat

The Japanese government has explicitly identified three states as potential sources of threat to the nation's security: the Soviet Union during the Cold War, and China and North Korea since the end of the Cold War. Since its test firing of a Taepodon ballistic missile over Japan in the summer of 1998, North Korea has been perceived as the most serious threat by both Japanese policy-makers and the general public, a perception compounded by the revelation in 2002 of the abduction by North Korean agents of more than a dozen Japanese citizens, many of whom had allegedly died in captivity.

Table 10.1 Public views of most serious foreign policy issues

What foreign policy issue or issues do you consider as most serious now? (as percentage)	
Terrorism	43
Global warming/environment	43
Relations with Asian nations	38
Stabilization of the world economy	38
Northern territories dispute with Russia	30
Disarmament/abolition of nuclear weapons	24
Economic/technical aid/cooperation	20
Participation in international humanitarian efforts	19
Strengthening US–Japan ties	18
Stabilization on the Korean peninsula	16
Framework-building for regional security in Asia	16
Stabilization of China–Taiwan relations	10
Response to US missile defence plans	7

Source: *Yomiuri Shimbun*, 31 October 2001: 20.

The 11 September terrorist attacks on the United States shocked the Japanese government and public and brought home to them the danger of international terrorism. As far as the Japanese public is concerned, however, the horror of terrorism was soon overshadowed, if not replaced, by the horrors of the war on terrorism fought in Afghan and Iraqi cities and villages and those caused by natural disasters, especially the 2004 Indian Ocean tsunami and the 2005 devastation of coastal communities in the southern states of the United States. In the years following 11 September, sources of threat thus multiplied and diversified in the perception of the Japanese public.

The US–Japan Mutual Security Treaty, originally signed in 1951 and revised and extended indefinitely in 1960, was implicitly aimed at the Soviet Union. Until the Soviet invasion of Afghanistan in 1979, however, few Japanese leaders considered the Soviet Union as a real and serious threat. The 1980 edition of the Defence Agency White Paper referred for the first time to a 'Soviet threat', a term subsequently repeated a number of times by Yasuhiro Nakasone during his prime-ministerial tenure (November 1982 to November 1987) (Maeda and Iijima 2003: 158). As he explained to a JCP member in the lower house Budget Committee in February 1983, Japanese defence policy was designed to counter-attack Soviet Backfire (TU-22M) bombers, bottle up Soviet submarines in the Sea of Japan by blocking all exits, and defend Japan's vital sea lanes with Japan's own ships (Maeda and Iijima 2003: 125; Kawakami 1996: 161–2). The fall of the Soviet Union and the end of the Cold War, however, rendered this presumptive Soviet threat doubtful and, as Berger points out, the Defence Agency White Paper stopped mentioning the Soviet Union as a threat after 1990 (Berger 1998: 240).

Table 10.2 Public opinion on Japan's neighbours

Do you have favourable images of the following countries? (as percentage)			
	January 1995	*August 1999*	*October 2001*
United States	75	70	79
China	55	47	56
South Korea	50	51	56
Russia	13	18	28
North Korea	10	2	6

Source: *Yomiuri Shimbun*, 31 October 2001: 21.

By comparison, most Japanese viewed China far more favourably even during the Cold War. A 1980 poll, for example, found nearly 80 per cent of the respondents holding friendly feelings toward China, although the percentage of such respondents sharply fell in a 1989 poll taken in the wake of the Tiananmen Square incident and remained at about the same level throughout the rest of the 1990s (Nihonjin wa chugoku ga kirai 1999; Kokubun 2001: 42–3). In fact, China was the second most popular country, next to the US, in *Yomiuri Shimbun*'s polls, until the mid 1990s when South Korea's popularity rose marginally above China's.

Nonetheless, the Defence Agency's 2000 White Paper expressed serious concern about China's growing military power, especially its growing arsenal of nuclear weapons and ballistic missiles (Boeicho 2000: 53). The 2005 White Paper warns against the threat posed by the increasing presence and activities of Chinese warships, including nuclear-powered submarines, within and just outside Japanese territorial waters, as well as the possibility that China may use force against Taiwan (Boeicho 2005).

Not surprisingly, right-wing academics point out the Chinese threat far more openly, forcefully and spitefully. Nakanishi (2003: 27) writes: 'There is a campaign under way to drive a wedge between the US and Japan, a campaign behind which lies the Chinese ambition to gain a hegemonic position and rebuild an imperial tributary regime in East Asia in the 2010s.' And Shigeharu Aoyama (2002: 45), another right-wing academic, goes a step further: 'China's Dongfeng-21 (East Wind 21) is an intermediate-range ballistic missile designed to be fired against Tokyo. This makes China a source of threat even greater than North Korea.'

However, by far the most frequently and boldly identified source of military threat to Japan in recent years has been North Korea. Serious Japanese suspicions about Pyongyang's intentions and plans against Japan were first aroused by the firing of a North Korean missile, Taepodon, in August 1998, which apparently flew over Japan and parts of which fell in the Pacific Ocean. These suspicions were then aggravated in March 1999 when a pair of officially 'unidentified' North Korean ships inside Japan's exclusive economic zone was detected off its Sea of Japan coast. When another unidentified ship was spotted in the same area in December 2001, a Japanese patrol boat pursued, fired on and sank it (Maeda and Iijima 2003: 256). Following these incidents, some in the Japanese government and public began to suggest a Japanese, or joint US–Japanese, pre-emptive strike against North Korea, although a more sober and pragmatic approach has prevailed so far (Fukagawa 2004; Izumi 2004).

The Japanese public also perceives North Korea as an important source of military threat. Asked which foreign country they thought threatened their country in an *Asahi Shimbun*–RDD/Harris joint poll conducted in Japan and the US in the fall of 2002, nearly half of the Japanese respondents, compared to almost none of the Americans, singled out North Korea, while less than 10 per cent of the Japanese, compared to nearly a quarter of the Americans, mentioned China and almost none of the Japanese, compared to nearly 30 per cent of the Americans, mentioned Iraq (*Asahi Shimbun* 8 September 2002: 5).

The abduction of Japanese nationals by North Korean agents in the 1970s and 1980s has compounded Japanese distrust of North Korea. These abductions had been widely rumoured in Japan since the early 1990s, but were stoutly denied by Pyongyang until September 2002. At that time, during Prime Minister Junichiro Koizumi's first visit to North Korea, Kim Jong-il admitted that North Koreans had kidnapped 13 Japanese nationals, of whom eight had died (*Asahi Shimbun* 18 September 2002: 1). The five remaining survivors returned to Japan within a month of Koizumi's visit and the American husband and two daughters of one of the five arrived in Japan via Indonesia in July 2004 (*Asahi Shimbun* 9 July 2004: 1). Many Japanese, particularly the families and friends of the eight declared dead, however, refuse to believe Kim's words and continue to claim that all or some of them are alive in captivity in North Korea.

In spite of their deep-rooted fear of North Korea's military policy, especially its nuclear weapons programme, and distrust of its highly autocratic and secretive regime, or perhaps because of such sentiments, a majority of Japanese seemed to wish in 2002 that the relationship between the two countries was normalized and stabilized as soon as possible (*Asahi Shimbun* 20 September 2002: 4). Japanese public opinion has subsequently turned increasingly sceptical about and wary of the costs and benefits of a closer and friendlier relationship with North Korea. By the middle of 2003, those opposing the normalization of diplomatic relations between Tokyo and Pyongyang outnumbered proponents and, by early 2004, those favouring economic sanctions against Pyongyang as a means to solve the nuclear weapons and abduction issues outnumbered those who favoured dialogue (*Asahi Shimbun* 24 February 2004: 5).

There is, however, a body of academic opinion in Japan that holds that the abduction and the nuclear weapons issues cannot be solved by punitive action against North Korea, but only by dialogue and negotiation. Those who subscribe to such a view argue that the Japanese who condemn North Korea's abduction of Japanese citizens should not forget that Japan brought hundreds of thousands of Koreans to Japan by force and used them as slave labour in Japanese factories and mines during the Second World War and that Japan still owes them an apology and compensation (Chosen minshushugi jinmin kyowakoku 2003). Nonetheless, in mid 2004, North Korea remained the source of the most serious, or the only serious, military and non-military threat in the minds of many Japanese, though probably not a majority of them.

Agency of threat

As indicated by the results of the *Yomiuri Shimbun* poll presented in Table 10.1, the Japanese public clearly perceived international terrorism as one of the most serious security threats in the wake of 11 September. The shocking television images of the burning and collapsing World Trade Centre buildings, however, have receded and been overtaken by the equally shocking images of Afghan and Iraqi towns and villages attacked and destroyed and their inhabitants, mostly civilians, forced to leave their homes or even shot to death, seemingly randomly, by invading US and coalition soldiers. In fact, even these images have been overshadowed by those of houses, cars and people tossed around and swallowed by tsunami, hurricane surges and destructive earthquakes. Not surprisingly, the focus of many people's attention has shifted, and so have their threat perceptions.

For the average citizen in today's Japan, domestic crimes and violence, potential accidents at nuclear power plants, unsafe or unhealthy foodstuffs, and the deteriorating environment, as well as natural disasters, such as earthquakes and typhoons, are more immediate and serious threats to personal security than international terrorism or North Korea (Urabe 2003; Ishibashi and Tamura 2005). In a recent poll, the Japanese public was asked whether Japan was a safer or less safe country to live in compared to five years earlier. An overwhelming majority of the respondents said Japan was a less safe country (see Table 10.3). In a set of 11-nation public opinion surveys conducted in 2002, Japanese respondents were more worried than their counterparts in other countries about nuclear wars and natural disasters (see Table 10.4). It thus appears that, in less than a year after 11 September 2001, Japanese were less worried than Americans about terrorism and much more worried about natural disasters, economic problems or nuclear wars.

Institutional and instrumental responses to threats

Post-Second World War Japanese security policy has been consistently framed bilaterally in cooperation with and in deference to the United States and decisions have been made on the basis of the original (1951) and revised (1960) United States–Japan Mutual Security Treaty. This preference for bilateralism has extended to Japan's economic aid policy, which has been used to an important extent as a component of the nation's security policy and, since the early 1990s, has led to its

Table 10.3 Public opinion on changes in personal safety in Japan

Do you think Japan has become safer, less safe or unchanged in the last five years? (as percentage)	
Safer	1
Less safe	81
Unchanged	6
d.k./n.a.	2

Source: *Asahi Shimbun* 27 January 2004: 17.

Table 10.4 Eleven-nation survey of public opinion on the state of security
(in percentage of respondents)

Respondents of:	Nuclear war	Terrorism	Natural disasters	Accidents	Violent crime	Health	Economic disaster
Japan	19	12	24	8	6	12	20
Brazil	1	0	3	2	84	4	1
Canada	4	8	17	14	24	14	3
France	4	10	14	8	46	8	1
Germany	10	9	8	2	14	3	4
India	5	19	13	8	24	5	16
Russia	15	13	10	4	22	9	6
South Africa	2	4	7	1	47	22	5
South Korea	6	3	21	12	6	14	10
UK	10	6	13	4	26	6	1
USA	5	15	13	11	22	6	2
All	9	11	14	8	23	9	6

Source: *Asahi Shimbun* 17 May 2002: 1, 16–17, based on surveys by Ipsos Reed for Liu Center for the Study of Global Issues, University of British Columbia, with the cooperation of the *Asahi Shimbun*.

Self-Defence Force troops' participation in peacekeeping operations around the world and in the US-led 'war on terrorism', despite widespread public opposition. By comparison, the Japanese attitude toward and resort to multilateral forums, such as the United Nations and the ASEAN Regional Forum (ARF), as alternative means of the nation's security policy, have been by and large ambivalent and perfunctory.

Interaction preference

The Japanese government and people would no doubt prefer, if possible, to make unilateral decisions and take unilateral actions in dealing with issues of vital interest to their own security. In practice, however, Japanese responses to perceived security threats, especially military threats, have been framed largely bilaterally on the basis of the half-century-old alliance with the United States. The only exception to this rule is the nation's response to threats arising from domestic sources with effects largely restricted to its own territory, such as most natural disasters, industrial accidents and domestic crimes. A more ambiguous exception is its foreign aid policy as a component of its security policy.

Japanese responses to earthquakes, typhoons, accidents at nuclear power plants and domestic crime have been predominantly unilateral in the past and will remain so in the future. So will responses to actual or potential attacks by home-grown terrorists or terrorist groups, although they are likely to involve increasingly international linkages, if not formal cooperation. Following the bombing attacks on underground trains and a bus in London in July 2005, for example, the Japanese Ministry of Land, Infrastructure and Transport developed a plan to install closed circuit television (CCTV) cameras at all or most subway stations in Tokyo (Tetsudo tero 2005; Kao ninsho shisutemu 2005). The move was no doubt inspired by the apparently effective use of a similar system in London and New York City's decision to introduce one for its subway stations.

Japan has for the most part unilaterally designed and implemented its foreign aid policy, which has been regarded and used as an integral and important tool of its foreign and security policies since the late 1970s (Orr 1990: 54–8; Yasutomo 1986: 4–5, 42). Yet, as Orr and Yasutomo document in considerable detail, Japanese aid policy had a bilateral element as well; at many critical junctures, the United States has placed considerable pressure on Japanese policy-makers to follow policies congenial to American interests.

It is in the area of conventional defence policy, with its primary emphasis on military security and reliance primarily on the use or threatened use of military force, that Japan's bilateral approach is most salient and consistent. As discussed subsequently, the US–Japanese alliance continues to serve as the essential and central pillar of Japanese defence policy, even as it has come increasingly under criticism in Japan since the beginning of the Bush administration's war on terrorism in Afghanistan and, especially, the invasion of Iraq.

The United Nations has frequently been mentioned in the Japanese government's official statements on a variety of security-related issues, but the mention has been almost invariably more rhetorical than substantive. Moreover, even the rhetorical deference has substantially declined in recent years, as the repeated Japanese calls for a 'reform' of the world organization, namely, the creation of new permanent seats on the Security Council, including one for Japan, have fallen largely on deaf ears among the occupants of the five such seats that currently exist (Watanabe 2004: 33).

During the last decade, Japanese governments have made a few limited and hesitant moves toward the construction of a regional multilateral framework for national security and international peace. Following the creation of the ARF in 1994, Japan joined the group as one of its seven 'dialogue' nations, along with the US and China (Mack and Kerr 1995; Hoshino 2001: 38–9). While the ARF is primarily a venue of discussion and exchange of information and ideas, rather than a mechanism for facilitating coordinated decision and policy-making, senior government officials meet to discuss wide-ranging issues of vital national and regional security interest (Hoshino 2001: 41). At its July 2004 meeting in Jakarta, the ARF endorsed a Chinese proposal to launch an Asian Security Community to help its members deal more effectively with issues related to military intelligence, maritime safety, etc. (*The Economist* 10 July 2004: 27). The Japanese Defence Agency's 2005 White Paper mentions the important role played by the ASEAN and the ARF, but does not discuss the 2004 Chinese proposal specifically (Boeicho 2005).

As suggested above, post-war Japanese security policy has been far more closely bound by and defined in reference to the US–Japan Mutual Security Treaty. Every LDP and LDP-led coalition government has steadfastly upheld and adhered to both the letter and the spirit of the long-standing military and political alliance. The present Koizumi government continues to do so with renewed commitment and enthusiasm, as witnessed by its prompt support for and participation in the Bush Administration's war on terrorism. Within a few weeks of 11

September, his cabinet had approved a Special Anti-Terrorism Measures Bill and a Basic Plan of Special Anti-Terrorism Measures, which authorized the SDF to assist American and British forces fighting terrorists in Afghanistan, and later in Iraq as well (Boeicho 2003; *Asahi Shimbun* 11 November 2003: 1).

In the wake of 11 September, Japanese public opinion, too, was overwhelmingly in favour of cooperating with the US in its war on terrorism (*Yomiuri Shimbun* 26 September 2001: 3). What most Japanese had in mind, however, was offering US troops medical, transport and provisioning services, information, funds and other forms of non-military support, but not Japanese troops or weapons (*Yomiuri Shimbun* 26 September 2001: 3; *Mainichi Shimbun* 26 September 2001: 2). The Japanese public strongly opposed the US and coalition forces' attack on Iraq in the spring of 2003. Despite the opposition of a substantial majority of Japanese citizens, the Koizumi government proceeded to take a series of legislative and executive measures to make it possible to send SDF troops to war-ravaged Iraq and, by January 2004, actually began to send SDF troops to a relatively peaceful part of southern Iraq. At that time, nearly two-thirds of Japanese had come to believe that the US and coalition forces had invaded Iraq without a legitimate cause (*Asahi Shimbun* 24 February 2004: 5). The war on terrorism, and especially the Iraq War, thus drove a wedge between the Japanese government and the Japanese public on a key issue of contemporary security policy. The wedge, however, does not seem to threaten, at least in the short run, either the half-century-old US–Japanese alliance or Japan's officially bilateral security policy that is based on it (see Table 10.5).

Instrumental preferences

As the world's second largest national economy after the US, Japan has also been, since the late 1970s, the second largest contributor to the UN budget, the second largest quota subscriber of the International Monetary Fund (IMF) and the second largest shareholder of the World Bank. While, in the eyes of many of its leaders, Japan has not been accorded status commensurate with its financial contribution at the UN – a permanent seat on the Security Council – it has long enjoyed a permanent seat on the Executive Directorate at the IMF and the World Bank. At the Asian Development Bank (ADB), Japan has not only been the largest shareholder, but has monopolized its presidency since it was founded in 1966, largely at Japan's own initiative (Yasutomo 1983).

A somewhat more explicit and direct use of its abundant economic power for foreign and security policy purposes has been Japan's foreign aid policy. For nearly

Table 10.5 Public opinion on US-led coalition forces' attack on Iraq (as percentage)

Do you approve of the US-led coalition's attack on Iraq?	
Yes, I do	31
No, I don't	59
d.k./n.a.	10

Source: *Asahi Shimbun* 23 March 2003: 4.

a decade, up to 2000, it was the top donor of official development assistance (ODA), its total annual disbursements surpassing those of any other member, including the US, of the then 21-member Development Assistance Committee (DAC) of the Organization for Economic Cooperation and Development (OECD). As the Japanese government itself admits, however, the nation ranked near the bottom of the group in terms of the grant component of the funds disbursed and the ratio of ODA to gross national product (GNP), suggesting that its aid policy was driven more by instrumental considerations than by purely charitable impulse (Japan MOFA 2001; *Mainichi Shimbun* 19 August 2002: 19).

The largest recipients of Japanese ODA – mostly in the form of yen loans – have been Asian nations, such as Indonesia, China, Thailand, the Philippines, India and Pakistan. The recipients during the Cold War, however, also included Turkey, Egypt, North Yemen, Sudan, Somalia, Kenya, Zimbabwe and others, which were considered important for the security interests of the US-led Western alliance, rather than for Japan's own economic interests (Yasutomo 1986: 4). Japan has also used its ODA as a tool of economic sanction against, for example, Vietnam, Cambodia, Cuba, Afghanistan, Ethiopia and others, by withholding aid altogether or reducing aid amounts to punish their policies or behaviour considered harmful to Japan's security interests. By the mid 1980s, Japan had inaugurated, as Dennis Yasutomo puts it, 'a policy of extending, or denying, economic assistance for strategic purposes to nations deemed important to international as well as Japanese peace and security' (Yasutomo 1986: 4).

As the Japanese economic miracle came to an end and a decade of virtually no growth set in at the beginning of the 1990s, economic power ceased to be as readily available a means of foreign and security policy. In 2001, Japan yielded the pride of place as the top ODA donor nation to the United States for the first time in nearly a decade (*Nihon Keizai Shimbun* 15 May 2002: 9). This period of Japan's economic trouble coincided with the period marked by rising calls abroad, especially in Washington, for Japanese contribution of manpower and services, as well as funds, to international peacekeeping operations (PKO). Under these circumstances, Japan began, in the early 1990s, to contribute SDF personnel and equipment to international peacekeeping or peace-building efforts. The dispatch of several minesweepers to the Persian Gulf in the wake of the 1991 Gulf War was followed by the participation of SDF troops in PKO-related activities in an increasing number of conflict-torn countries and areas, such as Cambodia, Mozambique, Rwanda, the Golan Heights and East Timor (Boeicho 2003). This trend has continued into the new century: SDF troops have participated, if only in non-combat roles, in the wars in Afghanistan and Iraq.

The earlier SDF involvement in PKO activities abroad was approved subject to fairly rigid conditions, such as that it was in response to an explicit UN request, limited to post-conflict sites and approved by the host nation or nations concerned. In the more recent cases, such as Afghanistan and Iraq, however, SDF troops were sent abroad in response to the request of the US government, rather than the UN, and to areas where violent conflict was still ongoing (Shimpojumu 2003: 45–6).

Many of the Koizumi government's post-11 September actions, however, appear to have been intended more to please the US and its coalition partners in their war on terrorism than to increase drastically the SDF's operational capability and reach. Ever since the Japanese contribution of funds, unaccompanied by a contribution of troops, to the US-led Gulf War in 1991 was widely criticized around the world, or was so reported by the Japanese media, the succession of Japanese governments have been eager to avoid the same 'mistake' and make a more respectable contribution to another US-led war, whatever its cause or consequences.[3] The Koizumi government was no exception and was determined to behave as the Bush administration's trustworthy ally (Yachi 2002). This interpretation of Japan's instrumental preferences is consistent with the remarkably constant level of resource allocation to defence-related budget items in general and the SDF manpower and equipment in particular.

Allocation of resources

Japan ranks among the half dozen nations with the largest defence budgets in today's world, after the US, China, Russia and France, and roughly equal to the UK and Germany (*Asahi Shimbun* 5 February 2004: 2). Nonetheless, Japan's significant defence budget – $45 billion in 2003 – is approximately 10 per cent of the American defence budget, a very modest amount for an economy nearly half as large. While it is true that the United States is an outlier on this score, Japanese defence expenditures consume a modest share of Japan's GNP (below 1 per cent) and account for slightly over 10 per cent of the annual government budget. Moreover, this share has been virtually a constant for nearly three decades since the mid 1970s (*Boei Handobukku* 2004: 315–17). This stability is generally attributed to the well-known 'immobilist' tendencies in Japanese politics in general and budget-making process in particular, which arise from the influence of powerful cabals comprised of ruling party politicians and government ministry bureaucrats, each intimately connected with and representing one major interest group or another (George 1988: 106–40).

The onset of international terrorism and the American-led war on terrorism has not caused any discernible change in the pattern of budget allocation in the Japanese government. Setting aside the occasional protestations of government leaders to the contrary, terrorism is not perceived as a serious and immediate threat to Japanese security. More importantly, the economic downturn and the fiscal crisis of the 1990s and early 2000s have forced the government to retrench even in an area vital for national security. The Koizumi government has committed itself to cutting expenditures in all areas without exception and keeping total general account expenditures in each annual budget below levels of the previous fiscal years (Katayama 2005). Consistent with these policy goals, the New Defence Policy Outline announced in December 2004 projects a negative average annual growth rate of minus 0.2 per cent for the defence budget during the period 2005–2009. The budget plan reduces the SDF's total force by 5,000 and the number of tanks and armoured vehicles by 300, but does provide funds to establish a modest 4,800-man rapid response group (*Asahi Shimbun* 10 December 2004: 2; and 11 December 2004: 1).

Table 10.6 Typology of perceived threats to Japanese security, 1992–2004

	1992–2001	*2001–2004*
Type of threat	Invasion by foreign conventional armed forces Domestic crime Natural disasters	International and domestic terrorism Infiltration and subversion by guerrillas and special operations forces WMD proliferation Domestic crime and violence Natural disasters
Agency of threat	State and non-state actors	State and non-state actors
Target of threat	Territory Social order and peace	Government operations Infrastructure Social order and peace
Geographical source of threat	Former Soviet Union space	Northeast Asia, particularly China, North Korea
Severity	Low	Low to medium
Type of response	SDF reinforced by US forces Minimum necessary military forces Strictly defensive force structure Operations within Japan and surrounding territory	SDF reinforced by US forces Acquisition and installation of precision-guided weapons and advanced information and communications systems Build-up of multifunctional response capability Regular participation in international peacekeeping operations
Instrumental preferences	Bilateral US–Japanese joint operations Foreign aid	Bilateral US–Japanese joint operations Participation in regional multilateral forums
Tractability	Practicable/no great dangers	Complex, but generally amenable to diplomatic solution

Conclusion

The famous peace clause of the post-Second World War Japanese constitution explicitly renounced not only the nation's right to maintain any form of military force, but the sovereign 'right of belligerency' itself. As a uniquely unarmed major power, Japan would seek to preserve its security and existence, as the Preamble to the Constitution stated, 'trusting in the justice and faith of the peace-loving peoples of the world'. The post-war world, however, was hardly a totally, or even normally, peaceful community of peace-loving peoples. Instead, the post-war period, in which evolved a bipolar system dominated by superpower rivalry and opposing alliance systems, to be transformed into an unstable post-Cold War unipolarity fractured by national and ethnic conflicts and violence. In order to survive Cold War bipolarity, Japan adopted and followed a complex and contrived security policy bifurcated into, on one hand, a conventional defence policy anchored to its bilateral military alliance with the US and, on the other, an amorphous security policy that relied mainly on the diplomatic and strategic use of Japan's economic power (Kato 1998: 78–80) (see Table 10.6).

Neither the 'peace constitution' nor the bifurcated security policy prevented post-war Japan from rearming itself in the name of self-defence. In fact, the SDF grew quickly into a respectable armed force within a few years of its creation in 1954. In the post-Cold War era, ushered in by the fall of the Berlin Wall in 1989 and the disintegration of the Soviet Union in 1992, however, this neatly bifurcated security policy ceased to be viable in a world where the Japanese economy experienced a protracted slump from which it is just now recovering, a heightened incidence of conflict, violence and asymmetrical warfare in geoeconomically critical areas of the world, and an intensified American demand for greater Japanese military or paramilitary contributions to international peacekeeping and anti-terrorism efforts. These factors combined to encourage Japanese politicians, academics and others to substitute a more orthodox and straightforward defence policy, where Japan depended openly on the exercise of Japanese military power, for the contrived Cold War-era security policy that relied almost exclusively on American protection. Such a change, however, was married to the parallel demand for the prompt revision of the constitution, particularly Article 9. The campaign to make such changes appears to be gathering momentum, but it is still too early to predict the ultimate outcome of the internal debate. Perhaps more important than the eventual outcome, however, is that this foreign policy and constitutional debate is taking place at all within the political mainstream.

In the immediate aftermath of the 11 September terrorist attacks on the United States, a very visible shift occurred in Japanese public opinion. However, that shift did not mark a visible and clear-cut watershed in the Japanese perception of security threats, judging either by the results of various public opinion polls or by the pattern of budgetary allocations and has not had a lasting impact on the fundamental issues at stake in reformulating Japanese security policy. Nor has it changed the post-war security culture that provided the parameters of Japanese security policy over the entire post-war period (see Table 10.7).

During the Cold War period, the Japanese government stuck fairly consistently to a 'civilian' security policy, as dictated by its constitution and as illustrated by its deliberate use of economic power for foreign and security policy purposes. However, it also depended on and used the military alliance with the US and, if only implicitly, the SDF as the principal means of territorial defence policy as a subsidiary instrument of post-war security policy. This duality made Japanese policy 'differentiated,' rather than purely 'civilian'. A notable shift is underway: Japan is moving from the post-war bifurcated security policy towards a more conventional and simpler defence policy cum security policy. If this trajectory continues, Japan will in all likelihood make the transition to a 'normal' state in the sense the term has been bandied around by the nation's conservative politicians (Ozawa 1993:102–5).

Table 10.7 Japanese security culture

Worldview of external environment	Generally pacific external environment Primary military threat emanating from North Korea and possibly China Power – economic and military – as the arbiter of conflict and instruments of persuasion
National identity	Strongly national with no evidence of Western cosmopolitanism Well-defined 'other' in Japanese political discourse Relatively insular culture and civilization
Institutional preferences	US – Japan Mutual Security regime; United Nations ASEAN Regional Forum (ARF)
Interaction preferences	Predominantly bilateral, particularly with US Weak multilateralism within ARF, UN, and six-party talks on North Korea

Whether Japanese security policy instruments – hitherto 'differentiated' but undergoing a shift in the post-Cold War period – match the nation's security policy goals is difficult to determine, because the goals themselves have been ill-defined and shifting. The SDF's expanding involvement in a variety of humanitarian, peacekeeping and anti-terrorism activities abroad clearly signals an expanding definition of security and security policy as understood by the Japanese government, if not by the Japanese public.

The constant share of the annual government budget allocated to national security over a period of nearly three decades, however, suggests that the shift may have been more apparent than real. A plausible explanation of this apparent policy shift unaccompanied by a corresponding resource shift is that the Koizumi government's effort to expand Japan's military capability and international role, if mainly to please Washington, has been frustrated by the notorious gridlock in the Japanese budget-making process in the 'lost decade,' an era of chronic revenue shortfalls and budget-making with a 'zero percent growth ceiling' (Mulgan 2002: 186–98).

This interpretation seems corroborated by the observation that the Japanese public in this period has been more seriously concerned about domestic threats to their personal security, such as the rising crime rate, the deterioration of the environment, accidents at nuclear power plants and natural disasters than threats emanating from the external environment. Yet, allocations to budget items and programmes directly relevant to such domestic problems have not increased but, with a few exceptions, decreased (Somusho tokeikyoku and Tokei kenshujo 2002: 210–11; Naikakufu keizaishakai sogo kenkyujo 2002: 150–5). The apparent mismatch between security policy goals and instruments, especially financial instruments, thus seems to result largely from a combination of structural and financial constraints beyond the government's control, rather than deliberate choice or simply policy miscalculations.

As Berger observes, Japan's security culture, like that of Germany or any other nation, is not static but evolves in response to internal and external developments.

If Japan becomes faced with a clear and present threat, especially a nuclear threat by an international terrorist group or a hostile state, such as North Korea, the security culture may change drastically (Berger 1998: 209–10). That has not happened so far and the majority of Japanese no doubt hope will never happen.

Notes

1   The *Asahi Shimbun* is the second largest of Japan's half dozen major national dailies, in terms of the number of copies sold daily, and marginally more liberal or progressive than the average. For consistency's sake, this newspaper is used here for the bulk of factual information on current affairs, especially as the source of public opinion poll results.
2   Conservative nationalists tend to write for such national dailies as the *Yomiuri* and *Sankei* newspapers and their affiliated magazines, such as the monthly *Bungeishunju,* and television and radio stations, while liberal internationalists tend to do so for the *Asahi* and *Mainichi* newspapers and their affiliated publications, such as the monthly *Sekai,* and television and radio stations. See relevant comments in Berger (1998): 55–6, 172, 181.
3   On the international, especially United States, criticism of the Japanese and German responses to the first Gulf War, see Berger (1998): 171–7.

References

Ampo yori shakaikozo ga tairitsujiku ni: Shugiin giin no ishiki katsudo chosa (2003) *Asahi Shimbun.* Available online at: <http://www.asahi.com> (accessed 27 August 2003).
Aoyama, S. (2002) 'Nihon kakubuso wo hinin suru', *Shokun* (August): 38–48.
Berger, T.U. (1998) *Cultures of Antimilitarism: National Security in Germany and Japan,* Baltimore: John Hopkins University Press.
Boei Handobukku: Heisei 16-nenban (2004) Tokyo: Asagumo Shimbunsha.
Boeicho (2000) *Boei Hakusho: Heisei 12-nenban,* Tokyo: Okurasho Insatsukyoku.
Boeicho (2001–2005) *Boei Hakusho.* Available online at: <http://www.jda.go.jp> (accessed 15 October 2005).
Chosen minshushugi jinmin kyowakoku mondai ni taishi nihon seifu ga torubeki funso yokushi seisaku no teigen (2003) *Sekai* 716: 74–7.
Fukagawa, Y. (2004) 'Kitachosen keizai wa mohaya shindeiru', *Chuokoron* 119 (1): 167–75.
George, A. (1988) 'Japanese interest group behaviour: an institutional approach', in J.A.A. Stockwin *et al.* (eds) *Dynamic and Immobilist Politics in Japan,* London: Macmillan.
Hoshino, T. (2001) 'Ajia taiheiyo chiiki anzen hosho no tenkai', *Kokusai Mondai* 494: 34–47.
Ishibashi, K. and Tamura, M. (2005) 'Taidan: Semarikuru genpatsu shinsai no kyofu', *Sekai* 741 (8): 218–25.
Izumi, H. (2004) 'Rachi no jubaku wa toreta ga kaku ga mada nokotte iru', *Chuokoron* 119 (7): 50–5.
Japan MOFA (Ministry of Foreign Affairs of Japan) (2001) *Role of Japan's ODA in Implementing the Comprehensive Cooperation Package to Address the International*

Digital Divide. Available online at: <http://www.mofa.go.jp/ policy/economy/it/oda/ role0106.html> (accessed 30 July 2005).

Kabashima, I. (2004) 'A nuclear Japan?', *Participation* (Bulletin of the International Political Science Association) 28 (1): 7–8.

Kao ninsho shisutemu: Raishun nimo chikatetsu de jikken (2005) *Mainichi Shimbun.* Available online at: <http://www.mainichi.co.jp> (accessed 30 October 2004).

Katayama, S. (2005) 'Jieitai nimo kozokaikaku ga hitsuyou da', *Chuokoron* 120 (1): 156–63.

Kato, K. (1998) *Tsusho kokka no kaihatsu kyoryoku seisaku,* Tokyo: Bokutakusha.

Kawakami, T. (1996) *Beikoku no tainichi seisaku: Haken shisutemu to nichibei kankei,* Tokyo: Dobunsha.

Kokubun, R. (2001) 'Reisen shuketsu go no nicchukankei', *Kokusai Mondai* 490: 42–56.

Mack, A. and Kerr, P. (1995) 'The evolving security discourse in the Asia-Pacific', *Washington Quarterly* 18 (1): 123–40.

Maeda, T. and Iijima, S. (2003) *Kokkai shingi kara boeiron wo yomitoku,* Tokyo: Sanseido.

Masumi, J. (1988) *Nihon seijishi 4: Senryo kaikaku, jiminto shihai,* Tokyo: Tokyo-daigaku shuppankai.

Mulgan, A.G. (2002) *Japan's Failed Revolution: Koizumi and the Politics of Economic Reform,* Canberra: Asia Pacific Press.

Naikakufu keizaishakai sogo kenkyujo (2002) *Keizai yoran (Heisei 14-nenban),* Tokyo: Okurasho Insatsukyoku.

Nakanishi, T. (2003) 'Nihonkoku kakubuso e no ketsudan', *Shokun* (August): 25–7.

Nihonjin wa chugoku ga kirai (1999) *AERA* 30: 26–7.

Orr, R.M., Jr. (1990) *The Emergence of Japan's Foreign Aid Power,* New York: Columbia University Press.

Ozawa, I. (1993) *Nihon kaizo keikaku,* Tokyo: Kodansha.

Shimpojumu: Hokuto-ajia no anzenhosho to kempo 9-jo (2003) *Sekai* 719: 44–64.

Somusho tokeikyoku and Tokei kenshujo (2002) *Nihon no tokei, 2002,* Tokyo: Okurasho Insatsukyoku.

Tetsudo tero taisaku de eki ni kao ninsho shisutemu: Kokkosho ga jikken kaishi (2005) *Yomiuri Shimbun.* Available online at: <http://www.yomiuri.co.jp> (accessed 22 October 2004).

Urabe, N. (2003) 'Intabyu: Honto no anzenhosho towa nanika', *Sekai* 721: 204–8.

Watanabe, A. (2004) 'Nihon ni totte kokuren to wa ikanaru sonzai ka?' *Chuokoron* 119 (5): 32–5.

Yachi, S. (2002) '11 September terokogeki no keii to nihon no taio' *Kokusai Mondai* 503: 6–8.

Yasutomo, D.T. (1983) *Japan and the Asian Development Bank,* New York: Praeger.

Yasutomo, D.T. (1986) *The Manner of Giving: Strategic Aid and Japanese Foreign Policy,* Lexington, Mass.: D.C. Heath.

11 Russia

Struggling for dignity

Katja Mirwaldt with Vladimir I. Ivanov

Russia boasts the largest territory in the world, stretching from the Pacific across Siberia far into the European continent. Historically, the country has long been one of the world's great powers with a foreign and security policy rooted in realpolitik. Imperial Russia, for example, customarily relied on varying military alliances to preserve a balance of power in Europe. Interventions in weaker neighbouring countries safeguarded a friendly belt around the Russian heartland. The Cold War between the Warsaw Pact and NATO represented the climax of such power politics. Russia provided the key security pillars for the Soviet bloc and it defined the foundations of Soviet defence policies through antagonism to the West. Moscow viewed massive investments in conventional and nuclear arms as the best deterrence against Western aggression.

Russian threat perceptions have changed dramatically since 1992. With the end of the Cold War, the risk of large-scale war with the West has practically disappeared. In the early 1990s, Russia's traditional Western opponents became partners, relations with China grew increasingly cordial, and Russia gradually joined the G7/G8 summitry. Russia's new relations with NATO were guided by the doctrine of partnership. However, from the Kremlin's perspective, the post-Cold War international architecture became too NATO-centric and dependent on the United States. Moreover, the dissolution of the Soviet Union and the Warsaw Pact greatly complicated the exercise of hegemony over Russia's traditional sphere of influence in Eastern Europe, the Caucasus and Central Asia.[1] Faced with this transformed security environment, President Vladimir Putin, in his 2005 State of the Nation address, called the collapse of the Soviet Union the 'largest geopolitical catastrophe of the century'.

Besides weakening Russia's international standing, the post-Soviet disintegration plunged the country into a deep domestic crisis. The 1990s witnessed Russia's economic free fall. The considerable loss of territory left more than 20 million ethnic Russians beyond Russia's new external borders. Simultaneously, the collapse of the Soviet Union triggered an 'epidemic of disintegration', and for a decade the threat of Russian break-up was grave. Many regional governors turned into mini-tsars, and regional autonomy – a policy used by Putin's predecessor Boris Yeltsin to consolidate his grip on power – became an invitation to separatism. A notable example of this threat to the Russian Federation was the instability in Chechnya and the surrounding area, which blurred the boundary between internal and external security risks.

Threat perception

The policy-makers

In December 1999, Vladimir Putin became President of the Russian Federation. Within weeks of taking office, he formally adopted the security policies set out in two key documents. The National Security Concept, which outlines the main internal and external challenges to Russian security, replaced the 1997 Security Blueprint. The long-awaited Draft Military Doctrine, which updated the 1993 Doctrine, identifies military security threats and appropriate responses to them. These two documents are a reflection of changing governmental threat perceptions and priorities.

The National Security Concept is evidence of a far-reaching notion of security, as it details both conventional security threats (mainly external) and non-conventional (mostly internal) challenges. The Concept identifies economic and social problems as the most urgent internal threats:

1   The dire economic situation: economic problems include a low GDP, weak research–technical potential and the one-sided export structure which is dominated by energy and raw materials.
2   Threats to the cohesion of the Russian Federation: these include poor centre–periphery relations, separatism and nationalism, as well as political and religious extremism.
3   The social crisis: the main social problems have their origin in deep social cleavages, poverty, unemployment, and the rapid population decline in Russia's Far East.
4   The criminalization of society: ineffective legal and enforcement instruments have facilitated the spread of corruption and organized crime to the public sphere.

The list could easily be extended to include illegal immigration, environmental hazards or infectious diseases. Internal weaknesses are interlinked and reinforce each other, leaving Russia with a very complex domestic security agenda. The National Security Concept attributes internal threats to fundamental flaws in the post-Soviet reform process.

External threats are characterized in the National Security Concept as 'attempts of other states to hinder the strengthening of Russia as a centre of influence in the multipolar world'. In this context, Celeste Wallander (2000: 4) draws attention to a departure from the 1997 Security Blueprint, which had stated that no external threats arose from deliberate actions or aggression. In contrast, the 2000 National Security Concept and Military Doctrine highlight three external sources of threat: (1) territorial claims and discrimination against Russians abroad, (2) the danger of losing Russia's international political, economic and military influence, and (3) armed conflict and military build-ups in Russia's vicinity (Russian Federation 2000b).

Separatism, other states' territorial claims, and the lacking legal confirmation of Russia's borders have been identified as principal threats to the country's territorial integrity. The border demarcation issues were successfully settled with China, but remained unresolved with Japan and Finland as well as Estonia and Latvia. Relations with the two Baltic republics are also tainted by their discrimination against their Russian-speaking minorities. Moreover, there is still a maritime dispute with the United States in the Bering Sea.

If the international environment is far from genial, Russia's influence over its immediate neighbourhood has also been diminishing. In 2004, the EU and NATO expanded into the former Soviet space. Baltic membership in NATO above all was seen in Russia as an encroachment upon the country's traditional periphery.[2] Moscow interpreted the outcome of Georgia's 'Rose Revolution' and the 2004 'Orange Revolution' in Ukraine as further evidence of a major trend towards Westernization. The Russian leadership was particularly alarmed about the active Western support for regime change. There was a perception that the West was keenly interested in seeing Russia weakened in its own neighbourhood.

In Russia, 'the West' is an emotionally charged term, which alludes to the hegemonic position of the United States – Russia's Cold War nemesis – and US leadership in organizations such as NATO. As the foremost Western security organization, NATO epitomizes Russia's insecurities vis-à-vis this 'West'. Since the first session of the joint North Atlantic Cooperation Council in 1991, the dialogue with NATO has been developing and Russian leaders and officials have confirmed on several occasions that NATO does not constitute a military security threat. Nonetheless, the Defence Ministry describes the Alliance as fundamentally 'anti-Russian' (cf. Defence Ministry of the Russian Federation 2003). Thus, the Russian position on NATO's expansion into Russia's traditional sphere of interest in Central and Eastern Europe has been described by Foreign Ministry official Andrei Kelin (2004: 21) as 'calmly negative'. Moscow suspects that NATO is marginalizing Russia rather than embracing it as a fully fledged partner. The NATO bombing of Yugoslavia in 1999 without a UN mandate constitutes a case in point. From the Russian perspective, these bombings proved that the allegedly defensive Alliance was willing to assault a non-member without previously being attacked. In Russia, this is interpreted as an:

> attempt to create a structure of international relations based on the domination of developed Western countries, led by the USA, in the international community and providing for unilateral solutions of the key problems of global politics, above all with the use of military force, in violation of the fundamental norms of international law.
>
> (Russian Federation 2000a)

The US withdrawal in 2002 from the Anti-Ballistic Missile (ABM) Treaty with the intention of putting into place a strategic missile defence system was interpreted in Moscow as another illustration of American unilateralist leanings. For Russia, the ABM Treaty had been a cornerstone of the arms control regime. In order to save it, Putin had signalled his willingness to make extensive amendments. George W. Bush's notice of withdrawal was therefore received coolly in Moscow. Moreover, in 2003, the American-led invasion of Iraq was heavily criticized in Russia: first, because it allowed the occupying forces to extend their influence further into Russia's neighbourhood; second, the fact that the invasion was pushed against the wishes of the UN Security Council was seen as yet another example of the US not taking Russia's security concerns seriously. It must be added, though, that Russia's opposition to the Iraq war was much more moderate and less divisive than France's or Germany's ardent resistance (Karaganov 2005).

Even though American global dominance is a steady source of Russian indignation and insecurity, Russian and American security interests have converged on the fight against terrorism. In the National Security Concept as well as the Military Doctrine, separatism is contemplated as a major source of terrorism. At the same time, terrorism is linked to external forces, including fundamentalist organizations and quasi-state actors providing support for guerrillas and terrorists.

In 2003, Defence Minister Sergei Ivanov published his 'Priority Tasks for the Development of the Armed Forces'. Ivanov's so-called White Paper reflects the Defence Ministry's and General Staff's security priorities. In contrast to the President's emphasis on internal threats, the Ministry tends to accentuate traditional strategic threats (Polikanov 2005). According to the White Paper, the foremost security threats are the proliferation of weapons of mass destruction (WMD), ethnic and religious tensions, terrorism and organized crime spilling across Russia's porous borders. The militant infiltrations in Chechnya with a possible link to al-Qaeda have shown how external agents can intensify internal hazards. The White Paper defines this new type of threat as transborder threats. These can be internal in appearance but external in nature, including:

- the operation of structures connected with international terrorist operations on home territory;
- the training of armed groups for operation on Russian territory or the territory of other states;
- transborder crime, including smuggling and other illegal actions, which require the use of border guards (Defence Ministry of the Russian Federation 2003).

It is questionable whether 11 September 2001 and the resultant war on terrorism had a strong bearing on the White Paper. The terrorist attacks on the United States offered the Russian leadership a chance to redefine the campaign in Chechnya as part of the international fight against terrorism. Before these attacks, Moscow had been relentlessly criticized on many fronts for human rights violations in the

Caucasus. Following 11 September and Putin's unconditional solidarity, Russia became a member of the ad hoc anti-terrorist coalition:

> What was striking about Russian collaboration was the extent of operational support involved. Putin broke new ground in the range and depth of help he provided for the US campaign against the Taliban. This operational help ranged from intelligence collaboration to aid in accessing military facilities in the region.
>
> (Pravda 2003: 43)

Against all domestic opposition,[3] Putin even consented to a – provisional – US military presence in Central Asia, as American troops were stationed in Uzbekistan for the 2001 invasion of Afghanistan. In return for Putin's assistance, the US temporarily ceased criticizing the Russian army's conduct in Chechnya. NATO General Secretary Robertson argued that the events of 11 September 2001 had helped the West to 'understand that Russia's warnings about the dangers of terrorism have not just been motivated by the need to dispel Western criticism of the Chechnya campaign' (Robertson 2002: 36). Overall, 11 September does not seem to have transformed Russian policy-makers' awareness of the terrorist threat that had been shaped during the second Chechen war. Rather, Putin seized the opportunity to capitalize on cooperation with the US when he saw a chance to advance Russia's security agenda in Chechnya and Afghanistan.

Table 11.1 provides an overview of governmental threat perceptions. In a reversal of the Cold War environment, external threats such as American unilateralism or NATO are now the least hazardous for the Russian state. Fierce disputes occasionally erupt in Russia's new relationship with the former adversaries. Nevertheless, these threaten Russia's international status much more than its military security. Conversely, instabilities along Russia's southern periphery pose a serious threat to military security while simultaneously endangering the cohesion of the Russian state. Separatism, terrorism, cross-border crime and religious extremism all fall under this definition of transnational threats. Most importantly, the list of internal predicaments is very long and, in the policy-makers' perception, these threats remain worryingly interlinked.

Public threat perceptions

The citizenry is in broad agreement with the government on the internal and transnational priorities. Table 11.2 displays the top ten dangers as identified by Russian adults in 2005. Apart from the foremost concern about terrorism, all subsequent threats are of unequivocally domestic origin. Russian citizens place external dangers much lower on the list of priorities. Examples include the loss of some territories (7 per cent of respondents), war with Western countries (7 per cent), military conflicts with the nearest neighbours (7 per cent), and loss of national sovereignty and American influence (6 per cent).

Table 11.1 Governmental threat perceptions

	External threats	Transnational threats	Internal threats
Type of threat	US unilateralism NATO expansion Circumvention of the UN Security Council	Separatism and terrorism Porous borders and organized crime	Weak state structures Economic vulnerability Socio-economic degeneration Environmental hazards
Agency of threat	US NATO	Separatists and Islamic fundamentalists Terrorists Organized crime	Incomplete and flawed reforms of economy and state organization
Target of threat	Russia's geopolitical rank Multipolarity	State integrity Civilian population	Economic interests Civilian population State structure
Geographical source of threat	US Westernizing former Soviet countries (Baltics, Georgia, Ukraine)	Central Asia North Caucasus	Russia
Severity	Low	High	Very high

Table 11.2 indicates that terrorism is the primary security threat in the perception of Russian citizens. Likewise, in a survey conducted in August 2005, 71 per cent of respondents considered a large terrorist attack in Russia possible (Angus Reid Consultants 2005a). Nevertheless, different opinion polls present different pictures on the importance attached to the terrorist threat. For example, in a 2006 survey conducted by the market research company ROMIR, a sample of Russians was asked to pinpoint the country's most urgent problems. As Table 11.3 shows, respondents identified the level of economic development and its social repercussions as the four most pressing items. Transnational issues, namely the situation in Chechnya and the fight against terrorism, appear much lower on the list of priorities.

Many indicators point to Islamic extremism as the link that Russians make between domestic, that is Chechen, and international terrorism. For example, when asked what the terrorist attack on London in July 2005 represented to them, a majority (44 per cent) considered it 'an attack on the entire civilized world, including Russia', although 30 per cent deemed it a retribution for Britain's support of the wars in Iraq and Afghanistan (Angus Reid Consultants 2005b).

The expression 'attack on the entire civilized world', reminiscent of world leaders' rhetoric after 11 September, conveys a sense of international conspiracy. An international poll conducted in spring 2005 demonstrates the level of alarm: Russia emerged as the nation most apprehensive about Islamic extremism, closely

Table 11.2 Top ten dangers identified by Russians (in percentage of respondents)

Which of these dangers causes the greatest fear to you personally? (several answers allowed)	
Terrorist attacks to strategically important targets	36
Extinction of the Russian population due to low birth rate	33
Sharp decrease in standard of living, hunger	30
Environmental catastrophe	21
Civil conflict in Russia	18
The disintegration of Russia into several independent states	15
Depletion of oil and gas, and other natural resources	14
Mass epidemics (cholera, AIDS, pneumonia)	14
Decline of culture, science and education	13
Immigration by people of other nationalities	12

Source: Angus Reid Consultants (2005) *Terrorism is the Main Concern for Russians*. Available online at: <http://www.angus-reid.com/polls/index.cfm/fuseaction/viewItem/itemID/7301> (accessed 26 September 2005).
Note: N = 1,600, conducted 23–24 April 2005. Margin of error is 3.4 per cent.

Table 11.3 The 15 most urgent problems identified by Russian citizens (in percentage of respondents)

In your opinion, which problems should be solved first? (several answers allowed)	
Economic development	45
Inflation	29
National welfare gain	28
Unemployment	21
Housing and municipal utilities	21
Struggle against administrative corruption	14
Public health	13
Decrease of oligarchs' influence on administration	11
Salary/pension delays	11
The Chechnya situation	10
Senior citizen care	9
Public assistance development	9
Fight against terrorism	8
Weakness of the administration	8
Environmental pollution	8

Source: Romir Monitoring (2006) *The Russians Speak about Hot Issues for the Nation*. Available online at: <http://rmh.ru/en/news/res_results/6.html> (accessed 28 January 2006).
Note: N = 1,500, conducted January 2006.

followed by India. Especially for the larger countries, some allowance must be made for sampling error. Even so, it is striking that Russian anxieties were more pronounced than in Spain, which had been shocked by the terrorist attacks on Madrid the previous year.

The reasons for Russian citizens' concern with Islamic fundamentalism are manifold. One obvious root lies in Russia's intense experience of Muslims' terrorist assaults, particularly the bloody school drama in Beslan that had sent shockwaves throughout the country in 2004. Instabilities around Russia's southern borders are also associated with religious extremism (Sukhov 2005). In this regional context, many Russians look with trepidation to Iran, fearing Iranian influence and endorsement of radical Islam in Central Asia. Suspicion of Islam is deeply entrenched in large parts of Russian society. Any government will have to take it into account when deciding how to respond to these threats.

Academic and expert threat perception

According to most Russian academics, internal threats lie at the root of Russia's security predicaments. The most frequently mentioned problems include societal cleavages and a criminalized economy, but also weak democratic processes. Kremenyuk (2004) argues that, in Western societies, strong democracy, sound economy and a safe environment constitute the basis for citizen security in the personal, economic, social and national spheres. He concludes that building a similar Russian system of national security preconditions a reliable societal foundation, which would have to be created in an extensive internal reform process.

Table 11.4 Concern about Islamic extremism in select countries
(in percentage of respondents)

How concerned, if at all, are you about the rise of Islamic extremism in our country these days?

	Very concerned	*Somewhat concerned*	*Not too concerned*	*Not at all concerned*
Russia	52	32	9	4
India	48	36	9	4
Spain	43	34	15	7
Germany	35	43	14	7
UK	34	36	22	6
France	32	41	18	8
United States	31	39	19	9

Source: Angus Reid Consultants (2005) *Russians, Indians Wary of Islamic Extremists.* Available online at: <http://www.angus-reid.com/polls/index.cfm/fuseaction/viewItem/itemID/8109> (accessed 25 January 2006).
Note: N = 9,325 in ten countries, conducted from 25 April to 29 May 2005. Margins of error range from 3 to 4 per cent.

'Only after such a basis appears in Russia and acquires a dominant position in politics and economy ... may [one] tackle the problem of creating an adequate and reliable mechanism of national security' (Kremenyuk 2004: 160).

Indeed, socio-economic problems and military security threats are intertwined around the Russian borders. There is a perception that armed conflicts near Russia's borders, possibly involving nuclear weapons, are a very real threat (Dvorkin 2005). The notion of an 'arc of instability' has been coined to describe the conflict-ridden neighbourhood: 'This area stretches from the Dniestr region in Moldova, to the Crimea, to the mountain ranges of the Pamirs and Tian Shan in Central Asia' (Arbatov 2004: 107). Poverty, tensions and crime, especially large-scale narcotics trafficking, haunt the states in Central Asia. The Caucasus remains a breeding ground for friction: no peaceful solution has been found in the conflict between Armenia and Azerbaijan, and nationalism and separatism as well as religious extremism continue to spread in the region. The upshots of these regional instabilities can spill into Russia and introduce illegal immigration, organized crime as well as religious and nationalist extremism.

Within the Russian Federation, the ongoing conflict in Chechnya is one of the most urgent concerns. Ethnic tensions and crime flourish in the trouble-ridden breakaway republic. Sukhov (2005) points out that the population has been radicalized by the continuing bloodshed, including the Russian army's incriminating use of violence against civilians. Chechnya is also identified as a hotbed for terrorism. Since 1999, Russia has been the site of several major terrorist assaults. The Moscow theatre siege in 2002 and the tragedy in Beslan two years later exposed Russia's ineffective response strategy when facing Chechen terrorism. In contrast to the public's fear of Islam, however, Russian scholars highlight socio-economic problems as catalysts for the proliferation of terrorist groupings in the North Caucasus. In her analysis of the terrorist threat to Russian security, for example, Stepanova (2005) argues that Chechen rebel groups are linked to organized crime much more than they are to Islamic fundamentalism. Fierce responses to 'international terrorism', accordingly, are likely to provoke an Islamist backlash and increase Muslim support for terrorism (cf. Satanovsky 2005).

As regards Islamic fundamentalism, there is a perceived danger that American-led operations in the Middle East, such as the Iraq war or a possible intervention in Iran over its uranium enrichment programme, are likely to further destabilize the region. This would hold obvious security implications for Russia: far from constituting a buffer zone, the weak states at Russia's southern border may instead act as transmission belts for regional conflict and religious extremism.

At the global level, American prevalence causes concern among Russian academics. Experts from the Russian Academy of Sciences have identified the US prevalence in international affairs as the primary external threat. As part of this research, Russia's long-term strategic risks in the political sphere were rank-ordered by degree of importance for maintaining and promoting Russia's national security. Some of the results stand in marked contrast to the policy-makers' threat perception:

1   US dominance in international affairs;
2   China's increasing power;
3   Russia's decreasing defensibility and weakness of the armed forces;
4   ·the possibility of ethnic and religious conflicts;
5   increasing military threats from the USA and NATO;
6   the possibility of regional and local military conflicts;
7   the proliferation of militant fundamentalism in Russia's South;
8   increasing international terrorism.

(*Strategicheskiye Riski Rossii* 2005: 163)

There is broad agreement with the policy-makers regarding transnational threats such as ethnic friction or regional conflict. However, some Russian scholars also perceive a military threat from NATO and the US. Most importantly, their priorities diverge from those of the policy-makers: these academics identify as the two foremost sources of strategic risk the American ability to intervene militarily, politically or economically in other countries' affairs and China's medium-term potential as Russia's rival.

This assessment reflects the country's uncertainties over strategic choice, namely the question of whether Russia should side unequivocally with the West or whether to concentrate on its role as an Asian power. In contrast to the government's comparatively optimistic outlook on Sino–Russian relations, many Russian academics contemplate China with apprehension. Russia's decline as a great power coincided with China's rise as the key Asian player and predictions hold that China's economic and military might in (Central) Asia will continue to expand. Dimitri Trenin, one of the most prominent commentators on Russia's foreign relations, points out the long-term potential for rivalry and discord (Trenin 1999). In his *End of Eurasia,* he warns:

Over the medium-term, Russia will increasingly be worried about several things: (1) Chinese migration into the Russian Far East and southern Siberia and (2) the growing economic attraction of China. Over the long term, the fundamental change in the balance of power between Russia and China could lead the border issue to resurface in a totally different way.

(Trenin 2002: 318)

By and large, Russian academics, policy-makers and the public agree on internal predicaments as the most pressing threat to the country's security. Regional instabilities, described by the Defence Ministry as transnational threats, are seen as a likely source of terrorism and military conflict. However, one can detect some disagreement between policy-makers and academics in the strategic sphere. Parts of the academic community are very cautious about cooperation with China. In contrast, the Russian government has proven eager to combine forces with China in responding to threats.

Responses to threats

The *National Security Concept* states a preference for non-aggression and non-military means to resolve conflict. In addition to a defensive guiding principle, the document professes a commitment to cooperation in multilateral institutions such as the United Nations and the OSCE. However, Russia's dedication to multi-lateralism, international institutions and cooperation is not rigid. The country's leadership frequently departs from these principles in order to pursue Russia's security agenda bilaterally, unilaterally and sometimes very assertively.

Interaction preference

In his State of the Nation addresses of 2003 and 2004, Putin laid down three key tasks for the following decade: doubling GDP, reducing poverty and military reform. Following the precept that Russia must rely on a favourable external environment in order to address the considerable number of internal threats, Putin stepped up the efforts to integrate the country into international structures. Thus, Russia introduced the possibility of membership in the WTO and filed an application for joining the OECD.

Relations with the European Union, Russia's key trading partner and consumer of energy exports, have been evolving. The Russia–EU agenda now includes the concept of the four common spaces,[4] agreements on a liberalization of the visa regime, and establishment of non-discriminatory trade relations. A new EU–Russia treaty to be negotiated by 2007 is expected to develop cooperation in joint crisis management and energy relations (EU Observer 2006).

In international affairs, Moscow cherishes the concept of a multipolar world, in which several powers would coordinate their foreign policies. The motives are psychological on the one hand, as Russia struggles to find its role in a world dominated by the former enemy and only remaining superpower. On the other, Moscow contends that American and NATO dominance cannot adequately reflect the global variety of interests. To counter this dominance, Russia stresses multilateral cooperation in the Commonwealth of Independent States (CIS), the Shanghai Cooperation Organization (SCO) and, above all, the United Nations. The Kremlin attaches particular importance to the UN as a forum for coordinating divergent interests. As a permanent member of the Security Council, Russia interprets unilateral actions without a UN mandate as an assault on Russia's voice in global affairs:

> Russia proceeds from the premise that the use of force in violation of the UN Charter is unlawful and poses a threat to the stabilization of the entire system of international relations. Attempts to introduce into the international parlance concepts as 'humanitarian intervention' and 'limited sovereignty' in order to justify unilateral power actions bypassing the UN Security Council are not acceptable.
>
> (Russian Federation 2000a)

Nevertheless, Russia's commitment to international institutions is flexible. For example, Putin was prepared to abandon multilateralism when membership in the American-led ad hoc coalition against terrorism was to be gained. Indeed, the most substantive of Russia's security relations tend to be bilateral. Nowhere is this more apparent than in the Commonwealth of Independent States. The CIS has been identified as a zone of strategic interest in improving Russian security. In the mid 1990s, the so-called 'Monrovsky Doctrine' declared the CIS space a region of exclusive Russian influence, provoking exclamations of national sovereignty on the part of many CIS states. Sceptical of Russia's dominance in the region, some members of the CIS, notably the GUAM grouping (Georgia, Ukraine, Azerbaijan and Moldova), have strong reservations about integration in a multilateral framework. The dilemma lies in Russia's international weight: too weak to act unilaterally, Russia is nonetheless too dominant for genuinely multilateral security cooperation in the CIS. However, the CIS framework proved useful in facilitating bilateral ties between Russia and other members. Cultural, linguistic and historical links are still significant. A low language barrier and economic ties allow Russia to maintain and strengthen cross-border cooperation with its immediate neighbours. Especially in the transnational security realm, interests tend to converge and produce joint policy decisions, as seen in the creation of integrated border guards (Willerton and Cockerham 2003).

Institutional responses

Despite its shortcomings as a multilateral body, Russia sees the CIS as one of the main instruments in countering security threats. The National Security Concept and the Foreign Policy Concept give priority to the neighbouring post-Soviet states, aimed at building a 'friendly policy belt' (Russian Federation 2000c). In the Russian view, conflict prevention should take the form of joint policing of borders, also in order to counteract terrorist networking. Russia aims to strengthen CIS cooperation in the fight against terrorism (Belov and Putintsev 2005) and transborder law enforcement, while also enhancing the Collective Security Treaty which still does not boast many multilateral security functions (Kay 2003; Willerton and Cockerham 2003).

The prospects for these new relations between Russia and other CIS countries are uncertain. Putin has abandoned Yeltsin's 'near abroad' rhetoric that had caused a lot of anxieties in Georgia or Ukraine. However, this does not automatically represent a greater forbearance in relation to these countries' orientation towards the West. Moscow appears reluctant to relinquish control and has been accused of exploiting Eastern Europe's dependence on Russian gas and oil for political ends. For example, in December 2005, the state-owned Russian energy giant Gazprom quintupled the price for gas deliveries to Ukraine. With Russia's close ally Belarus still paying a minimal rate, there was a strong perception that Ukrainians were being presented with a political bill for turning away from Russia and towards the West (cf. Gamova 2005). Moscow denied these allegations but the gas crisis conveyed the impression that Russia endeavours to preserve its influence over the CIS, albeit through 'soft' rather than military means.

In the sphere of external threats, the dialogue with NATO has been developing since Russia joined the Partnership for Peace programme in 1994. Joint NATO–Russian peacekeeping operations in Bosnia from 1996 were praised as highly effective (Yermolaev 2000). Moreover, the 1997 Founding Act was partly designed to alleviate Russian reservations regarding NATO's eastward enlargements. In theory, the Rome Declaration and decision to establish the NATO–Russia Council in May 2002 demonstrated a commitment to political dialogue on current security issues, notably the terrorist threat. But despite the regular consultations held in the NATO–Russia Council, consensus on security questions remains difficult to achieve. The lack of any practical achievements in jointly tackling terrorism and WMD proliferation in particular has been accentuated as a missed opportunity (cf. Weitz 2005).

Facing an ambiguous partnership with NATO and the US, the Kremlin seeks to keep all options open in Asia. For example, on 2 June 2005 in Vladivostok, Russia hosted the trilateral foreign ministers' talks with India and China (Ministry of Foreign Affairs of the Russian Federation 2005a). The three Asian powers experience similar problems in combating new threats and challenges. They have a common interest in regional stability and favour an international order based on cooperation and multilateralism.

There is a possibility that India, which currently has an observer status, could join the Shanghai Cooperation Organization (SCO).[5] Iran, Israel and Pakistan have also signalled an interest. The SCO developed into a viable regional body with a special focus on the factors destabilizing Central Asia (Ministry of Foreign Affairs of the Russian Federation 2005b). According to the General Staff, it could develop into a pillar of stability and cooperation, especially in the fight against radical Islamists and the interlinked concerns of terrorism and separatism (Lukin 2004). However, it is difficult for Moscow to lay out a design for the future development of the SCO. Hitherto, the evolution of the SCO has taken place only in areas of robust interest convergence. Moreover, India has so far displayed little zeal in the strategic 'Eurasian triangle' between Moscow, Beijing and New Delhi.

Most importantly, the future of the SCO will depend on the direction of Sino–Russian relations. Russia is slowly adjusting to the fact that China's power is growing. China could be a gigantic and long-term source of economic growth and regional development for Russia (cf. Karaganov 2005). But even stable and friendly relations could potentially create problems, depending on the dynamics of Sino–American and Sino–Japanese relations (cf. Trenin 2002). The US in particular has shown a tendency to distrust the SCO and its growing influence in Central Asia as Russia and China, the two key players in the SCO, 'use the advancement of multipolar international institutions to balance American power' (Kay 2003: 136).[6]

Instrumental preferences

The National Security Concept highlights the conventional military as a means of safeguarding Russia's national interests. However, during the years of economic decline, a weakened and outdated military had to shift the emphasis to strategic deterrence. Russia's nuclear arsenal serves as a deterrent against nuclear as well as conventional attacks. The 1993 Military Doctrine had been the first not to dismiss the option of a first nuclear strike. The 2000 version goes further and spells out that nuclear weapons can be used first in response to large-scale conventional attacks. However, Russia made a pledge not to use nuclear weapons against any of the signatory countries of the Non-Proliferation Treaty, except when such countries align with other nuclear states.

While stressing Russia's commitment to peace and the defensive nature of its military policy, four types of conflict are identified in the Doctrine: (1) a world war defined by the involvement of a sizeable number of states from different regions, (2) regional wars involving warfare between two or more states of the same region, (3) local wars characterized by partial force deployments in the conflict area, and (4) armed conflict involving irregular units that rely on sabotage and terrorist activities, and where local populations are caught up in the conflict. World wars and regional wars are deemed likely to escalate into nuclear conflict (Russian Federation 2000b).

The Doctrine introduces as a new element the use of the military forces inside Russia with the purpose of 'containing and neutralizing anticonstitutional actions and unlawful armed violence that threaten the sovereignty, territorial integrity and state unity of the Russian Federation' (Russian Federation 2000b). A blatant reference to Chechnya, this aspect of instrumental response ties in with Russia's difficulty to address the causes of conflict. Thus, Russia's strategic concepts locate regional conflict potential in the (North) Caucasus and Central Asia. But despite the perceived likelihood of tensions escalating in this region, the National Security Concept is conspicuously silent on strategies to defuse conflict potential within Russia and in the former Soviet Union area.

Troop deployments in peacekeeping operations were identified as an important crisis management tool. Throughout the early 1990s, Russian peacekeeping efforts in the CIS, such as the operations in Moldova and Georgia, were condemned as disguised pursuits of Russia's national interests rather than operations consistent with international peacekeeping norms (Yermolaev 2000). In contrast, peacekeeping missions under the auspices of the UN, such as the Russian contribution to KFOR in former Yugoslavia, reinforced Russia's readiness for international cooperation in this sphere of security policy. The Doctrine confirms Russia's continued commitment to peacekeeping missions, on condition that the UN Security Council authorizes them.

And finally, the energy sector is an important tool to safeguard Russia's geopolitical influence. As the Russian Ministry of Energy (2003: 2) puts it, Russia possesses a 'powerful fuel and energy complex, which is the basis of economic development and the instrument of carrying the internal and external policy'.

Particularly in Eastern Europe, dependence on Russian fuel raises concerns, as the Ukrainian gas crisis plainly illustrated.[7] But Western Europe, too, has been receiving mixed messages. On the one hand, Russia seeks to position itself as a reliable supplier of gas and oil. Thus, at a trilateral summit in September 2004, President Putin assured his French and German counterparts that Russia would maintain and expand its oil supply. On the other hand, in April 2006, Gazprom threatened to divert some of its gas exports to China or North America if prohibited from investing in Europe. Dick Cheney, the American Vice President, brusquely condemned such uses of energy resources for foreign political ends as 'tools of intimidation and blackmail'.[8]

In 2005 and 2006, Putin tried to seize the storm over Iran's uranium enrichment programme as an opportunity to combine two ends: to highlight Russia's competence in energy questions while avoiding a collision course with Iran. Always eager to maintain friendly relations with the Islamic Republic, Russia nonetheless has no interest in allowing Iran to acquire nuclear weapons. However, Iran did not accept Putin's offer to enrich uranium for Tehran on Russian soil, and the matter was taken to the UN Security Council in March 2006.

Table 11.5 summarizes Russia's preferred responses to security threats. As far as interaction preference is concerned, Russia stresses multilateralism and international institutions in order to solve its most pressing internal problems. Nevertheless, substantive security cooperation will normally take a bilateral shape, especially with the members of the CIS and the SCO. Russia stresses diplomacy and cooperative instruments in responding to external and transnational threats. At the same time, Russian policy-makers emphasize nuclear deterrence and optional military interventions within and outside of Russia as means of safeguarding the country's military security.

Resource allocation

Military reform was one of the crucial tasks outlined in Putin's 2003 and 2004 State of the Nation addresses. The transformed international environment and the economic crisis of the 1990s had badly affected the military. The losses incurred

Table 11.5 Russia's preferred responses to threats

Interaction patterns	Commitment to multilateralism Integration in international institutions (WTO, G8, OECD) Bilateral responses
Institutional preferences	United Nations CIS SCO
Instrumental preferences	Cooperation and diplomacy Nuclear deterrence Military intervention abroad and within Russia Peacekeeping Energy exports

during the first Chechen war uncovered the weakness of the armed forces. The recruitment problem of contract forces, augmented by the population decline, represented a major challenge to the post-Yeltsin leadership (Miller 2004). In August 2000, the tragic sinking of the nuclear powered submarine *Kursk* drew public attention to the hazardous ageing Soviet arsenal, which includes plutonium, uranium, and a large number of stored nuclear weapons. This arsenal also poses a long-term environmental risk.[9] The entire military organization required rationalization and a qualitatively improved technical base.

Moreover, some argue that the mass conscript army is a relic from the Cold War. Responding to new security challenges requires a mobile, well-equipped and professional army to perform 'various low-intensity operations, including peacekeeping, counterinsurgency, anti-guerrilla campaigns, and counterterrorism' (Miller 2004: 21). As it stands, a large share of the defence budget is spent on maintaining the ordinary forces alone. The Defence Ministry presses for greater professionalization, in addition to a reasonable level of pay and social conditions for the servicemen and their families. The aim is for contract-based units of permanent combat readiness that would constitute the core of the military force.

Russia ranks among the top ten global spenders on military expenditure. Measured in purchasing power parities, the official Russian defence budget is the fourth largest in the world (Sköns *et al.* 2005). However, official military spending excludes a number of defence-related items, namely military pensions and paramilitary forces such as the internal or border troops. For this reason, the International Institute for Strategic Studies (IISS 2004) estimates that the real

Table 11.6 Estimated Russian military expenditure in (constant 2003) US$ million

Year	Expenditure	% of GDP
1988	147,907	15.8
1989	137,145	14.2
1990	116,023	12.3
1992	27,159	5.5
1993	23,958	5.3
1994	23,172	5.9
1995	14,700	4.1
1996	13,300	3.8
1997	14,300	4.2
1998	10,300	3.1
1999	12,300	3.5
2000	14,200	3.7
2001	15,700	4.0
2002	16,900	4.2
2003	18,500	4.3
2004	19,400	n.a.

Source: Stockholm International Peace Research Institute (SIPRI). Available online at: <http://first.sipri.org/non_first/result_milex.php?send> (accessed 9 October 2005).
Note: Data for 1991 are not available from this source.

Russian defence spending remains second only to that of the US and roughly comparable to China's.

Table 11.6 illustrates the enormous cuts in defence spending that were made during the collapse of the Soviet Union. Russia's 1992 official defence budget was less than a quarter of what had been spent on defence in 1990. The 1990s witnessed a further downward trend. In view of these figures, Russian experts contend that spending is too low to even maintain the current low level of capability, while the available resources are spent inefficiently (Arbatov 2004). Predictably, the General Staff frequently plead for colossal increases in the defence budget. However, since 1999, there has been only a modest upturn that coincided with the start of the second war in Chechnya. The increases are not targeted at any particular area but rather serve to augment pay, research and development and procurement (IISS 2005: 170).

Russia's rearmament programme until the year 2010 gives emphasis to research and development as well as modern weapons procurement. Modernization involves intelligent weapons systems such as the tactical missile system Iskander-M, or equipment destined for counterinsurgency operations (IISS 2005). However, the majority of Russia's modern weapons production is destined for export (Reppert 2003), especially to India and – more disturbingly for Russian military planners – to China, Russia's likely future rival.

Consistent with the emphasis on credible nuclear deterrence, there are plans to upgrade Russia's nuclear arsenal by introducing new generations of strategic weapons. Intercontinental Topol-M missiles are intended to gradually replace older strategic weapons. New delivery systems were successfully tested in 2004. These state-of-the-art missiles move at hypersonic speed and their excellent manoeuvrability makes it impossible to predict their trajectory. Consequently, the General Staff claim, Topol-M missiles are immune to ABM defence mechanisms, including the planned US strategic missile defence system.

On the whole, however, the Russian government has only slowly embarked on a modernization process of the military forces, which were in a poor state after the collapse of the Soviet Union. These efforts are evidence of a piecemeal approach rather than the far-reaching overhaul that is sorely needed. The absence of any major military reform is not strategic choice. Rather, the military command resists any major restructuring and has so far been successful in prolonging the status quo. Putin's refusal to inflate the Russian defence budget confirms his preference for effective diplomacy and economic success as the safest route to stable external relations.

Conclusion

Over the past two decades, Russia's threat perceptions have changed dramatically. The end of the Cold War constituted an unparalleled sea change. The danger of large-scale nuclear war with the West – the defining factor in Soviet threat perceptions – disappeared from the security agenda. Simultaneously, the post-communist transformation process gave rise to an escalation of domestic

Table 11.7 Russian national security culture

Worldview of external environment	– relations with other states characterized by rivalry and fragile alliances – increasingly, transnational actors exploit Russia's internal weakness – aspiration towards a 'multipolar' world
Identity	– great power symbolisms clash with a pragmatic foreign policy – 'Eurasian' power characterized by uncertainty over geographic identity
Instrumental preferences	– emphasis on traditional military instruments and deterrence – increasing reliance on instruments of 'soft' power
Interaction preferences	– primarily bilateral ties and membership in ad hoc alliances – desire for greater integration in international multilateral organizations

security threats. Russian security planners increasingly have to take into account the structural or non-military threats that non-state actors pose to the civilian population, economic interests and the state's structure and integrity. There is broad consensus in Russia that the new internal and transnational challenges constitute the gravest threat to the country's security. However, ambiguities about adequate responses to threats reflect a tension between old-style defence postures and a thoroughly reformed security strategy as the basis for Russia's restructured security culture.

It is still uncertain what a new Russian identity that reflects the geopolitical changes after the Cold War would look like. Unlike his predecessor, Putin avoids referring to Russia as a great power. In contrast to Yeltsin's often erratic course, Putin stresses sobriety and pragmatism in Russia's relations with the West. Despite this reserve, Washington in particular has caused a lot of chagrin by disregarding Russian concerns. Resentment of what is perceived as American condescension goes hand in hand with a sense of betrayal, symbolized in the humiliating advance of American and NATO troops into Russia's traditional sphere of influence.

In the wider international context, the Russian leadership seems unsure about whether to look East or West. Stable relations with the West, especially trade relations, are deemed indispensable to any solution of the country's most pressing problems. The country's strategically vital location and its wealth in gas and oil are Russia's most valuable resources in fostering partnerships. Relations with NATO, in many respects a marriage of convenience, are the product of Russia's attempts to embed itself more deeply in the international institutions, including the OECD, the G8 platform and the WTO. And yet, US dominance of the West is disturbing for Russia and its ambition to represent one of multiple poles in the world. Looking to the East and forging ties with China, however delicate, can be seen as an attempt to compensate for this American primacy.

In terms of interaction preferences, there is a discrepancy between Russia's professed commitment to multilateralism and the primacy of bilateral ties with other states. The CIS space is accorded absolute priority. As Russia's immediate neighbourhood, this region is of foremost strategic importance. Only here can Russian influence be said to match, if not exceed, US authority. Indeed, Moscow is eager to preserve these traditional ties, sometimes with a vehemence that evokes unease about Russian hegemony in many CIS countries.

Overall, despite Russia's commitment to a pragmatic, low-key and cooperative security concept, a lot of importance is still attached to status symbols reminiscent of the country's former great power status. These include the permanent seat in the UN Security Council, the nuclear bomb and a sphere of influence in the immediate neighbourhood. The divergence between these two lines of thinking, namely the widespread attachment to a view of Russia as a force to be reckoned with, and the practical embrace of cooperative foreign relations, represents the dilemma inherent in Russia's struggle for dignity.

Acknowledgement

The authors would like to thank Boris Porfiriev for his comments on a previous draft of this chapter.

Notes

1   The Central Asian region is defined here as Kazakhstan, Kyrgyzstan, Tajikistan, Turkmenistan and Uzbekistan.
2   Moreover, Defence Minister Sergei Ivanov argued at the Munich Conference on Security Policy in 2004 that NATO enlargement to the Baltic states could jeopardize the Treaty on Conventional Armed Forces in Europe (CFE).
3   Foreign troops in Central Asia had long been a red rag to the Defence Ministry and the military, which feared 'encirclement' by unfriendly forces and American influence in the oil-rich Caspian Sea region. The Ministry's White Paper, for example, had made the stationing of foreign troops in friendly states dependent on Russian and UN Security Council approval (Polikanov 2005).
4   These are in the fields of economic and trade relations, law and order and internal security, as well as humanitarian contacts and external security.
5   'Interview of Russian Foreign Minister Sergey Lavrov' in *Vremya Novostei,* 6 June 2005.
6   In August 2005, a large-scale joint combat practice demonstrated the extent to which shared concerns over American influence can catalyse the progress in Sino–Russian relations (BBC News 2005).
7   A planned Russo–German gas pipeline under the Baltic Sea further illustrates the sensitivity of Russian energy policy in Central and East European countries: this pipeline deal of 2005 has been compared in Poland and Lithuania to the Hitler–Stalin Pact of 1939.
8   'Cheney hits at Putin over energy "blackmail"', *Financial Times,* 5 May 2006.

9 In order to address these problems, Russia's Western partners aid the dismantling of
Russia's old nuclear hardware. This includes the G7 US$20 billion contribution
towards safeguarding nuclear stockpiles and securing nuclear reactors. Of particular
importance since al-Qaeda's efforts to acquire nuclear weapons were exposed,
assistance also goes to the protection of nuclear materials from the access of militants
(BBC News 2002).

References

Angus Reid Consultants (2005a) *Russians Expect Large Terrorist Attack.* Available online
at: <http://www.angus-reid.com/polls/index.cfm/fuseaction/viewItem/itemID/8812>
(accessed 26 September 2005).

Angus Reid Consultants (2005b) *Russians Review Effect of London Bombings.* Available
online at: <http://www.angus-reid.com/polls/index.cfm/fuseaction/viewItem/itemID
/8201> (accessed 26 September 2005).

Arbatov, A.G. (2004) 'Military reform: from crisis to stagnation', in S. Miller and D.
Trenin (eds) *The Russian Military: Power and Policy,* Cambridge, MA: MIT Press.

BBC News (2002) *G7 to fund Russian arms control.* Available online at:
<http://news.bbc.co.uk/1/hi/world/europe/2069522.stm> (accessed 28 October 2005).

BBC News (2005) *China Russia games in final stage.* Available online at:
<http://news.bbc.co.uk/2/hi/asia-pacific/4175530.stm> (accessed 26 October 2005).

Belov, Ye. and Putintsev, O. (2005) 'CIS: countering threats to security and stability',
International Affairs 51 (1): 95–105.

Defence Ministry of the Russian Federation (2003) *The Priority Tasks for the Development
of the Armed Forces of the Russian Federation,* Moscow: Defence Ministry of the
Russian Federation.

Dvorkin, V. (2005) 'An outlook for joint countering of security threats', *Russia in Global
Affairs* 3 (4): 45–57.

EU Observer (2006) *New EU–Russia Treaty to Deepen Security and Energy Ties.* Available
online at: <http://euobserver.com/24/21105> (accessed 13 March 2006).

Gamova, S. (2005) *Russia: The Political Pipeline.* Available online at:
<http://www.gasandoil.com/goc/news/ntr60266.htm> (accessed 1 March 2006).

IISS (International Institute for Strategic Studies) (2004) 'Russia', *The Military Balance*
104 (1): 294–8.

IISS (2005) 'Russia', *The Military Balance* 105 (1): 151–72.

Karaganov, S. (2005) 'Russia and the international order', *Chaillot Paper* 74: 23–43.

Kay, S. (2003) 'Geopolitical constraints and institutional innovation: the dynamics of mul-
tilateralism in Eurasia', in J. Sperling, S. Kay and S.V. Papacosma (eds) *Limiting
Institutions? The Challenge of Eurasian Security Governance,* Manchester: Manchester
University Press.

Kelin, A. (2004) 'Attitude to NATO expansion: calmly negative', *International Affairs* 50
(1): 17–25.

Kremenyuk, V. (2004) 'Russian National Security Doctrine. Russia and NATO', in G.
Hinteregger and H.-G. Heinrich (eds) *Russia: Continuity and Change,* Vienna: Springer
Verlag.

Lukin, A. (2004) 'Shanghai Cooperation Organization: problems and prospects', *International Affairs* 50 (3): 31–40.

Miller, S. (2004) 'Moscow's military power: Russia's search for security in an age of transition', in S. Miller and D. Trenin (eds) *The Russian Military: Power and Policy,* Cambridge, MA: MIT Press.

Ministry of Energy of the Russian Federation (2003) *The Summary of the Energy Strategy of Russia for the Period up to 2020,* Moscow: Ministry of Energy of the Russian Federation.

Ministry of Foreign Affairs of the Russian Federation (2005a) *Alexander Yakovenko, the Spokesman of Russia's Ministry of Foreign Affairs, Answers Media Questions Regarding Upcoming Trilateral Meeting of Foreign Ministers of Russia, India, China in Vladivostok,* 1 June 2005. Available online at: <http://www.ln.mid.ru/brp_4.nsf/0/l38e 02edebf8501dc3256ff8003a23e4?OpenDocument> (accessed 24 October 2005).

Ministry of Foreign Affairs of the Russian Federation (2005b) Press Statement Following the Meeting of the Shanghai Cooperation Organization Council of Heads of State, Astana, 5 July 2005. Available online at: <http://www.ln.mid.ru/brp_4.nsf/0/5c6695 c5cac855cec3257036002629ee?OpenDocumen> (accessed 24 October 2005).

Polikanov, D. (2005) 'Russia's perception and hierarchy of security threats', *The Quarterly Journal* 4 (2): 85–91.

Pravda, A. (2003) 'Putin's foreign policy after 11 September: radical or revolutionary?', in G. Gorodetsky (ed.) *Russia between East and West: Russian Foreign Policy on the Threshold of the Twenty-First Century,* London: Frank Cass.

Reppert, J. (2003) 'Russia's threat perceptions', in S.K. Wegren (ed.) *Russia's Policy Challenges: Security, Stability, and Development,* London: M.E. Sharpe.

Robertson, G. (2002) 'A new quality in the NATO–Russia relationship', *International Affairs* 48 (1): 32–7.

Russian Federation (2000a) *National Security Concept of the Russian Federation,* 10 January 2000 version, No. 24. English version available online at: <http://www. fas.org/nuke/guide/russia/doctrine/gazeta012400.htm> (accessed 9 September 2005).

Russian Federation (2000b) *Draft Military Doctrine of the Russian Federation,* approved by the President 21 April 2000, No. 706. English version available online at: <http://www.fas.org/nuke/guide/russia/doctrine/991009-draft-doctrine.htm> (accessed 9 September 2005).

Russian Federation (2000c) *The Foreign Policy Concept of the Russian Federation,* approved by the President, 28 June 2000. English version available online at: <http://www.fas.org/nuke/guide/russia/doctrine/econcept.htm> (accessed 9 September 2005).

Satanovsky, Y. (2005) 'A no-compromise war', *Russia in Global Affairs* 3 (1): 122–30.

Sköns, E., Omitoogun, W., Perdano, C. and Stålenheim, P. (2005) 'Military expenditure', *SIPRI Yearbook* 2005.

Stepanova, E. (2005) 'Islamic terrorism as threats to Russian security: the limits of the linkage', *Ponars Policy Memo* 393: 165–70.

Strategicheskiye Riski Rossii: Otsenka i Porgnoz (2005) Moscow: Delovoi Express.

Sukhov, I. (2005) 'North Caucasian map of threats', *Russia in Global Affairs* 3 (4): 150–8.

Trenin, D. (1999) *Russia's China Problem,* Washington DC: Carnegie Endowment for International Peace.

Trenin, D. (2002) *The End of Eurasia: Russia on the Border between Geopolitics and Globalization*, Washington, DC: Carnegie Endowment for International Peace.

Wallander, C. (2000) 'Russian national security policy in 2000', *Ponars Policy Memo* 102.

Weitz, R. (2005) 'Revitalising US–Russian security cooperation: practical measures', *Adelphi Papers* 377.

Willerton, J.P. and Cockerham, G. (2003) 'Russia, the CIS and Eurasian interconnections', in J. Sperling, S. Kay and V. Papacosma (eds) *Limiting Institutions? The Challenge of Eurasian Security Governance,* Manchester: Manchester University Press.

Yermolaev, M. (2000) 'Russia's international peacekeeping and conflict management in the post-Soviet environment', in M. Malan (ed.) *Boundaries of Peace Support Operations: The African Dimension,* Monograph No. 44.

Part IV
Conclusion

12 Regional or global security co operation? The vertices of conflict and interstices of cooperation

James Sperling

Many of the contemporary threats facing the major powers are global in origin and consequence. Neither terrorism, naturally occurring pandemics, the proliferation of weapons of mass destruction nor the degradation of the environment respect national boundaries. These kinds of threats, which resist either national or regional solutions, have emerged as crucial concerns for the public and elites in the G8 countries and China; they are also of concern for others, including the European Union member states and other regional powers such as India, Indonesia, or Brazil. The relative saliency of the new security agenda as well as the immediacy of the traditional one varies across national boundaries, owing in large part to the national sense of (in)vulnerability to those threats and the evolution of the state towards a late or post-Westphalian identity (Sperling 2003 and 2007).

It would be a mistake, however, to overlook the divergent perceptions of threat which, in turn, define the content and source of security challenges for each state and the preferred ways in which those challenges can and should be mastered. In the United States, there are both theoretical and policy debates about the limits of American power and the American ability to address ostensibly global threats unilaterally, if need be. While the administration of President George W. Bush has declared war on 'global' terror, the military manifestation has been a largely unilateral affair, albeit with significant British and Australian assists. Only China has adopted a similarly unilateralist perspective. But Chinese unilateralism is muted by the need for conditional multilateral cooperation in order to offset the overwhelming presence of the United States in its own geopolitical neighbourhood. Moreover, 11 September had an asymmetrical impact on national security perceptions as well as the willingness to embrace or reject multilateral solutions to a problem generally considered to have an indefinite origin and global reach. That event impelled the American elite and public to reconsider the very nature of security, while it had at best an indirect affect on the security calculations of China (namely, the stationing of American troops in Central Asia) and Japan (which faces a negligible threat from Muslim terrorists). The recognition that global terrorism exists has not been sufficient for the crafting of a global solution to it; other global threats likewise resist a global solution. Instead, security cooperation has been largely regionalized with varying degrees of persistence and success.

The regionalization of security has been cited as a feature of the international system, particularly after the end of the Cold War (*inter alia* Lake and Morgan 1997; Adler and Barnett 1998a; Buzan and Wæver 2003; Ikenberry and Mastanduno 2003; Sperling *et al.* 2003; Allison 2004; Katzenstein 2005; Pempel 2005; Suh *et al.* 2004). Regional security institutions, ranging from NATO and the EU to the Shanghai Cooperation Organization (SCO) and the ASEAN Regional Forum (ARF), strongly suggest that states do perceive security problems as regional phenomena, owing to regional identities or geopolitical orientations as well as the belief that those security challenges are only tractable at the regional level among states with a presumed set of commonalities facilitating cooperation. Barry Buzan and Ole Wæver adopt this logic in their definition of regional security complexes: 'most threats travel more easily over short distances than long ones, security interdependence is normally patterned into regionally based clusters' (Buzan and Wæver 2003: 4). While the notion of a regional security complex provides a rationale for investigating the origins of security pathologies at the regional level, they unduly restrict their definition of which states *belong* to a particular regional security complex.[1] This restriction reflects, in turn, an apparent desire to divide the globe into the largest number of viable regional security complexes. While their taxonomy is consistent with their assumption that security externalities do not travel well, it obscures the interface of pan-regional and global security cooperation, and underestimates the important and intrusive roles that great powers play in geopolitically critical areas of the world.[2] This limitation is problematic given the current environment where security externalities are *not* necessarily limited in their geographic scope and the provision of security requires, at a minimum, pan-regional, great power cooperation.

The G8 member states and China interact and dominate the world's four major security zones: Europe, the Atlantic, the Asia–Pacific, and Eurasia. While each of these nine countries has a manifest stake in the security and stability of each region, the direct participation of each power in a specific region varies considerably and in many cases is indirect or marginal at best. The questions addressed in this conclusion are relatively straightforward: what factors facilitate or bar regional security cooperation? Should the major powers seek the ambitious goal of global security cooperation or must they settle instead for regional security cooperation? Can security cooperation in these four regions generate decentralized global security cooperation or can it only produce regions that are more or less secure? Towards answering these questions, four variables will be compared across regions: national assessments of threat and its origins; the dominant pan-regional interaction patterns of the major powers; the balance struck between the civilian and traditional forms of statecraft; the pattern of convergence and divergence in national security cultures. The values taken on by those four variables identify the vertices of conflict and interstices security cooperation, regionally and globally. In the concluding section, the prospects for global security cooperation in the early twenty-first century are assessed.

European security cooperation

There is a growing consensus that the EU constitutes a civilized security community (Harnisch and Maull 2001: 4). The EU itself meets the primary criterion of a security community established by Adler and Barnett (1998b: 55); namely, the common expectation (if not certainty) of non-violent conflict resolution. The existence of a security community and the collective identity attending it provides neither the necessary nor sufficient conditions for within-group security cooperation. Although states may manage security cooperatively within the community, in geographically removed regions cooperation may fail owing to divergent national interests, historical legacies, and global ambitions. Just as the prospect of war between Britain and France or Germany and Poland is unthinkable, the run-up to the Iraq war also demonstrates that France and Britain or Germany and Poland can disagree fundamentally on how threats are defined and the best means for meeting a threat, even if all parties agree that the threat exists.

Threat assessment and the source of threat: sources of conflict and convergence

Of the four regions under consideration, the greatest degree of convergence is found among the major European powers. The British, French, German and Italian governments share a common assessment of threat, although there are divergences in the rank-ordering of threats, the spectrum of threats, and the definition of threats having a European rather than an idiosyncratic national salience. Perhaps the most important event-shaping threat perception in the post-Cold War period is 11 September 2001. Terrorism had been an abiding concern of each European power over the course of the post-war period, ranging from secessionism in France (Corsica) and Britain (Northern Ireland) to revolutionary movements in Italy (the Red Brigade) and Germany (Baader–Meinhof). The al-Qaeda terrorist attack on the United States, however, accelerated the globalization of Europe's geopolitical orientation.

Prior to 11 September, Italy and Germany had parochial, regional concerns that reflected national interests – Italy was preoccupied with developments in the Mediterranean and south-western Balkans; Germany was concerned with the success or failure of democratic transitions along its eastern and southern peripheries. Both states have belatedly recognized that economic globalization has engendered the globalization of security. The impact on France and the United Kingdom has been less dramatic; both already possessed a broader geopolitical orientation. France has been a significant military and diplomatic presence in Africa during the entire post-war period, has sought a global role, and possesses significant force projection capabilities enabling it to back its diplomacy with force. The United Kingdom has played a global role owing to the economic and diplomatic legacy of its empire and its close diplomatic relationship with the United States. Britain, in effect, has provided diplomatic support and supplied a dependable expeditionary force serving American and by definition British interests.

Today, the four European powers share a common set of security concerns. Britain, France and Germany rank terrorism and the proliferation of weapons of mass destruction (WMD) as their first or second most critical security challenge, while Italy has ranked terrorism first and WMD as one of the top five security challenges.[3] They also have an overlapping concern with the maintenance of regional stability: Germany emphasizes the need for political stability and the emergence of regional democracies; Britain and France are preoccupied with the requirements of military stability; and Italy focuses on the challenge of economic stability, particularly in the Balkans and North Africa. These states also have idiosyncratic security concerns that are non-intersecting: France is particularly preoccupied with conventional war, Islamic extremism, and organized crime; Britain and Germany view environmental degradation as a security threat. Unsurprisingly, the European Security Strategy (ESS) emphasizes four security challenges where the Europeans can act jointly: terrorism, WMD proliferation, regional instability and conflicts, and organized crime. While France is the only country that rank-ordered organized crime as a critical security threat, the EU and its member states have implemented a broad spectrum of policies addressing that challenge, particularly as it relates to money laundering and trafficking of drugs, humans and small arms by transnational criminal organizations and terrorist groups.[4]

Despite the existence of a European security community *in conjunction with* a common or overlapping set of threat perceptions, differentiated geopolitical orientations limit that cooperation, if for no other reason that each faces budgetary and resource constraints. Britain, France, Germany and Italy identify the political evolution and stabilization of Central, Eastern and Southeastern Europe as critical to European and national security; each is also concerned with developments in the Middle East, although the Middle East is defined differently – some are preoccupied with the resolution of the Israeli–Palestinian conflict and others are preoccupied with the Persian Gulf, but have conflicting views of how to best meet the threats emanating from that region. The British, Germans and Italians also view Central Asia and the Islamic world generally as regions posing a threat to their security, while the British, French and Italians share a common concern with the stability of the Mediterranean. Britain also has a particular interest in the stability of the Indian subcontinent which is not a widely shared concern within the EU. The ESS reflects an aggregation of these geopolitical orientations, which lends the EU a global orientation without the political (and instrumental) capability to act decisively; the document ranks the Middle East and Central and Eastern Europe as the two most important sources of threat, a ranking consistent with the policies and perceptions of the four major states. The inclusion of Africa as a region of concern in the ESS reflects the particular interests of Britain and France, although Africa is essentially a threat to itself and only poses an indirect threat to British or French security interests.

Patterns of interaction

The pattern of interaction falls along a continuum bounded by unilateral action and institutionalized multilateralism. EU membership has conditioned a reflexively multilateral response to common security threats. France, Germany and Italy are rhetorically committed to the EU as the multilateral forum of first choice, while the British view the EU as second best to NATO. Yet, the British and French reserve the option of unilateral action, an option alien to German or Italian security discourse or policy. Moreover, Britain and Italy have repeatedly acted bilaterally with the United States on security matters or multilaterally in 'coalitions of the willing', whereas France and Germany have been reticent participants or abstained. Thus, these four states range from those operating along the full spectrum of interaction patterns (the UK and France) to those who operate within a very narrow range (Germany and Italy).

Even though all four states exhibit a preference for institutionalized multilateralism, the British favour action within NATO while the others favour cooperation within the EU. Moreover, while Italy and Germany rank-order NATO as the second most important multilateral forum for security cooperation, it ranks third for France. And just as Britain, Italy and Germany rank the UN as the third most important institutional venue, it ranks second for France. These institutional rank-orderings reflect two national assessments: first, the determination of which multilateral institution is most likely to deliver security successfully; second, the identification of the institution maximizing the returns on expended diplomatic capital. French influence within NATO naturally declined after its withdrawal from the integrated military command in 1966, but its veto on the UN Security Council remains intact; Britain, while it too has a veto, leverages its relationship with the United States and its force projection capabilities within NATO. Both Germany and Italy have diminished influence outside of the EU, although NATO lends more opportunities for shaping the security agenda (and restraining American power) than does the UN, where they are simply member states with one vote.

The balance between civilian and traditional forms of statecraft

Each country recognizes that the collective security challenges facing Europe can only be met with a balancing of the civilian and traditional forms of statecraft. The general acceptance of multilateral action obscures divergences between these states on the efficacy of each category of instrument in meeting specific security threats; each state demonstrates a reflexive preference for either civilian or traditional instrumental forms of statecraft. The British, in particular, appear most wedded to the traditional instruments of diplomacy, pre-emptive military engagement, and deterrence. France is likewise reliant upon military force and deterrence, but explicitly recognizes the central role that economic aid and civilian policing play in the contemporary security environment. Just as the British are wedded to the traditional instruments of statecraft, the Germans are equally wed to the civilian instruments. This civilian approach to security reflects the German desire to redress the underlying causes of instability, particularly along Europe's perimeter, while the continuing French and British reliance upon the military instrument reflects a preoccupation with redressing the symptoms or manifestations of insecurity. While all four states have an express preference for diplomatic solutions to security crises – the EU-3 negotiations with Iran are a case in point – the British and French are willing to resort to military action up to full-scale war, while the Italians and Germans are only willing to countenance peacekeeping or peace-enforcement operations.

Convergent or divergent security cultures?

The content of the four national security cultures varies markedly. The preceding examination of instrumental preferences and interaction patterns illustrates a number of divergences, but the two other critical aspects of security culture – the worldview of the external environment and the nature of the national identity – are likewise critical to the understanding of the presence and absence of security cooperation within Europe or any other region of the world.

These four European powers hold disparate worldviews that construct a significant barrier to security cooperation. The distribution and balancing of power continues to mesmerize the French foreign policy elite; security policy remains primarily directed towards states and the traditional security threats that states pose. In Britain, security is taken as a given in the European context; the concern with defending against asymmetrical warfare has displaced the traditional task of conventional defence. Moreover, British security policy focuses on regional instability outside Europe, in part reflecting Britain's investment position in the former empire as well as the calculation that political instability anywhere provides a haven for the operations of transnational criminal or terrorist organizations. Unlike France and Britain, which retain in different measure a state-centric understanding of the international system, Germany and Italy perceive the international system as best managed by the institutionalization of multilateral cooperation. This assertion does not suggest that German and Italian elites are unaware of the continuing importance of states, but rather that these elites actively seek an alternative to a state-centric system. Although each accepts the saliency of military force and power, neither state is willing to rely upon it or accepts its exercise as inevitable.

The persistence of national identities is the most significant barrier to deeper European security cooperation. Identity has been increasingly identified as the central causal variable for those seeking to explain the emergence and persistence of security cooperation, particularly within Europe and North America (Wendt 1999; Finnemore and Sikkink 1998; Checkel 1998; Hampton and Sperling 2003). Shared identities are linked to the process of interest formation; collective identities are claimed to create shared interests and normatively disciplined patterns of behaviour. As important, however, is the balance struck between collective and national identities: where a collective identity exists, cooperation will be facilitated and enduring, whereas the persistence of a national identity only admits episodic cooperation contingent upon overlapping or common national interests. While the major European states do accept the existence of a common heritage and history, national identities with foreign and security policy consequences remain more resilient in France and Britain than in Germany or Italy. France and Britain have not abandoned a national statecraft or definition of threat, even though Britain and France recognize the difficulty of achieving their security objectives unilaterally. Italian and German security policies have been relatively denationalized; elites in both nations have endeavoured to embed their security policies in the institutional frameworks of the EU, NATO and the UN. France and Britain claim the role of global powers; Britain, unlike France, has not yet reconciled itself to a European vocation as the foundation for the exercise of influence in the wider world. Italy and Germany – at least in the more traditional domains of security policy – have actively pursued European solutions to European problems, a strategy no doubt reflecting an accurate assessment of their power capabilities (Italy) and the debilitating inheritance of history (Germany).

Eurasian security cooperation

In Halford Mackinder's (1904) famous geo-strategic formulation, the state that controls the Eurasian heartland controls the periphery, and the state that controls the periphery controls the world. The Russian Federation and China are the two states capable of establishing control over the heartland, but the heartland remains one of the most geopolitically unsettled regions of the world.[5] The simple virtues of geographic proximity and power guarantee that these two states, along with Japan, will dominate the evolution of Eurasian security cooperation. With the exception of Japan, which has functioned as a civilian power and has progressed towards a late-Westphalian identity, China and Russia retain foreign policy preoccupations and identity of the Westphalian state. The major Eurasian states lack even a rudimentary common identity that could provide the basis for the collective definition of threat or enable them to transcend narrow calculations of national gain and loss. As an empirical matter, security cooperation is likely to remain limited to shifting rather than principled alliances and bereft of effective multilateral institutions.

Threat assessment and the source of threat: sources of conflict and convergence

As compared to the dissolution of the Soviet Union and the emergence of unstable yet geo-strategically important states such as Uzbekistan, Kazakhstan, Tajikistan and Kyrgyzstan, 11 September only indirectly affected the regional definition of threat or its agency. In the Russian and Chinese cases, the American 'global war' on Muslim terrorism provided a virtual diplomatic carte blanche for suppressing their own internal Muslim secessionists in Chechnya and the Xinjiang province; in the Japanese case, Muslim terrorism poses a negligible threat to Japanese security owing to Japan's culturally enforced social homogeneity, securely controlled borders, and the absence of an acute Muslim grievance against the Japanese. A second indirect effect of some consequence, however, has been the sequential American-led invasions of Afghanistan and Iraq. Both wars provided the Central Asian successor states of the Soviet Union an opportunity to reinsure their independence against the Russian Federation by inviting the United States to conduct operations from their territory, a development unwelcomed in Moscow and Beijing.

China, Japan and Russia only share two common security concerns: terrorism and domestic organized crime. While these two categories of threat have facilitated or produced cooperation in Europe, they have not done so in Eurasia: terrorism in all three countries is indigenous in origin without a significant transnational component; their concern with organized crime and domestic violence reflects very different calculations of cause and effect. Chinese elites, for example, increasingly fear an unsettled and disenfranchised underclass that may upend the existing political and economic systems; in Russia, a government sponsored or tolerated 'kleptocracy' in conjunction with the rise of powerful criminal organizations thwarts the consolidation of democracy, the rule of law, and the market economy. And for Japan, terrorism and organized crime have plagued society over the entire post-war period and represent a chronic condition threatening societal security.

China and Russia also share a common concern with the American military presence in the region; both countries have hegemonial ambitions that will remain unrealized so long as the United States is engaged and present in the region. While Russia and China can agree that American hegemony is undesirable, their own aspirations in the region are mutually exclusive. This diplomatic conundrum points to the fragility of Sino–Russian security cooperation even where a common interest exists. Moreover, the Japanese view the United States as the guarantor of their security, particularly with respect to China and North Korea. Thus, cooperation between these three states is stymied by their different assessments of the American role in Eurasia and their own conflicting ambitions.

The relative saliency of the new security agenda for each state provides a second barrier to security cooperation. As compared to Japan, neither Russia nor China is particularly concerned with environmental degradation, natural disasters, or threats to societal security.[6] Instead, both China and Russia are preoccupied with regional military instability, preparations for conventional or asymmetric warfare, and the avoidance of domestic political collapse or constitutional change. Moreover, the Chinese preoccupation with ensuring access to natural resources, particularly oil and natural gas, may deepen the enmity and distrust between China and Japan, particularly since both are seeking privileged access to Russian and Caspian Sea oil production (Choo 2003).

Even where there is some common ground on the nature of the security threat, there is an absence of agreement on where that threat originates. As noted, terrorism is a largely indigenous phenomenon that only provides a limited basis for cooperation: China and Russia only agree on their choice of anti-terrorist rhetoric and willingness to lend the other a free hand in coping with their respective Muslim secessionists. All three powers recognize the threat posed by organized crime. But the opportunity for cooperation is limited: only Russia serves as a haven for transnational criminal organizations and Russian organized crime targets the richer and more easily penetrated European and North American markets.

Just as China and Japan have a common concern with the evolution of the Korean Peninsula, Russia and China have a direct stake in Central Asia, particularly the emergence of the United States as a significant military player in the region. North Korea poses a military threat to its neighbours, while the American presence in Central Asia represents a barrier to the realization of Chinese and Russian ambitions in the region. Thus, the absence of common as opposed to intersecting security interests, in conjunction with the disparate assessments of where threats originate, limit the opportunities for sustained or institutionalized security cooperation.

Patterns of interaction

Multilateral security cooperation is weakly institutionalized in Eurasia. The SCO, the chief Eurasian security institution, was created as a response to the outstanding border conflicts between China and the successor states of the Soviet Union (Yom 2002; Kay 2003). The SCO member states have established a joint terrorism centre, but have refrained from extending one another any sort of reciprocal security guarantee. Bilateral security relationships are prevalent in the region: the post-war bilateral security treaty with the United States underpins the Japanese security strategy; Sino–Russian security cooperation is informed by a common concern for the stability of the former republics of the Soviet Union with which they share common borders as well as the American regional military presence; and each Eurasian power has a significant bilateral relationship with the United States, although the Sino–American relationship remains competitive if not adversarial, while the Russo–American relationship is cooperative as it pertains to Europe but less so in Eurasia. Unlike China, which has demonstrated a proclivity to act unilaterally when possible, the Russians and Japanese accept the importance and utility of entering into multilateral frameworks. However, the absence of enduring and common security interests – other than avoiding war – removes any incentive to broaden or deepen security cooperation.

The three Eurasian powers do agree, however, on the continuing relevance and importance of the UN. China and Russia, like France, view the UN as a forum enabling them to compensate for their relative power disadvantage vis-à-vis the United States owing to their status as permanent members of the UN Security Council. For Japan, the UN remains an important forum for protecting Japan's global and regional interests, but also offers the prospect of an eventual permanent seat on the Security Council and the possession of a unit veto. Aside from the ARF and SCO, these three states are also parties to the Six-Party Talks on North Korea, a weak form of security multilateralism contingent upon the persistence of the commonly perceived and acute security threat to Northeast Asian stability. The motives animating Russian, Chinese and Japanese participation are mixed: Japan is presently the most likely target of a nuclear-armed North Korea; China wishes to preserve its patron–client relationship without jeopardizing regional security in the process; and Russia is motivated by prestige as well as its direct interest owing to geographical propinquity.

The balance between civilian and traditional instruments of statecraft

China and Russia have a pronounced preference for the traditional instruments of statecraft. Both states are major military powers and China is undertaking a military modernization programme that includes the acquisition of a blue water navy. China remains preoccupied with the traditional security task of territorial defence and continues to distrust American intentions in the region, particularly as they pertain to the status of Taiwan. Japan has restricted itself to a limited military capability tailored to the requirements of territorial defence, but its military force is slowly undergoing a restructuring that will lend Japanese diplomacy greater flexibility outside Northeast Asia. Nonetheless, all three states remain committed to diplomacy as the foreign policy instrument of first choice. Although China, Japan and Russia use their economic assets to facilitate the realization of their foreign policy goals, China and Japan employ those assets to realize the 'in kind' objectives of guaranteed access to markets and raw materials. Russia uses the leverage derived from its oil and natural gas reserves as a diplomatic instrument serving political objectives with allies, friends, and rivals. Nonetheless, China and Russia continue to place the traditional instruments of statecraft in the service of the traditional security agenda. Japan, despite its status as a late-Westphalian state, relies upon the entire spectrum of diplomatic instruments and pursues a relatively traditional security agenda, largely owing to its geopolitical milieu.

Convergent or divergent security cultures?

The Russian worldview is characteristic of a classical Westphalian state: interstate relations alternate between rivalry and fragile alliances; war and diplomacy remain the most dependable and useful instruments of statecraft; and a multipolar international system will preserve the independence and autonomy of its constituent units, the state. This Westphalian worldview does not becloud the recognition that transnational actors pose a palpable and significant security threat to Russia. The rise of transnational criminal organizations and their penetration of the Russian economy and society as well as the bloody, interminable war of secession in Chechnya provide clear evidence that non-state actors seriously threaten Russian security.

The Chinese share the broad outlines of the Russian worldview. China, like Russia, prefers the emergence of a multipolar international system balancing America's currently unassailable position in the international system. Unlike Russia, Chinese animosity towards American power is not tempered by a direct stake in the evolution of the European security order, particularly the transformation of NATO into a collective security system. Rather, it is the continuing American support of Taiwanese political independence that intensifies China's grievance against American power. Despite the modest institutionalization of

Central Asian security cooperation with the SCO, China remains wary of security institutions and, like the United States, favours unilateralism over multilateralism.

The Japanese worldview has a 'European' flavour insofar as Japan has opted for a diplomacy based on persuasion and economic incentives. The Japanese aversion to the exercise of military power for anything other than self-defence remains unchanged, but not unchanging. The Japanese government has increasingly come to see military power as a useful and legitimate instrument of statecraft, although the Japanese armed forces have been restricted to support operations in theatres of war, peacekeeping operations under the auspices of the UN, and relief operations in the wake of natural disasters. But because Japan exists in a Westphalian environment where North Korea and China pose plausible threats to Japan's territorial integrity, the viability of the constitutional 'peace clause', which still places legal and psychological barriers to a militarized foreign policy, remains contingent upon the continued conflation of American and Japanese interests as well as the persistence of American military dominance in the region.

China, Japan and Russia possess strong national identities animating each state's security perceptions and calculation of interest. Unlike Europe, where there has been the evolution of a common identity cultivated within the EU, the Eurasian states have clearly defined and mutually exclusive identities. Consequently, security cooperation depends upon the coalescence of material interests rather than a pre-existing propensity to define interests in common. Put differently, the continuing differentiation of the national from the regional provides a significant barrier to sustained security cooperation although it does not preclude its epiphenomenal occurrence.

Japan and China both lack the elements of a cosmopolitan identity; neither possesses a sense that they share a common civilization or culture. Instead, their cultural and civilizational exceptionalism – if not chauvinism – is mutually antagonistic and exclusive. The Chinese exceptionalism is further exacerbated by its historically self-assumed status as the 'Middle Kingdom' for millennia prior to the age of European imperialism, the century-long 'humiliation' of China's dismemberment into exclusive zones of European economic control, the Japanese colonization of Formosa and Northern Manchuria as well as Japan's brutal occupation during the Pacific War, and its continuing exclusion from the inner circle of international powers, perhaps best exemplified by its absence from G8 summits. Moreover, China and Russia treat the other great powers as a well-defined 'other', while Japan's partial socialization into the American-sponsored system of multilateralism has muted the culturally conditioned predilection to do the same.

Russia remains a 'European' state, albeit one with an Asian hinterland. While Russia is a Eurasian power, Russians identify themselves as European in terms of their civilizational orientation, ethnicity, and religious conviction. This European identity, constructed – at least in part – in opposition to Asia, poses a serious barrier to the process of collective identity formation between the three Eurasian powers. That barrier is reinforced by outstanding Japanese grievances against Russia, particularly its occupation of the four islands off the coast of Hokkaido, and China's continuing distrust of Russian intentions in Asia. Even though China and Russia share the same self-assessment that both are great powers frustrated in their global and regional ambitions by the United States, this shared grievance, which reflects a zero-sum understanding of international politics, does not provide the basis for lasting bilateral cooperation.

Transatlantic security cooperation

NATO – and the transatlantic relationship more generally – has been the exemplar of institutionalized security cooperation in the post-war period. As the most successful collective defence organization in the twentieth century, it not only prevented a third European war but provided a framework for security cooperation that carried over into the post-Cold War period and facilitated the integration of the former Warsaw Pact states, including the Soviet Union, into the pre-existing Atlantic security order. Yet the fundamental geopolitical change occasioned by the end of the Cold War transformed NATO virtually overnight from a compulsory alliance that derived its cohesive power from a common Soviet threat into a voluntary alliance with no specific adversary. This development changed the alliance security referent from a well-defined and adversarial 'other' to an ill-defined and diffuse regional milieu. Moreover, not only has the consensus on the goals or purposes of the Alliance eroded, but the absence of a concrete 'other' has revealed divergent perceptions of threat on both sides of the Atlantic.

Threat assessment and the source of threat: sources of conflict and convergence

It would be difficult to overestimate the fundamental impact that 11 September had on the character of the transatlantic security system. The attacks dramatically and profoundly demonstrated to Americans their individual and collective vulnerability to transnational terrorism that had been previously conducted against off-shore American assets with a few exceptions. Not only did it alter the American perception of threat and remilitarize American foreign policy, but it underscored for the Canadians their own vulnerability to the actions of its southern neighbour. While the reorientation of the American foreign policy elite after 11 September created a new set of tensions within the Atlantic Alliance, it had the secondary impact of undermining the European perception of the American invulnerability to external attack. In combination with the American effort to press-gang Europe into a global war against terrorism and to impose a global military mission on NATO, pre-existing divergences outside the Atlantic area were inexorably manifested on security issues that were of common concern and well within the regional writ of NATO. Regardless of anyone's assessment of the clarity of purpose animating any NATO member-state foreign policy, it has become clear that there is a growing divergence of purpose rooted in different understandings of threat, the sources of threat, and the best methods for ameliorating or defending against those threats.

Prior to 11 September, the overarching foreign policy ambitions of the United States were largely consistent with the civilian ambitions of the Europeans, particularly as it pertained to the task of establishing democratic governments and competitive market economies in Central, Southern and Southeastern Europe as well as in the successor states to the Soviet Union. Both the Europeans and the Americans undertook measures to thwart the proliferation of nuclear, chemical and biological weapons, although the Americans had a greater concern than the Europeans with the threat of WMD proliferation while the European allies were more concerned with the more imminent threat of unsafe nuclear power plants in Central and Eastern Europe. Nonetheless, those interests were complementary and mutually reinforcing in the Atlantic context. An important divergence in American and European security perceptions, which has driven the transformation of the American armed forces and accounts for relatively high levels of defence spending, is the American concern with the rise of a peer competitor challenging American regional or global dominance. This divergence is as unavoidable as it is corrosive to the broadening or deepening of security cooperation in the Atlantic Alliance.

The American proclivity to define its interests and perception of threat as a national rather than collective problem was reinforced by 11 September, despite the universalistic rhetoric employed by the Bush administration. Even though there *is* a superficial commonality between Europe and America on the need to cope with Muslim terrorists, the United States (and until recently Canada) tend to define the threat as an external one, while the Europeans are forced to treat the threat as internal as well as external, a condition forced upon them by demographic trends and their own inability to assimilate citizens of non-European ancestry or non-Christian religious confession. Likewise, the threat posed by Muslim terrorists was conflated with other American concerns, particularly the proliferation of nuclear weapons programmes in the Gulf region that threatened not only its own strategic and economic interests but the very existence of Israel, a country that has deep emotional and religious importance for a large segment of the American public and political classes. The continuing concern with the rise of China as a peer competitor is of no direct concern for the major European powers, but deflects American attention from the pressing security concerns preoccupying the Europeans. The European concern with transnational criminal organizations, for example, does not figure as prominently in American security calculations unless it is explicitly linked to the financing or arming of terrorists. And the European concern with the environment, including the threat posed by climate change, has been treated with disdain by the current administration.

The United States has always had a global security orientation, while the Europeans have been largely satisfied with tending to their parochial concern with regional stability. The events of 11 September had the salutary effect of forcing the Europeans to adopt a more global view of security threats, but the direct European stake in developments outside the Mediterranean and greater Middle East remains negligible. This difference manifests itself in a divergent definition of the sources and agents of threat confronting the Atlantic Alliance. The United

States remains preoccupied with three classes of actors: rogue states, peer competitors, and transnational (Muslim) terrorist groups. While the Europeans have endeavoured to negotiate outcomes relieving American concerns with the problem of nuclear and missile proliferation in Iran, it is as plausible that the real target of Europe's diplomatic exertions has been the United States itself. The deep European scepticism of the American invasion of Iraq and its Middle Eastern diplomacy more generally, officially expressed in Germany and France and shared by the publics of all four major European powers, has only been validated by the continuing sectarian violence in Iraq, the rising number of defections from 'coalition of the willing' and the less than successful American occupation.

The geographic concerns currently preoccupying the United States are echoed in European chanceries, particularly the importance of negotiating a final settlement guaranteeing Israel's right to exist as well as creating a viable Palestinian state. While the Europeans and Americans broadly share these two goals for the region, the respective foreign policy elites tend to favour the other's antagonist – the United States unreservedly sides with Israel, while the Europeans have greater sympathy for the plight of the Palestinians. The Europeans also share the American concern with the stability of the Gulf Region; the Europeans are more dependent than the Americans on the stable flow of oil from the region. Yet, the Europeans are as likely to view the United States as a threat to the continuing supply of oil owing to the preoccupation with regime change in Iraq and Iran, two members of the Bush administration's 'Axis of Evil' and not insignificant sources of oil. Moreover, the United States has legitimate security concerns in Asia that are matters of relative indifference for its European NATO allies. The American preoccupation with Chinese military power diverts resources away from meeting those threats preoccupying its European allies, but as important, the American concern with Chinese military power reflects a desire to sustain America's global dominance – a foreign policy goal that many Europeans see as a barrier to their own goal of greater autonomy and the effective institutionalization of regional and global security cooperation.

Patterns of interaction

The execution of American foreign policy in the Atlantic area was predicated upon the successful institutionalization of security and economic cooperation; multilateral security cooperation with the major European states was both a substantive and instrumental foreign policy goal for those 'present at the creation'. The United States relied upon NATO to achieve its security goals in Europe during and after the Cold War. Even though the United States wielded disproportionate influence within NATO favourable to it, the European member states found the arrangement a useful mechanism for influencing American policy and linking American security to the security of Europe. Multilateralism within the Atlantic area, while a constant feature of the member states' foreign policies, did not preclude bilateral or unilateral policy initiatives on either side of the Atlantic. The recent American preference for unilateral responses when possible and for 'coalitions of the willing' only when necessary has eroded NATO's centrality in American security calculations; it has also driven the Europeans to seek defence and security autonomy. While it would be premature (and inaccurate) to argue that NATO no longer functions as the most important security institution in the Atlantic area, NATO has lost some of its lustre and utility for its North American and European members.

The balance between civilian and traditional forms of statecraft

On the surface, it would appear that within the Atlantic area there are two distinct forms of statecraft, the civilian (practiced by the continental Europeans) and the traditional (practiced by the United States and Britain). The Europeans have devoted vast sums of financial resources and technical expertise towards sustaining the transition to democracy and the market economy in Central, Southern and Southeastern Europe, addressing the root causes of regional instability, transnational crime and terrorism, and supporting regional and international institutions to mediate and resolve conflicts that arise between and within states. The Americans, on the other hand, reflexively turned to the Pentagon in response to the 11 September attacks. Rather than treating terrorism as a policing and intelligence problem, the threat of terrorism was transmuted into a global war naturally requiring the exercise of American military power. Moreover, the Americans and Europeans diverged in their rhetoric: the American government adopted the strategy of pre-emptive war, while the Europeans agreed upon a policy of preventive engagement to address the root causes of terrorism. With respect to security threats originating within the transatlantic area broadly defined or directly threatening Alliance members, however, there is little difference between the member states on the use of military force or the utility of international institutions; friction occurs primarily when the allies seek a common response to a security threat 'out of area'.

Nonetheless, the United States has relied upon the civilian instruments of statecraft to address a wide range of security threats, notably in the areas of health, WMD proliferation, organized crime, and energy. Similarly, the Europeans, particularly France and Britain, not only have a force projection and nuclear capability second only to that of the United States, but have demonstrated time and again their willingness to use force when all other options are exhausted. Even Germany, which had once been unwilling to participate in combat operations even when its interests were threatened, has steadily increased its military profile in areas as diverse as Afghanistan, Sudan and Kosovo. The United States and Europe clearly have different rank-orderings and assessments of which instruments are best designed to meet a specific threat, but the difference that does exist has been unduly exaggerated. There is a fundamental divergence within the Atlantic area on the importance of international law, treaties and conventions as mechanisms for conflict resolution or addressing common security threats, particularly on issues such as global climate change, the criticality of a UN resolution for justifying the use of force, and the legitimacy of extraordinary rendition and torture of suspected terrorists. Despite Britain's steadfast support of the United States since the invasion of Iraq, the United States is increasingly isolated from all of its major allies on the substantive importance of international law and the UN in particular.

Convergent or divergent security cultures?

The American worldview has always perplexed its European and Canadian allies alike. During the Cold War, the American obsession and fear of communism as a political movement befuddled those at the centre or on the left of the European political spectrum. Just as the Americans transformed the Soviet–American competition for regional and global hegemony into a Manichean struggle between good and evil, the more jaundiced European elite treated the competition for what it was – the perennial struggle for the mastery of Europe.[7] As grating for the Europeans was the proselytizing impulse to remake the world in the American image whether it was in the interests of the United States or the state targeted for American munificence. While European scepticism of American motives is the product of historical experience, many Americans attribute it instead to Europe's effete foreign policy and political elite, political turpitude or a by-product of a spent civilization. There has been a convergence of sorts after 11 September: a radicalized Islam has been similarly embraced as the primary threat to regional stability and domestic tranquillity. Yet, the members of the Atlantic Alliance do not share the same faith in the transformative power of democracy in the Islamic world as a panacea for eliminating Muslim terrorism. Moreover, Europeans and Canadians are less dependent upon a demonized 'other' in their framing of their security policies or their definition of threat.

It has been widely assumed that a common transatlantic identity – rooted in the shared values of the enlightenment and a common history – has contributed to the coherence and persistence of the Atlantic Alliance. That identity, fostered by elites on both sides of the Atlantic, reinforced the cement holding the Alliance together, the common Soviet threat to European stability. Elites on either side of the Atlantic have appealed to shared values and civilization as a rationale for continuing or deepening security cooperation even where the national interests of the member states overlapped only imperfectly. Over time, the existence of a common identity became an uncontested assumption and was commonly invoked to explain the depth and longevity of transatlantic security cooperation. It would be incorrect to argue that some form of common or collective identity does not exist within the transatlantic area or that it has not facilitated cooperation, but the importance of that transatlantic identity has been exaggerated; it has been found wanting as a unifying force when one state perceives an existential threat where the others do not. There is also a countervailing identity dynamic in the transatlantic area that overrides the collective identity forged over the post-war period; namely, an American identity that remains national, self-referential and inexplicably defensive that is matched by the cisatlantic admixture of national and European identities oftentimes deriving its sole content from an unflattering apposition to the United States.

Asia-Pacific security cooperation

The prospects for sustained security cooperation in the Asia-Pacific are limited. Chinese interests and ambitions are directly opposed to those of the other two major Pacific powers, Japan and the United States. China, as a revisionist power, is seeking to displace the United States as the dominant military and political actor in the region, while the United States and Japan, as the region's status quo powers, are determined to thwart Chinese ambitions and preserve American dominance as well as the privileged Japanese–American security relationship. The end of the Cold War in 1989 did not initiate a changed systemic context that unleashed the demand for the institutionalization of security cooperation between erstwhile adversaries or rivals. The major turning point in the evolution of the Asia-Pacific was the Sino–American accommodation initiated by the Nixon Administration towards the end of the war in Vietnam and the enlistment of China as an unspoken ally balancing Soviet power in Asia.

China and Japan's phenomenal economic growth throughout the last third of the twentieth century also signalled the growing importance of the Asia-Pacific for the United States. It harkened the onset of a Pacific century where the global balance of power and economic dynamism are shifting inexorably in Asia's favour and providing the economic wherewithal for China to emerge as a full-spectrum great power wielding ambidextrously the economic instruments of persuasion as well as the military instruments of coercion. China, like Japan before it, has become America's banker; its emergence as a trading power running a significant current account surplus with the United States and accumulation of vast foreign reserves invested in American Treasury bills together finance the modernization of the Chinese armed forces. Were China to realize its military modernization goals and to acquire a deep water navy, it would then possess the diplomatic resources enabling it to circumscribe American and Japanese influence in the region, if not displace the United States as the major guarantor of order in the region.

Threat assessment and the source of threat: sources of conflict and convergence

Just as the end of the Cold War in 1989 was a matter of relative indifference to the underlying dynamic of the region, the security consequences of 11 September only indirectly affected China and Japan. China was a diplomatic beneficiary of the 11 September attacks: it not only temporarily relieved the American preoccupation with China as a peer competitor, but extended China a free hand in its own efforts to suppress the separatist aspirations of its Muslim Uighur minority in the Xinjiang province as a part of the global war on terrorism. For Japan, 11 September only increased American expectations that Japan would 'normalize' its foreign policy and reintroduce military force into its diplomatic toolbox.

China, Japan and the United States share two interests in the Asia-Pacific: ensuring the existing territorial and political status quo on the Korean peninsula and preventing any change in Taiwan's legal status vis-à-vis mainland China. Each party has an interest in avoiding the militarization of the underlying conflicts. Yet, the major antagonists – North Korea and Taiwan – are the client states of China and the United States, respectively. Neither China nor the United States is totally sympathetic to the goals of their clients, but each has an interest in preserving those bilateral relationships even if it forms a barrier to Sino–American security cooperation elsewhere. Taiwan's unresolved status – the Taiwanese desire for full sovereign independence from mainland China and China's stated long-term objective of absorbing Taiwan as a province of the People's Republic – poses a greater likelihood of a great power confrontation. In the event of a Chinese gambit to occupy Taiwan militarily, it would spark a conflict drawing in the United States, more than likely as a combatant; Japan, by virtue of its bilateral security guarantee with the United States and the stationing of US Marines on Okinawa, would be likewise vulnerable to a widening Sino–American military conflict.

Japan and the United States continue to share a number of common security concerns: the North Korean nuclear weapons and missile programmes as well as the growing power and influence of China. Japan largely shares the American concern with the acquisition of nuclear weapons by rogue states, but that concern is directed primarily at North Korea rather than Iran. The overlapping Sino–American perception of Muslim terrorists as a security threat does not serve as the firm basis for broader, long-term security cooperation: the United States remains fixated on the threat posed by al-Qaeda and Arabic Muslim terrorism more generally and China is preoccupied with the specific threat posed by the Islamic Movement of Uzbekistan (IMU), which is active and conducts operations out of Kyrgyzstan and Tajikistan in support of China's Uighur separatists.

In many respects, the security threats occupying American, Chinese and Japanese political elites originate with at least one of the other major regional powers. The Japanese concern with the environment, for example, is not matched by China or the United States;[8] Chinese particulate and carbon dioxide emissions attending the burning of brown coal directly affects Japanese air quality and places Japan's environmental health beyond national control or remedy. Likewise, the Sino–Japanese competition to gain privileged access to Russian and Central Asian oil and natural gas production reflects their mutual concern over energy security and their competing strategies of diversifying their sources of supply. The militarization of regional disputes remains the greatest source of threat to the stability and tranquillity of the Asia-Pacific. The Japanese acquisition of significant force projection capabilities, for example, would disrupt the existing military status quo and sharpen the Northeast Asian security dilemma, while the Chinese modernization programme threatens American prerogatives in the region as well as the prospect of military conflict over unsettled territorial claims in the South China Sea despite the Chinese pledge to seek negotiated settlements.

Patterns of interaction

Unilateralism and bilateralism are the dominant patterns of interaction in the Asia-Pacific. The ASEAN-sponsored institutions, which include two or more of the Asia-Pacific powers – ASEAN + 3 (which includes China, Japan and South Korea) and the ASEAN Regional Forum (which includes inter alia the United States, Australia, Canada, India, Russia and the EU) – explicitly lack a security remit. Only Japan and the United States have a long-standing bilateral security arrangement, while the only multilateral security diplomacy currently linking China, Japan and the United States is the Six-Party Talks to dismantle the North Korean nuclear weapons programme.[9]

The balance between civilian and traditional forms of statecraft

The underlying dynamic of the Asia-Pacific is driven by the traditional security objectives of protecting territorial integrity from internal and external threats as well as balancing power between status quo and revisionist states. The balance of power regulates conflict between China, Japan and the United States; as noted above, the modernization of Japanese forces and China's eventual acquisition of a significant force projection capability are viewed as threats by each of the regional antagonists. Even though the source of threats in the region stem from the Westphalian preoccupation with territorial integrity and the conflicting imperatives of autonomy and influence, a diplomatic firewall segregates economic intercourse among these nations from their competing geopolitical interests and objectives.

Convergent or divergent security cultures?

The American and Chinese worldviews are not dissimilar. The foreign policy elites in each country view the underlying dynamic of the Asia-Pacific as a struggle conducted primarily between states seeking to maximize their power, influence and autonomy. Both also assume that non-state actors play a relatively minor role in mediating the relations between them, either as agents galvanizing cooperation or serving as a source of divisiveness. Neither state has anything other than the Hobbesian expectation of endemic interstate conflict punctuated by temporary alliances of convenience. Military power, the numeraire defining power and military force in the service of diplomacy, is the relevant and most effective instrument of statecraft. Japan, unlike the others, has opted for a more civilianized foreign policy despite the manifest military threats presented by China and North Korea; this foreign policy strategy is only possible owing to Japan's continued dependence upon the American security guarantee. Japan does share the others' state-centric understanding of the Asia-Pacific region, but relies upon the economic instruments of persuasion to achieve its goals.

The absence of a common positive identity reinforces the competitive dynamic inherent in these states' worldviews. China, Japan and the United States do not collectively share the characteristics commonly associated with a positive or collective identity. All three remain intensely national, if not parochial and insular, and claim a unique civilization or culture that is either a model for the rest of the world (in the American case), superior to all others (as in the Chinese case), or simply *sui generis* (as in the Japanese case). Regardless of each civilization's particular merit, these cultural differences form a barrier to security cooperation, even if they do not serve as important sources of conflict. While the Japanese–American relationship is marked by amity and high levels of commercial, scientific and cultural exchange and interpenetration, the same can not be said of their bilateral relationships with China.

Conclusion: prospects for regional and global security cooperation

Simply stated, the prospects for effective and institutionalized global security cooperation are poor. The major powers do share a common interest in avoiding war with one another, although their rejection of great power war is derived more from the conventional calculus of cost and benefit than from a normative aversion to it. Yet the majority of those major powers – China, France, Russia, the United Kingdom and the United States – have not rejected military coercion or war as a viable policy instrument in their relations with others, particularly weaker states with some geopolitical importance. This continued reliance upon the traditional forms of statecraft reflects a security agenda that is derived in large part from the competitive logic of anarchy and power that drives the international system outside the narrow ambit of Europe and the broader transatlantic area. The heterogeneity of purpose among the major powers cannot be explained fully by differentiated geopolitical milieu or the mere presence of idiosyncratic security threats. Instead, the diverse patterns of security cooperation among the major powers and regional forms of security governance can be better explained by the contemporaneous coexistence of Westphalian and post-Westphalian states in the international system.

Territoriality is the key characteristic of the Westphalian state and functions as the 'hard shell' protecting states and societies from the external environment (Herz 1957). Territoriality is increasingly irrelevant, particularly in Europe and North America. These states no longer enjoy a territorial 'wall of defensibility' that would leave them relatively immune to external penetration. The changed salience and meaning of territoriality has not only expanded the number and types of security threat, but shifted attention from the 'hard' to the 'soft' manifestations of power. The Westphalian states of Eurasia and the Asia-Pacific are preoccupied with protecting autonomy and independence, retaining a gatekeeping role, and avoiding external interference in domestic constitutional arrangements. Westphalian states, regardless of their objective ability to deflect or contain transnational disturbances, remain content with a national definition of security. Post-Westphalian states, by contrast, have largely abandoned their gatekeeper role owing to the interdependencies of economic openness, welfare maximization and political principle. Likewise, autonomy and independence have been devalued as sovereign imperatives and have been subordinated to the demands of the welfare state. The ease with which domestic disturbances are transmitted across national boundaries *and* the difficulty of deflecting those disturbances underline the strength and vulnerability of the post-Westphalian state: the ever expanding spectrum of interaction provides greater levels of collective welfare than would otherwise be possible, yet the very transmission belts facilitating those welfare gains serve as diffusion mechanisms hindering the state's ability to inoculate itself against exogenous shocks or malevolent actors. Those actors, in turn, are largely immune to sovereign jurisdiction as well as strategies of dissuasion, defence and deterrence. Consequently, broad and collective milieu goals have been substituted for particularistic, national security goals, conventionally conceived. Perforated sovereignty has rendered post-Westphalian states incapable of meeting their national security requirements alone. This category of state is more vulnerable to the influence of non-state actors – malevolent, benevolent, or benign – in international politics. Non-state actors fill or exploit the gaps left by the (in)voluntary loss or evaporation of sovereignty attending the transformation of the state, while others are purposeful repositories for sovereignty ceded, lent, pooled or forfeited. The changing nature of the security agenda, particularly its functional expansion and the changing agency of threat, necessitates a shift from coercive to persuasive security strategies as well as from national to multilateral solutions.

This post-Westphalian hypothesis challenges the assumption that states are homogenous actors with a common set of preferences (Waltz 1979). Post-Westphalian and Westphalian states seek alternative forms of security and practice alternative forms of statecraft – instrumentally and substantively. Just as the structural characteristics of post-Westphalian states are favourable to the institutionalization of security cooperation, the characteristics of the Westphalian state provide a significant barrier to security cooperation – even in the transatlantic area. States in the contemporary international system fall along a continuum bounded by the Westphalian and post-Westphalian forms. The major powers fall along the entire continuum: China and Russia are unalloyed Westphalian states; Canada, Germany and Italy possess in the fullest measure the characteristics of the post-Westphalian state; France, Japan, the United Kingdom and the United States are probably best described as late-Westphalian states.

These categories of states, owing to their structural characteristics in conjunction with liberal constitutional orders, exhibit disparate understandings of threat, the agents of threat, and the best means for ameliorating them. That disparity precludes, in turn, deep or sustained security cooperation where dissimilar categories of state occupy the same geopolitical space as is the case in the Asia-Pacific. The presence of predominately post-Westphalian states in Europe explains the emergence of the EU as a security actor and the sustained patterns of multilateral security cooperation among its member states.[10] Conversely, the persistence of the Westphalian state elsewhere in the world, particularly in Eurasia, explains the continuing force of anarchy and the continued reliance on epiphenomenal or tactical forms of security cooperation, regardless of domestic constitutional form. The uneven and eroding levels of security cooperation in the

Atlantic area, however, can be explained by the confluence of two developments: the globalization of security which has made it increasingly difficult for the United States to practice a bifurcated statecraft tailored to the preferences and expectations of its regional partners and antagonists; and the global role and responsibilities of the United States which require it, unlike the Europeans, to interact with and respond to Westphalian states still preoccupied with managing the traditional security dilemma attending anarchy.

Unipolarity has been heralded as an opportunity for the United States to make the world more secure or has been identified as the chief threat to the long-term stability of the international system. The invasion of Iraq, regardless of its under-lying purpose or rationale, is symptomatic of the arrogance and tragedy of preponderant power. But neither the evaporation of American preponderance nor the emergence of multipolarity would eradicate the variegated perceptions of threat, fundamental disagreements on the geographic origins and agents of threat, and incompatible national security cultures of the major powers. The empirical evidence indicates, if not demonstrates, that these intrinsic differences function as insurmountable barriers to global security governance. Yet the empirical evidence also provides some basis for concluding that there are good reasons to expect that the persistence of the different forms of regional security governance now in place will continue to minimize the probability of a militarized major power conflict.

Acknowledgement

I benefited greatly in the writing of this conclusion from the insightful observations made by Kostas Ifantis and Magnus Ekengren at the conclusion of the GARNET workshop held in Trento. My thinking about the problem of security governance also benefited from the contributions of those attending the workshop, particularly Mark Webber, Antonio Missiroli, Paolo Foradori and Mark Rhinard. I am most indebted, however, to Haru Fukui for his careful and judicious reading of the manuscript.

Notes

1   In their discussion of the East Asian security complex, for example, they assert that only Japan and China are members of that complex and that Russia and the United States are outside powers even though they are 'consistent participants' in the region (Buzan and Wæver 2003: 80). The exclusion of Russia, for example, from the Northeast Asian security complex is puzzling given the long Sino–Russian border and its status as a littoral state of the Sea of Japan. While a slightly better case can be made for excluding the United States on the basis of geography (ignoring the Aleutian atoll for the moment), it does not pass the common sense test: the United States is an integral part of the Northeast Asian security system.
2   The term pan-regional refers to the broadest category of regional security complex; for example, while there are Northeastern, Southeastern, and Central Asian regional complexes, there is also the Eurasian pan-regional security complex that encompasses all three.

3   These rank-orderings are derived from the country-study chapters.
4   This dimension of security cooperation is investigated in Kirchner and Sperling (forthcoming). For a fuller discussion of the ESS, see Chapter 6.
5   See Mackinder (1904). For a general assessment of the evolution of the Eurasian security system, see Sperling, et al. (2003).
6   In a recent Pew public opinion poll, 20% of Chinese respondents and 34% of Russian respondents expressed a deep concern with the threat of global warming; over a third of the respondents in each country expressed little or no concern with global warming. (Pew 2006: 5|). In a survey conducted by TNS Emnid, 44% of Chinese respondents identified global warming as a major threat, but only 28% of the Russians polled did so (TNS Emnid 2006: 18).
7   This characterization is drawn, of course, from A.J.P. Taylor's magisterial history of nineteenth century European diplomacy. See Taylor (1955).
8   In the United States, only 19% of those polled in 2006 identified global warming as a serious problem and 47% expressed little or no concern; the corresponding figures in Japan were 65% and 7%, respectively. The Russians occupied the middle ground, with 34% viewing it as a serious problem and an equal share expressing little or no concern (Pew 2006: 5).
9   China also is a member of the SCO (see section on Eurasian Security Cooperation) and has a bilateral treaty with the Russian Federation. Likewise, the United States, Australia and New Zealand are connected by the ANZUS Treaty, but only Australia has a direct security relationship with both.
10 Those post-Westphalian characteristics also provide a superior explanation for the existence of a security community than does a neo-Kantian reliance upon a single form of constitutional order, liberal democracy, as the sole explanatory variable.

References

Adler, E. and Barnett, M. (eds) (1998a) *Security Communities,* Cambridge: Cambridge University Press.

Adler, E. and Barnett, M. (1998b) 'A framework for the study of security communities', in E. Adler and M. Barnett (eds) *Security Communities,* Cambridge: Cambridge University Press.

Allison, R. (2004) 'Regionalism, regional structures and security management in Central Asia', *International Affairs* 80 (3): 463–83.

Buzan, B. and Wæver, O. (2003) *Regions and Powers: The Structure of International Security,* Cambridge: Cambridge University Press.

Checkel, Jeffery T. (1998) 'The constructivist turn in international relations theory', *World Politics,* 50(2): 324–48.

Choo, J. (2003) 'The geopolitics of Central Asian security' in J. Sperling, S. Kay, and S.V. Papacosma (eds) *Limiting Institutions? The Challenge of Eurasian Security Governance,* Manchester: Manchester University Press.

Finnemore, Martha and Kathryn Sikkink (1998) 'International norm dynamics and political change', *International Politics,* 52(4): 887–917.

Hampton, M. and Sperling, J. (2003) 'Positive/negative identity in the Euro-Atlantic communities: Germany's past, Europe's future?', *Journal of European Integration* 24 (4): 281–302.

Harnisch, S. and Maull, H.W. (2001) 'Introduction', in S. Harnisch and H.W. Maull (eds) *Germany as a Civilian Power? The Foreign Policy of the Berlin Republic,* Manchester: Manchester University Press.

Herz, J. (1957) 'The rise and demise of the territorial state', *World Politics* 9 (4): 473–493.

Ikenberry, G.J. and Michael Mastanduno (eds) (2003) *International Relations of the Asia-Pacific,* New York: Columbia University Press.

Katzenstein, P. (2005) *A World of Regions: Asia and Europe in the American Imperium,* Ithaca: Cornell University Press.

Kay, S. (2003), 'Geopolitical constaints and institutional innovation: the dynamics of multilateralism in Eurasia', in J. Sperling, S. Kay, and S.V. Papcosma (eds), *Limiting Institutions? The Challenge of Eurasian Security Governance*, Manchester: Manchester University Press.

Kirchner, E. J. and Sperling, J. (2007) *Governing European Security,* Manchester: Manchester University Press.

Lake, D. A. and Morgan, P.M. (eds) (1997) *Regional Orders: Building Security in a New World,* University Park: Penn State University Press.

Mackinder, H. (1904) 'The geographical pivot of history', *Geographical Journal* 23 (4): 421–44.

Pempel, T.J. (ed.) (2005) *Remapping East Asia: The Construction of a Region,* Ithaca: Cornell University Press.

Pew Research Center (2006) *No Global Warming Alarm in the U.S., China,* Washington, DC: The Pew Global Attitudes Project.

Sperling, J. (2003) 'Eurasian security governance: new threats, institutional adaptations' in J. Sperling, S. Kay and S.V. Papacosma (eds), *Limiting Institutions? The Challenge of Eurasian Security Governance,* Manchester: Manchester University Press.

Sperling, J. (2007) 'State attributes and system properties: security multilateralism in Central Asia, Southeast Asia, the Atlantic and Europe', in D. Bourantonis, K. Ifantis, and P. Tsakonas (eds) *Multilateralism and Security Institutions in an Era of Globalization,* London: Routledge.

Sperling, J., Kay, S. and Papacosma, S.V. (2003) *Limiting Institutions? The Challenge of Eurasian Security Governance,* Manchester: Manchester University Press.

Suh, J.J., Katzenstein, P.J. and Carlson, A. (eds) (2004) *Rethinking Security in East Asia: Identity, Power, And Efficiency,* Stanford: Stanford University Press.

Taylor, A.J.P. (1955) *The Struggle for Mastery in Europe: 1848–1918,* Oxford: Oxford University Press.

TNS Emnid (2006) *World Power in the 21st Century,* Berlin: Bertelsmann Stiftung.

Waltz, K. (1979) *Theory of International Politics,* New York: Random House.

Wendt, Alexander (1999) *Social Theory of International Relations*, Cambridge: Cambridge University Press.

Yom, S.L. (2002) 'Power politics in Central Asia', *Harvard Asia Quarterly,* 6(4). Available online at: <http://www.asiaquarterly.com/content/view/129> (accessed 27 October 2006).

Index

ABM Treaty 241
Afghanistan 15, 37, 39, 49, 58, 80, 82, 98,
   100–1, 106–7, 137, 147, 151, 213, 224,
   230–1, 242–3, 270, 277; *see also*
   Taliban
African Union 9–10, 57
African, Caribbean and Pacific (ACP)
   countries 122, 129
Albania 28, 71–2
Algeria 73, civil war 28
al-Qaeda 76, 139, 165, 171, 175, 241, 265,
   280
Armenia–Azerbaijan conflict 246
arms control 57, 59, 103, 210, 241
ASEAN 12, 14, 121, 201, 210–11, 229,
   264, 281; Regional Forum 12, 15, 175,
   211, 228–9, 264, 271, 281
Atlanticism 29, 99–108, 116, 122
Australia 149, 263, 281
'axis of evil' 52, 165, 171, 184, 276; *see*
   also Iran, Iraq *and* North Korea

Balkans 4, 35, 48, 51, 54, 71–2, 74, 80–1,
   118, 265–6; Stability Pact 82, 116, 122
Ballistic Missile Defence Programme 147,
   152, 241, 254
bilateralism 99–100, 108, 178–9, 188,
   205, 208, 227, 248, 256, 271, 280–1
bin Laden, O. 165
bipolarity 93, 149, 233
Bosnia and Herzegovina 35, 70, 94, 106,
   114, 116, 122, 166, 250; IFOR/SFOR
   71, 124; EUFOR 124
Bush, G.W. 52, 161, 165, 171, 174, 179,
   203, 241, 263; doctrine 114, 116, 179

Canada 17–18, 137–160, 274–5, 278,
   283; Ad Hoc Committee on Public
   Security and Anti-Terrorism 137, 143,

148; Canada Border Services Agency
148, 152; Canadian Security and
Intelligence Service 139–41, 146,
148–50; Department of Public Safety
and Emergency Preparedness 137,
144, 148; Integrated Threat
Assessment Centre 148–9; Privy
Council Office 148–9; Royal
Canadian Mounted Police 146, 148;
White Paper on National Security
139–41
CARICOM 10
Caucasus 73, 238, 242, 246, 251
Central and Eastern Europe 4, 95, 103,
   108, 162, 164, 171, 184, 238, 240, 252,
   266, 275
Central Asia 73, 97, 166, 171–2, 200, 202,
   208, 213, 238, 242, 245–6, 250–1, 263,
   266, 270–3
CFSP 33, 78, 101, 122, 126, 130; High
   Representative 11, 114, 124, 126; *see*
   also EU
Chechnya 241–2, 246, 251, 253–4, 269,
   272
China 12, 15–18, 162, 166–7, 171–2,
   199–218, 221, 231, 247, 263–4,
   269–74, 276, 279, 281–3; arms
   embargo 59; Communist Party 202,
   205–6, 216, 232, 250, 254–5; foreign
   humiliation 199, 215–6, 223–5;
   National People's Congress 205;
   People's Liberation Army 213–14;
   Revolution in Military Affairs 204,
   212, 214
Chirac, J. 29, 33, 37
civil liberties 141–2, 145
'civilian power' 16, 47, 125, 166
climate change 51, 120, 177, 223
Clinton, W. 161, 174, 178